JOHN PAUL II

For Kathy and Clive,
with many thanks for their help

JOHN PAUL II

Michael Walsh

HarperCollins*Publishers*

HarperCollins*Publishers*
77–85 Fulham Palace Road, London W6 8JB

First published in Great Britain
in 1994 by HarperCollins*Publishers*

1   3   5   7   9   10   8   6   4   2

A catalogue record for this book is
available from the British Library

ISBN 0 00 215993–7

Typeset by Harper Phototypesetters Limited
Northampton, England
Printed and bound in Great Britain by
HarperCollinsManufacturing Glasgow

CONTENTS

INTRODUCTION

SHORTLY AFTER Cardinal Karol Wojtyla, Archbishop of Cracow, was elected Pope in 1978 I was approached by a publishing company to write a book on the history of the papacy simply on the grounds, it transpired, that the company's sales force had told the editors that they could sell one. The papacy, with so charismatic a figure from central Europe on the throne of Peter, was big news. Many biographies were written, most of them flattering. Though my own contribution at the time was not a biography of an individual pope but a history of the office he held, none the less my book had to include a brief character study of John Paul II. This was 1979. When I submitted the chapter about the present Pope to my editor, the sales force was disturbed. My text was too critical. They wanted a much more upbeat assessment of Papa Wojtyla. I more or less obliged, though elements of my disquiet at the turn his papacy was taking can be seen in what I wrote only a year, or less, after his election.

As the years have gone by I have seen no reason to change my original judgement. There have been occasional books about him, and with some of them I have sympathized, such as David Willey's excellent *God's Politician*. Rather oddly, however, there has not been published for some time now, at least in English, anything that might be described as a biography. Willey's book, for instance, useful though it is coming from a man who knows Rome well and has frequently travelled with the Pope, is thematic in its approach rather than chronological. Carl Bernstein, he of Watergate and the *Washington Post*, is promising a study of John Paul, but his interest appears to centre upon the Pope as a world statesman, alongside Ronald Reagan and Mikhail Gorbachev, a role about which, as this book attempts to indicate, I am distinctly sceptical.

What I did not find, when I was again approached to write about the papacy, and this time specifically about the present Pope, was a biography which recorded, after his election, what he did, step by step, and why he did it, in so far as that information may be gleaned about a man who is still living and whose papers, other than those published (in Karol Wojtyla's case that is a considerable amount) are not open to inspection.

Apart from the opening chapters, which attempt to recount who Karol Wojtyla is, what sort of education he received, and what his intellectual interests may be, this book tells the story of his pontificate, year by year, and in chronological order as far as is consonant with providing a continuous narrative. Yet it does not deal with everything. When long periods are passed over in silence, the Pope was writing an encyclical, drafting a speech, receiving an ambassador – a growing number as will be seen – or addressing a group of bishops on their regular visits to Rome to report on the state of the Church in their dioceses.

He may also have been on his travels. Whenever the Pope left Italy I have recorded the fact and, for the most part, said where he was and what he was doing at any stage of his foreign tours. But he has also travelled around Italy – to Sicily, for example, to condemn the Mafia – and these I have had to leave out. There are other topics about which he showed an especial concern but which, on the whole, did not engage him publicly: the situation in mainland China is an instance. Of these, too, I have made little or no mention. I have, I think, given an account of all the major documents which the Pope has produced, or which have been produced by others to appear over his signature – encyclicals, apostolic constitutions and the like. I have also discussed a small number of other documents from Vatican departments of one kind or another, but which clearly reflected papal views – I am thinking particularly of the two 'instructions' on Liberation Theology which were published by the Congregation for the Doctrine of the Faith.

Here, then, is the public persona of the Pope. It is my view that the private persona is not all that much different. Popes have not made a habit of going skiing, it is true, or for that matter walking up the sides of mountains in the Dolomites. In such things John Paul is different, at least from his predecessors over the last two centuries, for before then popes lived a more leisurely style of life. But even these 'private activities' the Pope makes no attempt to conceal. It is not my impression that he is a particularly private person. He puts all of himself into whatever he does – as his philosophy would anyway tell him to do – and his personality can be discerned from his public acts and his published writings.

That, at least, is the conviction which has governed the writing of this book. I have recorded his public acts, recounted his published writings, and attempted to assess the Pope through them. For his public life I have relied heavily, as will quickly become apparent, upon that outstanding London-based weekly, *The Tablet*, and more especially upon its valuable 'Church in the World' section. But I have also gleaned information from the French *Documentation Catholique* (more recently in an English dress as *Catholic International*), the American bishops' *Origins*, the Spanish *Vida Nueva* and even from the Vatican's own *Acta Apostolicae Sedis*. To them all, but especially to *The Tablet*, I extend my thanks for the work they do. I would also like to thank Desmond O'Grady, Felix Corley and John Anderson for letting me see advance copies of their soon-to-be-published writings.

Heythrop College   Michael J. Walsh
Holy Saturday, 1994

W HEN THE Cardinal electors chose Karol Wojtyla to be Pope on 16 October 1978 they voted for the first non-Italian to be Bishop of Rome since the brief pontificate of the gloomy Dutchman, Hadrian VI. He had been elected in January 1522 and had died, largely unlamented, in September 1523. Hadrian, number 217 in a line which stretches back to the first century of the Christian era, at least had this much in common with John Paul II, number 263 in the same succession of Roman pontiffs: boths of them had been, and continued throughout their pontificates frequently to act as if they still were, university professors.

Hadrian we call Dutch because he was born in Utrecht. But the Netherlands were then, and long afterwards continued to be, a dependency of Spain. When Karol Jozef Wojtyla was born in Wadowice on 18 May 1920 that small town was indeed part of an independent Poland. But only just. The country had come back into existence as a political entity scarcely eighteen months earlier, on 18 November 1918.

Before Hadrian there had been French popes and German ones, there had been a Portuguese pope and even an Englishman. But there had never been a Slav pope, certainly not one from Poland. They had invariably come from states, when there were such things as states, which had played a central role in European history. Poland, on the other hand, for more than a century before the birth of Karol Wojtyla, had entirely vanished, as a national unit, from the map of Europe if not from the hearts of the people who lived on its traditional territory.

Poland had been at the height of its power in the sixteenth century: the Polish-Lithuanian Commonwealth then constituted the largest state in Europe. In the seventeenth it was under siege, most particularly from the Swedes. In November 1655 Carl Gustav X of Sweden, who had by that time conquered most of Poland, launched from Cracow an attack on the fortified monastery of Jasna Góra at Czestochowa in Southern Poland. Though it looked for a time as if the monastery was bound to fall – it was garrisoned by fewer than 200 soldiers and 68 monks – the Swedish commander called off the siege on 26 December. This marked a turning point in Polish efforts to free their country from Swedish domination. After his return to Poland King John Casimir, in a ceremony in the cathedral at Lvov, dedicated the country to the Black Madonna of Czestochowa, an icon of the Virgin (traditionally said to be have been painted by St Luke on the wooden table-top of Mary's house at Nazareth) which had been housed in Jasna Góra (Mountain of Light) since 1382. Our Lady of Czestochowa John Casimir declared to be Queen of Poland.

Ever since the lifting of the siege of 1655 the icon, damaged by swords of Hussites in the fifteenth century, has stood as a symbol of Polish unity. But little more than a hundred years after the Swedish armies withdrew, the country's unity was destroyed by a series of partitions, three in less than a quarter of a century. At first it was Prussia, the forerunner of modern Germany, which benefited most as Poland was divided out among Prussia, Russia and the Austrian Empire of the Hapsburgs. Under Napoleon what little remained as the Duchy of Warsaw became a dependency of France. In the aftermath of the Napoleonic Wars it was Russia which emerged as the main beneficiary of the partition of Polish lands.

The First World War destroyed all three Empires, those of Russia, Germany and Austria, and Poland emerged once again as an independent state. Russia was not prepared to let go and saw the newly-liberated country not as a buffer between itself and Germany – which was how the victorious powers looked upon it – but as a gateway to bring the Communist Revolution to the rest of Europe. They went to war, and were on the point of conquest until, against all odds, at the battle of Warsaw the Red Army was defeated. Whether it was the intervention of Mary, Queen of Poland, or the military skills of Marshal Pilsudski, to the Poles it was all one: the 'miracle on the Vistula' was a sign of God's favour upon the people.

It was into this intensely nationalistic world that Karol Wojtyla was born. His father, also called Karol, was an administrative staff officer, a captain at his retirement, in the Polish 12th Regiment of Infantry. But that was only after Polish independence. Earlier he had seen service in the army of Austria.

The place of his birth was Wadowice, a town then of some 15,000 inhabitants. It is situated in the foothills of the Beskidy mountains, part of the Carpathian range, and lies on a tributary of the Vistula called the River Skawa. It has a history which stretches back six hundred years. Until 1918 and the implementation of the Treaty of Versailles it had been, like the provincial capital, Cracow, only some fifty kilometres to the northeast, in that part of the Austro-Hungarian Empire known as Galicia.

Cracow was another reminder of the past greatness of Poland. When, through the marriage of Queen Jadwiga of Poland to Grand Duke Ladislas Jagiello of Lithuania in 1386, Kingdom and Grand Duchy had been brought together into a single commonwealth, Cracow had been declared its capital. The university of the city, founded in 1364 and one of the oldest in central Europe, was effectually refounded by Jadwiga and Ladislas in the year of their marriage. It is still named The Jagellonian. Jadwiga was later beatified, and is venerated at her tomb which lies within the cathedral beside the castle on the Wawel hill above the city of Cracow.

Even after the division of the country at the end of the eighteenth century Cracow remained the centre of nationalist aspirations and culture. Indeed, for the century before Wojtyla's birth Polish culture was all that survived, something of which he has been very conscious. 'I am the son of a nation that has lived through the greatest experiences in history,' he told a meeting of UNESCO in 1980, 'which though condemned to death by its neighbours, has survived and remained itself. It has conserved, regardless of foreign occupation, its national (as distinguished from political) sovereignty, not by depending on the resources of physical power, but uniquely by depending on its culture. As it happened, this culture revealed itself as being a greater power than all the other forces.'[1]

Captain Wojtyla's father Maciej, a tailor by trade, had settled in what was then a suburb, but has since become a part, of the city of Cracow. The family had originally come from Czanec, near Andrychow, and Karol senior had himself lived there for a time. After his marriage to Emilia Kaczoronowska, however, he settled at Wadowice.

It was, and is, a small town. For young Karol Jozef Wojtyla it was at first even more circumscribed. His father's military pension was tiny, and the family was poor. They lived in a three-roomed, first-floor, apartment in a short street alongside the church, which stands in the southwest corner of the town square. One of those rooms was the kitchen, through which one entered the flat. When Lolek, as Karol was familiarly called, was old enough to enter primary school he had only to walk round to the other side of the church. His secondary school, the Marcin Wadowita High School, to which he went in 1934, was only a little further away, just across the town square. On his way to school across the square Karol Wojtyla daily used to pause in the church for private prayer. Devout he may have been, and extremely well-behaved, but, by all accounts, pious in a sentimental fashion he certainly was not.

Tragedy was early added to Lolek's experience of poverty. When he was nine his mother died of heart disease. When he was thirteen his brother Edmund, a doctor in a hospital in Bielsko, died from scarlet fever caught from one of his patients. For much of his childhood, therefore, the Wojtyla family consisted only of father and son. Karol senior was deeply devout, and this communicated itself as a living force to Lolek. He did well at school in his religious lessons – but then he was a star pupil, and did well at all of the subjects. He was particularly good at languages – Latin, Greek and German: his mother's family had come from Silesia, so he learned German at home. He was an altar boy. For three years he was president of the sodality. Originally a Jesuit-founded institution to foster devotion to the Mother of God, by 1920 this was little more than a pious association found world-wide especially in Catholic schools.

Lolek is remembered as tall, lively and distinctly chubby. He was also a keen sportsman and has remained so with a particular passion for football: he played in goal. He loved swimming, skiing and skating and also walking in the hills. He was a keen cinema-goer, though he preferred the theatre.

That Karol Wojtyla is a playwright is now well known: the collected English edition lists six plays all of which he originally wrote, however, under a pseudonym. From the age of eight he was involved in amateur theatricals, at first running errands or trying to get the job of prompter. When visiting his brother Edmund he would act out scenes from plays for the patients in the wards. His earliest formal experience of acting was at school, where he was directed by Dr Mieczyslaw Kotlarczyk (1908–78), a teacher of history at the neighbouring school for girls. Kotlarczyk had completed his doctoral thesis in 1936 on early theatre criticism in Poland, Germany and France. Wojtyla took part in ten plays, invariably playing male lead, often also helping to direct. All but two of the plays with which he was involved either at school or in the town's Catholic Centre were from the Polish romantic and neo-romantic tradition, dealing with foreign oppression and liberation. In one he played the poet-hero Count Henryk: he was always given heroic, patriotic roles.

In the early part of 1938 school came to an end. Just before it did so, however, he was selected to read the address of welcome to Cardinal Sapieha, Archbishop of Cracow, who was visiting Wadowice. He much impressed Sapieha who expressed the hope, which then seemed unlikely, that Wojtyla would become a priest.

There was nothing to keep father and son in Wadowice (though Karol's year-group at school had been a particularly closely-knit one, and continued afterward to meet regularly), and they moved to Cracow. They took lodgings at 10 Tyniecka Street, in the part of Cracow just across the Vistula called Debniki, where they had relatives. It was a basement flat, small, dark and gloomy. Above lived two aunts, sisters of Karol's mother. Contact with them seems to have been slight, but their presence in the same house may explain the choice of place to live.

Karol joined other students for the summer at a camp building roads, then enrolled at the Jagellonian as a student of Polish philology. At the same time he signed up for evening classes in elocution: by now acting was clearly a passion. With a girl friend from Wadowice he was almost immediately involved in another theatrical production, staged at the end of the academic year in the courtyard of the library. Through this play, called *The Moonlight Cavalier*, an especially written allegorical work featuring actors playing the different signs of the Zodiac, he made new friends. Chief among them was Juliusz Kydrynski, who took the role of Aquarius: Karol Wojtyla was Sagittarius. The friendship with Kydrynski blossomed: they held literary evenings together in his flat in Felicjanki Street. Through him Wojtyla came to know Irena Szkocka, a widow who lived in Poniatowski Street alongside the Vistula. Her daughter Zofia was married to Jan Pozniak, who played the piano for their theatricals. Wojtyla could talk music – his favourite composers were Bach, Beethoven and Chopin – with Pozniak, who was a distinguished musicologist, or Polish romantic literature with Mde Szkocka. He even had the opportunity to learn French there – which he did from their lodger who was a teacher.

In the summer of 1939 Lolek had to do military training in the 'Academic Legion' made up of students. On 1 September 1939, as Wojtyla knelt in prayer in the Wawel cathedral, he heard the German planes flying in to bomb Cracow. The German army arrived in Cracow shortly afterwards. The Second World War had erupted.

By the end of the month the Soviet Union had annexed parts of Eastern Poland. Germany established a puppet government over much of what remained, though it, too, annexed part of the country, a strip which included Wadowice – and Auschwitz. In July of 1940 Poland, or what remained after the annexations by the USSR and Lithuania, was incorporated into a greater Germany. The country which had begun just shortly before Karol's birth had disappeared when he was only twenty years old.

One of the first acts of the German army of occupation was to close down the university. Many students and professors were despatched to Sachsenhausen. Few returned. None the less the university kept going clandestinely, with Wojtyla enrolled once more as a student of philology.

In the meantime, however, Lolek's father had died. Soon after Christmas 1940, which Karol and his father spent at Kydrynski's house, Karol senior was taken ill and stayed in bed in the apartment in Tyniecka Street. Karol junior would come home from work, collect food cooked for him by Kydrynski's mother and then, with Kydrynski's sister, go back to the flat. One day in March Wojtyla went to his father's room and found him dead. He was utterly devastated that he had not been there when his father died. He was buried in Cracow, in a military cemetery: later Emilia's coffin was also transferred there. Karol Wojtyla lived for a while after his father's burial with the Kydrynskis, but then went back to his flat.

At Kydrynski's lived Jadwiga Lewaj, the lodger who taught Karol French. He helped get him a job breaking stones in a quarry at Zakrzowek belonging to Solvay Chemical Works, once a Belgian company. Later, Karol was promoted to the rather more restful job of blasting the sides of the quarry with dynamite. The work may have been hard, but it had its consolations. In a letter of 7 August 1940, Wojtyla wrote to Kotlarczyk that as a labourer he felt satisfied with his physical work, that time flew by quickly, and that through work 'a man becomes a fuller man'.[2] His experiences inspired a poem entitled 'The Quarry', published after the war under the name of Andrzej Jawién. However, his work by day and his study by night took its toll on his health. One evening he collapsed in the street from exhaustion, was struck by a passing German truck and was knocked unconscious. He lay there all night and was not found until the following morning when he was rushed to hospital, where he stayed for some time.

In the winter of 1941–2 he was put to work at the water purification department of the Solvay factory near Cracow. It was a hard, repetitive job. The workers had to carry lime and other chemicals in buckets swung from yokes, to treat the water. Wojtyla took it upon himself to try to ameliorate these conditions by suggesting improvements to the workers' recreational and religious facilities.

Meanwhile his drama teacher Mieczyslaw Kotlarczyk had come back into his life – although Wojtyla had remained in touch by letter. Kotlarczyk had lost his job in Wadowice when the town was annexed by Germany. In June 1941 he came, with his wife and two daughters, to Cracow, and to Wojtyla's flat. Instead of history teaching he now became a ticket collector on the tramway. But he also, and in secret, returned to his first love – the theatre.

It was a world of bleak contrasts. Poland had been destroyed. German soldiers drank coffee in Cracow's beautiful main square. Meanwhile Jews were being herded into ghettoes. And not far away the notorious death camps were being constructed. Yet a gathering of intellectuals met regularly as a tightly-knit theatre group in the house of Mde Szkocka. When this was requisitioned by German troops, she moved across the Vistula with her daughter to a smaller house on Szwedska Street, not far from Wojtyla's own apartment. Tenuously, the theatre group survived. More extraordinary still was Wojtyla's role. He was only in his early twenties, yet the group had moved to be closer together around his flat in Debniki.

His friend Osterwa had planned new translations of classic dramas – he managed to do Sophocles' *Antigone*, and *Hamlet*. Under his influence Wojtyla translated *Oedipus*. Kotlarczyk and Wojtyla, with support from Tadeusz Tudlinski, founded the Rhapsodic Theatre on 22 August 1941, with five actors. Of these, three were women, all students, with whom Wojtyla had acted in Wadowice (Krystyna Debowska, Danuta Michalowska and Halina Krolikiewicz). Tadeusz Ostaszeewski was stage designer. Because of the enemy occupation, performances had to take place in private apartments, which meant that theatrical elements (stage, curtains, scenery and so on) were minimal to non-existent, though this fitted very well with Kotlarczyk's own ideas on stagecraft.

Writing in 1958 in the Catholic weekly *Tygodnik Powszechny* to solicit the reopening of the Rhapsodic Theatre which had been closed by the Communist regime, he seems to argue that the theatre's style was born of necessity rather than ideology. In an article entitled 'Drama of Word and Gesture' he said, 'Of all the complex resources of theatrical art, there remained only the living word, spoken by people in extrascenic conditions, in a room with a piano. That unheard-of scarcity of the means of expression turned into a creative experience.'[3] But the style adopted by the Rhapsodic Theatre was very much the creation of Kotlarczyk, with the active support and encouragement of Wojtyla. The spoken word was isolated, and made to carry the burden of the drama without benefit of props or scenery. It was all extremely cerebral and intellectual.

In the same newspaper an earlier article (April 1957) on the need to restore the Rhapsodic Theatre appeared under the pseudonym of Andrzej Jawién which Wojtyla used for his poetry. He defended Kotlarczyk's ideas – the spoken word transmits thought, scenery and props should be kept to a minimum. Writing again a year later ('Rhapsodies of the Millennium') he argued:

This theatre [the Rhapsodic], in which there is so much word and relatively little 'acting', safeguards young actors against developing a destructive individualism because it will not let them impose on the text anything of their own; it gives them inner discipline ... A group of people collectively, somehow unanimously, subordinated to the great poetic word, evoke ethical associations; this solidarity of people in the word reveals particularly strongly and accentuates the reverence that is the point of departure for the rhapsodists' work and the secret of their style.

These ideas he more than likely picked up from the Polish phenomenologist Roman Ingarden (1893–1970) whose lectures he had attended while at university. Ingarden maintained that the actor's use of words – with gestures, intonations, facial expression and so on – carry the dispositions of the actors.[4]

The power of the word was all; in such a theory of drama, the actor was little more than a mouthpiece.

Wojtyla's first play written in December 1939, *David*, is no longer extant. *Job* and *Jeremiah* were to follow, written respectively in the spring and summer of 1940. Both his plays and his poetry are very much alike, frequently containing dramatic monologues or dialogues. His plays are poetic drama, not concerned so much with outer events as with debate within the soul.

Job was written under the influence of the Young Poland literary movement, its language stylized, its lines very short. Wojtyla uses obsolete phrases and forms of address. Its prologue points to the parallel between Job's day and the Poland of 1940.[5] Its setting is described thus: 'Job: A drama from the Old Testament. The Action took place in the Old Testament/Before Christ's coming/The Action takes place in our days/In Job's time/For Poland and the World', while the prologue says of Job, 'he was righteous/before God and man – /he was righteous, and yet he is tried;/he was upright, and yet he is oppressed/so that his arms lose their strength,/so that his wrists turn limp./Behold, my people./Behold, my people – /and listen to the Word of the Lord,/you who are downtrodden,/you who are flogged,/sent to the camps, you– /Jobs – Jobs./Behold, my people – /and enter the sacrificial circle,/where an offering is made of he-goats ...' This is a description not only of Job, but it is also language used of Christ: in nineteenth-century romantic poetry dismembered Poland had been a figure of the suffering Christ.

In the end, of course, Job (and Poland?) is rewarded:[6] 'And the Lord gave twice as much – /lovely daughters, and brave sons, and/twice the possession he had before./But mind the other wondrous thing/that he discovered in his suffering, what the visions of the Lord revealed to him:/He sent the prophet

– listen, brothers – /and He sent His Son./And God's Son founded/a New Covenant,/on His sacrifice, passion, and suffering./This suffering transforms us,/puts the New Covenant in men's hearts,/like a new day of creation.'

This sounds remarkably like claiming for Poland a messianic role. Such an idea, however, was not far from Wojtyla's mind. On 2 November 1939, he wrote to Kotlarczyk, 'No matter how this has come about and who is to blame for it, one thing becomes obvious: in Europe, Poland has been the greatest martyr, she whom He had raised as Christ's bulwark for so many centuries ... I think that our liberation ought to be a gate for Christ, I think of an Athenian Poland, but more perfect than Athens with all the magnitude of Christianity, such as our great poets imagined, those prophets of Babylonian captivity. The nation fell like Israel because it had not recognized the messianic ideal, already raised like a torch – but unrealized.'[7]

A similar theme is explored in *Jeremiah*, which he clearly subtitles 'A national drama'. The first two acts of the play take place on Palm Sunday 1596, at the outset of Poland's greatest period of power: Wojtyla saw its role as a buffer between infidel Turk and schismatic Russian. The occasion is a gathering – a fictional device, for the people involved cannot all have been in the same place at the same time – for a sermon by Fr Piotr Skarga, a Jesuit priest renowned for saying that Poland would fall if it did not put its house in order. A major character in the play is another Jesuit, Saint Andrzej Bobola, a Polish aristocrat murdered by Cossacks in 1657 and canonized as a martyr in 1938. The play closes in 1620, with a Polish defeat. In his sermons the historical Skarga analyses the ills of society and condemns in particular oppression of the poor.[8] Skarga also equates Poland with Jerusalem, as does Wojtyla in the play.

Apart from writing plays there was performing in them. From 1941 to 1944 Wojtyla appeared in seven productions, giving twenty-two performances, and attending over a hundred rehearsals. The first, on 1 November 1941, was *King-Spirit*: its theme, the struggle for power between rebellious spirits and those divinely inspired. Partly an account of the clash between King Boleslaw the Bold (1039–81) and Bishop Stanislaw of Cracow (1030–79), the bishop is finally killed by order of the king and is subsequently hailed as Poland's patron saint. In a performance of *Pan Tadeuz* which opened on 28 November 1942, Wojtyla, as the dying Bernardine monk Robak, had to continue proclaiming his lines about having fought for Poland while in the background the Nazi loudspeakers were booming out news of a German victory on the Eastern front. His final appearance was in *Samuel Zborowski*, a drama by Slowacki about a rebellious Polish nobleman who was executed in the sixteenth century. Although Wojtyla played the title role in all performances in March 1943, he had already switched his course of studies from Philology to Theology, and he had already begun to seem more distant to his friends. None the less he continued to write to Kotlarczyk about the theatre, a correspondence that was to continue from Rome in later years.

Perhaps Wojtyla's decision to study for the priesthood should have come to his friends as no surprise. Yet it did. He had been a pious child and a devout young man: perhaps only the need to care for his father had prevented him from making the decision earlier. He took it not long after his father's death. But it is clear from his own writings at this period, and from the roles which he took in the plays he and his friends presented, that the Church provided a vehicle for his burning Polish nationalism. 'Let theatre be a church where the national spirit will flourish',[9] Wojtyla had written to Kotlarczyk on 2 November 1939. If theatre and church were to be custodians at least of the Polish culture, then the priesthood just as much as acting was a means to fight for the independence of the national spirit without resorting to arms. But as priests were disappearing into concentration camps (among them Maximilian Kolbe whom he was later to declare to be a saint), to play that particular role demanded great moral courage, and spiritual commitment. Whatever the precise trigger for his determination to abandon his studies in the underground university in order to take up theology, he could not have done so without considerable spiritual underpinning. That training of the spirit had come from a seemingly unlikely source.

Jan Tyranowski was a tailor. He had trained as an accountant, but from his father had inherited the machinery to make clothes, as well as the customers to whom to sell them. Like Wojtyla, he lived near Debniki Square and both of them attended the same Salesian church of St Stanislas Kostka. When Wojtyla met him in February 1940 he was in his forties. Formerly a key Catholic Action leader in Cracow, he was now playing a leading part in a theology discussion group that Wojtyla decided to join. He was to die a mere seven years later.

Joining the discussion group was a statement of Wojtyla's future intentions. Many young men of his age were engaged in guerrilla activities against the occupying forces, moving secretly about Cracow at night to assassinate those of their fellow countrymen who were collaborating with the Germans. Tyranowski's group was also actively engaged against Germany: but their only weapon was prayer. This was no pious platitude but an option positively taken. Under Tyranowski's inspiration a 'living rosary' was formed: fifteen young men (there are fifteen 'decades' of ten Hail Marys each in a full round of the rosary) met together for prayer, for mutual support, and to foster each other's devotion to Mary, Queen of Poland. The leader of each group met Tyranowski regularly. Wojtyla was one such leader. From him he learned something of the Carmelite spirituality which Tyranowski had made his own through the reading of the great Carmelite mystics, John of the Cross, Teresa of Avila and Thérèse of Lisieux. The tailor of Debniki Square, self-taught in the ways of the spirit, became the future pope's unofficial spiritual director, and set him on a course which would lead, not too many years later, to a doctoral study of the writings of John of the Cross. When he thought about becoming a priest his first choice seems to have been the Carmelites, but he was directed to the diocesan clergy.

For someone as devout as Wojtyla, the puzzle is not why he determined, in 1942, to begin the process which would lead to his ordination, but why he had not made the decision earlier. As has been remarked above (p. 4), in 1938 he had been introduced by one of the local clergy to Adam Sapieha, the Cardinal of Cracow, as a possible candidate for the priesthood. At the time Wojtyla himself was unwilling. It may have been that he felt much more drawn to the profession of acting; it can scarcely have been that he was actively attracted to the married state. There were girls in his life, but no romantic attachments.

One obstacle to choosing the priesthood may have been the bishop of the diocese whom, as a priest, he would be obliged to serve: Archbishop Sapieha himself. Sapieha was a complex figure. He was an aristocrat among the clergy, a prince by birth in addition to being, as a cardinal, a 'prince of the Church'. He had been educated in the Jesuit theological faculty at Innsbruck, Austria, and then in the aptly-named 'Academy of Noble Ecclesiastics' in Rome. He had taught in a seminary before being called to Rome. Here he worked closely with Pope Pius X throughout the campaign against the supposed theological deviancy known as modernism which Pius X and his collaborators suppressed with a ruthlessness little short of scandalous.

Back in Poland after the First World War, Sapieha found his intense nationalism at odds with his loyalty to the Holy See. He had snubbed the Apostolic Visitor to the country by barring his attendance at a meeting of Polish bishops. When that Apostolic Visitor became Pope Pius XI, he retaliated by banning Sapieha from membership of the Polish parliament. On the other hand, and perhaps against his personal preference, Sapieha backed the Pope in opposing the forced conversion to the Latin rite of three million Byzantine-rite Christians in the provinces restored to Poland after the War. This enforced 'conversion' was the policy which the head of State, Marshal

Pilsudski, wanted, as did many, if not most, Polish nationalists. It was not the only cause of friction between the marshal and the archbishop, for the former was neither an obedient, nor an observant, son of the Church. But Wojtyla senior had been a military officer, and his son bore as his middle name the Marshal's first name, Jozef. In comparison with that of Pilsudski, Sapieha's patriotism seemed compromised, his loyalty divided between Poland and Rome.

In 1942 the situation was very different. Sapieha had emerged as a national leader, and an opponent of the occupying Germans. He was making valiant efforts to tell a seemingly unheeding Vatican details of Nazi atrocities, particularly against the Jews. In Wadowice one of Karol Wojtyla's closest friends, Jerzy Kluger, was a Jew. His father was leader of the local Jewish community, and Lolek had known them well enough to remark very many years afterwards when he had become Pope, upon the physical similarity between Kluger's granddaughter and Kluger's sister, who had died in a Nazi concentration camp. Sapieha was party to a conspiracy to supply Jews in Cracow with baptismal certificates to attest their Catholicity and thereby, it was hoped, to guarantee their safety.[10] A priest from Wadowice was deeply involved in these rescue attempts, and Wojtyla was also implicated. He secretly moved about the city, helping Jews to leave their homes and identities and to take on new ones, taking them into hiding.

The seminary may have been underground, the seminarians were not. Wojtyla continued working at the chemical factory wearing, a fellow seminarian, Mieczyslaw Malinski, remembers, grey overalls and clogs without socks.[11] He took his books to work with him, struggling, in the autumn of 1942 just after he had begun his studies for the priesthood, with a book on metaphysics by Kazimierz Wais, a former colleague of Cardinal Sapieha. It was not until the new year that Wojtyla began to grasp the point of metaphysics, but his struggle with the test, he later admitted to Malinski, was the start of his philosophical career.

Then came the Warsaw Rising. In retaliation, on 7 September 1944 the German commander in Cracow ordered the arrest of all men in the city aged between fifteen and fifty. Oddly, the detail sent to Debniki failed to search Wojtyla's flat, where he was kneeling in prayer. He escaped arrest, but Sapieha that same day instructed all seminarians to take refuge in his house. For the remainder of the year Wojtyla resided, as well as studied, in the archiepiscopal palace. The drawing room was first turned into a dormitory, then rooms were found in the houses which made up the complex of buildings belonging to the Church.

In the remaining months of the German occupation – Soviet troops entered Cracow on 17 January 1945 – Wojtyla was, if anything, more at risk than he had ever been before. Sapieha continued his support for the resistance, and for the relief of Jewish refugees from the Warsaw Uprising. Wojtyla moved about the city distributing anti-Nazi newspapers. Now that he had abandoned his job at the Solvay chemical factory he was far more likely to come to the attention of the German overseers. After promptings from the cardinal, the manager of the factory conveniently lost Wojtyla's records.

With the retreat of the Germans the people of Cracow had to struggle to return their city to some semblance of normality. Wojtyla was able to publish his first book, a collection of poems entitled *Song of the Hidden God,* in March 1946: the publishers were the Carmelites of Cracow. But he had more mundane tasks than the writing of poetry. He was detailed to clean up the seminary which had been used by the Germans as a camp for French prisoners of war. At the same time he helped reclaim one of the halls of residence for students at the Jagellonian University. And he was himself soon back studying in the faculty of divinity, once it had reopened. But his studies were to be short-lived. He was ordained in the Wawel Cathedral on 1 November 1946, and celebrated his first mass on 2 November. Or masses, for it was the celebration of All Souls, when priests are permitted to say three. He offered them for his immediate family, father, mother and brother, and said them in the crypt at Wawel castle, surrounded by the tombs of Poland's monarchs and its heroes. But that was a private occasion. For his first public mass he chose as the venue the church of St Stanislaw Kostka in Debniki, and it was attended by several of those who had formed with him the Living Rosary, including Tyranowski. The reception afterwards took place in the flat of Mde Szkocka. On 15 November he departed for Rome for doctoral studies.

Cardinal Sapieha had chosen for him the Angelicum, a college in Rome run by the Friars Preachers, the Dominicans, which in 1963 became the Pontifical University of St Thomas (St Thomas Aquinas is regularly referred to as 'the angelic doctor' – hence the title of Angelicum). Living in Rome, Wojtyla would soon become at home in the Italian tongue. But quartered at the Belgian College meant that he could also improve his French.

It was a strange time to be in Rome. The Allied Powers had until recently been at war with Italy, and they were still the army of occupation. In Poland, under the Nazi occupation, Wojtyla's own education in theology had been spasmodic, and scarcely systematic or thorough. In Francophone lands, on the contrary, the German occupation had not prevented the continued development of Catholic philosophical and theological thought. Although the Church's educational system was formally committed to the study of the teachings of St Thomas Aquinas, there were vigorously distinct inter-pretations of what exactly this meant. There had grown up, especially in Francophone lands and particularly, though not solely, among the Jesuits a 'transcendental Thomism' which embraced the insights of modern philosophy and advances in the study of scripture. Most of all it saw the need to situate Thomas, or indeed any theologian, within his period and interpret him in the light of it.

In an article in the French Jesuit journal *Études* in 1946 Jean Daniélou S.J. wrote about the problems facing Thomism as a system of thought. The traditionalist Dominican theologian, Réginald Garrigou-Lagrange replied that same year in the *Angelicum*, the house-journal of his College. He titled the article, 'Where is the New Theology going?', and in so doing inadvertently gave the movement its name, the New Theology. Garrigou-Lagrange was the dominant figure at the Angelicum as Wojtyla arrived from Poland. The young priest, not a month ordained, walked straight into a battle between a severely conservative and a progressive interpretation of Thomism – an interpretation eventually so progressive it bore little relation to Thomas at all – that was to endure until the proponents of transcendental Thomism triumphed at the Second Vatican Council. And it was Garrigou-Lagrange who was the promoter of Wojtyla's doctoral thesis.

If he also chose the theme, the question of faith in the writings of St John of the Cross, it was one which appealed to his pupil. Wojtyla, as poet, actor and student of theology, could hardly not be attracted to the writings of a Spanish Carmelite mystic who expressed much of his thought on the ascent of the soul to God in verse. Tyranowski had led him earlier to the spirituality of the Carmelite saints. While Garrigou-Lagrange had already written on John of the Cross, the choice of thesis was to put Wojtyla's experiential knowledge into a solid theological context. The topic of faith, however, was one on which the more traditional Thomism of Garrigou-Lagrange differed from that of the transcendental Thomism of people such as Karl Rahner. Though Wojtyla's own version of the teaching of St Thomas developed along non-traditional lines, he has never aligned himself theologically with that interpretation embraced by Rahner and others.[12]

In July 1947 Jan Tyranowski died in Cracow, but Karol Wojtyla travelled to Belgium and France. Whatever his feelings about returning for the funeral of his spiritual mentor, his religious superior, Cardinal Sapieha, had different plans for him. There were important pastoral experiments taking place in

French-speaking lands: the cardinal wanted Wojtyla to learn about them at first hand. He went to France and to Belgium to investigate the worker–priest movement. That was not yet its name: to its participants it was still the 'Mission de France'. The decline of religious practice among the people of France had been studied in depth. The Archbishop of Paris, Cardinal Suhard, had founded a seminary specifically to train clergy to 'accompany' the people in their work places, for they had very largely ceased to frequent the churches. His campaign reflected, for those of clerical status, a similar outlook to that of the laypeople who formed the Jeuness Ouvrière Chretienne, the 'Young Christian Workers', whose secretary Wojtyla had met in Rome at the Belgian College. Earlier in his life, Tyranowski had been secretary to a parallel organization in Poland, but had abandoned it for a more contemplative approach to the life of faith. Wojtyla talked to Father, later Cardinal, Joseph Cardjin who had founded the 'Jociste', and discovered that Cardjin was not wholly in sympathy with the developing role of the 'worker priests', believing they were assuming a role which properly belonged to the laity. None the less, when he came to write about his experiences in *Tygodnik Powszechny*, the weekly started by Sapieha in 1945 as a Catholic voice on the political and social affairs of Poland, he advocated a more active priestly apostolate among the secularized masses, as well as a more committed lay apostolate alongside it.

He returned to Rome for the opening of the academic year 1947–8. On 30 April 1948 his thesis was approved, and he became a Doctor of Divinity. On 16 December of the same year, on the strength of his studies in Rome, he was made a Doctor of Divinity of the Jagellonian University.

NOTES

1. 'The World as an Environment for Humanity' in *Origins*, vol. 10, no. 4, p. 62, quoted in Williams, *The Mind of John Paul II*, New York, Seabury, 1981, p. 19.
2. Quoted Taborski, op. cit., p. 76.
3. Taborski, op. cit., p. 379.
4. Taborski, op. cit., pp. 11–12.
5. Just after the Warsaw uprising of 1944 the Catholic dramatist Jerzy Zawieyski (1902–69) wrote *The Perfect Man*, also on the theme of Job.
6. In *Salvifici Doloris* (11 Feb 1984) John Paul II wrote 'If the Lord consents to test Job with suffering, he does it to demonstrate the latter's righteousness.'
7. Quoted Taborski, op. cit., p. 73.
8. But he was no forerunner of Liberation Theology. He was in favour of

strengthening the power of the Polish monarchy, and of linking Church and state in a close union. He was also a prime mover in the Union of Brest-Litovsk which brought the Greek Orthodox under Rome's control.

9. Quoted Taborski (trs.). *The Collected Plays and Writings on Theater*, Berkeley, University of California Press, 1987, p. 5.
10. There is some dispute whether Sapieha believed the conversions to be genuine, albeit under duress, or a complete fiction: cf. Williams, op. cit., p. 85.
11. Mieczyslaw Malinski, quoted by Williams, op. cit., p. 87.
12. cf. Gerald A. McCool, S.J., 'The theology of John Paul II' in John M. McDermott (ed.), *The Thought of John Paul II* (Rome, Gregorian University Press, 1992), pp. 35ff.

TWO

1948–78

THE POST-WAR Poland to which Wojtyla returned in 1948 was a much more Roman Catholic country than the one into which he had been born. This was in part due to the tragic slaughter of its Jewish population and partly again because many non–Latin rite Christians had disappeared into the USSR when it annexed the Ukraine. The Communist Party and its Russian advisors had come to power in Warsaw in the wake of the 1947 elections. It had begun to nationalize industry and small businesses and had confiscated the property of the Church. It found itself, however, quite unable to pursue a rigorously anti-religious policy because of the strength of the Catholic commitment of the Polish people. Some religious newspapers and journals survived, and the Catholic University of Lublin remained for a generation the only institution of its kind behind the Iron Curtain.

On his return from Rome in 1948 Wojtyla, always loyal to his friends, visited the parish priest of Debniki and said mass in the church, but his first posting as a newly-ordained curate was to take him far from Cracow. In July Sapieha despatched him to the small village of Niegowic, 200 kilometres from the city. He was to assist an old priest who was on the point of celebrating half a century of sacerdotal ministry. The parishioners proposed painting the church for the occasion: Father Wojtyla persuaded them to build a completely new one. His passion for the theatre had not deserted him. Not only did he take parishioners on outings to the theatre in Cracow – the Rhapsodic Theatre included – he established in the parish an amateur dramatic society. He produced *The Expected Guest* by the Catholic writer Zofia Kossak (1890–1968). Wojtyla himself appeared as the guest, the central character, a beggar who turns out to be Christ.

The exile to the countryside was not to last long. In March 1949, after only eight months in Niegowic, he was called back to Cracow, to the parish of St Florian, one of the most important in the City. His father's sister, Stefania, with whom in the 1930s Wojtyla and his father had spent their holidays at Biala Leszczyny, came to help him run his house.

Under a Communist regime then at its most aggressively anti-Catholic he led as far as was feasible the typical life of a curate. He preached, often learnedly, sometimes at too great a length, always with a passion and skill in public speaking which reflected his abandoned career as an actor. He gave himself in particular to the young men and boys of the parish. He had never, and has never, lost his love for sport, and particularly for football which he played with the altar boys on fields on the outskirts of the town. He was thought by the parishioners to have little care for his personal appearance – his soutane being somewhat too dishevelled – and to engage in ascetic practices of an unusual kind – he was once discovered to be sleeping on the floor instead of upon his bed. But he had still not lost his taste for drama: one Palm Sunday he read the passion narrative as if it had been a performance.

He was a regular cinema-goer, rather, it seems, to his aunt's dismay. He was able to attend all new productions at the Rhapsodic Theatre and in 1950 he was present at the ceremonial laying of the foundation stone for its new building – though because of the tense political situation he was not allowed to say a prayer. But now, as well as going to the cinema or theatre he also had time to return to his own writing.

The first version of 'Brother Albert', which eventually became *Our God's Brother*, seems to have been composed as early as 1944 while Wojtyla was still working in the Solvay quarry and chemical works: he showed a draft to Fr Jozef Mtlak, the parish priest at St Stanislaw Kostka, the church in Debniki. The play may not have been completed until 1950, when he took it along to *Znak*. Its principal character is Adam Chmielowski.

Chmielowski had been born in August 1845 at Igolomia in the district of Miechów in southern Poland. In 1863 he joined the uprising against the Russian occupation, but the insurrection failed, and he was taken prisoner. His left leg was amputated, but he was allowed to return to Poland where he abandoned his earlier study of agriculture for that of art, though he also spent a year studying engineering. Though as an artist he had enjoyed considerable success, in 1880, a decade after the first exhibition of his paintings, he joined the Society of Jesus. The life of a Jesuit novice did not suit him: within six months he suffered a nervous breakdown and left the Order. Instead he became a Franciscan tertiary, working first in the countryside and then, after 1884, in Cracow. Though he continued for a while to paint, he gradually abandoned his art to care for the poor of the city, particularly for the homeless. Finally, in 1887, inspired by Rafael Kalinowski, another freedom fighter who had afterwards become a Carmelite friar, he adopted the name of Albert, donning a simple form of habit. A year later he took vows before the Archbishop of Cracow, Cardinal Albin Dunajewski, who had also joined the uprising of 1863. Albert promised that from then onwards he would completely dedicate himself to the service of the poor. He founded the Albertine Brothers – followed three years later by the Albertine Sisters – to care for the poor and the homeless. Both because of his holiness of life and his friendliness of character he attracted a great following, and his funeral in 1916 was attended by a vast mass of people, including the mayor of Cracow and the archbishop.

In the course of the play Max, a friend of Adam/Albert says (and Adam tends to agree with him): 'The individual makes himself and joins society as an individual. His task, his mission, is first of all individual. He has individual responsibility. Society's fate depends on whether the individual accomplishes his task, fulfils his mission, meets his responsibility, or makes a mess of it. If he succeeds, society will consist of a greater number of worthy individuals and will be rather more worthy itself'.[1] He goes on to say that 'upheavals are a rather antisocial phenomenon'. A Jesuit theologian, who has turned up with his mother to view Adam's picture, a portrait of Christ in the *Ecce Homo* scene, replies 'I admit that thanks to such upheavals mankind has moved forward rather than sideways, stretched like an army in retreat, and yet shrunk.'[2]

At the forefront of Wojtyla's mind must have been not only the upheavals of the Nazi invasion, but the subsequent imposition of a Communist regime. In *Our God's Brother* there is a somewhat mysterious character, a stranger, who rather rebukes Adam for dissipating his energies, not only on his painting but also on his individual acts of charity which, precisely because they are individual acts, will solve nothing. Adam is impressed by this presentation of the Marxist argument, but he responds, 'Man's poverty is deeper than the resources of all those goods you are talking about. All those goods man can aspire to by the force of his anger … man is to aspire to all goods. To all. To the greatest of them too. But here anger fails; here Charity is essential.'[3]

This high vision of human nature and purpose Wojtyla spells out more directly in the introduction he provided for his play: 'Between the man and the attempt to penetrate him there runs a line inaccessible to history. For it is a characteristic of man in general that it is not possible fully to fathom him historically. Indeed, an extrahistorical element in man lies at the very sources of his humanity. And any attempt to penetrate the man is connected to reaching to these sources.[4]

Wojtyla completed this play – which was not published (in *Tygodnik*

Powszechny) until after his election to the papacy – while serving as a curate in his parish in Cracow. There was a strong mystical element in his writing, no doubt reflecting his earlier studies. But there was also an equally strong ethical concern. It is not surprising that the first volume to which he gave his undivided attention when despatched to undertake a second doctorate was a work on ethics. Its author was the German Catholic philosopher Max Scheler (1874–1928). In order to comprehend it better, Wojtyla set about translating it from the German. When he finally came to write his doctoral thesis it was entitled *An Assessment of the Possibility of Building a Christian Ethic on the Principles of the System of Max Scheler.*[5]

The idea that he should start work on a second doctorate was not Wojtyla's, and he seems at first to have been opposed to the idea, preferring to remain as a pastor. It seems originally to have come from Ignacy Rózycki who had taught him in the theological faculty of the Jagellonian University. Cardinal Sapieha instructed Wojtyla to leave his post at St Florian's and go to live with Rózycki in Kanonicza Street, saying mass at St Mary's Church in the Rynek, Cracow's principal square. He asked to be allowed at least to work part-time in a pastoral post: the request was refused by Archbishop Eugeniusz Baziak, for Sapieha himself had died on 23 July 1951.

It was not surprising that Wojtyla was at first attracted to the philosophical ethics of Max Scheler. There was among the Catholic intellectuals of Cracow a strong interest in the writings of Emanuel Mounier and of those whom he had gathered around his journal *Esprit*. The 'personalism' which they developed as a system of thought was Christian in tone, but the group was ecumenical – including Jews, Orthodox and Protestant thinkers as well as Catholic ones like Mounier himself, or Jacques and Raïssa Maritain. They were left-wing, when it was not fashionable to be so. They were sympathetic to some aspects of socialism (though obviously unsympathetic to its militant atheism) and were critical of capitalist individualism. Jerzy Turowicz, a Polish intellectual who was later to be a close associate of Wojtyla's, attended the *Esprit* conference held in summer 1937, where he met Mounier and other leading personalists. Mounier's *Personalist Manifesto* was translated into Polish during the war years and Turowicz eventually organized the publication in Poland of many of Mounier's other works. In May 1946, under Turowicz's guidance, Mounier came to Cracow and gave a talk at the Jagellonian University. His experience led him to reflect upon Poland as a unique locus for a reconciliation of Catholicism and socialism. He worked hard for just such a reconciliation, and his journal became one of the leading exponents of Christian-Marxist dialogue. The personalists stood for a 'third way' between

Communism and capitalism, but 'while the personalist long-term political blueprint was relatively clear in what it opposed' it was not so clear 'as to what sort of political structures the new philosophy would establish if given a free hand'.[6] Mounier himself produced in 1934 *La révolution personaliste et communautaire*, but for his notions of community, and more especially for the spiritual dimension of the experience of community, he turned to the writings of Max Scheler.[7]

For one thing Scheler was, at least at the time of writing *Formalism and the Ethics of Substantive Values* – the book which Wojtyla translated – a Roman Catholic though scarcely an ideal one. His father was a nominal Lutheran, his mother Jewish. When he converted at the age of fourteen he was chiefly attracted to the Church by a highly utopian notion of the Middle Ages. His sexual adventures while lecturing first in Jena and then in Munich were such that he was removed from his post, and banned from teaching. He went to Göttingen to be near his philosphical hero Edmund Husserl (though Husserl was eventually to distance himself from Scheler's interpretation of his work), and there found himself in a circle which included the Polish philosopher Roman Ingarden, and Edith Stein, a Jew born in Silesia.

The 'Catholic period' of Scheler's thought began with his marriage to a devout Catholic in 1912, and culminated with a retreat in the Benedictine monastery of Beuron in the winter of 1915. After the retreat he once again started to frequent the sacraments. This was, of course, in the middle of the First World War, a conflict about which he had strongly-held views. He had little or no doubt of the righteousness of Germany and its allies, and he was particularly antagonistic to England, partly at least because of the links between England and the United States, a country he loathed even more, were that possible, than he loathed England itself. What he hoped for on the continent of Europe was an alliance of the continental powers, in a society restored on idealized medieval lines, revitalized by a renascent Church. The war against Britain, then, was something of a holy crusade.

It was a crusade which the supposedly Catholic powers finally lost. The collapse of Germany was followed by a rise in Scheler's fortunes when he was appointed a professor in Cologne. This was a post in a Catholic university, but Scheler's own Catholicism did not long survive. His disavowal of the faith no doubt sprang from his divorce and third marriage, but he attributed it to the incompatibility between his own phenomenology and the espousal of Thomism by the Church.

He was therefore a Catholic philosopher who was not in the Thomistic tradition and one whose thinking, therefore, presented Wojtyla with an entirely new philosophical perspective. It is tempting to see in Wojtyla's choice of thesis on Scheler the influence of Roman Ingarden. Ingarden, perhaps Husserl's most able pupil, had been a professor in Lvov before the War, and after it was appointed to Cracow. Though Ingarden is unlikely directly to have been an influence on Wojtyla, he was known to Rózycki who may have suggested the theme. In any case, though Wojtyla was to reject much of Scheler's approach (some of the terminology of 'personalism',[8] however survived), he found sympathy with Scheler's delineation of the five types of values, more specifically the fifth value, the holy, of which the saint was the exemplar.

The supreme saint is, of course, Christ himself. The New Testament therefore is the prime source of ethical teaching, Wojtyla argued, alongside tradition and the *magisterium*: the Catholic ethic must rest upon revealed truths. A Catholic's conscience has to take account of these external norms whereas in the conscience of an individual, according to Wojtyla's interpretation of Scheler, primacy is given to experience, to a 'feeling', and sentiment is the determining factor. The ethical philosophy of Scheler, concluded Wojtyla, was not an appropriate framework for Catholic ethics.

This did not imply that Scheler was to be totally rejected. Wojtyla picked up some of the terminology and conceptual models from the German philosopher. In particular, he came to think of the Church as 'almost a disciplined, unified, perfectionist sect, as it had been in times and places before – in pre-Constantinian antiquity, in England during the Reformation, in Ireland in the nineteenth century, and in Germany during the *Kulturkampf*.[9] The vital characteristic which linked these examples was that of persecution, just as that Catholic community was being persecuted within which he was at the time writing his thesis in preparation for a university post. His Church was not a highly structured, international corporation but an oppressed community to which people willingly belonged. The concept of a willing, therefore freely-chosen, membership of the Church has now so entered the consciousness of Catholics that it no longer seems remarkable. When Wojtyla was writing his thesis it was an uncommon perspective, one which he owed very largely to Scheler. It long continued to affect his thinking.

The thesis on Scheler was presented towards the end of 1953. Roman Ingarden was one of the examiners, another was Wladyslaw Wicher, a professor of moral theology at the Jagellonian. The third, who had become an unofficial supervisor of the young priest's work, was Stefan Swiezawski, formerly of the Catholic University at Lublin and a professor of medieval philosophy. By the time the thesis was approved, early in 1954, Wojtyla was already teaching social ethics in the seminary at Cracow, once more in touch with the student life he had so much enjoyed both as a student himself and as a young assistant priest. Wojtyla's was the last thesis to be approved before the Communist authorities closed down the faculty of theology.

He was now ready for university teaching, and in his friend Swiezawski he had a staunch advocate with strong links at the Catholic University of Lublin (KUL). This was an extraordinary institution. It had originally been founded in 1914 in St Petersburg to provide priests for the Poland that was under Russian domination, and for other Catholic communities elsewhere in Russian territory. In 1918, after the Revolution, it was closed and moved to Lublin where it flourished, partly at least in opposition to the only two other universities in Poland, which were of a secular bent. What was most remarkable about the KUL was its ability to survive under Communism. According to its constitution, the President of the University is the Primate of Poland; its Chancellor, however, is *ex officio* the Bishop of Lublin, and from 1946 to 1948 that bishop was Stefan Wyszynski, himself a former student. Neither Wyszynski nor successive rectors were disposed readily to give in to Communist pressure, and although KUL was stripped of some of its faculties, for the most part it managed to ride out the worst of the persecution. It could do so because it was the recipient of considerable donations from Poles living outside their country who regarded the University, alongside the Church, as one of the few bastions against a complete Communist take-over of their homeland. Throughout the period of Communist domination in Eastern Europe the Catholic University of Lublin survived as the only private university-level institution of the Eastern bloc.

Wojtyla first went there to lecture in 1953. It was a matter of a few addresses on the foundations of ethics given to students in the faculty of philosophy. There were, in all, three series of such lectures, of which the first has been published. He begins, not surprisingly, with Scheler.[10] The following year, 1954, he was asked to join the faculty of philosophy, and in 1956 he became a professor – not perhaps such a distinguished position as it might be at least in British universities. The faculty of Christian Philosophy, as it was called, had several of them. In the structures of the university there were several ranks of 'professor' and Wojtyla's chair was not in the first rank. None the less his appointment – which, incidentally, he has continued to hold as Pope, even reading doctoral theses on occasion – was no small achievement at the age of thirty-six.

As a university teacher Wojtyla was something of a success. Again not surprisingly, given his background as an actor, he was thought to be an outstanding lecturer. He did not take up residence in Lublin but commuted by night train to and from Cracow. This meant he was frequently late for seminars and lectures, and was constantly tired, so tired, indeed, that on occasion he was reported to have dropped off to sleep in seminars. But it also meant there was something of the exotic, something of the man of the world about him. He had, after all, but recently returned from the West.

He fitted well into the faculty, though he found his natural companionship at Lublin not among the clerics on the faculty, but with the younger lay lecturers, and among the students – to whom he eventually became known as 'Uncle'. He kept up his pastoral work in Cracow, which gave to the examples he produced in his lectures on ethics a certain immediacy missing from the stock in trade of the pure theoretician. He does not emerge in the stories told about him from those days as a man given to small talk, even though sport was one of his favoured topics of conversation. He would cheerfully debate moral issues, or declaim on the niceties of the theatre. He was once so lost in argument that he and his companions failed to notice they had been locked in the building when the porters made their rounds, and they had to climb out of a window. They had a difficult time proving to a vigilant policeman that they were not thieves.

His rapport with the students stretched beyond the confines of the lecture-hall. He remained a student chaplain, and he would spend his summers in the company of young people, walking in the mountains, or canoeing upon the lakes. It was while he was on just such a canoeing trip among the lakes of Mazuria that he was named auxiliary bishop to serve the diocese of Cracow, then under an Apostolic Administrator, Archbishop Baziak. The appointment was dated 4 July 1958. Wojtyla was given the formal title of titular bishop of Ombi. He was thirty-eight years of age, and Poland's youngest bishop.

The ceremony of ordination as bishop took place in the cathedral beside the Wawel castle in Cracow on 28 September 1958, performed by Archbishop Baziak. The vestments were supplied by a Jesuit priest who had left for the United States before the war, but who had remained in correspondence with the Kydrynski family: he was completely unknown to Wojtyla himself. Fifteen members of Wojtyla's family were present for the service, and immediately afterwards he went to see his godmother, living in Cracow but too ill to attend the cathedral. There was one untoward event in the course of the ordination. In the silence of the solemn ritual one of those who had worked beside him at the Solvay plant suddenly burst out, 'Lolek, don't let anybody get you down!' The sentiment, a biographer notes, was received with sympathy by congregation and Wojtyla alike.[11]

Up to this time had had been living still at Kanonicza Street with Fr Rózycki, doing pastoral work in Cracow and lecturing at Lublin. With the office of assistant bishop there came a flat at the official residence of the bishop attached to the offices of the archdiocese of Cracow in Franciszkanska Street. Wojtyla had to move, whatever his personal preference. Had the flat in the metropolitan curia remained empty, there was a good chance that the Communist authorities in Cracow would have requistioned it.

Although the office of bishop brought new responsibilities, it also appears to have given Wojtyla somewhat more time for writing. In December 1960 a new play, the first in a decade and the only work for the theatre to be published before he became Pope, appeared in *Znak* under the pseudonym Andrzej Jawién, one which Wojtyla used often. It was *The Jeweller's Shop*, a study of marriage, its hopes and its disappointments, set outside the window of a jeweller's shop. In the window are wedding rings, and the characters of the play reflect upon their own lives, the lives of their parents, and upon their hopes for life together. To call it a play is perhaps to overstate it – though it has been performed. (The world premiere was in Hammersmith, London, at the end of April 1979.) There is no action, precious little dialogue. The text consists of monologues spoken by characters when in each other's company, but not directly addressed to each other. Each person soliloquizes about his or her experience of love, or the lack of it, or its gradual destruction, but one, Adam, reflects upon it philosophically and theologically. 'The figure of Adam', Taborski comments,

> answers those who wonder how the author of the play, who never married or had a family, could delve into the problems of human love and marriage with such insight. The first act of the play refers to mountain hikes and rambles. As a priest Wojtyla used to go with young people on excursions to the country. They called him Uncle. Their companion and friend, he was also an adviser and witness to their friendships, budding loves, problems. Each year during the 1950s he undertook a two-week trip to the mountains and another around the Masurian lakes ... Witness, adviser, 'spokesman', and judge: all these functions are also implied in the duties of a confessor ...[12]

He clearly drew upon the same experience for his first book which was also published in 1960. If *The Jeweller's Shop* was concerned with the problems of love within marriage, *Love and Responsibility* turned its attention directly to sexual ethics. The topic was, of course, one that no lecturer in ethics could ignore, certainly no priestly lecturer at a Catholic University. It was also a topic where there was little room for manoeuvre, especially in 1960. One doubts whether Wojtyla wanted room for manoeuvre. Though he cites studies which are at odds with his own views, the young bishop expressly grounded his approach in Scripture, tradition, and the *magisterium* – the teaching of the Church authorities.

The book is aimed at the young laity whom he had served as chaplain. It was an educated, distinctly Catholic, elite, one to which a scholastic analysis of love relationships would not seem too incongruous. The book is extraordinary for what it leaves out, as much as for what it includes: there is no mention of abortion, none of pre-marital sex. There is nothing about the physically handicapped, perhaps because the socialist republic, of which Wojtyla was a member at least in theory, coped with such individuals frequently by removing them from contact with the generality of the population. There was no mention of homosexuality, possibly because there were – apparently – so few in Polish society.[13] It is a book written for an ideal group, ideal physically, mentally and, as Catholics, spiritually.

It is traditional in a scholastic treatise to cite the views of one's opponents, though only, of course, so that they may be held up to ridicule, and demolished. Of such *adversarii* Wojtyla has many, but it is significant that among them a large number are from the West – much more so than from the East – and include in particular English and to a slightly lesser extent American philosophers. He has an especial (but misplaced because he did not understand them) antipathy to the English puritans of the seventeenth century. He is also strongly opposed to situation ethics, roundly condemned by Pope Pius XII in the March and April of 1952. But situation ethics had been inspired in part by the personalist ethics of Max Scheler, and had been embodied in the novels of the Catholic authors François Mauriac and Graham Greene. Both depicted the central characters of some at least of their novels as having highly delicate consciences which they relied upon in morally unusual situations. Such an approach Pope Pius and Bishop Karol Wojtyla found dangerously relativistic.

Love and Responsibility sticks closely to the traditional Catholic view that marriage, though it may have many purposes, is primarily for the procreation of children (a position, incidentally, which a decade later the Vatican Council carefully avoided endorsing). Wojtyla also showed himself a protagonist of the controversial 'rhythm method' of birth control, going as far as printing tables to help distinguish fertile from infertile periods of a woman's cycle. In one modest way the book was ahead of its time – Wojtyla almost always mentioned the woman before the man – but in most others he was staunchly conservative, for 'devout and trusting surrender (to her husband) is the distinctive trait of the woman in love, [and] possession is the characteristic modality of the devotion of the man to the woman he loves'.[14]

By the time *Love and Responsibility* had been published, the Second Vatican Council had already been summoned. As Assistant Bishop to Archbishop Eugniusz Baziak he would in any event have attended this gathering of all the bishops of the Roman Catholic Church, but Baziak died in the June of 1962. Wojtyla was made Administrator of the diocese: he was not immediately created an archbishop. As Administrator he joined the other Polish bishops for the Council. With twenty-four others he flew to Rome on 5 October 1962: the Council met for its first session on the seventeenth of that month. He stayed at the Polish College, situated on the Piazza Remuria on the Aventine Hill: its Rector was Bishop Wladyslaw Rubin.

Though Wojtyla had taken an active part in the Polish bishops' preparation for the Council, he spoke only once during the first session (7 October to 17 December). On 7 November he urged the Council to consider the pastoral significance of the sacraments when discussing the document on the liturgy, stressing the importance of the sacraments of initiation, and in particular the notion of an adult catechumenate.[15] He also submitted two written comments. The first was on the document on the media, praising the 'instruments of social communication' as a 'great gift of God to the present generation', but warning of their dangers. They should, he said, serve 'true' human culture and improve people's interior lives, but very often they did not.[16] The second, at the end of the session, was on the Constitution of the Church, half of it devoted to the role of the Virgin Mary.[17]

By the second session (8 September to 4 December 1963) he was much more expansive. He had come to know others of the Council fathers, he had become acquainted with some of the *periti*, the theological experts who advised the bishops. He is recalled by one of his friends[18] as having praised in particular five of these experts, one Dominican, Yves Congar, three Jesuits, Riccardo Lombardi, Jean Daniélou and Karl Rahner, and a diocesan priest then embarking on what was to prove a turbulent career, Hans Küng.

On 21 October he intervened for the second time in the conciliar debates. His topic was the document which would eventually become *Lumen Gentium*, the Constitution of the Church. His argument was that there should be a statement about the whole people of God before descending to particulars and discussing the clergy as part of the people of God. He went on to say that the Constitution should make it clear that the Church was a

27

natural society, one made up of imperfect members, but in the supernatural order it was a perfect society, for it was possessed of every means to achieve its supernatural ends. He wanted a clearer distinction to be drawn between the universal priesthood of all believers, and the ministerial priesthood of the clergy.[19] He made further, written, comments on the Constitution on the Church.[20] When he spoke to the people of Poland by means of Vatican Radio at this period on 'Man as a Person', however, he chose to stress the dignity of the human individual, and the immense theoretical significance – not fully expounded by the Council as he admitted – of the recognition of the individual as a person in a world redeemed by Christ who 'has in a certain way united himself with each man'.[21]

Shortly after the close of the Council's second session Wojtyla went to the Holy Land – his visit preceding by a few days that of Pope Paul VI. But by the time Paul went to Jerusalem, Wojtyla knew that the Pope had appointed him Archbishop of Cracow. It was therefore as a Metropolitan that Wojtyla attended the third session, from 14 September to 21 November 1965, though while still formally an assistant bishop he made a number of written submissions, including one on the apostolate of the laity which urged that something be said about the apostolate of writing.[22] On 25 September in a debate about ecumenism he spoke on religious liberty, urging that civil liberty of religion be placed in the document on the Church in the Modern World. He argued none the less that the state had no right to interfere in the practice of religion, and that religious freedom included freedom of instruction. In the context of ecumenism, on the other hand, he insisted that liberty existed for the sake of seeking the truth. 'It does not suffice', he added, 'if the principle of religious liberty towards the separated brethren should appear only as a principle of toleration. For toleration does not so much have a positive sense as in some way a negative one ... Progress in the perception of the truth must be desired at the same time, for finally nothing other than the truth will liberate us from the various kinds of separations.'[23]

His next public intervention was on 8 October, when the Council fathers were discussing the document on the Apostolate of the Laity. There were groups in Poland (and elsewhere in the Eastern bloc) at that time claiming to be engaged in the lay apostolate, though their activities had the tacit, or in some cases open, support of the Communist government. Such groups, who wanted to subvert the apostolate for their own ends, he said, should be excluded from it. On the other hand he wanted the document to lay stress on the natural right of lay people to engage in the apostolate, saying that 'every human being has the right to know the truth and to communicate the same to others, either by word, or by writings, or by deed.'[24]

Two weeks later, on 21 October, Wojtyla was again addressing the Council on the topic of the Church in the Modern World, this time in the name of the whole of the Polish episcopate. He urged the fathers to use arguments drawn from reason and natural law (to a traditional Catholic, roughly the same thing) because only those would persuade. The Church, he said, should not appear omniscient or paternalistic, though he rather spoiled this by adding 'It is not in question that the Truth is already known to us; but [at issue] is in what manner the world will find it for itself, and make it its own'.[25] In the same speech he acknowledged that there was 'a plurality of worlds' to be addressed.[26]

At the end of the session Wojtyla returned to Cracow, but he had been appointed to work on redrafting the document on the Church in the Modern World. The meeting was in Ariccia, in February 1965, and on 12 February he broadcast to Poland over Vatican Radio, choosing as his theme 'The Council and the Work of Theologians'. For his Polish listeners he mentioned by name many of the most distinguished of the *periti* at work in the Council. The role of the theologian, he explained, was to understand the word of God, and to do so they needed to act as intelligent, free human beings.

The final session of the Council met from 14 September to 8 December 1965. The controversial document on religious liberty, held over from the previous session despite protests from many of the Council fathers, was the first topic for debate, and, on 22 September, Wojtyla was among the first speakers, having already made a written submission.[27] He insisted that the Church declaration on religious liberty should distinguish it from simple, liberal tolerance:

> It is not enough to say in this matter 'I am free', but rather 'I am accountable'. This is the doctrine grounded in the living tradition of the Church of the confessors and martyrs. Responsibility is the summit and necessary complement of liberty. This ought to be underlined so that our Declaration will be seen to be intimately personalistic in the Christian sense, but not as derived from liberalism or indifferentism. The civil powers ought to observe most strictly and with great sensitivity religious liberty as much in a collective as in a personal sense.[28]

A year before almost to the day Wojtyla, speaking on the same topic, had insisted that the state had no right to permit actions which were contrary to the natural law: liberty did not go that far. He carefully distinguished himself from the liberal point of view, for liberty was not to be mistaken for the indifferentism by which a government simply treated religious and ethical matters as entirely personal, and of no concern to the state as such.

Wojtyla's next intervention was on 28 September, while there was being discussed the section of the schema on the Church in the Modern World upon which he had himself helped with the revision at Ariccia earlier in the year. Its topic was the dignity of the human person, a typical Wojtyla theme, and in his speech he was careful to distinguish between an atheism systematically imposed from above (the Council fathers avoided talk of Marxism or Communism so as not to embarrass Church leaders from the Eastern bloc), and an atheism which was a personal conviction. It would be wrong to say that he displayed any understanding of an individual's commitment to atheism – which, he clearly believed, diminished the fullness of that person's humanity – but he was able to explain from his philosophical background in Marxism the problems that unbelievers might have in dialogue with believers, as much as believers in dialogue with atheists. This was his final speech. It was too long, and the chairman had to tell him his time was up.[29] There were two more written interventions, one on marriage and the family[30] and the other on culture.[31]

This was the last session of the Council, but there were a good many loose ends to be tidied up. The topic of birth control had been removed from the Constitution on the Church in the Modern World and a commission was established to discuss it, with Wojtyla as one of its members. He never attended.[32] (He did, however, establish his own, quite separate, commission of doctors and moral theologians in Cracow to study the whole question of marriage and sexual ethics.) He was also made a member of the Council on the Laity, one of whose tasks was to establish the important Commission on Justice and Peace: this he supported. In May of 1967 Pope Paul VI named him Cardinal, and he received the red hat in the Sistine Chapel on 28 June.

Later that same year the first Synod of Bishops was held in Rome. The hope which lay behind the establishment of these elected assemblies, representative (at least in theory) of Episcopal Conferences around the world, was that they would give concrete form to the doctrine of collegiality, elaborated during the Council, that all the bishops together with the pope exercised oversight over the worldwide Church. Cardinal Wyszynski, the Primate of Poland, was chosen to attend along with Wojtyla, but the Polish government denied him the requisite permission to leave the country. Wojtyla refused to attend if Wyszynski could not, so neither went, but a Polish Bishop, Wladyslaw Rubin, became secretary general to the Synod.

At home in Cracow there was much to concern him. There was a major celebration of a thousand years of Christianity in Poland, the climax of which was in Cracow between 6 and 8 May 1966. The commission on sex and marriage which he had established in 1966 reported in 1969, the year in which Wojtyla became vice-president of the Polish Episcopal Conference. Its findings were published – in French, presumably for wider consumption than Poland alone – in the *Analecta Cracoviensia*, the learned journal which Wojtyla had helped to found. A year before Paul VI had produced his encyclical letter condemning artificial means of contraception, *Humanae Vitae*. The commission's findings were immediately followed in the *Analecta* by an article by Professor Ignacy Rózycki, a priest who had once taught Wojtyla, arguing that Paul VI was perfectly within his papal rights to act as an exponent of natural law; that the papal utterances were binding on everyone precisely because they were based on the natural law; and that if not formally infallible, the encyclical was infallible in fact.

In 1969, in the spirit of Vatican II, Wojtyla organized a synod of his priests in Cracow. From 26 August to 11 October 1969 he made his first visit to North America. On his return he worked on a book, published in Cracow in 1972, revised and translated into Italian in 1979 by the Vatican's own publishing house shortly after his election to the papacy, and published in English in 1980 as *Sources of Renewal*. Its subtitle indicates its purpose: it addressed 'The implementation of the Second Vatican Council'. It was, indeed, a handbook for members of his ongoing pastoral synod in Cracow. It is a digest of the Conciliar texts, arranged in three major themes, 'The basic significance of conciliar initiation' (by which he means introduction into the spirit of the Council) 'The formation of consciousness', and 'The formation of attitudes'. It was not a history of the Council, nor a commentary upon its texts, but rather, as he called it in his introduction, 'a vade mecum introducing the reader to the relevant documents of Vatican II but always from the point of view of translating them into the life and faith of the Church'. It was dedicated 'to those who, in the Church at Cracow, give me their generous help and co-operate with me as their bishop in giving effect to Vatican II'.[33]

At least one commentator has seen this book as part of the neo-conservative reaction to the Council, well under way in the early 1970s,[34] and so indeed it may be. Wojtyla highlights the hierarchical structure of the Church, the distinctive roles of priests and laity, and is clearly traditional on such matters as the celibacy of the clergy, a topic then, as now, much debated. He quotes the Constitution on the Church § 10 which insists that the common priesthood of all the faithful and the ministerial or hierarchical priesthood 'differ from one another in essence and not only in degree'. He calls it a 'key passage'. He does not, however, comment that this sentence was added by Pope Paul under pressure from a conservative minority against the wishes of the Council: it was in line with the views which he had himself expressed in the Council debates. But Wojtyla's own contribution to the book is relatively brief, supplying continuity between the sections of the conciliar documents he chooses to quote. Most striking about the book, however, is the grasp he clearly had of the texts of Vatican II.

Sources of Renewal grew out of Wojtyla's experience of the Council and his desire to interpret it for his clergy. Several years before it was published he had produced his most significant work of philosophy. It has been called in English *The Acting Person*, and was first published in Cracow in 1969 as *Osoba I Czyn*, which more accurately translates 'Person and Act'. The English edition did not appear until 1979 and was considerably revised. To quote Williams, 'The goal and achievement of the book is, by means of a concerted effort in using the tools of phenomenological investigation, to demonstrate that man ... *is a person*. ... Such a person, body and soul, is not simply a rational and social animal, but a sovereign and enduring entity, self-determining and capable of responding to the revealed will of the Sovereign Person who created him after his image and likeness and capable also of participating with others in community'.[35]

Such a position is hardly startling, though when a conference was devoted to the book at Lublin in December 1970 in the presence of Wojtyla, some of the nineteen contributors praised it for its originality and daring. But it was also criticized, sometimes severely, among other things for too readily assimilating the terminology and the philosophical convictions of Aristotle and St Thomas. One of those who gave a paper confessed that though he had read the book twice, he was not sure he had understood it: there were jokes among the younger clergy that it would be required reading for Purgatory.

Whatever Karol Wojtyla felt about these criticisms, he seems to have realized that his book needed explaining, and in a number of conferences and articles over the following years he undertook this task, somewhat under the guidance of the Polish-born, though United States resident, Dr Anna-Teresa Tymienecka. Dr Tymienecka had studied at Cracow under Roman Ingarden immediately after the end of the war, but had gone on to the Sorbonne and the University of Fribourg. She had not known the young Wojtyla, but was greatly excited upon reading *Osoba I Czyn*. She used her considerable status as President of the World Institute for Advanced Phenomenological

Research, and as editor (and founder) of the *Analecta Husserliana*, to promote the Cardinal's work. In December 1974 she went to Cracow to negotiate for an English translation, to appear as a volume in the *Analecta*. This was agreed, and Wojtyla hired as translator Andrzej Potocki, who had been educated by the Benedictines at Downside Abbey, near Bath, one of England's leading public schools. The outcome is a very different work from that of which it is, in theory, a translation. Both the author and Dr Tymienecka were involved in rendering the text closer to the language of phenomenology, which does nothing to improve its comprehensibility to an English-speaking philosophical world little conversant with the type of thought the Cardinal was promoting. George Hunston Williams, in his study of the evolution of *Osoba I Czyn* into *The Acting Person*, a study written with not a little asperity directed particularly at Dr Tymienecka though Wojtyla is also included in the criticism, suggests that at least part of the problem arises because the author is basically a Thomist, and his philosophy has come to be clothed in an inappropriate language.[36] Another commentator agrees. Basing his argument that the difficulty of the text stems in part 'from its overly technical revision, more precisely from the frequency with which [Tymienecka] by differing paraphrases of scholastic terms, has supplanted an older technical language for another more contemporary one', Kenneth Schmitz concludes that the revision 'obscures the vitality which the author still finds in the intellectual traditions of medieval scholasticism'.[37]

The fundamental argument of *The Acting Person* is central to the understanding of much which Pope John Paul II has had to say about the importance of work, specifically in his encyclical *Laborem Exercens*. Williams summarizes it as follows:

> 'man-acts' are a narrow class of experience, and are only able to be performed freely through the use of self-determination; they are performed in reference to an objective truth, an absolute; they fulfil or do not fulfil the person's human potential, according to whether they are or are not true to a perennially valid ethical norm, thus making the person good or bad. The freedom or self-determination of a person thus depends ultimately upon his free choice of (the revealed) truth as to the good.[38]

As Williams comments, although the book is presented as a philosophical treatise, the above description of human acts presupposes a distinct Christian, not to say Catholic, understanding of free will, of the existence of absolute truth, and the moral value of every act – the last being a particularly significant feature of Thomistic ethics. The person therefore becomes (morally) good or bad through his or her actions.

The approach outlined above runs the risk of appearing self-centred. That is not what Wojtyla intends. A sovereign individual's human acts in most instances involve other sovereign individuals: there are 'communities of acting'.[39] In good Catholic style Wojtyla distinguishes two – the natural society (family or state) and voluntary societies which come together for particular purposes. About the value of the latter he has a curiously negative attitude, regarding them as organizations which exist to safeguard, selfishly, their members' interests which otherwise might be in jeopardy. He has, therefore, a somewhat Hobbesian view though without Hobbes' own pessimistic attitude to the individual's readiness to act in the best interests of others. It may be that his adult experience, limited almost entirely to a state under Communist domination, had not prepared him for a society in which voluntary groups worked for the good of others, though such groups are essential ingredients of Western democracies.

'Participation' (a favourite word) in a natural community is one of the essential activities of a truly sovereign individual. He recognizes the right of opposition within such a community, but it is not a topic upon which he dwells. He favours solidarity.

Reviewing the book in the columns of *The Tablet* in August 1979,[40] the distinguished English Jesuit philosopher Frederick Copleston was complimentary, but a touch cool. The treatise hinted, he said, at the possibility of a second volume but 'Now that he sits in the chair of St Peter, we obviously cannot expect him to find time for further philosophical writing of the kind represented by this book. But the loss thus incurred by the readers is more than compensated by his elevation to the position of Supreme Pastor of the Church'. Philosophy's loss, he appeared to be saying, was the Church's gain – but the professional philosopher did not seem to be too distressed by the thought.

The trip to North America in 1969 began in Canada, where there was to be celebrated the 25th anniversary of a Canadian Polish association. Wojtyla went first to Montreal, where he was greeted by Maurice Roy, the Cardinal of Quebec, President of the Council for the Laity of which Wojtyla was a member. He travelled widely around the country, and told a bemused gathering of young people in Toronto – about whose Catholicism he knew next to nothing – that their contemporaries in Poland probably had a firmer grasp of their faith than they. In the United States he sought out places of particular significance to Poles – a Polish seminary near Detroit, a centre where books on philosophy being produced by his faculty in Lublin were being translated. From the United States he went on to Rome for the 1969 Synod. The representative of the Polish bishops was Wyszynski: Wojtyla was appointed to membership of the Synod directly by Pope Paul.

Appropriately for a member of the Synod nominated by the Pope, Wojtyla re-echoed Paul's own views. He thought, along with Paul, that the document on collegiality (the topic of the Synod) was too weak, but he was quite clear that a Synod would have to be advisory to the papacy: in his scheme of things there was no room for a deliberative body. The bishops throughout the world were, however, a true 'communio' – the term Wojtyla used – or fellowship of different particular Churches. But, he argued, 'the multitude and even the multiplicity in respect of the fellowship should always be formulated from the angle of unity'. It is not exactly clear what Wojtyla was endorsing by the use of the word 'multiplicity'. One commentator has translated it as 'pluralism', and it is true that Wojtyla went on to talk of the bishops being 'gathered from different sides, representing the heritage of different people, cultures, and local Churches'. But however one understands this plurality or multiplicity, it is evident that for Wojtyla the overriding consideration was that of unity. His words made an impact. He was chosen as a member of the commission established to prepare the communiqué at the end of the Synod.[41]

Wojtyla returned from Rome to a politically very disturbed Poland. Vast numbers of Polish Jews had died during the war but some had escaped to Russia. They returned convinced Party members and soon rose to positions of influence. But the fact that they had not taken part in the Polish opposition to the German occupation caused resentment among those who had done so. The victory of Israel in the Six Day War (June 1967) was greeted with enthusiasm by Polish Jews – but it was a problem for the generally pro-Arab stance of the Eastern bloc countries. Poland broke off relations with Israel and there arose a strong wave of anti-Semitism (usually described as the politically more acceptable 'anti-Zionism') within the Polish Communist Party which continued on until 1969.

Meanwhile Alexander Dubcek had established a far more humane regime in Czechoslovakia than that of his Stalinist predecessor. Dubcek's achievements were watched with ill-concealed delight by non-Communist intellectuals in Poland. A nineteenth-century anti-Russian play had been attracting full houses in Cracow and Warsaw, its anti-Russian sentiments being cheered to the echo by the audience. In March 1968 the censors banned it, provoking an uprising among university students and their teachers. When the police found Jewish students among those arrested in the demonstrations, Gomulka used this as an excuse to step up his attack on the Jews. Both Wyszynski and Wojtyla protested against the treatment of Jews, showing concern not just for infringements of the Church's rights, but for those of society at large. And as for the Dubcek regime, in August 1968 Polish troops were sent to assist East German and Russian soldiers in putting it down.

In December 1970 the Polish government agreed with the government of the Federal Republic of Germany that the border between Poland and Germany should be the Oder-Neisse line, giving *de jure* recognition to the occupation by Poland after the Second World War of what had once been German territory. The German Chancellor Willi Brandt came to Warsaw to sign the treaty. It was a triumph for the Polish premier, Gomulka – and it was promptly followed by a rise in prices. There were riots among the shipyard workers and dockers of Gdansk and elsewhere, riots which brought the young, and recently-married, Lech Walesa into prominence for the first time. Much blood was shed in putting down the uprising, and Gomulka was deposed, to be replaced for the next decade by Eduard Gierek.

The setting of the border with Germany was of particular significance for the Polish Church. The Vatican had steadfastly refused, while the former German territories were still in dispute, to appoint bishops to the dioceses which lay within those areas. This was a matter of some annoyance to Poland's hierarchy. So was the general drift of the Vatican's *Ostpolitik*, its policy of attempting to win some concessions for the Churches in the Eastern bloc by reaching an understanding with the Communist regimes in those countries. The Polish hierarchy thought that it, rather than the Vatican, was best placed to handle the Polish government. That government, meanwhile, tried to separate the two cardinals, Wyszynski and Wojtyla. They thought the latter more manageable, and he had certainly suffered less than the Cardinal Primate.

Though Wojtyla kept up a show of solidarity with the Primate, others close to him were less circumspect. Jerzy Turowicz, editor of *Tygodnik Powszechny*, the paper founded by Cardinal Sapieha, wrote in 1969 about the crisis in the Polish Church, apparently criticizing Wyszynski for failing to implement adequately the decrees of Vatican II – specifically for failing to encourage the laity to play a greater part in the life of the Church. He followed that up with an open letter to the Primate complaining that Wyszynski kept the Polish Catholic intelligentsia, and more particularly those with seats in the Polish parliament, at a distance. Wojtyla, the letter suggested, was better informed than the Primate.

Wojtyla was in a difficult position. Turowicz was an old and trusted friend. On the other hand, it would be playing into the regime's hands were a public division to open up between himself and Wyszynski. Turowicz was rebuked, but at the same time, in May 1970, Wojtyla took advantage of a pilgrimage to Rome of Polish priests who had survived the horrors of the German concentration camps to explain to Paul VI the political situation in his country.

Meanwhile it was important that the Church in Poland should not seem to be divided, either politically or theologically. In September 1971 there was a Congress of Polish Theologians. Wojtyla congratulated them as having recognized that their proper task was to 'guard, defend, and teach the sacred deposit of revelation'. He was delighted that they did so in conjunction with their bishops, and in obedience to the *magisterium* – theoretically the Church's teaching, but by this time identified as papal teaching. He rejoiced that they had not called into question in the name of Vatican II (as theologians in the West were doing by this time, he appeared to think) the fundamental doctrines of the faith. Six months later Cardinal Wyszynski banned any further publication in Polish of the international quarterly *Concilium*, perhaps the leading exponent of a liberal interpretation of the doctrine of Vatican II. Potentially divisive theological speculation, which Wyszynski thought had helped to empty the churches in the West, was to have no place in Polish religion. 'We want a Polish theology for Poland,' he told the 1972 Congress of Polish Theologians.[42]

Shortly after the 1971 Congress Wojtyla went to Rome for the third Synod of Bishops, which discussed the priesthood and questions of justice and peace. In the course of it Maximilian Kolbe, a priest who had died in Auschwitz, was beatified, and Wojtyla, who had a particular devotion to the martyr, attended the ceremony along with other Polish bishops. At the end of the Synod he was made one of the three European members of the Synod's advisory council.

In 1973 he journeyed to Australia and New Zealand. The occasion was an International Eucharistic Congress held in Melbourne in February, and he travelled with two other bishop-delegates, one of whom was Wladyslaw Rubin. The invitation to Wojtyla to attend had come from Polish groups in Australasia, and it was very largely those groups he visited. He was becoming well-travelled, at least by the standards of Polish prelates, but for all the opportunities he had his range of experience was limited, a restriction which was to some extent self-imposed.

In September and October 1974 he was back in Rome for the fourth

Synod of Bishops, devoted to evangelization. The working document had been prepared by Bishop Rubin: Cardinal Wojtyla was chosen by Pope Paul to present its theological sections to the assembled Fathers. He came from what was often called the 'Church of Silence', he said, but questioned whether the silence arose from the bishops themselves, or whether it came about because bishops in the First World and the Third World did not pay any attention to them.[43] In the effort to spread the Gospel message, he went on, the Church rightly tries to adapt itself to the culture of the society being evangelized but, he warned, it must not do so to the extent that it damages communion with the successor of Peter, the Pope. He spoke of Liberation Theology as one of these forms by which the Church expressed itself in a particular society, that of Latin America, but as he understood it, liberation is primarily liberation from original sin. This interpretation made the concept into a personal rather than a social one, and in so doing undermined what the majority of Latin American theologians (and those from other regions of the world in their turn) were trying to achieve. The outcome of the synod was Paul VI's Apostolic Exhortation (after the debâcle of *Humanae Vitae* Paul never wrote another encyclical) *Evangelii Nuntiandi* (Proclaiming the Gospel). It is one of the finest documents to come out of Paul's pontificate, and Wojtyla is said to have had a hand in its composition.

It is a papal custom to invite a distinguished ecclesiastic to deliver to the pope and his household a Lenten retreat. In March 1976 the five days of retreat conferences were preached by Cardinal Karol Wojtyla to about eighty people (including cardinals and the Pope himself) who worked in the Vatican. They were immediately published as *A Sign of Contradiction*. One specific 'sign of contradiction' dwelt upon by Wojtyla in his conferences to the (entirely clerical) audience was that of Pope Paul himself for his encyclical *Humanae Vitae*. Paul was writing in defence of human dignity, said the Cardinal, but was frequently opposed even by Christians.

Back in Poland the situation was once again explosive. Food prices had been kept artificially low, but when, in June 1976, Eduard Gierek tried to raise them workers went on strike and there were riots in Warsaw and in Radom. In Radom, a city to the south of Poland's capital, workers attacked the Party building and discovered great quantities of supplies stored for Party workers. The police reacted brutally. In Radom there were at least seventeen deaths, hundreds were imprisoned. The Gdansk shipyard workers threatened to strike unless prices were reduced. Wyszynski told the workers that violent protest never solved anything; Wojtyla asked the government to rescind the price increases and stop attacking the workers. He also set up a fund for the families of the men who had been imprisoned, or been thrown out of their jobs.

The appeal voiced by Wojtyla and many others to the government was heeded. The price rises were cancelled and the strike of the shipyard workers was called off before it began. But repression of workers and intellectuals went on. There was an increasing number of arrests. In mid 1976 Jacek Kurón and thirteen others founded the Workers' Defence Committee (KOR). KOR brought both legal and material aid to those imprisoned and their families.

Throughout the summer of 1976 Wojtyla was again visiting the United States. There was a Eucharistic Congress in Philadelphia which he attended, but he also called upon leading US churchmen as well as a number of Polish centres. He lectured at Harvard and at the Catholic University in Washington. He worked on the translation of his book, *The Acting Person*, with Dr Tymienecka.

He returned to Poland on 5 September, and just over a week later was again presiding at the annual Congress of Polish Theologians. During the last week of November until early December he was back in Rome, then in March the following year he was lecturing in Milan on 'The Problem of the Constitution of Culture through Human Work'. Towards the end of June he was in Mainz to receive an honorary degree. He was back in Cracow briefly to preside at a conference on ethics, and then went to Paris. Back in Cracow in August powerful figures of the Catholic Church, Cardinals Volk of Mainz and Cooke of New York, came to visit him.

The fifth Synod of Bishops, on catechetical instruction, was held in Rome from the end of September to the end of October 1977. In the course of it the Cardinal of Cracow made a plea, which was decisively rejected, for the publication of a new catechism for the Catholic Church to reflect the teachings of Vatican II. While the Synod was meeting, Wojtyla travelled to Milan at the request of Cardinal Colombo to lecture. Late in June 1978 he was back in the same city again to lecture, this time at a congress to mark the tenth anniversary of the publication of *Humanae Vitae*.

The author of that encyclical, Pope Paul VI, died at Castel Gandolfo, the papal summer residence, on 6 August 1978. In the subsequent conclave Albino Luciani, Cardinal Patriarch of Venice, was elected Pope on the third ballot and took the name of both of his immediate predecessors, thereby breaking with papal tradition. He gave himself the title of Pope John Paul I. Wojtyla is said to have collected a number of votes in the course of the short election. It was a reflection of the way in which the college of cardinals had been so internationalized – there was by now only a minority of Italian cardinals – that a non-Italian pope looked a serious possibility.

Wojtyla had scarcely returned to Poland from the installation of the new pontiff than he was off again, this time with his Primate, Cardinal Wyszynski, and two other Polish bishops – one of whom was Wladyslaw Rubin of the secretariat of the Synod of Bishops – to make a visit of reconciliation to the German episcopate, who were to be gathered in conference at Fulda. The Polish delegation was welcomed in Cologne by Cardinal Joseph Höffner, attended by every other member of the German Bishops' Conference. In his reply to Höffner's greeting Wojtyla looked forward to the reshaping of Europe at the turn of the century and of the millennium. Again at Fulda itself Wojtyla recalled the coming of the millennium. In Munich, at the tomb of Cardinal Döpfner, Wojtyla mentioned Döpfner's initiative in founding a Carmelite convent at Dachau: he singled out for special mention in his address two of the many thousands who had died in concentration camps, Blessed Maximilian Kolbe and Edith Stein – choosing to remember Edith Stein as a pupil and then assistant to Husserl, as well as a Discalced Carmelite herself. It was a delicate balancing act, mentioning one Pole and one German who had died under the Nazi terror.

And then, after a pontificate of only 33 days, John Paul I died. It was 28 September 1978. On 16 October Karol Wojtyla was elected Pope. He took the name of John Paul II.

NOTES

1. Taborski, p. 180.
2. The portrait of Christ by Brother Albert in Act 1, his *Ecce Homo*, was placed in the church at Mistrzejoice in Nowa Huta of which Albert is the patron saint. The church was blessed by John Paul II in June 1983 and on 30 June 1985 Albert's relics were interred there.
3. Taborski, pp. 242–3.
4. Taborski, 159.
5. For a brief summary of Scheler's philosophy with reference to the Pope, cf. Robert F. Harvanek, S.J., 'The philosophical foundations of the thought of John Paul II' in John M. McDermott (ed.), *The Thought of John Paul II* (Rome, Gregorian University Press, 1992), pp. 2–16.
6. John Hellman, 'John Paul II and the Personalist Movement' in *Cross Currents* vol. xxx, no. 4, Winter 1980, p. 416. This section is a summary of Hellman's fascinating account of the origins of personalism in Poland.
7. art. cit. p. 413.
8. The subtitle to later, though not to the first, editions of Scheler's *Formalismus*,

the book Wojtyla translated, was 'a new attempt at the foundation of an ethical Personalism'. Personalism is somewhat briskly defined by Dr A. R. Lacey in his *Dictionary of Philosophy* (London, Routledge, 1976) as 'any of a wide variety of view emphasizing the primacy, in the universe, of persons (non-technical sense), whether human or divine', p. 157. For a more sympathetic treatment, which includes a discussion of Mounier, see 'The human person in contemporary philosophy' in F. C. Copleston, *Contemporary Philosophy* (London, Search Press, 1973), pp. 103–24.

9. Williams, op. cit., p. 139.
10. The first series has been published in Germany (Stuttgart, Seewald Verlag, 1981) as the *Lubliner Vorlesungen* with the secondary title, 'Act and lived experience'. They are discussed by Kenneth L. Schmitz in *At the center of the human drama: The philosophical anthropology of Karol Wojtyla/Pope John Paul II* (Washington DC, Catholic University of America Press, 1993), pp. 42ff.
11. Blazynski, op. cit., p. 69.
12. Taborski, op. cit., p. 270.
13. Williams, op. cit., p. 153.
14. Williams, op. cit., pp. 161–2.
15. *Acta Syndolia Sacrosancti Concilii Oecumenici Vatican Secundi*, (Rome, Vatican Polyglot Press, 1970–79, I:2, pp. 314–15.
16. *Acta Syndolia*, I:3, p. 609.
17. *Acta Synodalia*, I:4, pp. 598–9.
18. Malinski, quoted by Williams, op. cit., pp. 167–8.
19. *Acta Synodalia*, I:4, pp. 154–7. The speech was too long to be delivered in its entirety, and the final sections were handed over to the general secretary.
20. *Acta Synodalia*, II:4, pp. 340–2.
21. Quoted Williams, op. cit., p. 187.
22. *Acta Synodalia*, III:4, pp. 788–9.
23. *Acta Synodalia*, III:2, pp. 530–1; quoted Williams, op. cit., p. 172.
24. *Acta Synodalia*, III:4, pp. 69–70; quoted Williams, op. cit., p. 173.
25. Quoted Williams, op. cit., p. 174.
26. *Acta Synodalia*, III:5, pp. 298–300.
27. *Acta Synodalia*, IV:2, pp. 292–3.
28. *Acta Synodalia*, IV:2, pp. 11–13; quoted Williams, p. 177. A list of Wojtyla's interventions, written and oral, is given by John M. Grondelski in his appendix, 'Sources for the study of Karol Wojtyla's thought' to the book by Kenneth Schmitz, pp. 147–63. The list, which appears on p. 161, omits this last reference.
29. *Acta Synodalia*, IV:2, pp. 660–3.
30. *Acta Synodalia*, IV:3, pp. 242–3.
31. Ibid., p. 349.
32. See Robert Kaiser, *The Encyclical That Never Was* (London, Sheed & Ward, 1987).
33. Karol Wojtyla, *Sources of Renewal*, (London, Collins, 1989), pp. 11–12.
34. cf. Williams, op. cit., pp. 184–5.

35. op cit., pp. 192–3. For a summary of *The Acting Person*, see Peter Hebblethwaite, 'Pope John Paul II as philosopher and poet' in *Heythrop Journal* XXI (1980), pp. 123–36.
36. op cit., p. 200. There are a number of trenchant criticisms of the text on subsequent pages of Williams's book.
37. *At the center of the human drama*, p. 60.
38. op. cit., p. 207.
39. Williams, op. cit., p. 212.
40. 18 August 1979, p. 801.
41. For this debate, and the quotation used in the text, see Williams, op. cit., pp. 226–9.
42. cf. Williams, op. cit., pp. 232–4.
43. Williams, op. cit., p. 236.

THREE

1978-9

KAROL WOJTYLA was given cell number 91 for the duration of the conclave. Though his popularity had been high enough when Albino Luciani was elected six weeks earlier, the Cardinal Archbishop of Cracow made great play of not being '*papabile*'. Don't bother taking my photograph, he told a journalist from *Time* magazine, I won't be elected pope. He had even arranged to fly back to Poland directly after the election had taken place, without waiting for the installation of the new pontiff.[1]

But he could scarcely have failed to reflect that he himself might be a candidate, even if one with only an outside chance of election. His stance in Poland had earned him a degree of fame. His travels had brought him into contact with many of those who were to gather in conclave. The night before it began, the liberal-minded, much respected, Cardinal König of Vienna dined with Peter Nichols of *The Times* of London and Alain Woodrow, an Englishman working for *Le Monde* of Paris. Perhaps the time has come to elect a non-Italian, he told them. König had first encountered Wojtyla in 1961, when the Cardinal was crossing into Poland from Czechoslovakia, and Wojtyla, still an assistant bishop, had been sent to meet him at the frontier. He was immediately impressed, he said later,[2] by his intelligence, his humility, and his deep faith. The choice of a non-Italian seems to have come as a surprise to Nichols and Woodrow and to the wider world, but to König and to his non-Italian friends among the college of cardinals it was no new idea. They had considered it in 1963 when Giovanni Battista Montini was elected as Paul VI.[3] The preferred candidate was König himself, but he pleaded his age — he was then 73 — as an excuse.[4]

Wojtyla went into the conclave carrying a Marxist philosophical journal as reading matter. The first day of voting was 15 October, a Sunday. It soon became evident that the College of Cardinals (there were 109 voters) was sharply divided between the conservative faction who favoured Giuseppe Siri, Cardinal Archbishop of Genoa, and a progressive group who wanted

Giovanni Benelli, Cardinal Archbishop of Florence, but before that one of the most influential figures in the papal curia as the number two, though in effect the dominant figure, in the Secretariat of State under Paul VI. There were votes for other candidates, among them Wojtyla, but the main battle was still between two Italians.[5] After the seventh ballot, when no resolution of the impasse seemed in sight, the presiding cardinal urged the electors to reconsider their votes. Many of them did so. They switched them to an outside candidate: but they all chose the same one. Karol Cardinal Wojtyla, Archbishop of Cracow, was elected Pope on the eighth ballot with, it is said, 103 of the 109 votes cast. The outcome was utterly unexpected. It was greeted with a momentary silence, broken by an overcome Cardinal Wyszynski. *'Il papa è fato!'* he cried, 'The Pope is made!' and the cardinals began to make their allegiance to the new pontiff. He was 58 years old, the youngest pope since Pius IX nearly a century and a half earlier.[6]

Cardinal Felici announced the conclave's choice at 6.40 pm that day, 16 October, and then, hastily clad in an ill-fitting white soutane, Pope John Paul II, as he had chosen to be called, stepped out on to the balcony of St Peter's to deliver the traditional blessing. But his conduct was not all traditional. He first made a short speech. He used the singular, more personal 'I' rather than the customary, remote, pontifical 'We',[7] he described himself, in the third person, as 'this man from a far country', he confessed he had been afraid to accept the nomination – Wyszynski had told him he had to do so if elected – and he spoke in Italian: 'I speak to you in your – no our – language. If I make a mistake, please correct me', he said. There were great cheers from those gathered in St Peter's Square who, moments before, had been wondering who this Karol Wojtyla might be. The largely Italian crowd was won over by his identification with them, speaking of 'our language'. To others the gesture seemed contrived, not to say theatrical.

The following day the Polish bishops issued a statement: 'The servant of the Church of Krakow and of all Poland, the Deputy Chairman of the Conference of the Polish Episcopate, has been elected servant of the servants of God. We believe that it is the achievement not only of the Holy Spirit, but also of Holy Mary, the Mother of the Church, and Our Lady of Jasna Góra, whom the newly elected Pope loves so much, and we believe that it is the result of the prayers of the entire Polish people who have received this reward for their faith and the vitality of their religion.' They were sentiments of which Karol Wojtyla would have approved, especially the linking of the Polish national shrine of Jasna Góra with the new papacy.

The government of Poland attempted to claim some credit for itself. 'The

Pope is a Pole,' its statement read, 'a member of a nation which has passed through the hell of war, accomplished profound transformations in its country, and is advancing along the road of all-round development, which is a universally acknowledged fact.' The government gave the Catholic papers more newsprint to increase their print-runs, and granted visas to a thousand Poles to attend the papal inauguration. They even showed the mass in St Peter's Square on state television, the first time mass had been televised in Poland. But they could not but have been alarmed by Wyszynski's remarks when he returned to Warsaw after the election of Wojtyla: 'The Holy Father told me when I last saw him: "I have become Bishop of Rome, but I have not stopped being a Polish bishop." '

Among the Polish Romantic poets of the late eighteenth and the nineteenth centuries there was a strong sense of destiny. In an oppressed people without leaders they provided a different form of leadership and elevated the national consciousness of Poles to an heroic plane by portraying them as liberators not only of their own land but of other countries as well. Some put this into practice, fighting in the American and Italian revolutions, and they were not enamoured of popes such as Gregory XVI and Pius IX who, in 1830 and 1848 respectively, appeared to betray nationalist aspirations. One of the leading romantic poets, Juliusz Slowacki (1809–49), even wrote a poem on the flight of Pius IX from Rome in November 1848, foretelling the coming of a 'Slavic Pope', 'a brother of the people', who would be made of sterner stuff.[8] Karol Wojtyla was the first Slav ever to become Bishop of Rome. He was yet to be tested.

On the day after his election, John Paul spoke in the Sistine Chapel to the cardinals who had chosen him. His words, however, were addressed to all 'sons and daughters of the Holy Church [and to] all men of good will who now listen'. What he had to say amounted to a programme for his pontificate. His first concern was for the Second Vatican Council which, he insisted, had not yet been fully implemented, nor what was implicit in its texts yet been made fully explicit. He concentrated on one aspect in particular, that of the doctrine of the Church and, more especially, of collegiality.[9] He foresaw a development of 'those bodies, sometimes new, sometimes updated, which can secure a better union of heart, will and initiative in building up the body of Christ which is the Church'. He mentioned the Synod of Bishops, of which, as Archbishop of Cracow, he had been an active member. He did not refer to the development of national Episcopal Conferences.

On his own authority as a 'legitimate successor of Peter' he insisted that he would carry out his responsibilities with love, but he was firm that there should be fidelity 'to the teaching of Peter' in matters of doctrine, of liturgical practice, to the 'discipline' of the Church (a discipline which 'is not only a means of mortification, but also guarantees the right ordering of the mystical body'), and to the 'demands of the priestly and religious vocation'. He committed himself to the cause of ecumenism, along the path already mapped out, and to the pursuit of peace, development and international justice. He had no intention, he said, of interfering politically: his actions would be determined only by religious and moral considerations. He ended with a special greeting to Poland, and to the Catholics of Cracow in particular.

His predecessor, Albino Luciani, was a quiet, retiring, humble man who determined to avoid the pomp of a papal coronation with its overtones of earthly power. He chose instead simply to be invested with the pallium, the stole of lamb's wool which, since the fourth century, has been the symbol of papal authority, and one which he shares with senior ecclesiastics around the world as a sign of their communion with the Bishop of Rome. It would have been difficult for any pope to reinstate the crowning. It would not in any case have been in Wojtyla's character to do so – though it might have been attempted had another candidate been elected in his stead. John Paul's installation took place in St Peter's Square on Sunday 22 October, before a crowd of a quarter of a million – and before millions more by means of television. The sky, which had been threatening as the ceremony began, grew brighter as the long-drawn-out ritual proceeded. 'Here is a man of powerful energy who knows his own mind', commented one observer. 'The Vatican, the world even, is not a place where everybody is going to like the consequences, but they will never be dull.'[10]

The fourth of November is the feast day of Charles Borromeo, after whom Karol Wojtyla was named, and to whose memory Pope John XXIII was particularly devoted – he had prepared an edition of the Saint's *Acta* as Archbishop of Milan. On the first feast of St Charles after his election to the papacy, John Paul said, 'In his name my parents, my parish, my country intended to prepare me right from the beginning for an extraordinary service of the Church, in the context of today's Council, with the many tasks united with its implementation, and also in all the experiences and sufferings of modern man'.[11]

On 12 November the Vatican daily, *Osservatore Romano*, carried two articles written by Wojtyla as cardinal. One, a defence of *Humanae Vitae*, had originally appeared in *Analecta Cracoviensia* in 1969; the other, entitled (in Italian) 'Christ fully reveals man to man' had been published in *Osservatore* itself only two and a half years earlier. They were illustrated with a sixteenth-century Polish woodcut of the crucifixion. The first was an unequivocal sign of John Paul's adherence to the teaching on contraception of Paul VI. But it was not simply an act of loyalty to his predecessor: commitment to *Humanae Vitae* was taken as a test of loyalty to the Holy See, proof of obedience to Rome. It was clear that the new Pope envisaged no change. He was conscious of the authority invested in him, and was prepared to put it to use. He appeared puzzled when he conceived the idea of spending Christmas 1978 in Bethlehem, only to be told it was not possible.[12]

The tenor of his doctrinal authority was soon revealed. The Conference of United States Bishops had drawn up a directory to guide clergy and others in teaching the faith. It had been approved by the Conference in 1977, but only after heated discussion. One major issue was whether children might be permitted to receive communion before they had made their first confession: it was a matter on which one American bishop, Cardinal John Wright, formerly of Pittsburgh but by now in charge of the Vatican's Congregation for the Clergy which had jurisdiction in matters of religious instruction, had strong views.[13] There were four main criticisms of the Conference's directory *Sharing the Light of Faith*. First, it had to insist that confession was to precede communion; secondly, it was to make clear that general absolution (the giving of absolution for sins, without there being a personal confession of them to a priest) was to be used only in very exceptional circumstances; thirdly it was to make plain that Revelation had ended with the death of the last apostle; and fourthly it was to lay greater emphasis on the sacrificial nature of the priestly vocation, and to distinguish it more precisely from the common priesthood of all Christians.

Although this instruction of the Congregation to the US bishops to revise their catechetical directory came only six weeks or so after John Paul's election, it would not have been issued without his approval. Though at least one of the changes that were demanded was known to reflect Cardinal Wright's personal conviction, the remarks on the priesthood were in keeping with the views of the then Bishop Karol Wojtyla as he had expressed them in the debate on *Lumen Gentium* during the Council.[14] And as for priests themselves, immediately after his election the Pope put a sudden end to the grant of 'laicization' – the return of priests to the status of laymen – a permission which under Paul VI had been fairly readily given to those who petitioned Rome. It did not, however, put an end to priests abandoning their calling. They continued to leave the ministry, but the Pope's ban merely made them renegades in the faith they had once loyally served.

Shortly after his elevation to the papal throne, on 20 October, he received the congratulations of the diplomats accredited to the Holy See. In his address, John Paul II spelled out what was in effect to become an integral part of papal 'foreign policy': 'The Holy See seeks nothing for itself, it works, in union with local hierarchies, on behalf of the Christians or believers who live in your countries, so that, without special privilege, but in all justice, they can nourish their faith, enjoy freedom of worship, and be admitted, as loyal citizens, to a full share in the social life of the country. The Holy See does so equally in the interests of all men, whoever they may be, knowing that liberty, respect for life and the dignity of persons (who are never instruments), equality in treatment, professional conscientiousness in the task and united pursuit of the common good, the spirit of reconciliation, and openness to spiritual values, are fundamental needs for harmonious life in society, for progress of citizens, and for their civilization.'

Three months later the diplomats were back again *en masse* to offer him their good wishes for the New Year. In his message for the World Day of Prayer for Peace (1 January) he had made a passionate plea for peace in the world – he was, he said, taking up from Paul VI 'the pilgrim's staff of peace' – but had linked it above all to religious liberty: 'True religious feeling cannot fail to promote true peace. The public authorities, by recognizing – as they should – religious liberty, favour the development of the spirit of peace at the deepest level of people's hearts.' In an obvious reference to Communist attempts to hijack the peace movement he added 'Peace has become the slogan that reassures or is meant to beguile.' On 12 January before the diplomatic corps he returned to the central issue of the right to religious freedom and freedom of conscience. But he also made mention of the Holy See's efforts, to which he had directed his representatives, to resolving the squabble between the Argentine and Chile over the ownership of islands in the Beagle Channel. So impressed was the President of Bolivia that he wondered whether the Pope might not mediate also between his own country and Chile. Not so impressed was a group of Catholics in Buenos Aires who pointed out that the injustices being perpetrated under the repressive regimes in Argentina and Chile were of far more concern to the citizens of those countries than the Beagle Channel, and the Pope might think of doing something about that. In the meantime the Holy See, on 3 January, had signed the first concordat, or treaty, of the new pontificate between the Holy See and another country – in this instance, with Spain. The terms this time round were rather less favourable than last, but still, the Pope clearly thought, better than nothing: the negotiations had dragged on for two-and-a-half years.

He had also, diplomatically, to smooth down feathers in Hungary, ruffled by a visit to that country by Wyszynski. The aged but still combative Primate of Poland had rebuked the bishops of Hungary for being too ready to comply with the demands of the regime. John Paul wrote, on the other hand, to praise the role the Catholic Church had played in the life of Hungary, to stress the links between Hungary and Poland, and to hope that they would be able to continue their apostolate. Hungary turned out to be one of the earliest successes of the renewed Ostpolitik. Shortly before Easter 1979 it was announced that the Pope had been able to appoint to all four of the vacant sees, the result of two visits to Budapest by the Vatican diplomat Archbishop Luigi Poggi.

At the 12 January meeting with the diplomatic corps he told them what of course they already knew: that he was off on his first overseas trip to Puebla in Mexico, to attend the third gathering of the Conference of Bishops of Latin America, known to all and sundry as CELAM.[15] CELAM was, almost despite itself, an extremely controversial body. The first of their general conferences had been so unimportant that people found it hard to recall where it had taken place (Rio de Janeiro, in 1955). The second, at Medellín in Colombia, had placed Liberation Theology on the map. It had not meant to do so. The bishops of Latin America had called the conference simply in an attempt to apply the teachings of Vatican II to their continent, but the language of the documents was quite different. The experts at Medellín were not just theologians. They were, many of them, theologians rewriting their theology from the perspective of the poorest and most oppressed in society. And the tools of social analysis which they were using were, very frequently, those of Marxism.

Medellín did not use the expression 'the option for the poor' – by which was meant siding with the materially poor – but the concept was contained implicitly in the papers of the conference. These papers were swiftly translated and came to vie in popularity with the documents of Vatican II. A Peruvian priest, Gustavo Gutierrez, first published his *Theology of Liberation* in Lima in 1971. Like the documents of Medellín it was rapidly rendered into English and other European languages. It set the style for much of the most interesting theological work for the next decade, during which time Liberation Theology moved from its Latin American base to many other regions of the Third World, most particularly perhaps to Asia and to a lesser extent Africa, on both continents developing its own local style. That it should be local was of the essence of the approach: theology, said the protagonists of Liberation Theology, had to be done within a quite specific context if its purpose was not only to talk about God but to influence people's lives.

Though Liberation Theology as a method was spreading across the world, in Latin America itself it was running into difficulties. In the early 1970s there was a conservative reaction in the Church. When in 1974 elections were held for office-holders of CELAM, the staunchly conservative Bishop Lopez Trujillo became its Secretary General. Long before the gathering in Puebla it had become clear that the third assembly of CELAM was not to be the decisive force that Medellín had been. But bishops and their theological experts, many of them Liberation Theologians, were determined to do their best to make the meeting a confirmation of the documents of Medellín.

The schedule for this first major papal journey was punishing – but it was to become typical. The Pope arrived from Rome in Santo Domingo, the capital city of the Dominican Republic, at 1.30 pm, met the bishops, priests and leading laity, then went on to say mass at 5.00 pm. The next day there was mass in a small parish just outside the city, and then John Paul left for Mexico City. On 27 January he met the Polish community in Mexico, and paid a visit to the national shrine of Our Lady of Guadalupe. The Conference opened on Sunday morning with a papal mass, and a papal address in the afternoon. The next day he was back in Mexico City, flew South to Oaxaca, returned to Mexico City for a meeting of leading Catholics. On the following morning the Pope visited a school in Mexico City, went on to Guadalajara, visited the shrine of Our Lady of Zapopan, and returned to the city. Before he left for Rome on 31 January at 1.30 he fitted in a meeting with university students, a meeting with the press, and a sports display.

That was the itinerary. What of the message? The broadcasting correspondent of *The Tablet* criticized the television coverage. On the basis of a single phrase taken out of context, he complained, Jon Snow had claimed that the Pope had ordered the Church to stay out of politics. Mr Snow had got it right. The warnings were there from the very beginning, from the address to the assembled bishops on 28 January. They would have to take Medellín as their starting point, he told the gathering, but would have to beware of the 'incorrect interpretations at times made'. They had to 'be watchful for the purity of doctrine', to be on their guard against 'rereadings' of the Gospel based on 'theoretical speculation rather than authentic meditation', and he had particularly firm words for those who, or so he believed, passed over the divinity of Christ in silence, or presented him as a political, or as a revolutionary, figure. The Pope went on to develop a critique of what he took to be – without naming it as such – Liberation Theology. He accused its exponents of reducing the Kingdom of God to a simple, secular notion, of putting up a false dichotomy between the Church of the People and the official Church, and he called for 'a sincere reverence for the sacred *magisterium*'.

It was not that the Pope turned his back on the social involvement of the Church. Quite the contrary. In his addresses he stressed the Church's commitment to 'human advancement, development, justice, the rights of the individual' but, he added in a further swipe at the supposed errors of Liberation Theologians, the Church does not need to have 'recourse to ideological systems in order to love, defend and collaborate in the liberation of man', and to prove it he cited the social teaching of the Church, commending a study of it to all. It was a mixed message. The Pope's commitment to social justice, and to the Church's obligation to work towards it, was writ large, and repeated time and again as he criss-crossed the country speaking to workers, or to Indian peasant farmers. But he warned priests and other members of religious orders gathered to hear him in Guadalupe, 'You are not social directors, political leaders, or functionaries of a temporal power. So I repeat to you: Let us not pretend to serve the Gospel if we try to "dilute" our charism through an exaggerated interest in the broad field of temporal problems. Do not forget that temporal leadership can easily become a source of division ...'

As the Pope winged his way back to Rome (he arrived back there on 1 February) he left the bishops at Puebla fending off questions about whether John Paul had, or had not, condemned the involvement of the Church in politics. The bishops managed to end – the gathering lasted until 13 February – on an upbeat note. The programme they wrote for themselves, with its explicit mention of the central tenet of Liberation Theology, 'the preferential option for the poor', was in line with the programme begun at Medellín ten years before. But some at least of the enthusiasm which the election of a Polish pope had engendered less than six months earlier had already evaporated.

Not long after the visit to Mexico Pope John Paul produced his first encyclical. That he did so occasioned no comment. It had been expected. But it was the first such document in more than a decade. An encyclical is a papal letter addressed to all the faithful. It does not have the status of an infallible utterance, but in the range of papal pronouncements it ranks as one of the most solemn. The last encyclical had been Pope Paul VI's *Humanae Vitae* in 1968 in which, to the surprise of all but to the delight of some, he had condemned artificial contraception. There had been uproar. The ban was widely ignored, but ignoring it at the same time undermined the papal claim on the obedience of the Catholic faithful. As an exercise of authority it had failed, and Paul VI never tried again. John Paul II had no such inhibitions.

The encyclical is known, as is customary for papal documents, by its opening words *Redemptor Hominis* (The redeemer of mankind) and was published on 15 March. Roberto Tucci, the Jesuit in charge of Vatican Radio, acted as spokesman at the press conference to launch it. The Pope had written the encyclical himself, said Tucci. He had begun it in November 1978, but it represented views he had held throughout his priestly ministry. Tucci warned against misunderstanding that part of the encyclical which called for doctrinal orthodoxy: its aim was not so much to call the faithful into line as to give new vigour to the Church.

John Paul began his first encyclical with a reference to the coming of the year two thousand, and to the new millennium which would then dawn. Because of it, he said, 'We are in a certain way in a season of a new Advent, a season of expectation'. He identified himself with his two immediate predecessors, and dwelt for a time upon Paul VI's own first encyclical. He acknowledged that Paul's pontificate – which, he said, he had been able to observe closely – had been at times beset with criticism from within the Church. Criticism, he said, was good – but it should not go too far (how far that might be he did not define) lest it ceased to be constructive. Yet in spite of all appearances, the Church, he thought, was more than ever united. This unity he put down to the 'collegiality' of bishops and to the sharing of responsibility for the Church's wellbeing throughout the Church's members. He went on to commit himself, and the Church, to the search for unity among Christians, and to dialogue with non-Christian religions.

From this the Pope moved to the central theme of his encyclical, the effect of the redemption brought about by Christ. 'Human nature', he wrote, 'by the very fact that it was assumed, not absorbed, in him [Christ], has been raised in us also to a dignity beyond compare.' The God of creation, he went on, has been revealed as the God of redemption. The redemption restores human dignity and gives meaning to life.

Addressed to his fellow Catholics the sentiments may seem reasonable enough, little different from the common rhetoric of the faith. But this approach of the Pope's is radically new – at least, as said with such clarity and authority. It had been the teaching of the Church's philosophers and theologians for centuries that the dignity of the individual rested upon the natural law, upon a philosophical assessment of human need and capability, upon a conviction that ethics did not require a revelation. But 'the greatness, dignity and value' that belong to humanity, asserts the Pope, are to be found in the act of redemption. As the guardian of the Gospel message, therefore, the Church can claim a privileged status when the dignity of the person is to be debated. It also meant that there was no longer any common ground when talking of moral issues with those who did not share the Christian faith.

Pope John Paul then went on to talk of other religions as they had been treated in the documents of Vatican II, dwelling for a while upon Judaism, and discussed religious freedom which it was one of the great achievements of the Council to have affirmed, in contradiction to much of the Church's history. But in the Pope's view that freedom, unless it were the freedom of Christians, was marred: 'Since man's true freedom is not found in everything that the various systems and individuals see and propagate as freedom, the Church, because of her divine mission, becomes all the more the guardian of this freedom, which is the wisdom and basis for the human person's true dignity' (§12).

After a short section on 'man as the way for the Church', he turned to the threats to existence, to the paradox that the technological advances which human intelligence had made possible contained within them the seeds of human destruction. He did not mention nuclear weapons explicitly, but it is clear that he is thinking of these, and of threats to the environment. His message was a pessimistic one: 'man's situation in the modern world [is] far removed from the objective demands of the moral order, from the exigencies of justice, and still more from social love' (§16); 'this century has so far been a century of great calamities for man, of great devastations, not only material ones but also moral ones, indeed above all moral ones' (§17). He called upon human 'solidarity' to ensure the redistribution of wealth, and praised the efforts of the United Nations, as his predecessors had done.

The fundamental duty of power, he went on, is to serve the common good of society, and the common good is only achieved when citizens are secure in their rights – the Pope specifically mentioned the right to religious freedom, to which he added the right to freedom of conscience. He made an appeal for 'the rights of religion and of the Church's activity' to be respected (§17).

From this 'necessarily brief look at man's situation in the modern world' (§18), John Paul turned back to Christ, and to the Church as the 'social subject of responsibility for divine truth' (§19). In transmitting that truth, he made particular mention of the 'gift of infallibility'. He referred directly to the teaching of the first Vatican Council which had located that 'gift' squarely with the papacy. To say, as he went on to do, that theologians function correctly when they seek to serve the *magisterium* could, indeed, have a neutral interpretation: no theologian would wish to say that he or she was subverting the teaching office of the Church. The remark was in its context, however, a clear warning to theologians to fall in line behind the *magisterium*. He went on to speak of the doctrine of the Eucharist, and then turned to penance, praising recent efforts to highlight its community aspect, but emphasizing the need for personal conversion – and therefore personal confession. He spoke of the need for 'fidelity to one's vocation', a fidelity required of married people as much as of priests – but he chose to dwell upon the fidelity of the latter to their vocation. And he ended, as he has always done, with a eulogy of Mary.

This summary of *Redemptor Hominis* has been given at length because not only was it the first of John Paul's many encyclicals, but also because it was programmatic. This was not especially recognized at the time, and has become obvious only with hindsight. Popes were not expected to make 'state of the pontificate' addresses. They were not required to spell out a policy for the Church. Their emphasis, traditionally, had been to claim that they were simply repeating and developing what had been said by their predecessors. On this occasion Pope John Paul did likewise, building his encyclical as a commentary on various sections of Vatican II, and upon the teaching of Pope Paul VI. But there were differences, most importantly the implicit abandonment of the natural law as the basis of humanity's common moral code, and the sternness of tone in which was couched the demand that theologians subject themselves to the infallible *magisterium*. A correspondent to the London-based Catholic weekly *The Tablet* picked up the message perfectly: 'This message is that we now have as head of the Church a man determined to uphold its historical teaching and tradition, and to check the slide into Modernism and Protestantism which were denounced by Paul VI but which he was unable to halt.'[16]

Those who doubted the papal resolve did not have long to wait. For Maundy Thursday, the day on which is celebrated the institution of the Eucharist, John Paul II composed a letter to all the Church's priests. He insisted on the high nature of the priestly calling which – he said again, as he had said at Vatican II – differs from that priesthood shared with all the faithful not just in degree but also in essence. The priesthood, he said, was hierarchical, 'that is to say connected with the power of forming and governing the priestly people' (§4). 'The priesthood calls for a particular integrity of life and service', he said. It 'cannot be renounced because of the difficulties we meet and the sacrifices asked of us' (§4).

The Pope strongly reaffirmed the priestly obligation to celibacy, while recognizing that in this requirement the Latin Catholic Church was distinct from other branches of the Catholic Church. 'Celibacy is a sign of freedom that exists for service' (§8). 'The often widespread view that priestly celibacy in the Catholic Church', he went on, 'is an institution imposed by law on those who receive the sacrament of orders is the result of a misunderstanding, if not of downright bad faith' (§9). This is a strange statement. It is of course the case that celibacy is imposed by law. The Pope admits as much when he recognizes that in rites other than the Latin the obligation to celibacy among the clergy does not exist. What he appears to be saying is that celibacy is not imposed because it is freely chosen by candidates for the priesthood who have had several years to consider their vocation. When one accepts ordination, one accepts celibacy, and 'Keeping one's word is, at one and the same time, a duty and a proof of the priest's inner maturity; it is the expression of his personal dignity' (§9). Married people, said the Pope, have a right to expect from the clergy the same fidelity to celibacy that is expected from a couple by their marriage vows, and the need of people for the Eucharist in areas where there is a shortage of clergy should also encourage them to persevere in their vocation.

The letter begged a lot of questions. If there is a shortage of clergy to provide the Eucharist, why not, for example, ordain married men – or allow those who wanted to marry to remain in the priesthood? These are options that John Paul does not even consider. On the contrary, he seems almost, while denying he does so, to make celibacy part of the essence of the priestly vocation. In which case the candidate for ordination has no real choice: either he denies that he is called to the priesthood, or he embraces celibacy as part of the package. Rome was later to take extra steps to ensure that the obligation to celibacy was freely chosen: meanwhile there was a ban on dispensations from celibacy. Priests were no longer being allowed, as the official phrase put it, to be 'reduced to the lay state'.

There were protests. Hans Küng, a professor at the University of Tübingen and without doubt one of the Church's most able, if also most controversial, theologians, accused the Pope of denying the human rights of priests while posing as the champion of human rights elsewhere. French Protestants saw in the papal insistence on the hierarchical nature of the priesthood – which, they said, went beyond what was taught by Vatican II – a barrier to ecumenism, for it made far too sharp a distinction between the ministerial priesthood and the priesthood of all the faithful. There were, naturally, those who came to the Pope's defence – including Cardinal König who had played, as has been seen, an important part in John Paul's election to the papacy.[17]

When a pope is appointed his predecessor's 'cabinet' offer their resignation.

After John Paul I's election the new Pope had unhesitatingly reappointed Paul VI's chief ministers. John Paul II had thought about it for a week, but then confirmed all office-holders in their jobs. Cardinal Jean Villot was Secretary of State, the nearest thing the papacy has to a prime minister. He had been appointed in 1969 after serving as Archbishop of Lyons from 1965, and as Cardinal Archbishop from 1967. As Cardinal Camerlengo he had presided over the Church during the two interregna, and had wanted to retire. The Pope asked him to stay on so that the Church might benefit from his experience. That is certainly what he said, though rather oddly he said it in the form of an open letter. But then on 9 March Villot died, at the age of 73. The way was open for new appointments to determine the character of the new pontificate.

Archbishop Agostino Casaroli was appointed Secretary of State in May in succession to Villot. He was 64, and had been ordained in 1937. His entire working life had been in the Secretariat of State until, in 1967, he was appointed to the new Council for the Public Affairs of the Church, in which role he had been much involved in the Vatican's dealings with the States of the Eastern bloc, dealings which were collectively known as the Vatican's 'Ostpolitik'. A week later, further appointments were made. Bishop Achille Silvestrini replaced Casaroli at Public Affairs, but that, like Casaroli's own appointment, was only to be expected. Both were career 'civil servants' in the service of the Holy See. Both were experienced, and good at their job. They were like-minded, especially on the vexed question of detente, and Silvestrini in particular had shone at the Helsinki Conference as a skilful negotiator.

This far the appointments had been excellent, but predictable. Both Casaroli and Silvestrini were well-respected, and could have expected to achieve the positions they were now awarded. But the rest of the slate proved a surprise. Popes had for four and a half centuries been Italians. They were naturally concerned about Italian affairs. The second in command at the Secretariat was therefore traditionally an Italian prelate with a special responsibility for such matters. John Paul broke with tradition. As *sostituto*, or deputy, he chose a Spaniard, Archbishop Eduardo Martinez Somalo. He was a career diplomat and had served in Colombia, where he became a friend of Lopez Trujillo, the very conservative secretary of CELAM. The new under secretary at the Secretariat of State was Mgr Audryss Backis, a priest of Lithuanian origin who had worked for the Vatican's foreign service. The Pope had clearly set his sights on the Soviet Union and the Eastern bloc in general, and was preparing his team accordingly. The 'Italian question', on the other hand, and the links between the Church and the Italian Christian

Democratic Party, if not to be ignored in future, were, by the appointment of Somalo, made to appear as just another factor or two in the worldwide considerations of the new papacy. The appointments bode well for the Church, and there was genuine pleasure when Casaroli was created cardinal, along with 14 others (one of them *in petto*[18]) on 30 June.

The much-heralded papal visit to Poland began on a cloudless 2 June, when John Paul flew to Warsaw on board an Alitalia Boeing 727. His itinerary had been well prepared: the delay in publishing it – it appeared only a fortnight or so before the visit began – made it obvious that determining the papal schedule had not been easy. There had been regular visits to Poland by officials of the Roman Curia and no doubt the Communist authorities, who were awaiting the Pope's arrival with some trepidation, had believed they had done everything possible to minimize the effect of such a visit on their own, devoutly Catholic, citizens. They had already prevented the Pope from returning on what they considered a more volatile occasion. Saint Stanislaw of Szczepanow, Bishop of Cracow, had been murdered by Boleslaw II the Bold in 1079 for constantly upbraiding the king about his licentiousness. His feast day was 8 May, and in 1979 Polish bishops celebrated on that day the 900th anniversary of the canonization of Poland's first saint and the country's patron: his canonization had in fact occurred at Assisi in 1253. John Paul had wanted to go for that occasion, but the government said no.[19] While Catholic Poles venerated Stanislaw as their patron saint, a guardian of Catholic morality, and a martyr, the government saw in him (as Henry II in England had regarded Thomas Becket, to whom Stanislaw was often compared) as a rebel against legitimate authority. They did not want a Polish pope lending his authority to such – from their point of view – an ambiguous figure.[20]

It was a Saturday when the Pope arrived. The official reception at the airport was formal. Wyszynski entered the plane to welcome John Paul in the name of the hierarchy, and after kissing the tarmac in a gesture that had already come to be expected, the Pope greeted President Jablonski, and inspected the immaculately turned-out guard of honour. Jablonski's speech of welcome was unexpectedly warm, and full of Polish national pride in a Polish Pope. John Paul was clearly touched.

The seven-mile drive to the city was lined with cheering crowds. In Warsaw the Pope visited the cathedral and then went on to an official reception in the Belvedere Palace. This was a difficult moment. Eduard Gierek had certainly liberalized the state's attitude to the Church (he had approved a good many licences for the construction of new churches, for example, though getting them built was a different matter), but as First Secretary of the Polish Workers' United Party he could not have been expected to display the same warmth as had Jablonski, and he did not. As one commentator put it at the time, the Communists were 'treating the Pope as if he were no more than a peace movement activist, who had reached the top of the ladder in his organization'.[21] He went on to praise the Soviet Union for helping to solve Poland's problems, though, as both he and the Pope knew, Church and state together had an interest in ensuring that the Soviet Union's interest was not too immediate. The threat of direct intervention by the USSR was at this time always present.

The Pope's response was careful. 'Peace and the drawing together of peoples', he said, 'can only be achieved on the principle of respect for the basic rights of the nation, such as the right to existence, to freedom, to political self-determination for its citizens, and also to the formation of its own culture and civilisation.' The Church did not want privileges, he told the politicians and party members, but only that freedom necessary for it to carry out its mission. Its mission, however, in the Pope's eyes clearly implied a role in society which the Communist government was anxious to deny.

The next stop was Victory Square, where, a few days before, an altar dominated by a towering wooden cross had been erected. The Pope presided at a mass before a congregation of up to 300,000. In his homily he spoke of Poland that had 'in our times become the land of particularly responsible witness – that it is from here that the word of Christ must be spread with particular humility and firm faith'. His congregation quickly picked up on the political allusions: his remark that 'Christ cannot be kept out of the history of man in any part of the globe' was greeted with such prolonged applause he clearly thought it wise to cut the next sentence out of his sermon – it was even more directly anti-Marxist – in case the applause got out of hand.

At the end of the service Pope John Paul went back to the Cardinal Primate's residence to spend the night. The altar, and the immense wooden cross, were dismantled and removed as swiftly as they had been erected.

The following morning – Pentecost Sunday – there was a mass at St Anne's church. It was for students, and the authorities had tried to restrict numbers by issuing only a limited supply of tickets. Cardinal Wyszynski told the students to print up to 100,000, and they had done so. Then it was off to Victory Square, this time to be air-lifted to Gniezno, the ancient capital and, technically, the primatial see of Poland, where half a million people were waiting for him in a field about a quarter of a mile square. There was mass again, and a homily, and then John Paul was driven in his Popemobile through the crowds so that all could see him.

His next stop was Gniezno itself, and to the cathedral where the first Polish kings had been crowned and where St Adalbert was buried. John Paul is adept at exploiting symbols, and in St Adalbert, who had come from Czecho-slovakia in the tenth century at the invitation of a Polish king to convert the Baltic tribes only to be martyred by Prussians, he had an excellent example. Among the crowds outside the cathedral in Gniezno there was a group holding a placard saying 'Holy Father, remember your Czech children'. He could not forget them, he said, and perhaps God had chosen him, the first Slav pope, to bring an understanding of the Slav peoples to ears accustomed to hear other languages. He had a high conception of his own role: 'Is not the Holy Spirit disposed to see that his Polish Pope, this Slav Pope, should at this very moment reveal the spiritual unity of Christian Europe?'

There was yet another mass in the evening, again for young people. At its end the Pope, accompanied by Wyszynski and other bishops, appeared on the balcony of the episcopal palace. The crowd below, as crowds had done during the religious services in Warsaw and earlier in the field at Gniezno, broke into song. The Pope joined in, obviously enjoying the occasion enormously. He proposed songs himself, he sang solo, if only briefly, he added harmonies, his voice dominant over the loudspeaker system. The afternoon drew into evening. The crowd stayed until he sent them away.

Next morning it was Czestochowa for two nights and three days. Less people turned up than had been expected, possibly because of the refusal by the Polish authorities to grant holidays from work or from school during the visit, possibly because of the difficulties that were put in the way of those wishing to travel, and possibly, too, because a rumour (totally untrue) was circulating that a large number of people had been crushed to death in the masses that had gathered in Mexico to see the Pope. But chief among those who had come were the bishops of Poland, who had decided to hold their conference in the monastery at Jasna Góra during the papal visit.

When the Pope addressed the bishops it was in closed session – as it always has been on similar occasions around the world. It is known that he departed considerably from the prepared text, but it was none the less the prepared text which was issued to the 900 or so journalists who were accompanying him.[22] He chose as a major part of his theme the relationship between Church and state – not a theoretical issue, but his reflections on the situation which he had known about in Poland as Archbishop of Cracow. He highlighted the need for 'normalization' of relations between Church and state which had to be built on human rights. Dialogue, he said, 'must ensure all the rights of citizens, and normal conditions for the Church as a religious community', though he recognized the difficulty in dialogue because the partners in it come with such diametrically opposed views of the world.

He talked about the need for the Church to be clear about its moral principles, and said that the bishops had a particular obligation to preserve Polish culture. 'It is well known', he said, 'that it is precisely culture that is the first and fundamental proof of the nation's identity.' And he returned to the topic of European identity: 'Europe, despite its present long-lasting divisions of regimes, ideologies, and economic and political systems, cannot cease to seek its fundamental unity, must turn to Christianity. Christianity must commit itself anew to the formation of the spiritual unity of Europe. Economic and political reasons alone are not enough. We must go deeper to the ethical reasons. The Polish episcopate, all the episcopates and churches have a great task to perform.'

The third day in Czestochowa was given over to the official ministers of the Church, to the young clergy and religious in the early morning of 6 June, to older diocesan and monastic clergy shortly afterwards. In speaking to them he made a spirited defence of his Maundy Thursday letter to priests, calling the critics of that letter 'isolated voices', and claiming that, for the most part, 'the letter was received with satisfaction'. He had left Poland, he told his audience, with a very clear idea of what a model priest should be, and what was good for Poland, he clearly believed, was good for the rest of the Church.

During the three days in Czestochowa, three and a half million people came to see him from his old university in Lublin, from Silesia, from which part of his family had sprung. It was the spiritual heart of his journey. At the end of his stay he dedicated himself, his pontificate, the Church and Europe to the Black Madonna of Czestochowa, and then moved on.

He went to Cracow. If Czestochowa had been the heart, this was home. 'I discovered in Rome', he said, 'that it is not easy to leave Cracow behind.' The crowd gathered beneath his window in the episcopal palace that night and seemed disposed to stay until dawn. John Paul had to tell them firmly that it was time all of them, himself included, went off to bed, before finally shutting his window.

The following day he went to his favourite pilgrimage centre of Kalwaria Zebrzydowska, and then on to Wadowice, where he was greeted by Father Zacher, his old teacher of catechism. There was a simple buffet lunch in the presbytery, and then off by helicopter to Auschwitz. He prayed in the cell where Maximilian Kolbe had died, a Franciscan priest who surrendered himself to death to save the life of the married man first chosen by the

German guards for execution. As the Pope prayed that man, Franciszek Gajowniczek, stood outside. Then the Pope knelt at the spot where prisoners had been shot. He went on to Birkenau, said mass with 150 priests who had been prisoners in the death camps, and echoed the words of Pope Paul VI in 1965 to the United Nations, 'Never again war'. All those who took part in the mass at the site were deeply moved, the Pope included. Though the camps are most often remembered outside Poland as the killing fields for the Jews, within Poland they are remembered for all those Poles who had died there, one hundred and sixty-six of them Polish priests. The visit was on Polish television nationwide. Auschwitz was a symbol which the government did not want the people to forget – or to forgive those who had murdered there.

From Cracow the Pope went up into the mountains, to within a few miles of the border with Czechoslovakia whose citizens had been hindered from attending. He went to Nowa Huta, the steel town built without a church, whose workers had built one themselves and battled with the government to allow it to stay – Cardinal Wojtyla had finally consecrated it in 1977. He had indeed wanted to say mass there on this visit, but the government clearly thought that too much of a provocation, and the mass was said in a village on the outskirts. And one night, or rather, early one morning, when no one was about, the Pope wandered the streets of his former episcopal city.

He left Poland on 10 June. It was a Sunday. Two million turned up to the mass he said on a field outside Cracow before leaving for the airport. As he stood on the tarmac, a Russian-built plane of the Polish airline waiting to take him back to Rome, he was clearly moved to tears by the strain of leaving. His final farewell was a particularly emotional one, an unscheduled and wholly unexpected fond embrace of President Jablonski, whom the Pope had thanked for the efficient arrangements which had made his visit to Poland such an uncomplicated one. On the plane back to Rome, it was reported, the Pope drank a single glass of champagne.[23]

The Pope was to go back frequently to Poland. It seems reasonable that he should do so: it was after all to go home. But previous popes had scarcely travelled at all after their election, they had certainly not gone 'home', even if, as Italians, they had not needed to do so because they were already there. But there was little or no identification of the individual with a place. Perhaps it was difficult for a John XXIII or a Paul VI to dwell on their Italian background: it would have seemed unseemly as they played an international role in an international Church. John Paul II had no such inhibitions. From his thirty-two sermons and speeches on his first tour of Poland it was obvious that the Pope regarded his Polish nationality as an advantage to the Church because through it he could reach out to peoples who had hitherto been on the periphery of Europe, and bring them more to the centre.

Without doubt, the Pope's Polishness was of immense benefit for the people of Poland. It brought them hope. They were not alone in their struggle with the repressive Communist regime, but had in the Pope a voice who could speak powerfully in their support. How important this perception was, only became clear as the years passed. In the meantime there were those who, when they sat down to study what the Pope had said in the course of his visit, felt he might have gone further in his condemnation of the system under which they lived. But the Pope was a politician. Criticism of the government was there in his speeches for all to find, but it was not so great that Jablonski would have felt obliged to boycott the departure ceremony in protest. In the event, the sight of Pope and President embracing on the tarmac, a photograph which appeared on practically every front page the following day, was enough to encourage the Polish faithful to have hope that the situation might change. The Pope left Poland tearful and exhausted. He left behind a people saddened by his departure yet exhilarated that he had come. They knew that the visit was 'without doubt an unprecedented event, not only in this century but in the whole millennium, especially in view of the fact that it was a visit by a Polish Pope, who has the sacred right and duty to experience a deep emotional bond with his people'. That was the Pope's own summing up as he left Cracow airport. The visit had required, he said, great courage on both sides, but clearly he thought it had been worth the risk. He would be back. Meanwhile there were other tasks.

On 29 June, for example, the Pope received a delegation from the Ecumenical Patriarch of Constantinople led by Metropolitan Meliton of Chalcedon. This was a regular event, occurring annually on the feast of Ss Peter and Paul: Rome in return sent a delegation to Constantinople for the feast of St Andrew. This year the delegation was followed by one from the Coptic Orthodox, from Pope Shenouda III, Patriarch of Alexandria. These visits were followed in short order by an announcement that the Holy See was to establish diplomatic relations with the Greek government, something the Orthodox Churches hitherto had opposed. John Paul's interest in the East, which he had proclaimed on 17 January in his first major statement on ecumenism, seemed to be beginning to bear fruit.

Then he had to give thought to the Society of Jesus, the Church's largest religious Order of priests and its most powerful, but one which, under the leadership of Father Pedro Arrupe, had caused alarm both to John Paul's immediate predecessors, and to John Paul himself. The Society had, the Pope told the Jesuit General at an audience on 22 September, caused confusion to Christians, anxiety to the Church, to the bishops, and even to the Pope himself. Just what it was that was worrying him, John Paul did not spell out, but there were clues. Members of the Society of Jesus were among the Church's leading, most innovative, theologians, and had played an important role at Vatican II. The Pope did not question their orthodoxy, but urged that they safeguard orthodox teaching in fidelity to the *magisterium* (i.e., the theological views of the Roman Curia). Jesuits were also prominent in Latin America, not only as exponents of the Theology of Liberation but active in a practical apostolate of achieving justice for the poor. They must exercise the apostolate appropriate to their Society, the Pope told them, and an apostolate appropriate to their priestly character. The Jesuits had heard it all before.

In late September, just before the Pope set out on his visit to Ireland, Cardinal Silvio Oddi was nominated to succeed the late Cardinal Wright as prefect of the Congregation for Clergy. Oddi had a long career in papal diplomatic service, ending as Nuncio to Belgium and Luxembourg, before going to Rome. He was 68 at the date of appointment. For those watching anxiously for signs that the Pope was about to reform the Roman Curia, it came as a severe blow. The outspoken Cardinal Oddi was one of the curia's most conservative figures.

News that the Pope was thinking of visiting Ireland – though only as a stopover on a trip to the United States – had emerged in July. The Secretariat of State told the British Minister to the Holy See that the North of Ireland would not be on the itinerary, but not before the Reverend Ian Paisley had announced that should a visit to the North be proposed he would organize a general strike. The Moderator of the Presbyterian Church, William Craig, said he would not agree to meet John Paul should he be invited to do so, on the grounds that the papal office and the Pope's Marian devotion, already abundantly evident both from the Pope's constant references to Mary and from the large unheraldic 'M' that was prominently displayed on his coat of arms,[24] were contrary to the Gospel, but otherwise he was not opposed to the visit. Other Non-Catholic Church leaders on both sides of the Irish border made rather more welcoming noises.

The itinerary was announced at the beginning of September: John Paul was to arrive in the morning of Saturday 29 September and leave for Boston on the following Monday. On 3 September the Irish bishops issued a pastoral letter, comparing Ireland's devotion to Mary with that of Poland, but spending more time warning the faithful against materialism and, in equal measure, on condemning terrorism: it was only a few days earlier that a member of the British royal family, Earl Mountbatten, had been assassinated in a motor boat off the coast of Sligo, together with two boys and a woman.

Their words on terrorism were re-echoed by the Pope. At a mass for young people at Galway on 30 September he warned them 'do not close your eyes to the moral sickness that stalks your society'. At Limerick the following day he warned the government (all of whose members, together with the Irish president, received communion at the first papal mass, celebrated in Dublin's Phoenix Park) not to introduce civil divorce, because that was the slippery slope leading to ever greater instability in marriage.[25] To priests and nuns, seminarians and brothers gathered at the seminary at Maynooth, he returned to the topic of fidelity to their vocation at all costs, the theme of his Maundy Thursday letter, while at Knock in the West of Ireland he managed to give the impression that not only his visit to Ireland, but his earlier visit to Mexico, had been inspired chiefly by the desire to pay homage at each country's chief Marian shrine.

But most attention was caught by an impassioned plea for peace made at Drogheda, the nearest point to the border with Northern Ireland which the Pope reached. Before a gathering of some 200,000, many of whom had come over the border from the North for the occasion, he preached:

Violence is a lie, for it goes against the truth of our faith, the truth of our humanity. Violence destroys what it claims to defend, the life, the freedom of human beings. Violence is a crime against humanity, for it destroys the very fabric of society. I pray with you that the moral sense and Christian conviction of Irish men and women may never become obscured and blunted by the lie of violence, that nobody ever may call murder by any other name than murder, that the spiral of violence may never be given the distinction of unavoidable logic or necessary retaliation. Let us remember that the word remains for ever: 'All who take the sword will perish by the sword'.

And, as if foreseeing the rejection by the IRA which swiftly followed of this plea for an end to the killing, he concluded,

Do not lose trust that this visit of mine may be fruitful, and that this voice of mine may be listened to. And even if it were not listened to, let history record that at a difficult moment in the experience of the people of Ireland, the Bishop of Rome set foot in your land, that he was with you and prayed with you for peace and reconciliation, for the victory of justice and love over hatred and violence.

These were sombre words, but the rest of his visit was not in this vein. It seems likely that at least half the population of Ireland attended one or more of the papal gatherings. The mood, especially among the young at Galway, was, as one commentator described it, 'boisterous exuberance'. For two-and-a-half days a carnival atmosphere prevailed, which even touched John Paul himself – he was seen on at least one occasion to wipe away a tear when, in response to his 'I love you', the Galway crowd bawled back 'We love you too.' The huge cross which rose over the papal altar at Knock was later re-erected in the precinct of the Knock basilica. A plaque on its base, recording the coming of the Pope, describes his visit as 'the most important event in Irish history since the coming of St Patrick'.

The ensuing American trip was rather more complicated. It began well enough. John Paul arrived in Boston from Ireland to be greeted by Cardinal Humberto Medeiros, Archbishop of Boston, and by Rosalyn Carter, the wife of the US President. It was pouring with rain when the Pope said mass for 200,000 on Boston Common, but the weather did not dampen their enthusiasm. Nor it seems did the Pope's address, which contained a stern warning to the young not to try to escape responsibility as, he suggested, too many try to do – 'escape in selfishness, escape in sexual pleasure, escape in drugs, escape in violence, escape in indifference and cynical attitudes'.

The following day, 2 October, he was in New York to address the United Nations – of which more in a moment – but he was also given a ticker-tape procession along Broadway, addressed 20,000 young people in Madison Square Garden, said mass at the Yankee Stadium and the following day, with admirable impartiality, spoke to a packed crowd in the Shea Stadium. He went on to Philadelphia, where he visited the cathedral of the Ukrainian Rite (whose canon law permits a married clergy) before addressing priests and nuns on the permanence of the priestly state, and the need for a celibate priesthood.

He went on to visit the small-town church of Cummings, Iowa, and then to Des Moines. On 5 October in Chicago he met the US bishops in the by now customary closed session and then, in a published address, reminded them of his own 'exhilarating experience of collegiality in an ecumenical council'. In that spirit of collegiality he had come, he said, 'to strengthen you in your ministry of faith as local pastors, and to support you in individual and joint pastoral activities'. He listed some of those pastoral activities – their stand against racism, divorce, abortion and euthanasia – as well as their 'pastoral interest for your people in all their needs, including housing, education, health care, employment and the administration of justice'. On the teaching of the bishops, he warned them that their task was to transmit the *depositum fidei* in union with the *magisterium* of the Church.

On Saturday he went to the White House, to spend some time with President Carter and his family, before attending a gathering of government officials on the White House lawn. Early the next morning he went to America's National Shrine of the Immaculate Conception, situated on the campus of Catholic University, Washington, where he met a thousand young people who had spent the previous night in a prayer vigil. He addressed a large group of priests and then of nuns, reminding them, *en passant*, that 'your consecration to God should be manifested in the permanent exterior sign of simple and suitable garb. This is not only my personal conviction, but also the desire of the Church, often expressed by so many of the faithful'.

This turned out to be a fateful meeting. The Pope was welcomed to the gathering of women religious by Sister Theresa Kane, then president of the Leadership Conference of American Religious. She began by praising John Paul's commitment to the poor but, she added,

> I urge you to be mindful of the immense suffering and pain which is part of the life of many women in these United States ... As women, we have heard the powerful messages of our Church addressing the dignity and reverence for all persons. As women we have pondered upon these words. Our contemplation leads us to state that the Church in its struggle to be faithful to its call for reverence and dignity for all persons must respond by providing the possibility of women being included in all the ministries of our Church.[26]

The Pope did not then respond, but was clearly displeased. The women's issue had firmly been placed upon the table.

The visit to Ireland, the trip around the United States, had all been peripheral to the visit to the United Nations. 'Waldheim [then the UN Secretary General] invited me to take part in the General Assembly of the United Nations in September 1979', the Pope told David Willey, the BBC's correspondent in Rome, in 1989. 'But this would have been a purely political visit and it had to be pastoral in nature. So that is how a visit to the northeast United States came to be added to attending the United Nations. Then, at the suggestion of my secretary, Father [now Bishop] John McGee from Ireland, we added Ireland to the itinerary.'[27]

He could, of course, have declined the invitation, but the idea of doing so seems not to have crossed his mind. As a world spiritual leader he would on that platform have the opportunity of addressing the world's political leaders – and, in the event, only South Africa and Albania stayed away. Pope John XXIII wanted to go to the United Nations to launch his great social encyclical, *Pacem in Terris*, but he was too ill to consider it and sent Cardinal Suenens instead. Paul VI went on 4 October 1965, the day, the feast of St Francis of Assisi, being especially chosen to emphasize the Church's commitment to the poor. He made an impassioned appeal for peace, and begged that the money saved by running down armaments should be spent on solving the problems of hunger in the developing world. But, he said, people had other needs, those the UN proclaimed, 'fundamental human rights and duties, human dignity and freedom – above all religious liberty'. It was very well received, all except a plea that 'Your task is so to improve food production that there will be enough for all the tables of mankind, and not press for an artificial control of births, which would be irrational, so as to cut down the number of guests at the banquet of life.'[28]

John Paul II followed Pope Paul, though without raising the issue of birth control. He quoted his predecessor's plea for peace, 'No more war, war never again'. He called, again as Paul had done, for international guarantees to safeguard Jerusalem, 'a heritage sacred to the veneration of millions of believers of the three great monotheistic religions'. He quoted Pope Paul's *Populorum Progressio*: 'If the new name for peace is development, who would not wish to labour for it with all his powers?' but added that

the task must also be served by constant reflection and activity aimed at discovering the very roots of hatred, destructiveness and contempt – the roots of everything that produces the temptation to war, not so much in the hearts of the nation as in the inner determination of the systems that decide the history of whole societies.

The plurals were significant. One of the impressions which American commentators in particular took away from the papal speech was that John Paul had even-handedly condemned both capitalism and Marxism, the former for its subordination of human rights to the material interests of a few, the latter for denying the pre-eminent values of the spirit. Neither material nor spiritual good, said the Pope, were fairly distributed. People must become aware, he went on, that economic tensions with countries and in the relationship between states and even between entire continents contain within themselves substantial elements that restrict or violate human rights. Such elements are the exploitation of labour and many other abuses that affect the dignity of the human person.

John Paul was warmly applauded as he left the podium. Marxists and capitalists alike had not immediately realized that he had called down a plague on both their houses. It did not take long, however, for the light to dawn.

The Pope returned to Rome, and the anniversary of his election as Rome's Bishop passed with a spate of assessments of Karol Wojtyla's first year in office as John Paul II. They were varied. He had certainly made some effort to be, precisely, Rome's Bishop. Shortly after his election, on 10 November 1978, he had been visited by Cardinal Ugo Poletti, the papal vicar for Rome, who presented him with a depressing report on the state of his diocese. It reminded him of Cracow, said the Pope, and undertook to visit the diocesan offices for half a day a month. He also embarked on a programme of visits to each of the parishes nominally under his control. Moreover he engaged in public catechesis in Rome, even if the vast majority of those who came to listen were tourists. From September 1979 to May 1980 he lectured his regular Wednesday audience on love and sexuality, presenting his teaching as a commentary on Genesis. It was a *tour de force* of papal catechesis. It was not so much that the lectures displayed immense erudition, ranging over biblical exegesis and modern theology and employing the insights of anthropology as well as psychology, but that the catechesis happened at all. Here was a bishop, pontiff of the universal Church, who was going to teach. Many commented on his progressive social teaching, his defence of human dignity and his plea for a fairer distribution of the world's goods. But others noticed his conservatism, that he spoke well of ecumenism but seemed to have done little; that he claimed to be a bishop among brother bishops but had done nothing to curb Roman centralization; that his stern teaching on sexual morality as evident in his Wednesday addresses was alienating him from the membership of his Church. One thing, however, was clear, he fully intended to be the *magister* of the *magisterium*.

John Paul's stance was defended on German radio by Cardinal Josef Ratzinger, Archbishop of Munich. The Pope, he said, could not change traditional Catholic teaching. He did not have the right to do so. 'It is the Pope's duty', he said, 'to preserve the faith intact for our time, and to criticize the ills of Western society which [Hans] Küng [mentioning one of the Pope's sharpest and most articulate critics] singularly fails to do.'[29]

On 26 October he received the forty members of the International Theological Commission. They must not, he said, simply repeat the theological formulations of the past (not that any theologian worth his or her salt would dream of doing so), but help the Church to deepen its knowledge. They must not, on the other hand, make use of philosophical views which are incompatible with the faith – a clear reference to the Liberation Theologians' alleged use of Marxism to gain a clearer understanding of what Christianity might mean.

At the end of September the Pope had called a meeting of cardinals – neither a consistory (when cardinals are created or someone is approved for canonization) nor a conclave (to elect a new pope). In centuries past such gatherings had advised popes on matters of policy, but the practice had fallen into desuetude. Now Pope John Paul seemed about to revive it. Some commentators thought it would devalue the Synod if a meeting of cardinals became an advisory body to the Pope. The Roman Curia, on the other hand, was afraid that if the Pope turned to the cardinals for advice, the Curia itself would be undermined. In the event the meeting proved to be one of the first significant power struggles of the pontificate.

It took place from 5 to 8 November. The Pope appeared to suggest that it might be a regular occurrence, an exercise in collegiality such as had existed for a thousand years,[30] but would discuss only those issues about central organization which fell outside the scope of the Synod of Bishops. The cardinals then discussed, or rather had reported to them, the structure of the Roman Curia, the purpose of the pontifical academy of sciences and the financial situation of the Vatican. It was the last which was causing the Pope and his advisors anxiety, and he had asked for a balance sheet of the Vatican's finances to be prepared, so it was reported, for publication. It was the first time such an exercise had been undertaken, and it revealed a deficit of some $20 million. The two topics, curial reform and finance, were linked. Conservatives wished to see a reduction in the staffing levels of the 'new curia', those institutions set up in the wake of Vatican II, and especially the secretariats which dealt with Christian Unity, with Non-Christians and with Unbelievers. They were prepared to argue that at least an amalgamation of them was needed in order to save money.

Explaining the Vatican finances was a task allotted in the first instance to the two cardinals most closely involved, Cardinal Egidio Vagnozzi, who was President of the Prefecture for the Economic Affairs of the Holy See, an over-arching body set up by Paul VI and supposed to provide a picture of every aspect of the Holy See's financial position, and Cardinal Giuseppe Caprio. Caprio was President of the Administration of the Patrimony of the Holy See (APSA), a body which looked after all the Vatican's financial resources, including those which had come to it as a result of the Lateran Pacts of 1929 which had established the Vatican City State.

What is often called the Vatican Bank stood apart from APSA. Its proper name was, and is, the Institute for the Works of Religion, though that name was given to it only in 1942. Before 1942 its task had been to gather funds for church work throughout the world. After that date it was also permitted to hold money on behalf of religious Orders and other charitable institutions, to act as a merchant bank, and to act as a clearing bank for anyone associated with the Vatican. At the time of the cardinals' meeting it had some 11,000 clients, and a turnover of c. 200,000 million lire a year. Its president was Archbishop Paul Marcinckus.

In the event, Caprio and Vagnozzi proved unwilling to be as open about the Vatican's financial position as the cardinals – and Pope John Paul – required. The Pope instructed Cardinal Casaroli to address the assembly and be more forthright. He did so, but the cardinals remained dissatisfied, especially about the role of the Institute for the Works of Religion. They asked for still more information, and went home to think about the restructuring of the Curia. Perhaps John Paul had believed that, by acquainting the cardinals throughout the world of the difficulties of the Vatican's cash flow, greater funds might materialize from the local churches. If so he was to be proved wrong. The financial health of the central organization of the Roman Catholic Church was to become a constant preoccupation. It has not been helped by the Pope's constant travelling, even if the greater part of that burden fell on the churches being visited.

John Paul's final journey for 1979 was to Turkey, where there was no local church to share the cost. It was, on the face of it, a strange destination, but one dictated by ecumenical considerations. Rome regularly sent a delegation to the Orthodox Patriarch of Constantinople,[31] that is, of Istanbul, for the feast of St Andrew, Constantinople's patron saint, on 30 November. This year, the Pope chose to go himself. The Patriarch Dimitrios I was by no means as significant a figure ecumenically as had been his predecessor Athenagoras whom Paul VI had visited at the Phanar (Istanbul's equivalent of the Vatican) in July 1967. But because Paul had gone, John Paul told David Willey, he felt he had to do likewise.[32] It was also important for the policy of his pontificate that the first significant ecumenical visit should be one to Eastern Orthodoxy.

The Pope arrived in Istanbul on 28 November. He met the Patriarch, did some sightseeing and, the following morning, went to the liturgy in the cathedral of St George. In the afternoon he went off to Ephesus where is preserved the house allegedly lived in by the Virgin Mary in the latter years of her life. In front of the house he said mass – in Latin and in Turkish. The next day was the feast of St Andrew. The Pope attended the solemn liturgy in St George's cathedral presided over by Dimitrios, and preached the homily. During the first millennium, he said, the two churches of Rome and Constantinople had grown up side by side but during the second millennium, since the Great Schism of 1054, they had grown apart.

> Now we are coming to the end of that second millennium. Surely the time has come for us to hasten our attempts to achieve perfect fraternal reconciliation, so that when the third millennium begins it will find us standing side by side in perfect communion.

Not everyone in Turkey was delighted to welcome the Pope. The right-wing press in that country carried numerous articles opposing the visit. One member of the neo-fascist Grey Wolves, recently escaped from gaol where he had been sent after confessing to the murder of Abdi Ipekci, the editor of *Milliyet*, wrote to that paper:

> Fearing the creation of a new political and military power in the Middle East by Turkey along with its brother Arab states, Western imperialism has ... dispatched to Turkey in the guise of a religious leader the crusade commander John Paul. Unless this untimely and meaningless visit is postponed, I shall certainly shoot the Pope.

It was signed by Mehmet Ali Agca.[33]

This year the Vatican spokesman, to dispel rumours that John Paul was going to Bethlehem for Christmas, announced in good time that the Pope would definitely be celebrating midnight mass in St Peter's.

NOTES

1. Blazynski, George, *John Paul II: a Man from Krakow* (London, Weidenfeld & Nicolson, 1979), p. 2.
2. cf. *The Tablet*, 17 November 1984, p. 1148.
3. cf. Peter Hebblethwaite, *Paul VI* (HarperCollins, 1993), p. 324.

4. Giancarlo Zizola, 'The cardinals' role', *The Tablet*, 8 December 1979, p. 1200.
5. One of whom, Benelli, was to die soon afterwards: his election would have led to yet another short pontificate.
6. The doings of the cardinals in conclave are secret, but now that only cardinals up to the age of eighty are allowed to be present, the secrecy has become rather less absolute, for the electors feel obliged to tell their older colleagues what happened, and the over-eighties are not bound by the conclave oath. The foregoing account, however, is still based on Roman gossip.
7. John Paul I had used the first person singular when speaking to journalists shortly after his election, but *Osservatore Romano* had quoted him as using the plural of traditional papal style.
8. cf. Williams, op. cit., pp. 42–5. The stanza referred to runs as follows:
    To bear our load – this world by God designed –
    That power we need;
    Our Slavic Pope, brother to all mankind,
    Is there to lead!
   For the whole poem, plus commentary, see *The Tablet*, 20 January 1979, pp. 63–4.
9. 'Collegiality' of bishops means that the whole body, or college, of bishops, in union with the Bishop of Rome, have oversight of the whole Church.
10. *The Tablet*, vol. 222, 28 October 1978, p. 1039.
11. *Osservatore Romano*, 5 November 1978, quoted Williams, op. cit., p. 165.
12. Williams, op. cit., pp. 270–1.
13. cf. my article 'First confession in controversy' in *The Month*, CCXXXV, 1277 (January 1974), pp. 439ff.
14. cf. above, p. 27–8.
15. Conferencia Episcopal de Latina Americana.
16. *The Tablet*, 28 April 1979, p. 409. 'Modernism' was condemned by Pius X at the beginning of the twentieth century. It arose at least in part from the attempt to understand historically the development of the Church's doctrine. In doing so it was revealed that the particular ways in which doctrine was formulated were frequently of fairly recent date, and did not have the sanction of antiquity. This was regarded as subversive. One doctrine which certainly does not have the sanction of antiquity is that of the *magisterium*, as it is currently understood to mean the pope and his Curia.
17. For summary, see *The Tablet*, 5 May 1979, p. 438.
18. 'In the breast', i.e., the name of the candidate was not revealed – which suggests that news of his appointment might be dangerous to him.
19. When, at Christmas time, John Paul had written a letter to his diocese, the censor in Poland had cut out all reference to Bishop Stanislaw. Such was the storm of protest when this become known that permission had to be given for the text of the letter to be printed in full.
20. Stanislaw was indeed an ambiguous figure, who may have been slaughtered as much for his politics as for his moralizing.

21. Christopher Bobinski, *The Tablet*, 9 June 1979, p. 549.
22. Originally rather more had been expected: the charges levied by the Polish government seem to have deterred a great many. The official Polish press service went to great lengths to attempt to control the media (each journalist was assigned a 'minder' with the task of ensuring only an officially acceptable version of events got through), but without much success.
23. John Whale, ed., *The Pope from Poland*, p. 171.
24. The design was the work of Mgr Bruno Heim, then Apostolic Delegate to England, and the Vatican's expert on heraldry. When Archbishop of Cracow, the Pope's motto under his shield was 'Totus tuus', 'Wholly yours' – meaning the Virgin Mary.
25. A particularly controversial statement in the context of the Republic of Ireland, where the Church could grant a decree of nullity of marriage, while the law insisted on the permanence of the union.
26. A rival organization to Sister Kane's Leadership Conference afterwards described her words as 'provocative' and 'open dissent from the official teaching of the Catholic Church on the ordination of women'.
27. David Willey, *God's Politician* (Faber, 1992).
28. On this, see Peter Hebblethwaite, *Paul VI* (HarperCollins, 1993), pp. 437–9.
29. In October Ratzinger vetoed the appointment of the theologian Johannes Baptist Metz to a professorship in the theology faculty of the University of Munich – under the 1924 concordat between Bavaria and the Holy See such appointments required the approval of the local bishop. Karl Rahner S.J. sharply attacked Ratzinger's interference, calling on him to publish his reasons, and suggesting that what lay behind the veto was that Metz's theology had been, at least in part, the inspiration for Liberation Theology in Latin America. 'Twenty-five years ago', wrote Rahner, 'the Holy Office in Rome forbade me to write anything further on concelebration [i.e., the saying of mass by a number of priests together – a practice which became common]. That was a senseless, unscientific manipulation by church bureaucrats. I judge your action against Metz to be of the same category' (*The Tablet*, 1 December 1979, p. 1189).
30. That is what the Pope said, but the history of the cardinalate is rather more complicated, and consistories had not met as advisory bodies to popes since the setting up of the Roman Curia towards the end of the sixteenth century. On the history of the cardinalate, see Stephan Kuttner, 'Cardinalis: the history of a canonical concept' in *Traditio*, vol. 3 1945), pp. 129–214.
31. cf. above, p. 62.
32. Willey, op. cit., p. xi.
33. Herman, Edward S. and Brodhead, Frank, *The Rise and Fall of the Bulgarian Connection* (New York, Sheridan Square, 1986), p. 52.

FOUR

1980-1

O N 14 JANUARY 1980 began the Synod of the Dutch Church, announced in June just before the Pope set off for Poland. John Paul had ordered it to be held in Rome, and its agenda had been drawn up not by the Dutch themselves but by Joseph Tomko, general secretary of the Synod of Bishops. Cardinal Willebrands, Archbishop of Utrecht and president of the Dutch Conference of Bishops (there were only seven of them), was to preside jointly with Godfried Danneels, Bishop of Antwerp since 1977 but just appointed to succeed Cardinal Suenens as Archbishop of Malines, the Belgian primatial See. The appointment of the presidents lay in the hands of the Pope. At a press conference three days before the Synod was to open Tomko announced that the Pope had also invited six of his 'closest collaborators', all cardinals, to attend. They included Franjo Seper, Prefect of the Congregation for the Doctrine of the Faith, the watchdog of orthodoxy, and Sebastiano Baggio of the Congregation of Bishops. The balance of the Synod had clearly been weighted in favour of conservatism. Willebrands would not have been surprised. When a year earlier (25 January 1979) he had explained the problems of the Dutch Church to the Pope, John Paul had listened sympathetically, but had then asked to see immediately the two conservative members of the hierarchy, Simonis of Rotterdam and Gijsen of Roermond, and called the other four afterwards, and separately.

The Synod was, moreover, taking place against the uproar which followed the condemnation of Hans Küng. He had his *missio canonica*, his authority to teach as a Catholic theologian, withdrawn by a statement of the Congregation for the Doctrine of the Faith on 15 December 1979. The statement claimed that 'Professor Küng deviates from the complete truth of Catholic belief. For this reason he cannot be regarded as a Catholic theologian as such'. What was at issue was his book on infallibility. Two days later the German bishops explained that 'the dogma of infallibility may be at first regarded as a phenomenon marginal to the whole corpus of the faith, but in reality it includes fundamental problems such as the knowledge of truth, interpretation of revelation, its linguistic form and its tradition, the certainty of faith and the justification for the official authority of the Church'. Bishop Georg Moser of Rottenburg-Stuttgart, the diocese in which Küng lived, demanded that he be sacked from the theological faculty of Tübingen, under the terms of the 1933 concordat between Hitler's Germany and the Vatican.

Archbishop Ratzinger's veto of the appointment to a chair at Munich of Johannes Baptist Metz (see above, p. 73,n.29) was also simmering on, but Küng had a much higher profile than Metz, and was vigorously backed by the whole board of editors of *Concilium*, a progressive journal published in a number of different language editions but in origin a Dutch publication, and by a number of distinguished, individual theologians. The Dominican Yves Congar explained in the French newspaper *Le Monde* that Küng had never refused to go to Rome to enter into dialogue with the Congregation for the Doctrine of the Faith – the statement of the German bishops had given that impression – but had said that he would attend under a number of conditions. The Congregation accepted all but three. They could not agree that he might see the dossier which had been drawn up about him; they could not permit him to know who it was who would be appointed to defend him; and they could not grant him right of appeal.

Hans Küng was not the first theologian whose writings had been examined and found wanting by the Congregation for the Doctrine of the Faith.[1] But he was the one with the widest reputation, and someone whose writings were accessible to people other than professional theologians. Protestants as well as Catholics protested at the treatment of Küng. The case of Küng, even though it had begun long before John Paul was elected,[2] focused attention on the regime in Rome as no other similar incident had done.

In media terms it was bigger news than the Dutch Synod, despite the fact that in the Synod a whole local Church was being put on trial. The problem had arisen because of the speed of the changes in the Church in the Netherlands in the aftermath of Vatican II. Holland had been among the most conservative, most structured, of Catholic societies. Seemingly overnight the bonds burst. It became the most progressive, least constrained of local churches. As priests left to get married, they were replaced in their posts by lay people, sometimes even by married priests. There was a series of national pastoral conferences, dominated by the laity, which urged on Rome the acceptance of a married clergy, and even the ordination of women priests.[3] The number of men putting themselves forward for ordination dropped sharply, even more dramatically than in other countries suffering a similar decline – which was everywhere in the Western world.

But in Holland there was an additional problem. In order to attempt to reimpose a more traditional pattern of Church life upon the Dutch, Pope Paul VI made two episcopal appointments (and remember that the entire episcopacy numbered only seven bishops) which were extremely controversial. Mgr Simonis was sent to Rotterdam in December 1970 and shortly afterwards Mgr Gijsen was nominated Bishop of Roermond. They brought disunity to the tiny Bishops' Conference (Gijsen on one occasion denounced the remainder of the hierarchy as being of doubtful orthodoxy). It was this disunity, all of them agreed, and at least on this they were at one, which was the prime reason for the calling of the Synod by the Pope.

According to Willebrands, John Paul played a very active role in the Synod, which dragged on for a further four days beyond the official terminating date. But he failed, or was unwilling, to bring Gijsen into line, and allowed the Bishop of Roermond, or rather the complaints of the Bishop of Roermond and like-minded conservatives, to set the agenda, much to the distress of the remainder of the hierarchy. What was therefore discussed at the Dutch Synod, under the eye of the Pope and in the presence of six curial cardinals, were topics which hitherto had been handled within the Dutch Episcopal Conference itself. The outcome was something of an anti-climax. Much of what went on in the discussions remained secret. The official communiqué was relatively bland – except that it had an extraordinary provision, apparently added as an afterthought, stating that

> The Bishop of Roermond will collaborate once more with the other bishops in the matter of the A[ssociation for the] P[ropagation of the] F[aith], the Lenten campaign and the collection for Dutch missionaries.
>
> The bishops are aware of certain difficulties between the Bishop of Roermond and persons and institutions in the threefold domain mentioned. They are ready to help him find a solution to those difficulties.

That may have seemed to disinterested observers as a snub for Gijsen. It was not how many Catholics in Holland saw it: there had been an expectation that he would be removed. Instead there was increased control by Rome over the decisions of the Dutch Church, and clear indications that the role played by laity in the pastoral administration of the parish, and by married clergy, would be brought to an end. The married priests and pastoral assistants promptly organized themselves in opposition. When meetings were called to debate the conclusions of the Synod, bishops were excluded.

It may have been a disaster as far as the majority of Catholic laity in Holland were concerned, but in so far as it brought the Dutch Church back under the control of the Roman Curia it was voted a success by the Church's central authorities. There was already a Synod on the Family scheduled for the autumn – on 23 February John Paul warned the Council of the Synod secretariat against 'useless publicity' which presents 'in an over-simplified and superficial way problems that are essentially difficult and profound', and it was to be avoided before and during the session – and then he convened a Synod of the Ukrainian Church to meet on 24 March.

This was a bold step to take, particularly bold, perhaps, for a Polish Pope. The Ukrainian Church in communion with Rome had come into being in 1596 when it acknowledged the authority of the papacy while retaining its own Byzantine-Slavonic rite. It had officially ceased to exist in 1946 when it was absorbed into the Russian Orthodox Church. After the Communist takeover it survived underground, but it also survived, and very actively as a focus for Ukrainian nationalist aspirations, in Western Europe and, more especially, in North America. In 1980 its undisputed leader was 88-year-old Cardinal Josef Slipyj, whose indigenous title, as it were, was Major Archbishop of Lvov. In 1945 he had been sent by the Russians to a labour camp and released into Roman exile in 1963. He was none too pleased either by his exile or by Paul VI's attitude towards his Church. He wanted recognition as Patriarch of the Ukraine, which would have given him stronger authority over the bishops belonging to his rite. Paul VI refused, saying a Patriarch could exercise authority only over his own territory, while Slipyj's clientele, 823,000 of them, was scattered over the globe. John Paul was of the same mind. He had, none the less, to make provision for succession to the aged Cardinal.

Hence the Synod, called at only six days' notice, and lasting just four. This gave the Pope the opportunity of saying that the Ukrainians were choosing their own leader, while at the same time ensuring that it all happened under the eye of the Roman Curia. The choice was unsurprising. On 12 November Mgr Miroslav Lubachivsky had been appointed Ukrainian Metropolitan in Philadelphia. The Ukrainian Church of the Diaspora was divided between those who wanted a patriarchate, and those who did not. Lubachivsky was a Pope's man, rather than a Slipyj supporter. John Paul proposed to appoint him as an assistant, with right of succession, to Slipyj but needed the backing of the Ukrainian Synod if he was not to appear to be riding roughshod over historic claims. Lubachivsky was chosen by the Synod and honour was satisfied all round, though Slipyj still did not have his patriarchate. I want to see unity restored, said the Pope, not only between Rome and the Ukrainians, but within the Ukrainian Church itself. Whatever may be said for the success of the Synod in achieving the latter aim – and dissension remained – papal manipulation of a Uniate Church brought about a tighter bond with Rome.

The tightening of links with Rome was, of course, a major preoccupation of Pope John Paul as he went about his extensive travels. At the beginning of May he made his first visit to Africa. There were six countries on the itinerary, and the trip lasted ten days. The first stop, however, was by far the most important: on Friday 2 May he arrived in Kinshasa, the capital of Zaire. Zaire is not only one of the largest countries in Africa, it is also one of the most Catholic: half its population owe allegiance to Rome, and it had the largest Episcopal Conference – fifty-six bishops – of any country the Pope had so far visited.

But Africa represented, and still represents, one of the greatest challenges the Roman Catholic Church has to face. Worldwide, it is not only the largest single Christian Church, it is the largest unified religious group. That statistic, however, is being seriously challenged by the inexorable spread of Islam – if Islam can be described as a unified religious group. Catholicism may be growing fast, but Islam is growing faster. Nowhere on the African continent is Roman Catholicism the dominant force in a country, whereas in several Islam is the state religion. One response to the spread of the Moslem faith would be to adapt the practices of Catholicism more closely to the traditions of the peoples of Africa – Africanization, as the general theory of 'encul-turation' would be described in this context – but there are limits to how far the Pope is prepared to go.

David Willey has sensed a particular delight in the Pope about Africa and things African. 'Relaxing for the occasional moment on tour he can frequently be observed tapping his feet to African rhythms. When lecturing Africans on their moral failings he treats them gently, much more gently, I noticed, then when castigating, for example, the "hedonists" of some Western European countries.'[4] But there are limits. The Cardinal of Kinshasa, Archbishop Joseph Malula, was eager to ordain married men to the priesthood: that proposal got nowhere. Though during mass the Pope had to listen to tom-toms beating and to watch African priests dancing around the altar, he demanded that there should remain 'a substantial unity with the Roman rite'. Speaking to young people in Kinshasa on 3 May he insisted that the monogamous, permanent union of equal partners was ordained by God, and was not a style of marriage invented by the Europeans and imported unnecessarily into Africa.[5] Though he admitted in an address to the bishops of Zaire that 'the Gospel is not identified with any culture, and transcends them all', he added 'Africanization covers wide and profound areas which have not yet been sufficiently explored, whether it is a question of the language in which to present the Christian message in such a way as to touch the minds and hearts of Zairians, of catechesis, of theological reflection, of the form of expression most suitable for the liturgy or sacred art, or of the forms of Christian community life'. Cardinal Malula clearly did not think the process was proceeding fast enough. He told the Pope that he would have liked him to experience the full impact of the 'Zairian rite' – but the Congregation for Divine Worship back in Rome had vetoed the proposal: for the Pope to attend such a eucharistic service, in which clergy wore native headdresses and altar servers carried spears, would seem like pontifical approval, and that had not been given. Indeed, shortly after John Paul's return to Rome the Congregation for the Sacraments and Divine Worship issued an Instruction, tightening up the rules to be followed in celebrating the Eucharist, and laid down new guidelines for eucharistic services other than mass.[6]

From 1967 to 1974 President Mobutu of this former Belgian Congo had pursued an anti-Church policy, leading eventually to the exile of Cardinal Malula for safety's sake. Mobutu had modified his hostility only when a deteriorating economic and security situation made him turn to the West for support.[7] Before the Pope's departure the Belgian Justice and Peace Commission had called upon John Paul to boycott their former colony on the grounds that the papal presence might add a veneer of respectability to a basically corrupt regime. Every condemnation of 'corruption' in a papal speech got a roar of applause from the long-suffering populace,[9] as John Paul went about delivering his fifty major discourses in the course of this African trip. None was addressed pointedly at Mobutu.

However oppressed Zairians might have felt, there was little sign of it in the infectious enthusiasm with which they greeted John Paul's arrival. The celebrations got out of hand on 4 May, when the Pope went to a public square to celebrate Sunday mass, intending in the course of it to consecrate nine new bishops. Nine people were killed and seventy-two seriously injured in the crush, and the ceremony, together with the rest of the day's programme, was cancelled.

From Zaire John Paul went briefly to the Congo, from the Congo to Kenya where he addressed the diplomatic corps, himself carried a spear, and wore, a touch self-consciously for all his acting talent, a native headdress. He told the diplomats that Africa should be left to solve its own problems and appeared – guardedly – to favour democracy though he had said while in the Congo that the Church was not allied to one form of political regime against any other. In Ghana, the next stop, John Paul told the President on 8 May that 'Africa has something special to offer the world', though in what exactly this something special consisted he was rather more vague, taking refuge in the unity-in-diversity of its culture, its respect for the sacred, its links between nature and the Creator, and a certain *joie de vivre* which the Pope had clearly found to be to his liking.

In Accra on 9 May there was a morning (9.00 am) meeting between John Paul and the Archbishop of Canterbury, Robert Runcie, who happened to be in the Ghanaian capital at the same time. Their communiqué afterwards said that 'time is too short and the need too pressing to waste Christian energies on pursuing old rivalries', a sentiment which must have been reinforced by the drive to Christianize Africa. But, as will be seen later, these expressions of goodwill foundered before the reality of dialogue with the Anglican Communion, and more especially with the decision taken piece-meal by member Churches of that Communion to ordain women to the priesthood. 'I must say till this time I did not much think about this denomination', the Pope told Peter Hebblethwaite on the plane to Zaire.[9] That was to become very evident.

From Accra the Pope went on to Upper Volta and finally to the Ivory Coast where the President, Houphouèt-Boigny, had married his long-time partner just a week before the papal coming (Mobutu in Zaire had done likewise). 'The first-fruits of my pastoral visit', said the Pope, as his plane flew Romewards[10] from Abidjan.

His stay in Rome was short. Within three weeks he was off again, this time to Paris to address UNESCO, though protocol required that he both make at least a token visit to the Church in France, and pay a courtesy call on the President, M. Valéry Giscard d'Estaing. There was mass at Notre Dame – or rather, in front of Paris's cathedral – on Friday 30 May, immediately after the Pope's arrival. There was a breakfast meeting with French intellectuals the following day and, later the same morning, a garden party at the Elysée Palace. There was mass in the basilica of Saint Denis where French monarchs had been buried and where – for it stands in what is now a working-class suburb with a large immigrant population – he spoke on social justice. 'Today closed systems of ideas are not enough, on the contrary, such narrow systems can sometimes obstruct the way rather than open it up, as for example when it is a question of the victory of one system or party rather than the real needs of man', he said, in a passage which might have been taken as critical of both capitalism and Marxism (the Communist mayor was in the crowd outside the basilica, where the homily was delivered). There was, however, implicit criticism of the class war ('The world of work must be a world of love and not hatred'), though he quoted the passage from the *Magnificat* about casting the mighty from their thrones.[11] Worse still, there were evocations in the homily of the slogan of the wartime regime of Marshal Pétain, work-family-nation, chosen to replace the Revolutionary liberty-equality-fraternity.

It is unlikely that either the reminiscence of the Pétainist regime or the apparent snub to 1789 were intentional, but they were noticed,[12] and they were all of a piece with the general tenor of the papal visit. France, the most secularized of the one-time Catholic countries of Europe, was addressed by its ancient title of 'eldest daughter of the Church', and at the mass outside Notre Dame the Pope made great play with the saints of France's past – François de Sales, Vincent de Paul, Jean Eudes, Jean Vianney – though he also mentioned the controversial worker-priest movement, to which he gave apparent support. Just before he left on the Monday he paid a visit to the shrine of Ste Thérèse at Lisieux.

Not that John Paul was unaware of the statistics documenting the steep fall in the practice of French Catholicism. He could scarcely have failed to notice it. An attendance of one and a half million had been expected at a mass on Sunday 1 June at Le Bourget airport. In the event it poured with rain, and less than a quarter of that number turned up, though all the bishops were there. The Pope spoke of a 'crisis of growth' in French Catholicism, though a 'crisis of decline' would have been nearer the mark. He attacked progressives for being 'impatient to adapt even the content of the faith, Christian ethics, the liturgy and the organization of the institutional Church to changing attitudes', and the conservatives (in deference to France he called them '*integristes*') who 'commit abuses such as we are obviously the first to reprove and correct' – though the most significant of these *integristes*, Archbishop Lefebvre, was still at this point in apparently amicable dialogue with the Holy See – and, at his request, had been received by the Pope within a month of his election. To counter the supposed ravages of the progressives, John Paul advised the bishops to keep strict control over theological journals.

John Paul's address to UNESCO – where the Holy See had maintained a permanent observer since 1951 – was appropriately devoted to culture, its relationship to human existence on the one hand ('It is thanks to culture that man lives a truly human life … Man cannot do without culture. Culture is a specific mode of man's "existing" and "being". Man always lives according to a culture which is proper to him and which, in its turn, creates between men a bond which is also proper to them, in determining the interpersonal and social character of human existence') and religion on the other. 'It would certainly be no exaggeration to affirm in particular', said the Pope to the assembled delegates, some at least of whom would not have been overjoyed to hear it, 'that in a multitude of instances Europe as a whole, from the Atlantic to the Urals, in the history of individual nations as well as in that of the community as a whole, bears witness to the link between culture and Christianity'. It was a remarkable claim. In Paris, at the centre of the European Community, the Pope was insisting that the true hegemony of Europe extended so far as to include the whole of the Warsaw Pact countries except that part of Russia which lay in Asia; and that hegemony was created not by politics or economics but by a culture which was founded on Christianity.

Two days after John Paul returned to Rome the fragility of the unity of his own Church was demonstrated at the Katholikentag, the congress of German Catholics held every two years. The gathering took place in Berlin, in both halves of the divided city. But the meeting was also itself divided. Two years before in Freiburg the chief speaker had been Professor Johannes Baptist Metz. He was again invited, but declined the invitation. He attended instead an alternative congress, held in the same city and at the same time, at which the inaugural speaker was Professor Hans Küng. Metz followed Küng to the platform. The Pope, he said, was 'energetically stabilizing the Church backwards', working for 'a restoration of a fundamentally Eurocentric orientation' in the Church's pastoral practice. It was a neat, if unintentional, counterpoint to the Pope's address to the delegates at UNESCO.

Shortly afterwards, however, a small step was taken towards that Christian hegemony which the Pope so much desired. On 12 June the Holy See formally established diplomatic relations with the government of Greece, a move which the Greek Orthodox Church had hitherto discouraged. That it no longer opposed the agreement was seen as a sign of a positive attitude on the part of that Church towards the Vatican, and as evidence that links with the Churches of the East in general were improving. There had indeed recently been a meeting between Roman Catholic cardinals and theologians and representatives of fourteen autocephalous Churches of the Orthodox tradition. They met initially on Patmos where, it was claimed, John had written the Book of Revelation, and then on the island of Rhodes.

There were, meanwhile, matters to attend to in Rome. Cardinal Sergio Pignedoli, one of those cardinals thought likely to succeed to the papacy in the elections after the death of Paul VI and John Paul I, had himself recently died. Archbishop Jean Jadot was recalled from the United States, where he was Apostolic Delegates to replace Pignedoli at the head of the Secretariat for Non-Christians. The Rector of the Institut Catholique in Paris, Bishop Paul Poupard, was brought back to Rome to run the Secretariat for Non-Believers. A Polish Cardinal, and close friend of the Pope's, Wladyslaw Rubin, who had come to prominence as the secretary general of the Synod of Bishops, became Prefect of the Congregation for Eastern Churches, while Cardinal Pietro Palazzini went to head the Congregation for the Causes of Saints.

These announcements were made on 27 June. Three days later the Pope was in Brasilia. Brazil is the largest of all Roman Catholic countries, and it has the largest number of bishops of any single state. Its people were, at that time, among the most cruelly governed by the state and, as far as the Church was concerned, charismatically led – by Cardinal Evaristo Arns, Archbishop of São Paulo, who had opened his churches as refuges for demonstrators hunted down by the police.

The Bishops' Conference had wanted the Pope to begin his visit symbolically by arriving first of all in Fortaleza, the poorest and most oppressed part of the country. In the event Vatican insistence on diplomatic protocol meant he arrived in the Brazilian capital, itself an extravagant folly in a nation which could not afford it, to meet the President, General Figueiredo. 'We know that in many cases the information that reaches the Vatican about the Church in Brazil', Archbishop José Pires of Paraiba told the Spanish weekly *Vida Nueva*, 'does not convey the full reality of the situation and fails to bring out the anguish and hardship experienced by many priests and pastoral workers in their search for valid methods for the liberation of the oppressed.'[13] There were specific complaints. Cardinal Lorscheiter, as President of the Episcopal Conference, had written to the Pope requesting a speeding up of the process by which priests returned to the lay state – John Paul had not replied. The Bishops' Conference had asked for adaptations to be made to the liturgy: the Vatican had turned them down. A proposal that *ad limina* visits – the routine reporting – in person – of bishops to the Vatican should be suspended for a year and the money thus saved be donated to the needs of the Nicaraguan Church was rejected by the Holy See.

In the event, the visit, which had first been proposed as a visit to the national eucharistic congress being held in Fortaleza, became one of the most political of papal tours, even though John Paul told Figueiredo on his arrival that his visits have 'a definite apostolic character and a strictly religious purpose'. The President was less comfortable as the Pope continued, 'The Church preaches ceaselessly those reforms that are indispensable if the values without which no society worthy of the name can prosper are to prosper and be safeguarded'. And he added a warning, something of which the Brazilian President was already well aware, that if the reforms were not granted they would be demanded by force. Though the Pope warned, he clearly distanced himself from those who took such violent action. As he told young people in Belo Horizonte on 1 July, and reminiscing about his own experience in Poland at the outbreak of war, 'I learned that a young Christian ceases to be young and *a fortiori* to be a Christian when he allows himself to be seduced by teaching or ideologies which preach hatred or violence'. He was most outspoken when addressing agricultural workers in Recife on 7 July. The right to property is legitimate in itself, he told them, but must be used for the common good, which takes precedence over private considerations: unexceptionable assertions in themselves, but dynamite in Brazil especially when coupled, as the Pope coupled them, with demands for agrarian reform. Yet when addressing workers in São Paulo he re-interpreted the option for the poor as proclaimed at Puebla, making of it a determination to evangelize the poor rather than a commitment to stand alongside them in their oppression. That he spoke out vigorously – though in general terms – on behalf of workers' rights was balanced by the fact that in his address at Fortaleza behind closed doors to the 340 bishops of the Episcopal Conference, he instructed clergy to stay out of politics. They were to preach the Church's social doctrine, but not to get involved in putting it into practice. Their social programme, he told them, 'cannot be based on preconceived ideas which, despite the merits and qualities which one willingly recognizes in them, are basically contrary to the Catholic truth'. Again unexceptionable sentiments, but what (or whom) was he getting at?

The visit, ending (almost) with a meeting between John Paul and leaders of eighteen Brazilian tribes, was an extraordinary feat. Twenty million saw the Pope in person, countless millions more saw him on television. To mark the papal visit President Figueiredo declared an amnesty for prisoners with terms of four years or less. Those in gaol for political offences were not included.

Even when John Paul was back in Rome he had not quite done with Brazil. In his packed twelve-day tour he had not had time to deliver himself of all the thoughts that had crowded in upon him as he prepared for the trip. He left behind at the secretariat of the Bishops' Conference the text of an address which, had there been space, he would have read to representatives of base communities. His overriding concern was that such communities should remain loyal to the Church and retain their 'ecclesial' nature – a term he returned to time and again. It laid heavy emphasis on the hierarchical nature of authority within the Church, and under the guise of praising them ('they have made a notable impact on the world outside'), warned them to toe the line: the task of a community leader is 'to accept diligently from the Church what she wants to say'.

Not, for the most part, that they had not been doing so. But accusations abounded, no matter how vigorously their religious superiors, Cardinal Arns of São Paulo prominent amongst them, had been defending them. It was a wearisome business. In the Borgo Santo Spirito the Jesuit General was tired of likewise having to defend the priests of the Society of Jesus against wild charges of fomenting revolution. In 1980 Pedro Arrupe, perhaps the most charismatic and widely loved superior of the Jesuits since the Founder himself (oddly, Arrupe bore a remarkable physical similarity to Ignatius Loyola), had been General for fifteen years. He was 73 years old, was planning to retire. The Congregation of the Society which had elected him had made provision for just such a move though hitherto Generals had been elected for life. The election of a new General required the calling of another Congregation. It had been set in train. Then, on 1 August, the Jesuit HQ announced it was all off. John Paul II said he wanted the General Congregation suspended until he could find time to talk to Arrupe about it. The meeting, planned for 1981, would, he said, be 'inopportune for the good of the Society and the good of the Church'.

The Pope knew about inopportune meetings. In 1971 he had been elected to the Council of the Synod of Bishops, and the group met for the first time from 29 February to 3 March the following year. Discussion turned on how best to implement the decisions of the previous gathering: Cardinal Wojtyla insisted that it was the Pope's job to draw the conclusions of the Synod and put them into effect. He also made it clear that marriage, and the problems surrounding Pope Paul's encyclical on birth control, *Humanae Vitae*, should be high on the agenda of any coming Synod. By the next meeting of the Council marriage and the family were likely candidates for the next meeting of the Synod, though Wojtyla wanted Religious Life added to the list of possible topics because it was, he believed, in a state of crisis. In the end Evangelization was chosen as the theme, and Wojtyla was put in charge of presenting the position paper to the gathering. Paul VI was persuaded that, so soon after the apparent rejection of *Humanae Vitae* by so many, to return to the debate would do no one any good. It would be inopportune.[14]

What Cardinal Wojtyla thought of that argument at the time has not been recorded. In May 1978 Wojtyla, as Archbishop of Cracow, presided over a meeting of the Synod's Secretariat at which it was again suggested that the theme of the next gathering should be 'the family in the modern world'. This time the proposal was accepted by Paul VI, and later endorsed by John Paul I. 'The Role of the Christian Family in the Modern World' was the topic which, as Pope, Karol Wojtyla shortly after his election selected for the 1980 Synod. The Vatican produced '*Lineamenta*', an outline paper which was circulated to Conferences of Bishops throughout the world for their comment. The comments were occasionally complimentary, sometimes neutral, often highly critical. The document was, said the Brazilian bishops for example, long on theory and short on practicalities, while the bishops of Indonesia complained that it did not speak of the joys of marriage and spent far too much time rehashing the arguments of *Humanae Vitae*, which had already failed to convince.[15]

The Brazilian response was particularly interesting, for it undermined the whole basis on which the Synod had been called. The Church emphasizes the role of the family while failing to give due account to the social and economic structures which dominate the lives of individuals and of families. There is a danger, they pointed out, that the Church had an image of an ideal family, far removed from the reality of everyday living, and in pursuing that image they weakened the Church's mission. Moreover, the Church was intent on treating the family as the *object* of pastoral action, and rarely considered it as the *subject* (i.e., itself the actor) of such action.

The make-up of this, the Pope's first Synod, was illuminating. It is simpler to consider the synodal fathers as falling into two categories. There were those who were directly elected to attend by their Episcopal Conferences, and there were those who were there either by 'right' (e.g., superiors general of [male] religious orders) or by personal appointment of John Paul II. Of the first category, twice as many came from the Third World as from the First; when both categories are taken together, by far the largest representation came from Europe.[16]

The Synod began on 26 September and proceeded with admirable openness to the press (which had been promised an unheard-of two briefings a day)[17] and, for the first two weeks greatly heartened the participants. The Pope was present as often as he possibly could be, and regularly had lunch with Synod members. He took copious notes, but said nothing. 'You could have pulled a face or shown disapproval', Cardinal Emmett Carter, Archbishop of Toronto, told him on 20 October, 'But you did nothing of the kind. You left the Synod free.'[18] By that time, however, Cardinal Carter and the other participants knew the Synod was heading for trouble.

It all began on 14 October, when the bishops decided to present 'Propositions' to the Pope. The Pope was consulted about this idea, and a group of experts under the guidance of Cardinal Ratzinger was put to work drawing up such Propositions. These were put to the Synod the following day – and were promptly rejected, the bishops apparently believing that the Vatican bureaucracy was trying to usurp their synodal function. At this point the press statements ceased.

The fathers of the Synod met in their discussion groups[19] and made proposals, some of which were distinctly radical. The final forty-three propositions, approved on 24 October though some bishops complained that the final texts did not represent their discussions, were scarcely radical – though, for instance, a passing reference to studying the practice of the Eastern Church over the matter of divorce suggested a possible softening of the Western Church's stance in this matter and, as *The Tablet* put it at the time, the bishops had not approached *Humanae Vitae* 'in a fundamentalist manner'.[20]

The Propositions were supposed to remain secret, a brief to the Pope for some post-synodal document. But it was John Paul II who broke the embargo. In his final sermon on 25 October he made some stinging remarks about the proposals of the Synod. His sitting among the members of the Synod had seemed a collegial act: his unilateral attack on their conclusions was anything but. Many, if not most, bishops left disheartened by their experience of Vatican manipulation.

They had to wait over a year for the publication of the papal document, an 'Apostolic Exhortation on the Family', *Familiaris Consortio*, which purported to present a reflection on the Synod's deliberations. It appeared on 15 December 1981, though it was dated 22 November: the delay in responding to the Synod was no doubt a result of the attempt on the Pope's life earlier in the year. Superficially the Exhortation reflected the Synod's deliberations and its 43 Propositions, but it could have been written whether the Synod had taken place or not. The bishops had, collegially, contributed their pastoral experience to the Church's deliberations. They had called for greater understanding of local variations in the practices of marriage and family life: for more 'enculturation' of the Church's teaching and liturgy. This was given recognition by the Exhortation – then firmly placed under central Roman control. 'There is nothing taken positively from the Propositions', conclude Grootaers and Selling, 'which did not represent established, official teaching and practice.'[21] One wonders, therefore, why the Synod happened at all. The Pope was eager to call the gathering, one can only assume, because he wanted the Church, in the persons of the bishops elected to the Synod, to endorse the views which he already held.[22] In fact they showed themselves much more open and sympathetic than he to the pastoral problems of marriage among Catholics. Unlike the Propositions, in *Familiaris Consortio* 'There is no spirit of inquiry, no initiation of further study or willingness to rethink fundamental presuppositions'.[23]

For the British world at least, attention on the work of the Synod was diverted by the visit to the Vatican, on 18 October, of the Queen and Prince Philip. The Pope, in his official address, praised Britain's repeated defence in the twentieth century of 'the ideals of freedom and democracy', and commented on the spread of English as a world language. He was, he said, looking forward 'with great anticipation' to his pastoral visit to the Catholics of Great Britain, and both he, and the Queen in her reply, spoke of greater cooperation among Christians in the British Isles.

But in the meantime another, and potentially very difficult, visit was looming. The Pope was to go to Germany. It was going to be delicate enough as it was: the German Bishops' Conference made it worse. They commissioned a booklet on the history of the Church in their country which had some distinctly unecumenical words penned by Professor Remigius Bäumer on the subject of Martin Luther. The embarrassed bishops promptly disavowed Professor Bäumer's views and claimed they had never read his chapter before it got into print. But it was an unauspicious preliminary. Then the Evangelical Church, by far the largest non-Roman Catholic denomination, found it had been lumped together with other church groups in a delegation to meet the Pope: they were given their own slot and were mollified. Next there were unseemly squabbles in Bavaria over paying for the trip, and declaring a public holiday in honour of the Pope's visit. And finally there was the affair of the theologians' letter.

Some 130 German-speaking theologians, Hans Küng amongst them, signed a letter delivered to the Papal Nuncio in Bonn just five days before the Pope's arrival. The letter raised six issues: (1) a request for a revision of the Church's teaching on birth control, particularly in light of the poverty in the Third World brought about by high birth rates; (2) a rather obscure demand that since religion was at the root of, or contributed to, tension in the world, the Church ought to take a lead in resolving conflicts; (3) a demand for intercommunion, the removal of the impediment to marriages between Catholics and those of other Christian denominations, and the recognition of the Protestant ministry as having valid orders; (4) a proposal that the canon law regarding the remarriage of a forsaken partner be revised (an idea that they had picked up, no doubt, from the Synod where it had already been aired and had been received unsympathetically); (5) a suggestion that married men and women be ordained; and (6) that the proceedings of the Congregation of the Doctrine of the Faith be revised 'in a way that corresponds with the principles of law and justice'.

The trip to Germany, already problematic for a Polish Pope, seemed set to become even more contentious. John Paul II handled the situation with consummate skill. The avowed reason for going on 15 November was to celebrate the 700th anniversary of the death of St Albert the Great, the teacher of Thomas Aquinas and said to be something of a hero of the Pope's. Unfortunately, in the run-up to the celebrations a theologian, and a woman theologian at that, had demonstrated Albert to have been both anti-Semitic and anti-feminist. Cardinal Höffner, Archbishop of Cologne, the city where Albert lay buried, had vigorously defended Albert. John Paul took a wiser course. He said that St Albert's work was 'time-bound', but he was exemplary in uniting faith and reason, in which he was a model for us all today. Today, he claimed, the Church defended reason against irrationalism, freedom against tyranny and progress against pessimism.

The following day in Osnabrück, where the Catholic population was very largely composed of immigrants, he thanked Protestants for lending Catholics church buildings until they were able to put up their own. The Evangelicals when they had their audience on Monday 17th were delighted by very respectful references to Luther. His address certainly impressed them, especially by his careful citations of Luther's lectures on Romans (delivered before the break with Rome). John Paul went to Fulda, where he told bishops, priests and seminarians that there was going to be no change in the discipline of celibacy, but that priests needed support in order to live celibate lives. Still in Fulda the following day he told assembled laypeople that, in theological matters, they had to accept the decisions of the pastors of the Church who were responsible for protecting matters of faith. He was then off to Altötting, a Marian shrine in Bavaria, when he compared his visit to the shrine to Mary's visit to St Elizabeth and Zachariah. In Munich, on the last day of his stay, the Pope celebrated a mass in the open air for young people. The temperature was bitter (when it wasn't raining, which it did most of the time the Pope was in Germany, it was freezingly cold) but they came just the same and were electrified by the address of Barbara Engl who was to speak on behalf of Catholic youth organizations. She had a prepared text, but departed from it briefly to address the Pope directly about priestly celibacy and the role of women in the Church. The Archbishop of Munich was

Cardinal Ratzinger: he hustled John Paul away before he could reply. The Pope went home to publish his second encyclical.

Dives in Misericordia (Rich in mercy) was dated 30 November 1980. One commentator has described it as 'a philosophical essay on justice and mercy',[24] which indeed it is, but to describe it as 'philosophical' rather implies a dry treatise whereas the encyclical is a very moving, very personal, very revealing statement about the relationship of human beings to God and to each other. The more the Church's mission is centred upon men and women, the Pope insisted, the more it must be directed in Christ toward God the Father. The God revealed in Christ is the Father of mercies, especially close to people when they are suffering or under threat. Jesus' love was nowhere more evident than when he was in contact with suffering, injustice and poverty – and he demands that his followers do likewise. In a meditation on the parable of the Prodigal Son, the Pope argued that what was being taught was not the virtue of justice but that of mercy – the father owed his son nothing – and the exercise of mercy led on the part of the son to a conversion of heart: 'Conversion is the most concrete expression of the working of love and of the presence of mercy in the human world.'[25] John Paul then goes on to list the threats to the human race, a theme he had already developed in *Redemptor Hominis*, including among them the danger of mass destruction by nuclear arms, fear of that oppression which will 'deprive him of his interior freedom', and the dangers arising from inequality in the distribution of wealth. While the Church will continue, he says, to urge justice for all, justice alone is not enough: 'in the name of an alleged justice (for example, historical justice or class justice) the neighbour is sometimes destroyed, killed, deprived of liberty or stripped of fundamental human rights. The experience of the past and of our own time demonstrates that justice alone is not enough, that it can even lead to the negation and destruction of itself, if that deeper power, which is love, is not allowed to shape human life in its various dimensions'.[26]

There could be no doubt that the target of the Pope's criticism in *Dives in Misericordia* was the socialist system imposed upon the Eastern bloc as he had experienced it in Poland. In Poland, meanwhile, the independent trade union Solidarity had just been allowed to come into legal existence under the leadership of Lech Walesa. When Walesa signed the agreement permitting the existence of the unions, he did so with a souvenir pen from the Pope's 1979 visit, which sported a picture of John Paul upon it.[27] The threat of Russian invasion to put down the unrest, particularly in the shipyards of Gdansk but elsewhere as well, seemed to recede. Perhaps it had never been very real. Russia, already desperately stretched over Afghanistan, could scarcely afford it. As one Polish dissident prophetically noted in *Robotnik*, 'the very fact of war in Poland would stir up all kinds of forces in the Soviet Union. For there, as various evidence shows, the conflicts between nationalities are getting stronger and the economic situation worse'.[28]

It could be no secret in Rome that the Pope's attention was elsewhere. In his lengthy message for the World Day of Peace, 1 January 1981, he reminded his listeners that 'freedom is not something that is given. It is something to be constantly won'. He reminded them, too, in an Apostolic Letter of 31 December 1980 that the concept of Europe embraced the Warsaw Pact as well as NATO by declaring Saints Cyril and Methodius, the ninth-century apostles of the Slavs, co-patrons of Europe with St Benedict. Benedict had been declared patron of Europe by Pope Paul VI because the monks who had followed his rule, said Pope Paul, had forged a spiritual unity from the Mediterranean to Scandinavia, from Ireland to Poland.[29] Saints Cyril and Methodius extended that unity to Albania and Georgia, to Slovaks and Ukrainians. But there was a second purpose. It was in the context of dialogue between the Orthodox and the Catholic Churches, the Pope remarked on 21 January during the Octave of Prayer for Church Unity, that the apostles of the Slavs had been added to Benedict.

On 24 January Pope John Paul addressed the Sacred Roman Rota, the highest tribunal in the Church for the hearing of marriage cases, though these could also be heard, and most frequently were, in the lesser 'courts' of diocesan tribunals. What was worrying the Pope was the ease with which, apparently, annulments were being granted.[30] He spent much time, as he spoke to the assembled prelates and officials of the Rota, stressing the indissolubility of marriage, and cited the recent Synod as evidence of the alarm bishops were feeling with the increasing number of annulments.[31] He hoped – and his hope would be treated as an instruction – that those working on the final stages of the revision of the Church's Canon Law, begun under Pope John XXIII in 1959, would heed the fears expressed at the Synod. Above all, diocesan synods were to take their lead from Rome: 'any innovation of law, substantive or procedural, that does not correspond to the jurisprudence or practice of the courts and dicasteries of the Holy See is reckless'.[32] The Vatican Council under Pope John and Pope Paul had begun to devolve authority to bishops in dioceses. Pope John Paul wanted it back.

And then he was off once more on his travels, for a nine-day trip to Asia. His first stop was the Philippines. The visit had been proposed two years before and Cardinal Sin personally, and the Filipino bishops collectively, were claiming the honour of having issued the invitation. Not that it mattered all that much, for the person determined to make the most of John Paul's presence was the President, Ferdinando Marcos. As John Paul disembarked from the aircraft he walked between a row of Filipino officials on one side and a row of Asian cardinals on the other to be greeted at the end by the President's daughter and a bouquet. There was then much shuffling to the podium which was built just large enough to hold the President and his wife Imelda, and the rather more bulky ecclesiastical figures of Cardinal Sin and the Pope.

It must have been an uncomfortable huddle. By this time the Cardinal of Manila and many, though certainly not all, of the country's bishops were actively opposed to the Marcos regime which was, until shortly before the arrival of the Pope, governing the country through martial law. The jockeying for position on the podium was re-echoed in the jockeyings for position between Marcos, who was determined to make political capital out of the papal visit, and the Pope, who was just as determined that he should not. In the event, in the afternoon of his arrival (17 February) he read the President a stern lecture on human rights, and the following day claimed, in an address in a poor, waterfront area of Manila, that 'defending the human dignity of the poor and their hope for a human future is not a luxury for the Church, nor is it a strategy of opportunism, nor a means for currying favour. It is her duty ...' He was, however, short on the practicalities: 'The road towards your total liberation is not the way of violence, class struggle or hate; it is the way of love, brotherhood, peaceful solidarity'.

When he arrived John Paul had announced that the purpose of this pastoral visit was the beatification of Lorenzo Ruiz, a married man, half Chinese, who though born in Manila was martyred in Japan in 1637. This he undertook and afterwards met a group of Chinese Christians. Through them he addressed the Chinese government, assuring Beijing that Catholics would fully pull their weight in building up their country 'since a genuine and faithful Christian is also a genuine and good citizen'. Cardinal Casaroli, meanwhile, dropped a hint that the Vatican might be prepared to forgive and forget in the case of the Patriotic Catholic Association in China, that part of the Church which had reached an accommodation with the regime and was allowed openly to practise. It has not yet happened, and relations between China and the Vatican are as chilly as ever.

The Pope travelled around the Philippines, preaching on the sanctity of family life in Cebu City on 18 February, and two days later to sugar plantation owners and workers in Bacolid City. His message was for the owners rather than the workers, insisting that the produce of the land might not be used only for the benefit of the few. He warned the workers against using violence to solve social conflict.

On 23 February Pope John Paul set off for Japan where, the following day, he met representatives of non-Christian religions in the nunciature. The Catholic Church was, he said, ready to collaborate with them in the defence of human dignity – especially that of the unborn child. He was in Hiroshima as a 'pilgrim of peace' on 25 February, but reserved his most substantive address for the United Nations University where he talked about the responsibility of science and technology. He warned his hearers against three temptations – to pursue technological development for its own sake 'as if one should always do what is technically possible'; to use technology solely in pursuit of non-stop economic development and 'with no care for the true common good of humanity, making technology into an instrument at the service of the ideology of "having" '.

The Pope returned to Rome via Alaska after his twelve-day tour,[33] leaving Cardinal Casaroli in Hong Kong, attempting to negotiate with China. He met, not Chinese government officials but Bishop Dominic Tang, apostolic administrator of Canton, and the only prelate on mainland China who was *persona grata* with both the Chinese government and the Holy See. Casaroli made it clear that there might be ways of bringing back the Patriotic Association into the fold (there were, he said, a variety of different rites in communion with Rome, thereby suggesting a somewhat flexible link between the Vatican and Chinese Catholics). But the sticking point was the Holy See's diplomatic recognition of the Taiwanese government. The Pope, who had lived in a semi-free Church under a Communist government, understood that, in China, compromises might have to be made. But there were limits, and breaking off the Holy See's diplomatic links with the Taiwanese regime was one of them.

One of the Pope's constant themes in his addresses both in the Philippines and in Japan was abortion. It was much on his mind in the early months of 1981 as Italy prepared itself for a referendum on the law which legalized abortion, passed only a few months before Wojtyla became John Paul II. The referendum was scheduled for 17 May. Voters were asked to choose between two alternative propositions, one restricting the law the other broadening it. In the event, the Italians chose the latter by a large majority (67 per cent), despite the fact that the Pope had actively campaigned for the former. His high profile in what was seen in Italy as an entirely domestic issue was much resented by politicians who had themselves, for the most part, refrained from speaking on abortion, treating it as a non-political issue. The Communist

Party leader complained in the party newspapers that it was 'excessive and inopportune for the Pope to put himself at the head, with almost daily appeals and with mass meetings, of a movement conducting a campaign to modify the legislation of our Republic', while a Socialist Party spokesman used the term 'Vatican interference'.[34] The fact that the papal position was so overwhelmingly rejected has not in the least daunted the Pope's zeal on the matter of abortion, but it has dented the Church's credibility in Italy.

15th May 1981 was the ninetieth anniversary of the encyclical *Rerum Novarum*, Pope Leo XIII's letter on the condition of the working class which was hailed at the time as the 'charter of the working classes'. Subsequent popes had honoured the fortieth, seventieth and eightieth anniversaries with social encyclicals of their own. Pope John Paul was confidently expected to do likewise. On 13 May he was to give the first of a series of talks building up to the celebration of *Rerum Novarum*. The address was never delivered.[35] At 5.17 pm that day, as the Pope was being driven across St Peter's Square, Mehmet Ali Agca shot him. John Paul II collapsed into the arms of his private secretary, Fr Stanislaw Dziwisz. Two others in the crowd were wounded in the shooting, but not seriously.

There was, as a matter of course, an ambulance standing by behind the Arch of Bells. The Popemobile sped to it, and John Paul was rushed to the Gemelli hospital, over twenty minutes away, and promptly operated upon. Agca, a Turk, was arrested, and brought before Italian magistrates. He told them he was a nationalist atheist, an enemy of the Catholic Church and equally of American and Russian imperialism. He had, it transpired, already written a letter to the Turkish newspaper *Milliyet* (whose editor he had assassinated) saying that he was going to kill the Pope during his visit to Turkey (cf. above, p. 71). On that occasion John Paul had been too well guarded. In St Peter's Square he was an open target though only moments before he had plucked from the crowd a blonde, four-year-old girl whom he had hugged.

Loudspeakers kept the crowd in the Square informed of what had happened. There were tears, hymn-singing, much saying of the rosary. It was soon learned that the Pope, though badly wounded, had not been killed. Indeed, he had remained conscious up to the time of the operation, asking, bewildered, why did they do it, and calling upon the aid of Mary.

Mary was in his mind again when he broadcast his first message after the attempt on his life. It was 17 May, and his words were recorded: 'Dear brothers and sisters, I know that in these days, and especially in this moment of the *Regina coeli*, you are united with me. I thank you for your prayers and

I bless you all. I am particularly close to the two people injured at the same time as me. I pray for the brother who attacked me, whom I have sincerely forgiven. United with Christ, the priest and victim, I offer my sufferings for the Church and the world. To you, Mary, I say again *Totus tuus ego sum*: I am entirely yours.'

The following day, 18 May, was his 61st birthday. He was moved out of intensive care to a room from which he could catch a glimpse of the dome of St Peter's. Later that same day he learned that the Italians had voted to retain the law on abortion which he had campaigned so hard to have repealed. He returned to the Vatican in the evening of 3 June and appeared at the window of his room shortly afterwards to bless the crowd in the square beneath. He had been in hospital for just twenty-one days.

Meanwhile speculation mounted – and has not yet entirely abated – about the conspiracy to kill Pope John Paul. Even *L'Osservatore Romano* talked about 'unresolved questions'.[36] Was Agca acting alone, or was he part of an elaborate KGB conspiracy intended to rid the world of the one man who might inspire rebellion in Poland of a sort not to be stopped lest, in the 'domino' theory once so beloved of US geo-politicians, it lead to the rejection of Communism elsewhere in the Eastern bloc?

The latter interpretation was well-suited to the hard-line politics of the recently-elected Ronald Reagan, but it rests on no evidence. At his first trial in July 1981 Agca claimed to have been acting alone; at a later one conspiracy charges against six Turks and three Bulgarians were rejected by a Roman jury after a hearing lasting almost a year.[37] Gustave Weigel, of the Ethics and Public Policy Center of Washington, considers Agca's links with the Bulgarian secret service to have been 'proven',[38] and David Willey finds the coincidence distinctly suspicious of the only large pantechnicon for which the Bulgarians asked diplomatic immunity in 1981 leaving the Bulgarian embassy for Sofia just two hours after the assassination attempt.[39] If there were a conspiracy involving Bulgaria, most would agree, then it certainly could not have happened without the approval, and probably under the inspiration, of the KGB. This speculation had the backing of Henry Kissinger, the former US Secretary of State, who went so far as to blame Yuri Andropov, the head of the KGB who was, rather over a year later, to become the Soviet leader. He would have gone to any length, opined Kissinger, to counteract John Paul's influence in Poland. But no proof of the KGB's involvement has emerged, despite the opening up of so much of their archives. It is far easier to believe that, if Agca did not operate alone (and it seems unlikely that he could have done), then he was backed by the neofascist Turkish 'Grey Wolves' organization to which he was certainly linked. He had once before threatened to take the Pope's life, wholly unaided by the KGB or their Bulgarian equivalent: what need was there to implicate them later?[40]

Whatever the truth of the matter, the assassination attempt, followed shortly afterwards – on 28 May – by the death from cancer of Cardinal Wyszynski, cast an atmosphere of gloom over the Polish people. On 12 December that year the new head of the Polish State, General Wojciech Jaruzelski, declared war against his own nation. The tanks rolled in Warsaw and elsewhere, and in Gdansk Solidarity's leaders were arrested. It was almost as if, with the Pope incapacitated, the Communist regime felt itself all the stronger.

The Pope's recovery was not without its setbacks. When the doctors had operated on him immediately after the shooting they had established an intestinal bypass, scheduled to be reversed in June as his injuries healed. It did not take place, for he caught an infection which led to his return to hospital on 20 June. A medical bulletin issued four days later announced that he was suffering from cytomegalovirus, a virus infection which he might have picked up from blood transfusions immediately after the shooting. It was debilitating but not in itself life-threatening – large numbers of people, it was claimed, incur the infection some time in their lives. But it was slowing his recovery. The Spanish bishops seemed resigned to the cancellation of the papal visit to Spain scheduled for October. Even the English bishops signalled that the papal visit to Britain proposed for the end of May 1982 might have to be curtailed, something that seemed even more likely when a further two months of convalescence were imposed after the delayed operation took place on 4 August. He was released from hospital ten days later. On 26 August he spoke to pilgrims from the balcony of the papal summer residence at Castel Gandolfo. Three months after the assassination attempt he was back in business.

Not that he had been unoccupied in his hospital bed. The Curia had gone on functioning. There were appointments to bishoprics made and Vatican committees met. John Paul was kept closely informed by, especially, Casaroli. And there was an encyclical to which had to be added the final touches. *Laborem Exercens*, dated 14 September, closes with a paragraph noting that 'I prepared this document for publication last 15 May on the ninetieth anniversary of the encyclical *Rerum Novarum*, but it was only after my stay in hospital that I have been able to revise it definitively'.

As a celebration of Pope Leo's encyclical, *Laborem Exercens* was a curious document because *Rerum Novarum* is not even footnoted, and other papal or conciliar texts are rarely quoted. It marked a considerable break with the past, despite lip-service to the tradition of social teaching. Whereas earlier popes had appeared to favour some form of capitalism, Pope John Paul criticized both capitalism and Marxism. Whereas previously there had been a heavy emphasis on private property (albeit modified slightly under Pope Paul), Pope John Paul seems to accept the need for state ownership. Like his predecessors, he is opposed to 'class war', but accepts that conflict between classes may be inevitable. What he presents is more a philosophy and theology of work, than a discussion of social issues, and although there are occasional references to the writings of Thomas Aquinas, the Natural Law approach, which had underlain the Church's social teaching hitherto, was largely absent. And as for taking sides, he constantly insists upon the priority of labour over capital.

The prolonged convalescence had given the Pontiff time to reflect on a good deal more than workers' rights. On 7 August the much-loved[41] and highly respected Superior General of the Jesuits, Pedro Arrupe, had suffered a grievous stroke. Though he appeared to be making a slow recovery (in fact he lived for almost another decade but never did recover), there was no possibility of his continuing to govern the Society of Jesus. In the normal course of events the American Vincent O'Keefe, who had been Vicar General of the Society, running it from Rome in Arrupe's absences during visits to other parts of the world, would have been expected to continue in that office until a new Superior General could be elected. The procedures for a General Congregation to elect someone to replace Arrupe were already under way: the gathering was expected in 1982. But then Pope John Paul took a hand. In an entirely unprecedented move he appointed his own 'delegate', Fr Paolo Dezza, S.J., to run the society and to supervise arrangements for the General Congregation, thereby superseding Vincent O'Keefe.

Jesuits were aghast. Vincent O'Keefe was well-known in the Society, and well liked. Paolo Dezza was also well-known. He had spent most of his working life in Rome, serving as Rector of the Jesuit Gregorian University from 1941 to 1951. Generations of Jesuits had been brought up on his textbook on metaphysics. He was active as a consultor to a number of Vatican departments. He had been the conservative candidate at the 1965 Congregation which elected Pedro Arrupe as Superior General. He was, at the time of his appointment, aged 79 and almost blind, though otherwise in fairly robust health. Members of the Society feared that through a malleable Fr Dezza the Pope would be able directly to govern the Society. Possibly to soften the blow, John Paul gave Dezza an assistant, Fr Giuseppe Pittau. Pittau, like Dezza, was an Italian, but had worked closely with Arrupe in Japan, serving as President of the Jesuit Sophia University in Tokyo before being appointed Provincial Superior of the Jesuits in Japan. He was known to share Arrupe's vision.

Dezza took over the reins of power on 1 November, though Arrupe remained officially Superior General. Jesuit provincial superiors made a brave attempt to present the papal action in a positive light, though the French superior admitted that it was 'useless to disguise the fact that what is taking place now is outside the normal course of the law according to which we live'.

It is not possible that so drastic a course of action could have been initiated by anyone in the Vatican other than the Pope himself, and in the history of the Pope's relations with religious Orders it was to prove not to be an isolated incident. So why did he do it? There are two sorts of answers, readily compatible with each other. First of all, the Pope has not shown himself to be particularly sympathetic towards religious. They were not strong in Poland – certainly the Jesuits were not – and when still Cardinal of Cracow Wojtyla had appeared suspicious of their relative autonomy (known in Roman Catholic legal jargon as their 'exempt' status) with regard to diocesan bishops. At a council of the Synod meeting in 1974 Wojtyla had suggested as the next topic for discussion by the bishops religious life in the Church. He claimed it was in crisis, and that the best cure for this crisis would be to bring the Orders more closely under the supervision of bishops. He had, it was said, been irritated when the Jesuits refused to associate themselves with the general seminary for all students for the priesthood, religious as well as diocesan, that he was trying to establish in Cracow: he could not instruct them to cooperate if they did not want to do so.

Secondly, the Jesuits were a particular problem. They were, and are, the Church's most powerful religious Order. Many other Orders of both men and women look to the Society as a model both in the way they organize their lives, and in the way they manage their apostolate. In Latin America Jesuits had been closely linked to the Theology of Liberation, with its background in a Marxist analysis of society, an approach unpalatable to the Pope from Poland. Everywhere they were shedding their religious habits and, true to their traditions, were investigating new methods in the apostolate. They were closely associated with the reforms instituted at Vatican II if only because the general congregation which elected Pedro Arrupe had met in the immediate aftermath of the Council and had legislated in its spirit. Perhaps had Arrupe not been taken so seriously ill, John Paul might have delayed his attempt to bring the Jesuits into line. But in October 1981 the Society was unusually vulnerable, and the Pope acted.

John Paul had yet another surprise in store before the year was out. On 25 November he called Cardinal Joseph Ratzinger from his post as Archbishop of Munich, to be Prefect of the Congregation for the Doctrine of the Faith, the Vatican's doctrinal watchdog, and the successor to the Inquisition. It was a remarkable choice. The head of the Congregation meant to safeguard the purity of the Church's doctrinal teaching had rarely himself been a distinguished theologian. Cardinal Ratzinger was certainly that. He had begun teaching theology in 1952 and had held professorships at a succession of German universities. At the Council he had been in attendance on Cardinal Frings, then Archbishop of Cologne, as Frings' personal theologian. He had written a great deal, much of it, by the standards of the time, highly radical material – which those who were later to suffer at the hands of his Congregation were to quote with relish. He had been appointed to the Archbishopric of Munich in March 1977, and made a Cardinal the following June. But it was not the demands of ecclesiastical office which had moved him away from his former views. He had, it seems, already shed those, in the wake of student unrest in the late 1960s. The problem with Cardinal Ratzinger's appointment – as commentators were quick to point out – was, first, that it was something of a case of poacher turned gamekeeper and secondly as in his own right a distinguished theologian, it would be difficult to separate the Cardinal's personal doctrinal views from those of the Congregation which he headed. The latter problem has proved to be a serious one, but as Ratzinger's views appeared on the whole to be remarkably like those of John Paul, this was not an issue which troubled the Pope.

NOTES

1. The Congregation had been called by that title only since the end of 1965. From 1908 to that date it was known as the Holy Office, and its headquarters were (and are) located in the 'street of the Holy Office', close to St Peter's. Before 1908 it was the 'Universal Inquisition', created in 1542 to oversee doctrinal orthodoxy. When Paul VI changed its name at the end of the Vatican Council he had given it the additional task of promoting good theology. This role it has undertaken largely through the International Theological Commission, set up in 1969, which consists of distinguished theologians from around the world.
2. He was suspect even from his doctorate in 1957, cf. Herbert Haag, 'The Küng

dossier' in *The Tablet*, 16 February 1980, p. 152.
3. cf. Jan Bots, 'The conflict today' in *The Tablet*, 5 January 1980, p. 6.
4. op. cit., p. 157.
5. cf. Peter Hebblethwaite, *The papal year*, pp. 66–8.
6. *Inaestimabile Donum*. Among its concerns was to ensure that distinctions between the role of the laity and that of the clergy did not become blurred. It also banned girls serving at the altar, a directive which has just (April 1994) been rescinded.
7. *The Tablet*, 17 May 1980, p. 488.
8. Peter Hebblethwaite, *The papal year*, p. 72.
9. ibid., p. 76.
10. ibid., p. 72.
11. Hebblethwaite, *The papal year*, p. 86.
12. ibid.
13. Quoted, *The Tablet*, 28 June 1980, p. 635. Archbishop Pires was the country's only black bishop.
14. Hebblethwaite, *Paul VI*, pp. 593–8. Hebblethwaite suggests that one of the chief dissuaders of Paul VI from calling a Synod on the Family was Archbishop Worlock of Liverpool.
15. The Synod on the Family and its aftermath is discussed in detail in Jan Grootaers and Joseph A. Selling, *The 1980 Synod of Bishops 'On the Role of the Family'*, Louvain, Leuven University Press, 1983, hereafter referred to as Grootaers.
16. Grootaers, p. 68. There were 43 lay *'auditores'* also invited, mainly if not wholly chosen for their conservative views on family planning (ibid. pp. 80–2).
17. Press relations were the responsibility of the Scottish Franciscan Bishop Agnellus Andrew, Vice-President of the Vatican's Pontifical Commission for Social Communications, or media commission. He had learned his journalistic trade as a regular broadcaster for the BBC from the early days of World War II.
18. Quoted Hebblethwaite, *The papal year*, p. 107.
19. These were organized on a language basis.
20. *The Tablet*, 25 October 1980, p. 1041.
21. op. cit., p. 337. see Grootaers pp. 332–8 for a detailed comparison between the text of the Propositions and *Familiaris Consortio*.
22. He had the same view about the usefulness of sociology: 'The Church values sociological and statistical research when it proves helpful in understanding the historical context in which pastoral action has to be developed and when it leads to a better understanding of the truth', wrote the Pope. That assumes, commented Peter Hebblethwaite, 'that the truth being sought is known in advance and the only role left for sociology is to provide confirmation' ('The Pope on the family', *The Tablet* 9 January 1982, p. 29).
23. ibid.
24. Paul Johnson, *Pope John Paul II and the Catholic Restoration* (London, Weidenfeld & Nicolson, 1982), p. 82.
25. *Dives in Misericordia*, §6:4. The text being used can be found in Michael Walsh

and Brian Davies (eds.), *Proclaiming Justice and Peace* (Mystic, CT, Twenty-Third Publications, 1991), p. 347.

26. ibid., §12:2, p. 349.
27, George Weigel, *The Final Revolution* (New York, Oxford University Press, 1992), p. 141.
28. Jacek Kuron, quoted in *The Tablet*, 3 January 1981, p. 6.
29. Apostolic Letter of 24 October 1964, commemorating the reconsecration of the Abbey of Monte Cassino after its destruction during the Second World War.
30. 'Annulments' are legal statements made by the church tribunals that a marriage has never existed, and therefore the apparent legal bond is set aside. There are a number of grounds for annulment, perhaps the easiest to understand being non-consummation of the marriage, though a much more common one would be the determination that one of the two parties was, at the time of the wedding, psychologically incapable of making, or living up to, the commitment entailed in the sacrament. Annulments are the nearest thing the Catholic Church comes to providing divorce.
31. In 1969 there had been only 427 marriage cases brought before US tribunals. Ten years later there were over 53,000.
32. Cited in *The Tablet*, 7 February 1981, p. 136.
33. On his way to the Philippines he had said mass in Karachi, where he met President Zia, and between the Philippines and Japan he had landed at Guam.
34. *The Tablet*, 9 May 1981, p. 459.
35. Though it was later reported in *L'Osservatore Romano*.
36. Issue of 24 July 1981, in an editorial comment on the front page.
37. From May 1985 to the end of March 1986: the jury consisted of two judges and six lay assessors. In contrast the earlier trial lasted only three days. At the end of it Agca was sentenced to life imprisonment, the first year of his sentence to be served in solitary confinement.
38. *The Final Revolution* (Oxford University Press, 1992), p. 144.
39. *God's Politician*, p. 38.
40. See Edward S. Herman and Frank Brodhead, *The rise and fall of the Bulgarian Connection* (New York, Sheridan Square Publications, 1986), passim, but especially chapter 3.
41. John Harriott, a former Jesuit, wrote of him 'Pedro Arrupe is a very good man indeed, a saintly and captivating human being with exceptional breadth of vision and intense warmth of heart. Historians will probably recognize him as the greatest general of the society since Ignatius himself, and certainly the best loved' (*The Tablet*, 14 November 1981, p. 1110).

FIVE

1982-3

T HE NEW YEAR began with the traditional papal statement for the World Day of Peace. But this time the statement was longer, and, as the government of Poland faced threats of sanctions especially from the USA[1] over their declaration of a state of martial law, their suppression of Solidarity and the arrest of Solidarity's leading members, it seemed more heartfelt. While he urged Christians to work, and to educate, for peace he insisted that 'Christians are aware that plans based on aggression, domination and the manipulation of others lurk in human hearts ... Christians know that in this world a totally and permanently peaceful human society is unfortunately a utopia, and that ideologies which hold up that prospect as easily attainable are based on hopes that cannot be realized ... Christians are convinced, if only because they have learned from personal experience, that these deceptive hopes lead straight to the false peace of totalitarian regimes'. It was a powerful and moving plea for peace, addressed to all believers whatever their faith. There were those who noticed, however, that though the nuclear threat, which at the beginning of 1982 had never seemed more real, was abhorred, nuclear weapons as such were not condemned.

In the recent past Italian popes, Pius XII and Paul VI particularly, had involved themselves deeply in Italian politics, but never had it been so outspoken and obvious as John Paul II's preoccupation with Poland. His anxiety found its way into addresses to general audiences, and into the annual allocution to diplomats accredited to the Holy See. The Cardinals of Warsaw and of Cracow, and the Bishop of Wroclaw came to Rome to discuss the situation personally with the Pope. It was a major concern of the Vatican's own diplomatic service. On 19 January President Reagan claimed he had papal support for US sanctions against Poland. Not so, said the Vatican, indicating that Reagan had telephoned John Paul (on 15 December), and twice written to him (on 17 and 29 December), to explain American policy, but the Vatican did not say that Reagan's doings had received papal approval.

On Friday 12 February, however, John Paul had to put his worries about his native country behind him as he set out on his second visit to Africa. He arrived in Lagos that same day, to be met by the President of Nigeria as well as by ecclesiastical dignitaries. In a speech in Lagos he warned Nigerians against the corrupting influence of wealth, and looked forward to the day when Africa might govern itself, free from the intervention of foreign powers. The next day he went on to the cities of Enugu and Onitsha in Ibo territory. Only six or seven per cent of Nigeria's 100,000,000 population is Catholic, but of those that are, the majority are Ibos, and the Pope could be guaranteed a warm welcome. It was different the following day in Kaduna which is Moslem dominated. There were, of course, Catholics to greet him, but it had been hoped he would also meet an Islamic delegation. In the event the delegation never appeared. The Vatican's explanation was that the differing factions among the Moslems could not agree on a final communiqué and the Pope, when leaving Kaduna, spoke of his hopes that Christians and Moslems could work more closely together in promoting justice and peace: in 1987 one hundred and fifty churches were destroyed in Kaduna state when rioting broke out between Moslems and Christians, and there is an open threat to make Nigeria an Islamic state as a means to unify the country.[2]

The Pope's next stop was Benin, governed for the previous decade by Mathieu Kerekou. The official ideology of the country was Marxist, and the half million Catholics, though not by 1982 being persecuted, were little able to make a contribution to public life: the Pope diplomatically stressed the Church's commitment to health care and education. That was Wednesday morning. In the late afternoon John Paul flew on to Gabon, where Catholics make up a quarter of the population, where Church–state relations were good, and where the President was a convert from Christianity to the minority Islamic faith. The next day John Paul was in Equatorial Guinea. There Catholics make up by far the largest part of the small population, and the Pope promised the Church's help to rebuild the country after a ten-year tyranny under the former president. The Church had been suppressed, missionaries expelled and native-born clergy imprisoned. Again the Pope offered the Church's assistance with education and welfare services. From Guinea he flew back to Rome, and a crisis meeting of Provincial Superiors of the Society of Jesus.

Since the bombshell of the appointment of Dezza as the Pope's man to govern the Jesuits, John Paul had made considerable effort to demonstrate his affection for the Society. He had, for instance, spent the previous New Year's Eve with them (one member of the Jesuit community in their headquarters across the Piazza of St Peter's from the Vatican confided to the Pontiff that they did not usually eat quite so well); he had visited Pedro Arrupe, who had promised the Society's obedience to the Holy See. There had, on the other hand, been a letter signed by the Society's, and perhaps the Church's, most distinguished theologian, Karl Rahner, together with others, telling the Pope not to interfere with the internal governance of the Jesuits.

Against this background the Pope's speech to the meeting of Provincials on 27 February was awaited with distinct anxiety. He began in Italian, went on in French, switched to English and ended, rather oddly, in Catalan. The Provincials need not have feared. They were not castigated for deviant Marxism, loss of discipline or disloyalty either to the Holy See or to local bishops – though the Pope placed great emphasis on how important such loyalty was in the life of the Church. John Paul recalled the Society's history with obvious admiration, and with equal admiration spoke of how the Society had humbly accepted the appointment of Fr Dezza. The nearest thing to a rebuke was perhaps the warning not to play the part of doctor, politician, social worker or trade unionist, though even here he acknowledged there might be exceptions. He ended by saying, and this was the Catalan bit, that the general congregation to elect a new Superior for the whole Society would begin before the end of the year. The Provincials, when the Catalan was translated for them, heaved a collective sigh of relief.

The question remains, however, why John Paul had chosen to intervene in this manner. As far as the Society was concerned he had achieved little or nothing, except to put their loyalty to the test. It may be as some commentators at the time believed that he was acting at the instigation of a group of conservative Latin American churchmen. Yet if so, then it had backfired, for his speech to the Provincials was regarded as an endorsement, rather than a criticism, of Fr Arrupe's policies. What John Paul had demonstrated, however, was that he could take on even the most powerful of the Church's religious Orders and not be daunted by it. The Jesuits were the first Order to endure papal intervention. They were certainly not the last.

In England on 29 March the two co-chairman of the Anglican-Roman Catholic International Commission, which for a dozen years had been studying doctrinal disagreements, or presumed disagreements, between the two Churches, presided at a press conference to launch ARCIC's *Final Report*. There had been other 'reports' – on the Eucharist in 1971, on ministry and ordination two years later, on authority in 1976 and, in 1982, a further discussion on authority, on matters which had not been settled six years before. The co-chairmen were cautious. The document, they said, would have to be examined by their respective Churches over the next few years. What was at issue in the second statement on authority was papal jurisdiction and infallibility, matters which clearly touched the Vatican closely. Under the energetic presidency of Cardinal Ratzinger, the Congregation for the Doctrine of the Faith published its first response the following day. Substantive agreement between the two Churches had not been reached, the CDF's press release declared. What was worse, apparently, was that 'some formulations in the ARCIC report can still give rise to divergent interpretations', as if that were not true of very many dogmatic statements. The two Churches had to keep talking, said the CDF, which clearly did not want the opprobrium of putting an end to ecumenical debate, but there was a long way to go: some of the ARCIC conclusions, thought the CDF, 'do not seem to be easily reconciled with Catholic doctrine'. It was also true, as the *Final Report* made clear, that there were some elements of Catholic doctrine not readily acceptable to Anglicans.

The speed with which the CDF had responded to ARCIC was no doubt a function of the forthcoming visit of the Pope to Britain. Although billed as a 'pastoral visit' to British Roman Catholics, there was to be an ecumenical dimension with a visit by John Paul to the Archbishop of Canterbury, presiding in his own cathedral, and meetings with other leaders of other Churches. The Vatican knew there would need to be a successor to ARCIC: it therefore had to respond, if only briefly, to the *Final Report* so as to make its own position clear. Some Catholic commentators tried to put a benign interpretation upon the CDF's statement. Generally it was greeted with dismay.

The problem of having a learned theologian rather than a bureaucrat at the head of the CDF was promptly illustrated when Cardinal Ratzinger gave an interview to a German Catholic news service. He spoke at length about the papal role, on which, he clearly believed, the ARCIC report had fudged. He remarked that the two Churches still had much to discuss – and he made a special point of mentioning moral theology. But, he also commented, the whole question of Anglican Orders would have to be tackled once again, not this time from the angle of an arid argument over validity, but from an understanding of the way Anglicanism had developed, theologically and liturgically. In the light of the CDF's official comments, Ratzinger's remarks were regarded as encouraging. The Prefect's views, it seemed, were not to be identified with those of his Congregation. It was all somewhat confusing.

That was at the end of March and the beginning of April: John Paul was due in May. Souvenirs, from folding chairs to commemorative gold watches produced by the Crown jewellers, were already on sale. A production of *The Jeweller's Shop* was scheduled to open at the Westminster Theatre on 25 May. But now there was a serious doubt that he would come at all. Argentina, which had long claimed the Falklands, or Las Malvinas, as part of their territory, chose this moment to invade the islands. General Galtieri, the Argentinean President, had no doubt reasoned that the islands were too far distant from Britain for much of a response, other than diplomatic. He seriously miscalculated. A massive task force was sent, and war broke out. The Pope, it was presumed, could, or certainly would, not visit a country at war – more especially, perhaps, when the enemy was itself a formally Catholic nation.

Before he was to come to Britain, hostilities permitting, the Pope was to visit Portugal. More specifically he was going to visit the Marian shrine of Fátima, where the Virgin Mary was reputed to have appeared to three children on 13 May 1917. To add piquancy to the papal devotion, Our Lady of Fátima was commonly believed to have urged prayer against Communism, and for the conversion of Russia.[3] The attempt on the Pope's life – coincidentally on the Feast of Our Lady of Fátima – was by now widely, if erroneously, regarded as Russian-inspired, if not Russian-led.

On 12 May, John Paul arrived in Fátima.[4] 'As soon as I recovered consciousness after the attack in St Peter's Square my thoughts turned instinctively to this shrine', he told the pilgrims at Fátima, 'and I wanted to express here my gratitude to our heavenly mother for having saved my life … In this coincidence I recognize a divine call – though in the designs of Providence there are no mere coincidences.' The following day, still in Fátima, he consecrated the world to the Immaculate Heart of Mary.

The visit to Fátima was clearly a very personal pilgrimage for the Pope. In 1984 he presented the shrine with the bullet which had nearly killed him. It was set in the crown of the Virgin's statue at Fátima, alongside 313 pearls and 2,679 other precious stones.[5] None the less, the papal visit contained much of the mixture as before, with an address to trade unionists, defending their right to exist – the reference was clearly to Solidarity in Poland rather than to the situation in Portugal – and telling them not to strike for political reasons. (A Communist-led trade union in Portugal had called a general strike on the eve of the papal visit, though it guaranteed travel facilities for the pilgrims.)

Meanwhile the English, Welsh and Scottish bishops were engaged in a considerable diplomatic effort to save the papal visit to the islands of Britain. On 22 May there was a mass in St Peter's presided over by John Paul with, among the concelebrants, cardinals and archbishops from England, Scotland and Argentina. 'Peace is a duty', said the Pope in his homily, 'because all the inhabitants of the earth, wherever they were born, whatever the language in which they learned to express their thoughts and feelings, whatever the "credo", political or religious, on which they base their lives, still belong to the one family of the human race.' The difficulties may seem insurmountable, said the Pope, but in reality they could not be so. It was a particularly eloquent plea for peace between the warring nations, and British and Argentinean prelates pledged themselves to peace and reconciliation. John Paul sent identical telegrams to the President of Argentina and to the British Prime Minister: Margaret Thatcher continued to demand the unconditional withdrawal of Argentinean troops. Three days later it was announced that the Pope's visit would go ahead as planned despite the conflict. John Paul, however, in a display of strict impartiality, said he would pay a brief visit to Argentina at the end of his tour of Britain.[6] On 28 May, therefore, just after 8 o'clock in the morning, he was kissing the tarmac at London's Gatwick Airport.

By common consent, the visit to Britain, after all its vicissitudes, was one of the most successful of papal journeys. Even the sun shone, at least for most of the time, much, it seemed, to the surprise of the Pope himself.[7] There was naturally enough a constant call, even from the moment of his landing at Gatwick, for peace between Britain and Argentina, but the programme had been meticulously planned to emphasize its pastoral nature. There were to be no lectures on the Church and politics: instead, a celebration of the seven sacraments (so, for example, four people were baptized during his mass in Westminster Cathedral and a large number of priests ordained by him in Manchester). The Pope had been well-briefed in English Catholic history.[8] The visit to Canterbury and the meeting with the Archbishop of Canterbury on 29 May was an especial triumph, no little assisted not only by the weather but by brilliant television coverage. The Pope, already taken aback by the sunshine, was visibly moved at Canterbury by the splendour of the cathedral as it came into view. With Archbishop Runcie in a Common Declaration he committed the two Churches to a further round of ecumenical dialogue.

The crowds, especially of the young, were vast and enthusiastic. The Pope clearly enjoyed himself. It seems churlish, then, to comment that, when John Paul left Cardiff airport in the evening of 2 June, he left behind a Church which was considerably in debt over the visit. The crowds may have been immense; sales of the souvenirs that were supposed to recoup the costs were well below expectations. When figures were finally released in mid-

December 1984 it was revealed that the visit had cost nearly £7 million. Officially approved souvenirs earned the Church only just over a quarter of a million pounds: £1 million had been expected. The company set up by the Church in Britain to 'market' the visit, Papal Visit Limited, earned £526,000, just enough to pay for the policing of private property (policing of public areas was paid for from public funds).

On 11 June, with the good wishes of the bishops of England, Scotland and Wales, he was off to Argentina. The Pope arrived in Buenos Aires in the pouring rain, and was swamped by uniformed officialdom. The visit was arranged at the last moment, and preparations had necessarily been somewhat perfunctory. The Pope's message was of peace and reconciliation. When he spoke to priests, nuns and bishops in the cathedral of Buenos Aires he praised love of one's own nation, but reminded his hearers that such nationalism had to take account of the patriotism of citizens of other nations. The Church in Argentina, unlike that in Britain, had been unhesitating in its support of the war in the Falklands. While the Pope spoke, Argentinean flags waved on all sides and placards held by the crowds demanded the Holy Father's blessing on 'our just war'.

At this point of the year the Pope was still expecting to go on his second visit to Poland for the 26 August celebrations of the 600th anniversary of the arrival in Czestochowa of the icon of the Black Madonna. The country was, however, still in a condition of martial law. Józef Glemp was the late Cardinal Wyszynski's successor as Archbishop of Warsaw and Primate, but he did not have Wyszynski's stature, either physically or psychologically. What is more, he was ill at ease with the press. Just before John Paul went to Argentina Glemp spoke to mass-goers in Warsaw cathedral. He remarked that the papal visits to Britain and Argentina were a clear indication that such visits could not be seen as an endorsement of a nation's government or political system – he would even, he said, travel to a country governed as was Argentina by a 'military junta who keep many people interned in camps'. The Catholic community, he went on, would demonstrate that it was capable of receiving the Pope in peace and order. The government was not so sure. Archbishop Luigi Poggi arrived from Rome four days later to negotiate with the government. The situation, he said, had to be normal before the Pope could come. It was, in mid-June, anything but normal.[9]

The diplomatic pace was hectic. As John Paul arrived in Argentina Cardinal Casaroli, the Secretary of State, was reading an address from the Pope to the Special Session on Disarmament of the United Nations in New York. 'Peace is possible', said Casaroli in the name of John Paul, 'and since peace is possible it is a duty. A very grave duty, a supreme responsibility', but 'if efforts at arms reduction are not accompanied by a parallel effort at moral recovery, they are destined to fail.' It was only the recovery of moral principles that could guarantee peace. On one issue, however, he deeply disappointed the vigorous peace campaigners within the Catholic Church, that of nuclear deterrence. 'Under present conditions, deterrence based on equilibrium – certainly not as an end in itself but as a stage on the way to progressive disarmament – can still be regarded as morally acceptable.' To his critics this seemed very close to saying that the end justified the means, a principle which Catholic moral theologians had constantly condemned.

On the 15th, John Paul was in Geneva, addressing both the International Labour Organization (the ILO) and the European Centre for Nuclear Research (CERN). He chose the latter occasion to announce that he was setting up a Pontifical Council for Culture. There had in the past been tensions between religion and scientific research, he said, but those days were now over. The search for truth was 'one of the great values which are capable of uniting human beings of today across their diverse cultures'. He did not return, except in passing, to the question of nuclear arms – the Church, he commented, had already made known its views about the danger they posed.

There was a somewhat similar theme in the speech before the 2,000 delegates at the ILO's conference: the solidarity of workers united them across frontiers. Their solidarity had been forged by the experience of injustice. The situation may have improved but there remained 'various systems based on ideology and power [that] have allowed flagrant injustices to persist, or have created new ones'. Work, he claimed in words that echoed *Laborem Exercens*, was intimately bound up with the meaning and dignity of human existence. He was, in effect, commending his latest encyclical to the international representatives of the work force to which it had, primarily, been addressed. John Paul was not about to let an opportunity slip effectively to advocate the views he had expounded at greater length in his encyclical. The views were equally anti-Marxist and anti-liberal capitalism. But when the body of Roberto Calvi, president of the Milan-based Banco Ambrosiano, was found bizarrely swinging under London's Blackfriars Bridge in the early morning of 18 June, the Vatican's own murky involvement with liberal capitalism began to unfold.

The links between the Vatican Bank, more correctly the Istituo per le Opere di Religione, or IOR, and the shady world inhabited by Roberto Calvi and Michele Sindona long predated the pontificate of Pope John Paul II.[10] Ironically, it may have been the very fact of the Pope's desire for openness where the Vatican's finances were concerned that precipitated the crisis. In November 1979 he had called an extraordinary conclave of cardinals to discuss the precarious state of the Vatican's finances. He told them that the Vatican was more than $20 million in deficit, and that the Vatican's revenues were unable to cope with the cost of running the Church. He – or his advisors – expected an even bigger loss in 1980.

This report was seen by Graham Garner of Coopers and Lybrand, the auditors of the Ambrosiano subsidiary the Cisalpine Bank, based in Nassau in the Bahamas. Garner was worried by the extent of the Cisalpine's involvement with the IOR, and with other shadowy companies linked to the IOR: the president of the IOR, Archbishop Paul Marcinckus, was a director of the Cisalpine. The reported deficit at the Vatican alarmed him because he feared that the Vatican would not be in a position, even should it feel so obliged, to make good the IOR's debts. Indeed, the Vatican's own need to meet its commitments might have a deleterious affect upon the stability of the IOR itself.

The IOR scarcely behaved, even in John Paul's pontificate, with the high moral standards which the Pope's encyclicals constantly demand. In October 1982 *L'Osservatore Romano*, the Vatican's daily newspaper, published a summary of a report, claimed to be the IOR's own, into its dealings. The first point made was that 'The Institute for the Works of Religion has not received either from the Ambrosiano Group or from Roberto Calvi any funds, and, therefore, does not have to refund anything'. The statement was a straight-forward lie: the Ambrosiano was at that very moment paying off its debts to the Ambrosiano group.[11]

Marcinckus returned home to the United States at the end of 1990. He had escaped prosecution, and it has been suggested that the protection he received from the Vatican came in part from his friendship with the Pope, who found himself, rather like Marcinckus, an outsider in an Italian-dominated bureaucracy.[12] This does not ring true. The Pope may have been an outsider, but there is little evidence that he felt awed by the Roman Curia, or unable to handle it. Quite the contrary. From the first moment of his accepting the papacy he had stamped his character upon the Vatican administration. The protection vouchsafed to Marcinckus was simply the clerical caste defending its own – or a desire to avoid the workings of the IOR being opened to public scrutiny. According to Charles Raw, Marcinckus's dealings had cost the Vatican a total of half a billion dollars.[13]

The parlous state of the Vatican's finances, and the IOR's embarrassing debts to the Ambrosiano which it did not wish to acknowledge, may have had the curious side-effect of encouraging the Pope to call a Holy Year for 1983, despite the fact there had been one only eight years before, on the rather spurious grounds that it was 1,950 years since the death of Christ. Pilgrims seeking the Holy Year indulgences would come to Rome, it was hoped, in their millions. Their presence would not only be good for their souls, it would also replenish the coffers of the Vatican and enrich the shopkeepers and hoteliers of Rome.[14]

On 29 August, Pope John Paul visited San Marino, the tiny republic entirely surrounded by Italy: it was his shortest ever 'foreign' journey. Immediately afterwards he went to Rimini to preside at the closing mass of a conference jointly organized by two Catholic lay organizations, Communione e Liberazione and Movimento Popolare, the latter being the political wing of the former. He spoke in praise of the two bodies, describing them as a dimension of church life, the work of the laity, which had been fostered since Vatican II. He gave them his blessing, but his presence at the event was controversial. A group of Catholic scout leaders, some members of the Young Christian Workers, and a number of professors from the Catholic university in Milan signed a joint letter regretting the Pope's apparent support for two organizations with distinctly rightward-leaning political views. Did the Pope's attendance not constitute, they asked, 'a dangerous alignment which goes counter to the idea of pluralism in the political views of Christians affirmed by Vatican II?' Not long before – the fact was announced by the Vatican press office on 23 August – Pope John Paul had approved the creation of Opus Dei as a 'personal prelature', a unique status in the Church.[15] It was widely regarded as a sign of papal favour on this conservative, powerful and secretive organization, and further evidence of papal right-wing sympathies.

More significantly, the granting of an audience to Yasser Arafat on 15 September was similarly looked upon, by the State of Israel, as evidence of papal favour of the Palestine Liberation Organization which Arafat headed. It certainly marked a change of heart on the part of the Pontiff. In his years at school, and later in Cracow, Wojtyla had known many Jews, and had a number of close friends among the Jewish community. When he came into office he was more sympathetic towards Israel than his predecessor-but-one, Pope Paul VI, had ever allowed himself to be: but then Paul had been a diplomat all his life, working his way up the Vatican's career structure within the Secretariat of State. Though no stranger to politics, as his years dealing with the regime in Poland bore witness, Wojtyla was none the less unskilled in international affairs. His earliest remarks about conflict in the Middle East did not dwell upon the problem of the Palestinians. He met prominent Jews from round the world, and in April 1979 the Director of the Israeli Ministry of Foreign Affairs: the communiqué expressed the hope that, as a result of the meeting, contact between the Vatican and Israel would be more frequent. A meeting arranged with the Palestinian mayor of Bethlehem (a Christian) in the early summer of that same year was abruptly cancelled, causing much resentment among Palestinians.

The Pope was undoubtedly anxious for a settlement of the situation of conflict in the Lebanon, in which Arab Christians were among the warring parties, and he recognized that a solution to the Palestinian problem was tied up with the Lebanese civil war – he said as much in his United Nations speech in October 1979. He made the same link in his address to US President Jimmy Carter, when Carter visited him in the Vatican on 21 June 1980, but he did not call for justice for the Palestinians.

Among the concerns voiced on that occasion was the status of Jerusalem as a holy city, regarded as such by Christians and Moslems, as well as by Jews. The Vatican wanted international supervision of the city, but on 30 July 1980 Israel annexed Jerusalem, and made it their *de jure* capital. The UN Security Council called for the removal of all foreign embassies from Jerusalem (the USA abstained from the otherwise unanimous vote), and the General Assembly condemned the Israeli action.

After the annexation, the Pope began to speak more openly and forcefully about the rights of the Palestinians. There were growing contacts with the moderate Arab states, particularly Jordan, and a PLO leader, Farouk Khaddoumi, was received in the Vatican, though not by the Pope personally, in 1981 and early in 1982. The Israeli government maintained its own diplomatic pressure. The Foreign Minister, Itzhak Shamir, was supposed to call on the Pope in February 1981. The visit was called off at the last moment, and only took place a year later, in January 1982. Shamir stressed his government's commitment to protecting the holy places, but ignored John Paul's urging to negotiate with the Palestinians. The Israeli invasion of Lebanon in June 1982 destroyed almost entirely the goodwill towards Israel that Wojtyla had brought with him to the papacy. On 29 June 1982 Pope John Paul asked Catholics to pray that the right of the Palestinians to their homeland be recognized.

Receiving Arafat, then, was only one step further along the road the Pope had been travelling in his understanding of the conflict in the Middle East. The communiqué claimed, somewhat disingenuously, that there was no political significance to be attached to what was only a twenty-minute audience: the name of the PLO was not even mentioned. The US government was taken aback, and disapproving. Western European governments, on the other hand, had already backed the Palestinians' claim to the right of self-determination, and sympathized with the papal initiative. The state of Israel was furious, but the Vatican's standing among Arab states was, not surprisingly, very much enhanced.[16]

On 10 October, Pope John Paul canonized Maximilian Kolbe. Kolbe, a Franciscan priest, had died in Auschwitz when he offered himself as a substitute for a family man who had been arbitrarily condemned to death – the man he thus saved was present at the ceremony in St Peter's Square which was attended by many thousands of Poles. The Pope had wanted to celebrate the canonization in Poland, had the Polish government let him in, but they had of course refused to do so, regarding the proposed timing as inopportune. A governmental delegation was present none the less. It was distinctly frostily received by the worshippers and by John Paul alike. In his homilies, both during the ceremony itself and in a special audience the following day, the Pope referred to the banning of the Solidarity trade union, saying that such an act violated basic human rights, and the rights of working people, which the Church would always strive to uphold.[17] The day before the canonization, the Polish President had invited the Polish Primate to confer with him about a new date for the Pope's next visit to Poland. The date for his return – 18 June 1983 – was agreed by Glemp and Jaruzelski and announced by a government spokesman in Warsaw on 8 November, two days before strikes and demonstrations planned to protest against the banning of Solidarity. It looked like an attempt to defuse the situation with, this time, the Church as an accomplice of the state.

John Paul's next overseas journey was to a country where the Church had recently ceased to be an accomplice of the state, and was wondering what would happen next. The papal visit to Spain had been postponed because of the Spanish general election. Three days before John Paul flew to Madrid, in the afternoon of Sunday 31 October, the people of Spain had elected the first socialist, and moderately anti-clerical, government since the civil war nearly fifty years previously. Though on his arrival he was careful to stress, as always, the strictly religious and pastoral nature of his visit, when he was in Granada addressing a large gathering of teachers, he insisted that there should continue to be religious lessons in state schools, and that such lessons ought to remain publicly funded. As the Socialist Party had already committed itself to reducing the massive impact of the Church in education this was a clear political statement. Likewise, at a mass for families – and attended by some two million people – held in the open air in Madrid the Pope attacked contraception, abortion and divorce. Nothing surprising in that, perhaps, but those topics had, in one way or another, been part of the platform which had persuaded almost half the country's electors to vote for the Socialists.

The invitation to Spain had been extended by the country's hierarchy to mark the fourth centenary of the death of St Teresa of Avila. The Pope has a particular penchant for Christian anniversaries. Their celebration is a high point in the memory of the people, reminding them of the Christian roots of their culture. Their traditional shrines are likewise symbols of those Christian roots. Spain has such shrines in abundance. He went to Avila soon after his arrival, and on 6 November he visited the Jesuit shrines of Loyola and Xavier. There were Marian shrines also. He paid homage to the original Virgin of Guadalupe in a village in Extremadura whence the conquistadores took the devotion to Mexico, to the Virgin of the Pillar in Zaragoza, and to the Virgin of Montserrat in the mountains near Barcelona, a particular devotion of Catalan nationalists.

In Barcelona he spoke to workers, in Valencia to members of religious Orders. He flew each day to and from the papal nunciature in Madrid, a punishing schedule that left him drained of energy. None the less he left what turned out to be, perhaps, the most significant of his addresses to the end of his visit. John Paul's embracing of the Christian past does not need to distinguish fact from foundational myth, and among the foundational myths of Spain is the Apostle St James, who came to evangelize and now lies buried in a town which bears his name, Santiago de Compostela. The shrine is on the furthest edge of Europe. In the city's cathedral, before he departed for Rome on 9 November, the Pope presided at a 'European Act' or 'event', attended by academics, clerics, members of European organizations and other members of the intelligentsia from all over the continent. John Paul told them to rediscover their Christian past, and the spiritual unity of Europe. 'You can still be a beacon of civilization', he told them. Santiago, with its great thurible swinging from the roof of the magnificent cathedral, obviously impressed the Pope. He would be back. Meanwhile he had to go to Sicily.

He arrived in Palermo on 20 November. Its Archbishop, Cardinal Salvatore Pappalardo, was a vigorous opponent of the Mafia, and the Pope was expected to echo the Cardinal's condemnations. So he did – up to a point. He denounced the violence in his first address, as well as expressing his dismay at the delays – largely due to Mafia corruption of politicians it was widely believed – in restoring the damage suffered by villages in Sicily in the 1968 earthquake. The following day, however, two passages were dropped from the papal address, for want of time, said a Vatican spokesman. The passages left out would have expressed his support for the anti-Mafia stance of the Sicilian bishops and condemned *omerta*, the Mafia's code of 'honour'.

Palermo was conveniently close to Rome. The Pope was therefore not jet-lagged when he opened an extraordinary session of the college of cardinals, 97 of them in all. They had a considerable agenda, which included reform of the Roman Curia and the revision of Canon Law, but there was in practice adequate time for only one topic – the finances of the Holy See – and that had been sewn up in advance. The course of the gathering was dictated by a letter, dated 20 November, which Pope John Paul had sent to Cardinal Casaroli though 'internal evidence'[18] suggested that Casaroli had written it to himself.

The letter was interesting in revealing a little more about the finances of the Holy See. It was claimed that in 1981 there had been an excess of income over expenditure, which news must have come as a relief to those cardinals who headed dioceses, and were afraid of yet more pressure to produce money to keep the papacy in business. In fact, it was claimed, money had been rolling in, more than $15.25 million in Peter's Pence, a tax invented for the English in Anglo-Saxon times and gradually extended to the whole Church. Peter's Pence, together with income from the settlement made upon the Holy See by the State of Italy in 1929 when the Vatican State was formally recognized,[19] made the Holy See financially independent of the Vatican Bank, the IOR. All this was no doubt very true, but by spelling it out so formally the papacy seemed to be trying to distance itself from the fate of the IOR. There was, however, somewhat more to the letter than that. The Pope explained the provisions he had been outlining for the world at large applied equally in the Vatican City State. Well, not quite equally perhaps. The Vatican Employees Association, the nearest thing the Vatican had to a trade union, was to be granted official recognition (though it was warned against engaging in class conflict). Clerics, however, were not allowed to belong. There were, in all, 3,395 people employed by the Vatican at the time, the salaries of whom accounted for 55 per cent of the Vatican's total expenditure. In addition, over fifteen hundred were in receipt of pensions.

There was a flurry of activity on the international scene towards the end of 1982. The Italian authorities declared that they suspected the Bulgarians of having been behind the plot to assassinate the Pope,[20] the Polish government announced that martial law would end on 31 December; and the official Soviet newsagency, TASS, disseminated an attack on the Pope, which had recently been published in an official Soviet Communist Party monthly, according to which he was a fanatical anti-Communist, considerably more reactionary than his immediate predecessors, and personally responsible for the situation in Poland. A couple of weeks later TASS was citing with obvious approval the Pope's otherwise unremarkable (though as usual lengthy) peace message for the start of 1983.

On 5 January it was announced that, on 2 February, the Pope would create eighteen new cardinals. This time the list was particularly interesting. Only two members of the Vatican's bureaucracy, the Roman Curia, were promoted to the rank of cardinal, which was probably less than the Curia, ever concerned to ensure its officials receive due recognition, would have expected. The raising to the purple of the Archbishops of Paris, Malines and Milan was only to be expected, so was the appointment of Archbishop Glemp of Warsaw. There were cardinals from Bangkok, Abidjan and Lubango (Angola). Bishop Julian Vaivods of Riga was the first Soviet citizen ever to receive the red hat, and to complete a trio of appointments from the Eastern bloc, the Archbishop of Zagreb also became a cardinal. There was one appointment from the United States (Bernardin of Chicago) and one from Wellington, New Zealand. The patriarch of the Maronites, an Eastern-rite church in communion with Rome, was also given the red hat. There were two new cardinals from Latin America, the Archbishops of Caracas and of Medellín. The latter, Archbishop Alfonso Lopez Trujillo, was the youngest of the new cardinals and perhaps the most controversial. He was remembered by some as the Latin American prelate most influential in the decision by the Pope to visit Britain during the Falklands crisis. By others he was remembered as the most conservative of the executive members of CELAM, the Conference of Latin American Bishops, which he had served first as secretary and, since 1979, as president. He was a staunch opponent of Liberation Theology.

The most remarkable appointment, and one which gave great delight to many, was that of the Jesuit priest, Henri de Lubac. De Lubac had implicitly been condemned for his views on the relationship between nature and grace in Pope Pius XII's encyclical *Humani Generis* of 1950.[21] He survived a temporary exile from teaching – it lasted until 1954, during which period he wrote books on Buddhism and a 'Meditation on the Church' – to become one of the most influential experts at the Second Vatican Council. By that time he had become rather less of a radical, and had rewritten the works which offended to take more account of traditional Thomism. The conferral of the red hat was a gracious gesture by John Paul to a writer he had much admired, though it was not clear which period of de Lubac's theology appealed to him the more. Despite his eminence as a theologian, the red hat for the aged Jesuit was quite in keeping with the generally conservative nature of the appointments to the cardinalate.[22]

The elevation of Archbishop Lopez Trujillo gained in significance as the Pope made his preparations for what was possibly the most difficult of his journeys so far, a week-long trip to Central America. Among the documents which he had to master before he left Rome on 1 March for Costa Rica were two somewhat contradictory reports on the situation in the region. The first had been drawn up by Pax Christi, the Catholic international peace campaign. It criticized governments which repressed the human rights of their citizens, and disclosed that the Sandinistas in Nicaragua were really rather better behaved in this regard than the regimes in the majority of neighbouring countries.

This conclusion incensed Archbishop Lopez Trujillo, who complained to the Pope. John Paul wanted a new report drawn up by the bishops of Central America, but they refused. Lopez Trujillo then got CELAM to undertake the task. Its five-man team toured Central America in late 1981. As Lopez Trujillo said in the covering letter presenting the report, they had talked only to those 'who were in harmony with the Church or in some way in relation with her'.[23]

The report was not very enthusiastic about Archbishop Romero of San Salvador, widely regarded by the poor of Latin America as a whole as a martyr in their cause. The report failed to commit itself to the guilt of the military for Romero's assassination, though this was generally believed and has since been demonstrated beyond doubt; they were not too enthusiastic, either, about the role of Romero himself. The report insisted that in Honduras, where was located the base for the US-backed 'contras' and was therefore the US frontline against supposed Marxist advance, there were Marxists among the clergy, and that priests had joined in the armed struggle – neither of which assertions, said the Honduran bishops, was true. Worst of all, in Nicaragua there had grown up the *iglesia popular* (the people's church) which the Pope believed – and had said so in a letter to the bishops of Nicaragua in June 1982 – to be an absurdity. He believed it represented the outlook of only one class in society, and was therefore a party to the class struggle, which he abominated. Separated from the hierarchy, the *iglesia popular* was open to ideological tendencies at odds with Catholicism, and to the acceptance of violence. That was the papal view. The Pope does not understand, said Nicaraguan churchmen. Unfortunately, at the time of the Pope's arrival, there were five such churchmen in the Sandinista government despite John Paul's attempts to prohibit clergy from holding political office. It was not a situation that was likely to make him sympathetic to the Sandinista revolution, or to the *iglesia popular*.

The Central American tour started quietly enough on 2 March in San José, Costa Rica, where the Pope met the bishops of the region, all 67 of them, and, the following day attended a reception for members of the Inter-American Court of Human Rights. The Pope as always constantly stressed the pastoral nature of his visit, but when greeting him in Managua, the capital of Nicaragua, on 4 March, the leader of the Sandinistas, Daniel Ortega, used the occasion to launch a spirited attack on US policy in the region. But he also pointed out that the Sandinista revolution, unlike other revolutions, in overthrowing the hated Somoza regime had done so with the backing of Christians, including churchmen and women. Later in the day the Pope celebrated an open-air mass in the Plaza 19 Julio against a backdrop of pro-Sandinista placards. He congratulated the congregation on their heroism – but it was, he made clear, their heroism in the face of natural disasters, and not in overthrowing Somoza. Instead of support for the revolution, there was a homily on the unity of the Church, and an attack on the *iglesia popular*. The congregation began to chant Sandinista slogans – eye-witnesses believed the chanting to have been orchestrated. This may have been true, but it was also true that they were dismayed by the Pope's apparently wilful refusal to address what was their most important agenda, their victory over Somoza and the continuing war, in which many of those present had lost relatives, against the US-backed contras. Interrupted in his homily, for once the Pope lost his cool, and raised his voice to upbraid the people below him. It was an unmitigated disaster. Earlier, as the Pope arrived at the airport to be greeted by a string of eminent personages, he was seen publicly to rebuke, with an admonitory wave of a finger, the highly respected Fr Ernesto Cardenal, a poet-priest with a modest post in the government.[24] Cardenal had attempted to kiss John Paul's hand: the Pope would not allow him to do so.

The next day the Pope went to Panama, and the day after to El Salvador. No visit to the burial place of Archbishop Romero had been included. On his way from the airport, the Pope made a flying visit to the tomb. As David Willey comments, 'his act of homage to what had already become an important shrine for many Latin American Catholics was almost surreptitious'.[25] In the mass which followed he called for reconciliation, but made no mention of the murdered Archbishop who had died by an assassin's bullet in 1980 because he had called upon the government troops to lay down their arms and refuse to oppress the people. (At the time of his murder the Pope had described him as 'zealous', which had seemed to those hundreds of thousands in El Salvador who had hung on the Archbishop's words to be something of an understatement.)

That was Sunday. On Monday the Pope was in Guatemala where he spoke out against violations of the rights of the Indians, and seemed publicly to criticize the President, General Efrain Rios Montt, a born-again Christian, when he insisted in a sermon that faith and works could not be separated. Then he returned to Rome, by way of a stopover in Haiti where there was a Eucharistic Congress and, in the Congress's aftermath, where CELAM was holding its 19th General Assembly. David Willey confessed himself 'struck by [the Pope's] bold message that the time had come for change',[26] and by the Pope's trenchant criticism of the regime of 'Baby Doc', Jean-Claude Duvalier. The criticism was all the more surprising because it was, and is, rare for the Pope directly to attack even the most repressive of regimes in countries he visits. As in his address in Guatemala, there were frequently indirect remarks through which the Pope could distance himself from the government and thereby give encouragement to those working for change (that there was need for change in Haiti had been the theme of the Eucharistic Congress), but he also had to remember that the bishops had to continue to minister in the country after his plane had left.

But perhaps the most important factor in moderating his criticism was the fear of violent revolution. Violence, he appears to believe, can never be justified (though, as has been seen, he appears prepared to tolerate nuclear deterrence, cf. above, p. 109). This sets him apart from some at least of the Latin American church leaders – including the late Archbishop Romero – who had come to regard the armed struggle as a last-resort form of self-defence against the institutionalized violence of the ruling classes. And that was another problem for the Pope. He considered, with good reason, that an armed struggle was a struggle between classes in society, and wide open to ideological manipulation by Marxists. To associate Catholicism with that struggle, as had happened most notably in Nicaragua but also in El Salvador, was to instrumentalize the Church, and to betray its true identity.

There were two ways to stop that happening. One was to remind churchmen and women, as he had constantly done since almost the very first words of his address to the Latin American bishops at Puebla on his first journey out of Rome, that they had to stay out of politics. The second way was to ensure that the hierarchy of authority in the Church was preserved. Hence his detestation of the *iglesia popular*, a phrase which he seemed to translate as 'the church from the people', rather than the more neutral 'the church of the people'. He continued his polemic even though numerous Latin American prelates assured him that the people's church was for the most part unwaveringly loyal to the authority of the local bishop. CELAM, meanwhile, decided to undertake a full-scale study of the phenomenon.

Does the Pope ever learn anything from his journeys? 'The high moral responsibility that is his in the world and his own wisdom will surely keep him open to the possibility of enriching his judgements, as he comes into contact with the concrete reality of each place that he visits', commented the Sandinista authorities after the Pope had left. It is difficult to believe that they do. Speeches are prepared beforehand, so the message relates to what the experts have told him. But who chooses the experts? On 16 March, reflecting on his Central American tour during a general audience when back in Rome, he commented on the violence of the region, and in particular in El Salvador: 'This struggle has been conducted to a considerable extent with the help of foreign forces and of arms provided from abroad against the will of the vast majority of the people, who are longing instead for peace and democracy. This I was told by one of the best-informed bishops in that country.' But it is hardly surprising that people prefer peace to war, and he should not have needed to be told that Archbishop Romero, for one, had constantly called for a cessation in the supply of arms to the government troops of El Salvador. What the Pope did not learn, or certainly did not address publicly, was whether the people of El Salvador wanted the overthrow, by armed struggle if all else failed – as it had – of the regime of oppression under which they had been living. As Christine de Montclos has observed,[27] the Pope seems less preoccupied by the dictatorships of the right, possibly because they are not durable, than those of the left, which are, and the lack of material goods counts for him rather less than do the dangers posed by regimes which attack spiritual freedom. That, says de Montclos, accounts for the severity of the Pope's words in Managua, and his refusal to talk about the triumph of the revolution. The regime had used the Church for its own ends and, he believed, had separated the *iglesia popular* from the hierarchical Church. Hence the homily, which seemed so out of place to those who heard it, on the importance of maintaining the unity of the Church. Ecclesial identity, Christian culture, was not to be found in heroes of the revolution but in saints, in exemplars of holy living from within the Church.

The Pope talked constantly of saints, and of their role in the founding and preservation of Western civilization. They are in his eyes, and the minds of many, models of Christian living whom, through its official procedures of beatification and canonization, the Church sets before the faithful for emulation. Shortly before the Pope left for Central America it was announced that the procedures for making saints was to be simplified. One reform was intended to switch emphasis from the Vatican's Congregation for the Causes of Saints to work done at local level in the dioceses. It would have been a rare example, in the present pontificate, of a decentralization of authority – but if that was the intention, it has not happened. Other reforms (such as halving the number of miracles required for canonization) have, however, considerably speeded up the process and, in an attempt to have people declared saints whose lives have a contemporary relevance the time lapse between death and canonization was reduced to a minimum of ten years.[28]

Although other motives have been attributed to it (see above, p. 110-11), the declaration of the beginning of the 1983–1984 as a Holy Year was also part of that Christian culture, dating back to the first such event, proclaimed by Boniface VIII in 1300. In the late afternoon of 25 March, with the rain sweeping down across St Peter's Square, John Paul hammered on the 'holy door' of St Peter's basilica. The masonry was chipped away and the door swung open. The theme of holy years has always been that of prayer and penance – and the gaining of indulgences which would let one off time spent in purgatory serving time for one's sins. The Pope may still have believed in the efficacy of indulgences – one of the flashpoints of the Lutheran Reformation[29] – but they no longer figure large in the average Catholic's devotional life. A pilgrimage to Rome to gain an indulgence, even in the comparative comfort of a jet plane, no longer holds the same attraction. And the associated penance still less.

In May 1981 John Paul had established the Pontifical Council for the Family. Two years later, at the end of May and beginning of June 1983, it met for the first time in plenary session. The Pope told the assembly that there were three things to be kept in mind in all its deliberations. The first was that there was an 'indissoluble link between conjugal love and the service of life' – which is to say that to be truly Christian as the Pope understood the term husbands and wives had to be faithful to the teaching of *Humanae Vitae* in rejecting artificial means of birth control. There could not be a conflict between the doctrinal teaching on the matter, said the Pope, and pastoral needs, because the Church's task was simply to tell the truth, and it was not the author or arbiter of that truth. Secondly, once children had been born, it was the duty of the family, first and foremost, to educate them. Thirdly, the relationship of the family to the state had to be defined, so that the state respected the family unit, and did not attempt to swamp it. Clearly the Pope, who for much of his childhood had not had a family in the sense of two parents and a number of siblings, had a highly idealized notion of what in practice families were.

In mid-June the Pope began his trip to Poland, postponed from the previous year. The Vatican had said he would not go unless the situation was right, but it was doubtful whether it had much improved. Solidarity was still banned, and there seemed little likelihood of its being approved; martial law was suspended, but had not technically been rescinded. Still, the Pope went, arriving in Warsaw on 16 June, to be met by Cardinal Glemp and the Polish President. He left the country from Cracow on 23 June. The 16th and 17th he spent in Warsaw. On the 18th he visited Niepokalanw, founded by Maximilian Kolbe, and celebrated mass in honour of the recently-canonized saint. Later that day he went to Czestochowa where the jubilee celebrations had been extended into a year-long festivity, so that he could be present at the closing. He stayed at Czestochowa for two nights, though in between he visited other Marian shrines. In Cracow on 22nd June he went to his old university, the Jagellonian; he beatified Rafael Kalinowski, Ursula Ledochowska and Adam Chmielowski; he dedicated a church to Kolbe, and attended the closing ceremonies of the provincial synod of the archdiocese of Cracow.

Had it been anywhere else other than Poland, the itinerary would have seemed typically tiring (John Paul was reported to have fallen fast asleep as soon as he sat in his aircraft seat for the flight from Cracow to Rome) but unexceptional. Ecclesiastically, perhaps the most remarkable feature of the journey was the beatification of no fewer than three Poles at one time, two of whom (Kalinowski and Chmielowski) were Polish patriots who had taken part in the nineteenth-century insurrection against Russian domination[30] (see above, pp. 18-19).

In the particular situation of Poland, however, John Paul had to struggle to keep the people's feelings under control. On the first evening of his visit, after a mass in memory of the late Cardinal Wyszynski in Warsaw's cathedral, a crowd of some 20,000 chanting pro-Solidarity slogans paraded past the Communist Party headquarters. The following day, after mass in the stadium at Warsaw, he called upon those present to depart quietly. They did so. Later demonstrations were smaller and quieter, though Solidarity banners were frequently to be seen. Papal pragmatism was further in evidence when John Paul met General Jaruzelski. In a speech which was televised and whose meaning would not have been lost on the Poles themselves, he expressed his hope that the 'principles so painstakingly worked out in the critical days of August 1980 and contained in the agreements will gradually be put into effect'. 'Gradually' was significant: that was part of the Polish Church's pragmatism. The principles themselves included recognition of Solidarity, but also of the leading role in the country of the Polish Communist Party. That, too, was pragmatism.

The only occasion apart from the demonstration at the end of the mass in Warsaw cathedral when it seemed possible that the crowd might get out of hand was at Nowa Huta. There the Pope dedicated to St Maximilian Kolbe a church that the steelworkers themselves had struggled to build in the face of harassment from officialdom. But the ceremony took place without any provocation from the Pope. Quite the opposite. On an occasion at which, on past performance, he might have been expected to make a plea for the rights of workers, he restricted himself for the most part to reminiscences about the priest who had fought to have the church built, but who did not live to see it completed. As one commentator remarked at the time, in Nowa Huta he appeared to play the role of the Polish bishop he once had been as much as that of universal pontiff he had since become.[31]

It was rather in the latter role that he had requested conversation with Lech Walesa. The authorities had demurred, not allowing Walesa a break from work at the Gdansk shipyards to join the crowds going to see the Pope. Eventually, however, they relented. There was a four-hour meeting on the morning of 23 June – the Pope had seen Jaruselzski for the second time on the previous evening. What the conversation was about has remained a matter of considerable speculation, but Fr Virgilio Levi had no doubts: Walesa had been asked by John Paul to retire from leadership of Solidarity, thus sacrificing himself for the good of the country. 'Sometimes the sacrifice of inconvenient people is necessary for the greater good of the community', he wrote. It was where the article appeared as much as what it said that gave credence to Levi's views. Levi was deputy editor of L'Osservatore Romano, the Vatican's daily newspaper, and the piece had appeared, signed by Levi, in its columns. Levi never retracted the story that the Pope had asked Walesa to step down. He was, however, summoned to see Cardinal Casaroli, the Secretary of State, and Archbishop Silvestrini, head of the Council for Public Affairs, and later resigned from the paper. No one but the Pope could have had the deputy editor so summarily removed. Clearly John Paul was incensed by the story, but that does not make it inaccurate. Despite an apparent touch of hesitancy, however, Lech Walesa stayed, to the annoyance of the Polish government which had made it abundantly clear it had no intention of negotiating further with Walesa.

A week after the Pope got back to Rome Cardinal Glemp came too, together with bishops from dioceses John Paul had visited on his tour. There was no talk of a new trade union to replace Solidarity, said Glemp, nor had Walesa been told to stay out of politics as Virgilio Levi had reported. The Church, however, might find money to finance a central fund for the support of agricultural cooperatives, Glemp told the press.

The Polish Pope had no problem with the bishops of Poland. Their Synod notwithstanding (cf. above, pp. 75-6) he still was not satisfied with the loyalty of the bishops of Holland. On 8 July it was announced in Rome that Pope John Paul had appointed the Bishop of Rotterdam, Adrianus Simonis, to succeed Cardinal Willebrands, the highly respected Archbishop of Utrecht, and President of the Vatican's Secretariat for the Promotion of Christian Unity. The Dutch hierarchy was small – seven bishops in all. Simonis, with one other, Johannes Gijsen, were of the minority conservative faction on the Episcopal Conference. Utrecht was the sole metropolitan diocese, and informally the primatial see. His appointment gave Simonis, who said he had told the Pope there were better qualified candidates than he, an enormously influential role in the Dutch Church. The choice was clearly directly that of the Pope. It was evident from the reactions of the remaining bishops, Gijsen apart, and of the laity that there was deep disappointment at Simonis's elevation. Papal control of episcopal appointments throughout the world was one of the more effective means by which, little by little, John Paul could hope to impose his own personal outlook upon the Church. Rarely had the papal prerogative been so crudely exercised than in this choice of Archbishop for Utrecht.

So far Poland had been the only country twice to have received the Pope. France was next. A trip to France had been planned for the summer of 1981, for the Pope to attend the Eucharistic Congress then being held in Lourdes. The attempt on his life meant that the visit to the world's most important Marian shrine had been postponed. He finally made the trip in August 1983, arriving at Tarbes airport to be greeted by President Mitterand in the late afternoon of the 14th and returning the following day. After a conversation lasting three-quarters of an hour with the French President, John Paul went straight on to the shrine, spending time in prayer at the grotto and leading the torchlight procession in the evening. At the end of the procession he spoke of the place of suffering in the world and highlighted the suffering of those persecuted for their religious beliefs: it is typical of the Pope that religious freedom always dominates his catalogue of human rights and their abuses, but whereas his immediate predecessors had understood religious freedom to be about liberty of conscience, John Paul tends to equate it with the right to religious education.[32]

On 2 September the delayed General Congregation of the Jesuits met to begin the process which would lead to the appointment of a successor to Pedro Arrupe as its General Superior. Naturally there was a mass. The Pope presided, and for well over half an hour preached successively in Italian, French, English and Spanish. While praising the Society, he reminded its members to keep their specific purpose in mind – and that specific purpose he linked to the fourth vow (taken only by an elite, but a fairly large elite) which committed those who took it to a mission to go wherever the Pope should require. He dwelt in particular on a number of aspects of the Society's role: to promote the Second Vatican Council as it had promoted Trent;[33] to focus on dialogue with non-Christian religions and with 'cultures'; and to promote justice. With regard to the last, however, he wanted them not to forget that their vocation was a priestly one, and they should not take on work proper to the laity, thereby confusing roles. He left the 211 delegates to their task, and on 13 September they elected Pieter-Hans Kolvenbach, a 54-year-old Dutchman who had worked in Beirut and who, in keeping with his involvement in the Eastern-rite Churches, sported a beard. He was, the newspapers claimed, the first Jesuit General to have done so – since their Founder, that is.

But in the meantime the Pope had been to Austria. He arrived in Vienna on 10 September. The first event was the celebration of Vespers in the presence of some eighty bishops from all over Europe. Christianity, said John Paul, was the reason why the arts and sciences had so flourished in Europe, and he could not forbear to point out that it was a Pole, John Sobieski, who had lifted the siege of Vienna and turned back the Turks (and, of course, Islam, though he did not say as much) from spreading across the Continent. It was the 300th anniversary of the raising of the siege, an event a Pope who loved anniversaries could not overlook. Choosing to emphasize the European dimension in Vienna, once the capital of the Austro-Hungarian Empire and so close to the borders of the Eastern bloc, John Paul was once again insisting that the true Europe was a continent which included the Communist East as well as the capitalist West. And of it all, in his reading of history, a Pole had been the saviour.

He stayed in Austria until the 13th, taking part in the closure of the Austrian national Catholic Congress on the 11th, talking to scientists and other intellectuals in the early part of the 12th, and to Polish exiles in the evening and, on the 13th before flying back to Rome, visiting the Marian shrine of Marizell where he recalled that Mary was revered as Mother not just of Austria, but of Hungary also, and of all the Slavic peoples.

Four days later in Rome there occurred a small incident, not much remarked at the time, but of considerable long-term importance. One would not have expected any pope so close in time to Pope Paul VI's encyclical of 1968 *Humanae Vitae* to come out in favour of artificial means of contraception. But John Paul carried the Church's campaign against it to new levels. Speaking to fifty clergymen who had been attending a seminar on 'Responsible Procreation', the Pope claimed it to be a denial of God, that is to say, equivalent to atheism, to suggest that artificial contraception might ever, in any circumstances, be justified. To advocate contraception, he argued, was to put oneself in the place of God, determining which human beings might be brought into the world. What the fifty priests, debarred from procreating by their calling, and by that same calling committed to proclaiming the Gospel, made of reducing the test of faithfulness to God to obedience to a single commandment (and a commandment not to be found in Scripture): 'thou shalt not use artificial contraception', can only be guessed at. Meanwhile, as all the statistics relate, many millions of Catholics went on practising contraception and, perversely, believing in God.

On 29 September the sixth Synod of Bishops opened, on the theme of 'Reconciliation and Penance in the Church's Mission'. The Archbishop of Liverpool, Derek Worlock, was chief among those who made a brave attempt to breathe into this topic an element of social awareness. He was ignored. When the Superiors General of religious Orders of men suggested that the treatment of confession should reflect more on the community aspect of the sacrament, they were told that what had to be safeguarded at all costs was the traditional form of private confession. By canonical legislation under Pope Paul VI there were three forms of the sacrament of confession: absolution for the sinner could be given privately (the most traditional mode); there could be a common liturgical celebration with individual private confessions as part of it; and there could be liturgical celebrations during which absolution was given to all and sundry without the requirement of individual confession of sins. In the Western world, as numerous prelates bore witness, this last had proved remarkably pastorally effective in bringing people back to confession. It was viewed with considerable hostility by bishops from the Eastern part of the Church, and basically damned by Cardinal Ratzinger in a stern theological lecture made from his eminence as Prefect of the Congregation for the Doctrine of the Faith, the doctrinal watchdog. Bishops in the Third World wanted 'general absolution', as the final rite is generally known, because it solved problems of logistics in lands with too few clergy to cope. Just to emphasize where he stood, on 16 October, a date deliberately chosen to coincide with the Synod, John Paul canonized a Capuchin friar from Croatia, Leopold Mandic, who had spent the last thirty years of his life hearing confessions in Padua, and whose confessional box had since his death become a centre of pilgrimage.

Back in the synodal hall several of the fathers, most notably Cardinal Arns, the diminutive Archbishop of São Paulo, argued for the recognition of the evils of 'social sin' – the injustices of social structures which keep people oppressed, of racism, of terrorism, of the economic imbalance (as Arns stressed) between the rich North and the far poorer South. He was promptly scorned by Cardinal Trujillo (not an elected delegate but a personal invitee of the Pope's) who said that 'so-called social sin' was in danger of putting personal sin into second place. As far as the Synod was concerned, Cardinal Arns' views (and to be fair, those of very many other bishops) won the day. When they came to compose their message to the world, there was a great deal about the Church's reconciling mission understood in terms of its commitment to justice, and there was little about sacramental confession. The Pope's final message to the Synod fathers, however, put the emphasis exactly the opposite way round, stressing personal guilt and need for forgiveness, and saying that social sin was 'sin' only by analogy. One could not accuse the Pope of not having listened to the Synod debates, but it was difficult to see that he had learned very much from them.

On 6 October, despite vigorous opposition from Spanish bishops, the parliament in Madrid had approved a law permitting abortion where the mother's life was threatened, the foetus was malformed, or the conception had been a consequence of rape. Less than a fortnight later, on 15 October, Felipe Gonzalez, the Spanish prime minister, called on the Pope in the Vatican to discuss Church-state relations, rarely at so low an ebb in Spain since the ending of the Civil War. On 17 October the Prefect of the Congregation for the Causes of Saints announced that the beatification process for those killed in the Spanish Civil War was to be resumed. It had been shelved by Paul VI because of the old wounds such a ceremony would be likely to reopen in Spain, especially with a Socialist government in power. If such niceties were lost on John Paul II (and it is hard to believe that they were), to announce the reopening of the process just two days after a fraught meeting with the Socialist prime minister could surely only have been a direct snub.[34]

The Pope was not only taking on the government of Spain, he was also about to tackle the Catholic Church in the United States. *Newsweek* went so far as to carry a headline, 'The Pope vs the US Church'. There was ample evidence. John Paul had ordered a study of seminaries with the aim of tightening discipline, and enforcing obedience to the bishops. He had told the bishops to be firmer in enforcing the ban on artificial contraception, and he did not want them supporting those agitating for the ordination of women. He was also exhorting them to exercise greater surveillance over members of religious orders in their dioceses even though, technically, they had no right to do so.

But all that was of no consequence if he could not trust the bishops. One of the most wayward, from a Vatican perspective, was Archbishop Raymond Hunthausen of Seattle. He was a man of progressive views on war and peace, and had been withholding 50 per cent of his federal taxes, which was the sum he calculated would be spent on armaments. And if that was not bad enough, he seemed to be too tolerant towards homosexual groups. The conservative Archbishop James Hickey of Washington, DC, was asked to examine the allegations.[35] Apart from the Hunthausen enquiry, the Vatican seemed particularly concerned with the presence at US altars of girl altar servers, and with the role of women religious in seminaries. There were, one would have thought and many people said, far more important pastoral issues in the US Church demanding attention. But to focus attention upon nuns in this way was likely to be counterproductive for the US Church as a whole. The Church depended heavily upon them for the support of the parochial school system. Without their largely voluntary labour it would prove (and is now proving) too expensive to maintain.

NOTES

1. In Britain the Prime Minister Mrs Thatcher voiced prompt approval of the US sanctions, but her views were not shared by European governments at large.
2. David Willey, op. cit., p. 147.
3. In fact, prayers for the conversion of Russia and against Communism played no part in the original 'revelation', but seem to have been added to the 'message' c. 1928, cf. Michael P. Carroll, *The cult of the Virgin Mary* (Princeton NJ, Princeton University Press, 1986), pp. 136–40.
4. On the first evening of the visit to Fátima a Spanish-born priest, Juan Fernandez Krohn, made a further attempt on the Pope's life, though the guards prevented him from reaching John Paul. The priest's political views were violently anti-Communist; his religious ones he took from Archbishop Lefebvre, who had ordained him in 1978.
5. cf. Willey, p. 24.

1982–3

6. The proposal that the Pope should visit Argentina after Britain was, it seems, originally suggested by Tom Burns, then editor of *The Tablet*, to the Archbishop of Westminster, Cardinal Hume, cf. Burns's autobiography, *The use of memory* (London, Sheed & Ward, 1993), p. 163. Burns's youngest son Jimmy was at the time *The Financial Times*' correspondent in Buenos Aires.

7. On the balcony of Westminster Cathedral, his first stop after arriving at Gatwick airport, John Paul appeared to indicate his surprise at the bright sunlight to Cardinal Hume, who was standing beside him.

8. Though the pernickety took umbrage at the words, in the homily at Westminster Cathedral, 'This fair land, once a distant outpost of the pagan world …'. They pointed out with some justice that Britain had been converted to Christianity several centuries before Poland.

9. Conditions for the papal visit, demanded by the Church, included an amnesty for Solidarity activists and a relaxation of martial law. These were unlikely to be met, as the Polish leader, General Jaruszelski, was not himself in favour of the visit in August. The Church prudently extended the anniversary of the Black Madonna's arrival to encompass a whole year of celebration, thereby allowing the Pope plenty of time to attend. Glemp announced the postponement in a sermon in the Polish chapel of St Peter's in Rome, on 21 July.

10. See Robert Cornwell, *God's Banker: The Life and Death of Roberto Calvi*, (London, Gollancz, 1983) and Charles Raw, *The Money Changers*, (London, Harvell, 1992). The latter publication has the explanatory sub-title 'How the Vatican Bank enabled Roberto Calvi to steal $250 million for the heads of the P2 Masonic Lodge'.

11. Raw, op. cit., p. 10.

12. Raw, op. cit., p. 12.

13. op cit., p. 4.

14. This is not an unduly cynical remark. The first Holy Year in 1300 had undoubtedly been thought up for just that reason. There had been a Holy Year in 1933 to celebrate the 1900th anniversary of Christ's death.

15. Michael Walsh, *The Secret World of Opus Dei* (London, Grafton Books, 1989), pp. 79ff.

16. Andrej Kreutz, *Vatican Policy on the Palestinian-Israeli Conflict* (New York, Greenwood Press, 1990), pp. 151–9.

17. The canonization itself was not without its controversial side. The Pope clearly wanted Kolbe declared a saint, but the process of doing so would, in the normal course of events, have taken many years because it would have involved minute study of Kolbe's voluminous writings. By switching him from the rank of 'confessor' to that of 'martyr', however, that particular hurdle was avoided.

18. Peter Hebblethwaite, 'The cardinals meet in Rome', *The Tablet*, 4 December, 1982, p. 1227.

19. The money is handled by the Administration of the Patrimony of the Holy See, or APSA.

20. See above, p. 95–6.

21. His book on the topic, *Surnaturel*, was published in 1949.

22. The consistory at which the new appointments were to be formally confirmed took place on 2 February. A week earlier, on 25 January, the Pope launched the new Code of Canon Law, the rule book by which the Church was to be governed. The revision of the 1917 Code had been initiated by John XXIII in 1959, and the proposals that were made by the revision committee had been widely discussed: John Paul was quite correct when he said, in his Apostolic Constitution *Sacrae Disciplinae Leges* introducing the new Code, that it had been a collegial act. He also added that 'it is impossible perfectly to transpose the image of the Church described by conciliar doctrine [i.e., by Vatican II] into canonical language'.

23. cf. Peter Hebblethwaite, 'The Pope faces Central America', *The Tablet*, 26 February 1983, pp. 193–4. What follows is based on this article.

24. His brother Fernando, a Jesuit, had a much more high-profile position.

25. Willey, op. cit., p. 118.

26. Willey, op. cit., p. 135.

27. *Les voyages de Jean-Paul II* (Paris, Centurion, 1990), p. 268.

28. For an excellent account of the system, see Kenneth Woodward, *Making Saints* (London, Chatto & Windus, 1991). Anthropologically, the role of the holy man or woman in society is a complex one, much more so than the activities of the Congregation for the Causes of Saints would lead one to suppose.

29. The Pope had chosen as his Holy Year, surely by chance, the year in which Germany celebrated the 500th anniversary of the birth of Martin Luther.

30. Kalinowski had also served as a priest in the Pope's home town.

31. Christopher Bobinski, 'After the Pope's visit', *The Tablet*, 2 July 1983, pp. 624–5.

32. P. Blanquart, 'Quand l'apologétique se fait au nom d'Auschwitz' in *Le rêve de Compostelle*, edited by René Lueau (Paris, Centurion, 1989), p. 203. See also de Montclos, *Les voyages*, p. 98.

33. This view of the Pope's, that Jesuits were protagonists of the reforms of Trent, and of the Counter-Reformation, is commonly held, but it is not entirely accurate. Cf. John W. O'Malley, *The first Jesuits* (Cambridge MA, Harvard University Press, 1993), p. 17, and *passim*.

34. On 19 February 1984 the Pope beatified 99 martyrs of Angers who had been guillotined during the French Revolution for their refusal to take an oath of loyalty to the newly-established Republic.

35. John Deedy, 'US church under scrutiny', *The Tablet*, 12 November 1982, p. 1104.

SIX

1984-5

1984 OPENED with a flurry of diplomatic activity. New ambassadors (Burundi, Senegal and the Sudan) were received, and it was announced that the United States was to establish formal diplomatic links with the Holy See. This decision had been accompanied by an unprecedented degree of controversy – unprecedented, that is, in other countries with which the Holy See sought to establish such formal links. A strong American lobby, though not strong enough, had argued that the move would violate the Church-state divide they believed to be enshrined in the Constitution.

More significant, perhaps, was what the US Catholic bishops thought. It is a public policy issue, said one, and has to be decided in that forum – a remark of skilful neutrality. Archbishop Hickey had no such doubts, and took time off from his investigation into the pastoral policies of his colleague Archbishop Hunthausen to assert that the appointment of an ambassador to the Holy See would give the US access to 'the widespread humanitarian and peace-making agencies' of the Vatican. Sceptics wondered whether the existence of an ambassador (nuncio, or pro-nuncio[1] in the language of the Vatican) would allow the State Department more direct lines of complaint when the US bishops appeared hostile to the White House – as indeed they were at the time hostile over US policy in Central America, and over nuclear arms.

The expansion under John Paul II of the Holy See's diplomatic representation has been considerable – there were at this point 108 nations having representatives of ambassadorial status accredited to the Holy See (including countries of the size of Belize), and no doubt reflects the enormous impression made by the Pope himself.[2] An embassy at the Vatican, the world's smallest state, can scarcely carry out the usual roles of such offices elsewhere. But governments wished to establish them none the less. Whether local hierarchies were quite so enthusiastic is a totally different issue. The role of papal diplomats had been a controversial one at Vatican II, for they seemed to place between local hierarchies and the Holy See a theologically unjustified level of authority. In the worst scenario they removed debate with government away from the local bishops and transferred it to the Holy See. While such an outcome might be regarded as a benefit to a centralizing papacy, it was not something which local bishops could be expected to view with anything but suspicion. The Pope, on the other hand, was delighted with the expansion of the Vatican's diplomatic corps, and told assembled ambassadors so on 14 January, adding in what seemed like a reference to the Eastern bloc, that he looked forward to greeting representatives from nations with a 'secular tradition'.

The Vatican chalked up a modest diplomatic coup when Argentina and Chile signed, at the Vatican, a declaration about the Beagle Channel, an area in dispute between the two countries. Negotiations, mediated by the Holy See, had dragged on for six years and the document approved on 23 January was not yet a final agreement. The foreign ministers of Argentina and Chile were received by the Pope after the document had been signed. He would visit their countries after a final solution to their dispute had been reached, he told them.

Another diplomatic achievement, though of a rather different kind, was the settlement of a new concordat with Italy. Hitherto relations had been conducted in accordance with the concordat signed at the same time as the Lateran Treaty of 1929 which had established the Vatican City State. According to the Treaty, Catholicism was recognized as the religion of the Italian State. Negotiations had dragged on for a decade, with the place of religious instruction in state schools and the role of the Church in marriage as two of the chief difficulties in the search for an agreement. Signor Bettino Craxi, Italy's first socialist prime minister, piloted a new concordat through parliament which preserved religious instruction in schools, but gave parents the opportunity to withdraw their children if they believed this appropriate. Teachers of religion were to be appointed by the State, but they needed Church approval. The 1929 concordat gave full legal status to the provisions of the Church's canon law concerning marriage. Church marriages were to continue to have civil effect, but the privileged status of church courts in determining the nullity of marriage was no longer preserved. A great many details, including financial issues, were left to be settled after agreement on the main provisions.

Papal thoughts at this time, however, were very largely on Eastern Europe. On 26 February he went to Bari on the southeast coast of Italy, to the tomb of St Nicholas, Bishop of Myra. The ecumenical service in Bari was attended by the Metropolitan of Myra, representing the Eastern Orthodox tradition, and in his address the Pope spoke of Rome and Constantinople as the spiritual homes of the two traditions which have shaped Europe. There was a special mention of Russia of which St Nicholas (as well as being the personage behind – at a considerable distance – Santa Claus) is the patron saint, and of Albania which was just across the Adriatic and where all religious observance was banned. On the following Sunday John Paul presided at a mass in St Peter's in honour of the patron saint of Lithuania, St Casimir.[3]

The Pope had also let it be known that he had a strong desire to visit what was then Yugoslavia. The Communist authorities were not keen, and neither was the Serbian Orthodox Church. Patriarch German of the Serbian Church had refused Cardinal König's invitation to the ceremonies in Vienna in 1983 to mark the 3rd centenary of the lifting of the Turkish siege of the city (cf. above, pp. 125). The Patriarch's refusal, it seems, sprang from the intention of the Pope to meet the head of the Macedonian Orthodox Church, which had broken away from that of Serbia in 1967: the Serbian Orthodox Church refused to recognize its existence.

But there were other problems. The Serbian Orthodox bishops wanted the Catholic Croatian bishops to apologize for atrocities carried out during the Second World War by the Pavelic regime which, at the very least, appeared to have the blessing of the Catholic Church. The Croatians refused to apologize, both alleging similar atrocities by the Serbian Orthodox against the Catholics, and arguing that for the bishops to apologize would be tantamount to admitting it was indeed the Church, rather than the regime, which carried out the massacres of countless members of the Orthodox Church.

The ecumenical service in Vienna had also been a test for religious liberty in Czechoslovakia. No one from Slovakia, alleged the clandestinely-consecrated Bishop Jan Korec,[4] had been allowed to attend the occasion. While in a thirty-year period in Communist East Germany some 3,000 books had been published for Catholics, the number published in Czechoslovakia over the same period could be counted on one's fingers. This statement of Korec – written in the form of a letter to a newspaper – found its way into a newspaper published for Czechoslovak exiles shortly before a visit to Prague by the Vatican's special envoy to Eastern Europe, Archbishop Luigi Poggi. Immediately after that visit the Communist Party newspaper *Tribuna* published, on 28 March, an editorial describing John Paul as 'one of the most reactionary popes of the century'. The paper attacked the Pope in particular for having appointed, the previous year, two bishops to minister to the exiled Czechoslovak community. On 11 April Cardinal Tomasek, the Archbishop of

Prague, announced that he had invited the Pope to visit the country for celebrations to mark, in 1985, the 1100th anniversary of the death of the apostle of Bohemia, St Methodius. He said that he would be discussing details with both the Vatican and Czech government officials. There was no word from either, but young Catholics in Slovakia demonstrating in favour of a papal visit had been arrested.

In the midst of all this the Pope produced two lengthy documents. On 11 February there appeared an apostolic letter on the meaning of suffering, entitled *Salvifici Doloris*.[6] It was addressed to all the faithful and was presented very much as a personal meditation by John Paul on the problem of evil, though he concentrated not so much on the question of physical evil, of pain and of suffering in the more obviously experienced sense, but on the suffering which derives from separation from God. That separation has been overcome in Christ, the Pope argued, by his death upon the Cross – but that death united physical suffering, the pain of the crucifixion, with the moral evil of sin which he took upon himself: 'For our sake he made himself to be sin who knew no sin', as St Paul put it. 'Suffering is, in itself, an experience of evil', wrote the Pope, 'but Christ has made suffering the firmest basis of the definitive good, namely the good of eternal salvation'. The letter concluded – apart from a brief summary in the final (eighth) chapter – with a meditation upon the parable of the Good Samaritan. The Good Samaritan, wrote the Pope, 'does not stop at sympathy and compassion alone. They become for him an incentive to actions aimed at bringing help to the injured man. In a word, then, a Good Samaritan is one who brings help in suffering, whatever its nature may be. Help which is, as far as possible, effective'. This was vintage Wojtyla: a central problem for all those who believe in God, the problem of evil, explained immediately and unapologetically by reference to Christ's act of redemption in the suffering of the passion. It would not persuade unbelievers, but would bring consolation to Christians experiencing suffering.

On the feast of the Annunciation (25 March) there was released an 'apostolic exhortation' *Redemptionis Donum* (The gift of redemption) addressed to men and women in the religious Orders. He praised both the active and the contemplative forms of religious life, and called upon young people to assume this particular vocation, lived out under the vows of poverty, chastity and obedience. On chastity he quoted St Paul, that those who marry do well, but those who choose virginity do better. All religious bear witness to the love of Christ: 'Your mission must be seen', he told them.

Changes at the top of the Vatican's bureaucracy were somewhat overdue.

The theory was that officials held office for a maximum of five years before being moved on or reappointed. New appointments were announced on 9 April. They were not remarkable apart, perhaps, from the promotion of the first black African Cardinal, Bernardin Gantin, to head a major Vatican department, the Congregation for Bishops. The position of Cardinal Casaroli was confirmed as Secretary of State. He was also given powers to act in the name of the Pope in all that concerned the Vatican City State, though the position of president of the commission which governed that State was given to the conservative Cardinal Sebastiano Baggio. The Archbishop of Marseilles, Cardinal Roger Etchegaray, was set at the head of the Pontifical Commission for Justice and Peace, one of the Pope's most inspired appointments. More typical, however, was the choice of the very conservative Dominican Archbishop Jerome Hamer to replace the liberal Argentinean Cardinal, Eduardo Pironio, as Prefect of the Congregation for Religious and Secular Institutes: Hamer had been secretary to Cardinal Ratzinger's Congregation for the Doctrine of the Faith. Then, having put his house in order, Pope John Paul was off on his next far-flung tour.

He left Rome on 2 May for Seoul, South Korea. En route he stopped at Fairbanks, Alaska, where he was greeted by President Reagan who assured John Paul of the United States' dedication to human freedom and dignity. He arrived in Seoul on 3 May to be greeted by President Chun Doo Hwan. President and Pope both expressed their regrets at the division of Korea into two states, and the Pope won the hearts of many of his hearers by speaking of the philosophy of Confucius which had deeply influenced their country's culture even though a fifth of South Korea's population was Christian and Confucianism was now in retreat. North Korea, meanwhile, condemned the papal visit as an attempt further to divide the two parts of the peninsula.

Vast numbers of Koreans lined the route from the airport to the capital, but at the university students were demonstrating against the authoritarian rule of President Chun. Tear gas launched by the police to quench the demonstrators' ardour drifted on to the papal motorcade, and affected the Cardinal of Seoul, Stephen Kim. On 4 May the Pope went first to a baptismal ceremony in Kwangju and then to a leper colony on the island of Sorokodo, where he went on a walkabout among the patients, rather to the confusion of his bodyguards. In the evening he returned to Seoul, to address a gathering of diplomats. The following day there was an ordination ceremony in the town of Taegu. The Pope urged the thirty-eight new priests to dedicate their lives to the service of the poor and the oppressed, warning them, in an apparent reference to the proliferation of Christian sects in the country, 'not to be deceived by other messages, even if they are proclaimed in the name of Christ'. The trip to Taegu was immediately followed by one to South Korea's second city, Pusan, where there was the by now traditional gathering of workers. South Korea was undergoing a particularly rapid transition to an industrial economy. The Pope spoke of the workers' struggle for justice: Pusan had been the site of considerable industrial unrest.

The high point of the trip occurred on 6 May. At an open-air mass attended by some 200,000 the Pope canonized 103 Koreans who had died in persecutions in their country between 1839 and 1867, along with some French missionaries. The event, which was also intended to commemorate the 200th anniversary of the arrival of Christianity, was remarkable not only for the number of new saints created on one occasion, but because it was the first time since the Middle Ages that such a ceremony had taken place outside Rome. That evening there was a rally for young people, at which some participants were given the opportunity to address the Pope. One of them seized the chance to speak forthrightly about the appalling situation of the workers in Korea, while a university student spoke of the way in which people were being imprisoned for their views, something which simply drove them further to the left in their political ideology.

On 7 May John Paul left for Port Moresby, capital of Papua New Guinea, a country which he had visited ten years before when Archbishop of Cracow – and when it was still a colony of Australia. The Pope's message, delivered (or some of it) in Pidgin English, was much less political than it had been in South Korea. On 8 May, the eve of his departure for Honiara, capital of the Solomon Islands, the Pope spoke to the hierarchies of both countries, praising cooperation among bishops. 'There is need', he said, 'for a forum in which bishops can share their insights and experiences, pool their resources, and draw up programmes for meeting the urgent challenges and problems of the Church and society.' When he arrived in Honiara the Governor General revealed that, on the previous day, the government of the Solomon Islands had decided to establish diplomatic relations with the Holy See.

The final stop on the papal tour was in Thailand, but in the course of the Pope's flight from Honiara to Bangkok a message from John Paul to the people of Vietnam was released, calling for freedom of religious practice in the country, and pledging help in the reconstruction of Vietnam after the war. Vietnamese 'Patriotic Catholics' also issued a statement, denying that the government of their country was hostile to Catholicism.

Thailand is a country of 50 million, where only some 250,000 of the population are Catholics. In his audience with the King on his arrival the

Pope praised not only the country's religious tolerance but its hospitality to many thousands of refugees. Some of these encountered the Pope on 11 May, when he travelled to a processing centre outside Bangkok which contained some 18,000 refugees from Indochina – whom he addressed in English, his words being translated into Tai, Khmer and Vietnamese. Refugees, he told diplomats and government officials in the afternoon, have a right to return home: 'They have a right to all the cultural and spiritual relationships which nourish and maintain them as human beings'. Soon after this last address John Paul took plane for Rome, arriving back on 12 May.

On 17 May there was a commemoration of the 40th anniversary of the battle for Monte Cassino. Polish troops had played a major role on the side of the allies, and both the Polish Primate, Cardinal Glemp, and the Polish President, Henryk Jablonski, came to Rome. John Paul met Jablonski for private conversations on 19 May. There had been some hope that a Church-state agreement, opening the way to the establishment of diplomatic relations, might emerge. In the end nothing of significance came of the conversations, while the situation in Poland worsened as the government insisted on crosses being removed from schoolrooms and other public places. As fast as they were taken away the people put them back.

Papal diplomacy was making little headway in Poland and as far as South Africa was concerned it took a step backwards when, on 11 June, John Paul received in audience the Prime Minister of that country, P. W. Botha. It was a private audience and, in accordance with its own conventions, the Vatican issued no statement afterwards of the contents of the discussion. Such was the hostility aroused by the audience, however, that there was a communiqué of sorts. It said that the Pope never turned down requests for audiences from heads of government; that the granting of an audience did not imply approval of a government's policy; and that the Pope had expressed his abhorrence of racial discrimination and of colonialism. The Catholic Bishops' Conference in South Africa likewise felt the need to answer critics, which they did with similar arguments, though they recognized that many South Africans had been totally opposed to the granting of the audience. One of those critics was the Anglican Assistant Bishop of Johannesburg, Desmond Tutu. It was, he said, a 'slap in the face' for all who suffered under apartheid. John Paul went some way to repairing the damage by receiving on 27 June Mr Sam Nujoma, the president of the South West Africa People's Organization (SWAPO), the Namibian independence movement and, just over a week later (7 July), by calling for Namibian independence and condemning South Africa's violation of human rights in an address to a UN committee on apartheid.

But before then, on 12 June, he had been off again, though this time only as far as Switzerland. It was billed as a pastoral visit to the Catholics of the country, but it began with a visit to the headquarters of the World Council of Churches, followed immediately by a visit to the Orthodox centre at Chambésy. The Pope's message to the WCC was uncompromising: 'To be in communion with the Bishop of Rome is to give visible evidence that one is in communion with all who confess the faith, with those who have confessed it since Pentecost'. Dr Philip Potter, the shortly to retire General Secretary of the WCC, was apparently unfazed by this reassertion in Geneva, the city of Calvin, of papal claims. He was more relieved that the papal presence, and papal words, backed the WCC's international campaign for justice and human rights then under attack, especially from the United States. But outside the WCC there were many who were not happy. The President of the Federation of Protestant Churches, for instance, insisted that it was pointless praying with the Pope for unity when the Catholic Church denied the Eucharist to other Christians. There were advertisements in the press opposing the visit, and the Catholic attempt to establish two new dioceses in traditionally Calvinist areas also aroused hostility.

But it was not only the non-Catholics who were unhappy. The Catholics failed to turn up in any great numbers to hear the Pope. And those that did put in an appearance were not always happy with what they heard. The bishops (there were only six of them) were told that they were not properly in command of their Church; the faithful were rebuked for allowing their seeming peaceful tolerance to disguise both racist attitudes and an intolerance of conscientious objectors. Some of those who spoke to the Pope, on the other hand, gave expression to equally forthright thoughts. At Einsiedeln, an ancient Marian shrine, he was told that it was about time the Church approved the ordination of married men, and allowed women to be raised at least to the rank of deacon. The five-day tour was not a success.

On 11 July the Pope embarked at his weekly general audience on a series of addresses on Paul VI's encyclical on contraception, *Humanae Vitae*. It was an unlikely forum for such quite technical discourses, and John Paul asked a number of theologians to brief journalists so that any misunderstanding, or misreporting, of his words might be avoided. There was, said one Vatican official, considerable confusion about the doctrine, a confusion added to by a number of dissident theologians. Mgr Carlo Caffarra, the President of the Pontifical Commission for the Family which is located at the Lateran University, made the official's general accusation more specific, naming Charles Curran of the Catholic University of America, Hans Küng of

Tübingen, Franz Bockle of the University of Bonn and the late Marc Oraison as among the chief offenders. The ban of the use of artificial means of birth control, insisted the Pope, applied not only to Roman Catholics but, because it rested upon the basis of the natural law, to everyone throughout the world. He was, he revealed in the 5 September address, opposed even to 'natural birth regulation' if its aim was simply to avoid having children. There had, he insisted, to be other grounds – health, the welfare of the family, the good of society. Anyway, said the Pope on 24 October, periodic continence for married couples can be a good thing: 'In the case of married couples, continence deepens their understanding of the language of the body. They grow in the ability to give themselves to one another as a gift'. One cannot help wondering how he knew. The talks, which came to an end on 28 November, would be published as a thousand-page book by the Pontifical Institute for Marriage and the Family, said Mgr Carlo Caffarra, the Institute's head.

The context for these discourses was the International Population Conference, called by the United Nations, and held in Mexico City at the beginning of August. International agencies should not make their assistance to developing countries depend upon the achievement of strict control of population growth, the Pope had told the secretary of the conference, Rafael Salas, on 7 June. That was the position of the seven-man delegation, under Bishop Jan Schotte, sent by the Vatican. The conference began on 6 August and ended on the 14th. The conference ruled out abortion as a method of family planning, which the Vatican's representatives hailed as a success. On the other hand the Vatican refused to endorse the conference's concluding statement not simply because it supported birth control programmes and called for more investment in them, but because it stated that not only couples but individuals should have access to information to help them plan their families.

That was in Mexico City. Elsewhere in Latin America the Vatican was more successful in putting on pressure. In Nicaragua, the three priests who served in the government of the Sandinistas as minister of culture (Ernesto Cardenal), minister of education (Fernando Cardenal, S.J.) and the foreign minister (Miguel d'Escoto) were told on 12 August by the Holy See that they were in violation of canon law, and had to abandon their portfolios. They refused to do so. Meanwhile Leonardo Boff, a Brazilian priest and distinguished theologian, was summoned to Rome to explain his views to the Congregation of the Doctrine of the Faith.

Boff, a Franciscan, was a leading, perhaps *the* leading, exponent of the

Theology of Liberation. The view on such theology of Cardinal Ratzinger, Prefect of the Congregation for the Doctrine of the Faith, was a matter of record. At a meeting with Latin American bishops at the end of March he had already expressed criticism of it, which he repeated at a press conference on 13 April where he described Liberation Theology as 'in the final analysis unacceptable'. The basis of this rejection was the use of Marxist analysis to interpret not only society but the Scriptures and Christian doctrine. Such an outspoken condemnation (it was repeated in an article in the magazine of *Communione e Liberazione 30 Giorni*) by someone who was, in effect, to be the presiding judge at the 'trial' against Leonardo Boff could scarcely be regarded as doing anything but prejudging the proceedings. But then Boff supporters sprang a surprise. It was announced that he was to be assisted in his defence by Cardinal Aloisio Lorscheider, like Boff himself a Franciscan and president of the Brazilian bishops' theology commission. This pitched cardinal against cardinal though Ratzinger was, of the two, the more accomplished theologian: he had even been the director of Boff's doctoral studies. Boff also drew support from the head of his Order who insisted that not only was he a conscientious member of the Franciscans, but someone of whom the Franciscans were proud.

It was at this juncture, on 6 August, that the Congregation for the Doctrine of the Faith chose to issue a lengthy 'Instruction on Certain Aspects of the "Theology of Liberation" '. Its purpose was 'to draw the attention of pastors, theologians, and all the faithful to the deviations, and risks of deviations, damaging to the faith and to Christian living, that are brought about by certain forms of Liberation Theology which use, in an insufficiently critical manner, concepts from various currents of Marxist thought'. As the document proceeds, however, it becomes clear that no application of Marxism is acceptable: 'If one tries to take only one part, say analysis, one ends up having to accept the entire ideology', and this ideology 'contains errors which directly threaten the truths of the faith regarding the eternal destiny of individual persons'. A number of errors of the Liberation Theologians are specifically mentioned, such as the charge that they embrace the 'class struggle', that they put liberation from earthly servitude before liberation from the slavery of sin, that they radically question the nature of ethics.

This was a document from one of the Vatican's Congregations, not emanating explicitly from the Pope himself. Cardinal Casaroli took the extraordinary step – for a senior Vatican official – of distancing himself from it. He could not do otherwise, for its description of Communism was enough to jeopardize the whole of the Secretariat of State's efforts to improve relations with the Eastern bloc. Even so, there is no doubt that John Paul's weight was behind it, for it reflected views he had already expressed, especially when visiting Latin America. He had experienced the impact of Marxism upon a Catholic culture. He could not stand by and, as he clearly believed, allow Marxism, with the support of the Church, to make inroads into the Catholic culture of Latin America. The Pope was speaking out against Marxism, said Cardinal König, the Archbishop of Vienna, because that was what believers in the Eastern bloc wanted from him. He had been hesitant to do so at first while he waited to see what might be the impact of the election to the papacy of someone from a Communist country, but now he was attempting to influence the younger generation in the Soviet Union.[6]

On 7 September Boff was questioned for four hours by the Congregation[7] – he was accompanied during the last hour and a half not only by Lohrscheider but by Cardinal Evaristo Arns, the Archbishop of São Paulo and acknowledged leader of the Brazilian Church. Like Lohrscheider and Boff, the diminutive Arns is also a Franciscan. The focus of the interview with Ratzinger was Boff's book *Church, Charism and Power*, described by the Congregation as 'dangerous'. But Boff was far from being the founding father of Liberation Theology. That title has generally been conferred upon Gustavo Gutierrez, and Fr Gutierrez is a Peruvian. Part of the Vatican's tactics in opposing Liberation Theology was to attempt to persuade the Peruvian bishops to condemn Gutierrez. Ratzinger, in March 1983, had sent a document to them critical of Liberation Theology. The bishops could not agree, and set up a committee to discuss the issue: five of the six members sided with Gutierrez. On 1 October they were summoned to meet the Pope, on the 4th he addressed them publicly. In between they had turned down a document prepared by the Congregation for the Doctrine of the Faith which condemned propositions taken from Gutierrez's writings. But one had to read the Pope's address with care, and with considerable understanding of the Latin American situation, to believe that what he said was not a condemnation.[8]

Between Boff's questioning and the visit of the Peruvian bishops, John Paul had been to Canada – his 23rd overseas trip. He arrived in Quebec on 9 September amid strict security, and left on 20 September from Ottawa. In Quebec he spoke French, and visited the Marian shrine of Ste Anne-de-Beaupré, an especial place of pilgrimage for Canada's native peoples. On the 14th he attended a Polish rally, on the 15th he visited the Slovak cathedral. On the 16th it was the turn of Ukrainian Catholics in the cathedral church of Sts Vladimir and Olga, in Winnipeg. While he reminded the Poles and the

Slovaks of their cultural heritage, and urged them to cherish it, to the Ukrainians he gave the task of working towards better ecumenical relations with the Russian Orthodox. There could scarcely have been a message they wanted to hear less, the Russian Orthodox being quite reasonably regarded as major persecutors of the Ukrainian Byzantine Church in communion with Rome. They would have been more appreciative of a word or two promising them a patriarchate (cf. above, p. 77), or for permission to have a married clergy, according to their tradition.[9] The Canadian Bishops' Conference was one of the Church's most politicized: the Pope chided them. 'The entire renewal of the Church', he said, 'depends on the personal conversion which is sealed in a personal encounter with Christ.' Just before he left he told them that it was the laity's task to carry 'into society the principles of social doctrine which your [i.e., the Bishops' Conference] documents emphasize'. But he was outspoken in his condemnation of abortion – only to be expected, perhaps, but in Canada at the time it was an election issue.

On 10 October Pope John Paul was off again, this time to the Dominican Republic and a meeting of the bishops of the Conference of Latin American Bishops (CELAM). En route he stopped off in Spain, spending the night of the 10th in Saragossa. He was greeted by the King and Queen of Spain, and made another of his non-political political speeches, calling for the independence of church schools then very much under threat from the socialist government. Half a million people cheered him when, outside the city's floodlit cathedral, he spoke of the right of parents to choose what kind of education they wanted for their children.

He had made a stopover in Spain because, he explained, Spain had first brought the faith to Latin America, and a major part of the agenda of the CELAM conference in Santo Domingo was to discuss preparations for the celebration of the 500th anniversary of the arrival of Columbus in the New World. It gave the Pope a perfect opportunity to return to the topic of Liberation Theology (though he mentioned the term only once, and then in reference to the document – which he commended – from the Congregation of the Doctrine of the Faith). Amid the bishops, and addressing a congregation of 100,000 gathered for an open-air mass in the Hippodrome of Santo Domingo, he spoke of the conditions under which the Church must work: fidelity to the Gospel, 'which prohibits recourse to ... violence', an option for the poor which included all who wanted to abandon sin; a vision of the poor not as a class engaged in struggle; rejection of a society which would impose on citizens a programme of atheism or of practical materialism'. The first liberation, he said, was from sin, the moral evil which gives rise to social sin. The defence of the poor and especially of native peoples, he claimed, went back to the evangelizing activity of the first missionaries to the American continent. On 12 October Pope John Paul went on to Puerto Rico before returning home. He had been away from Rome three days, and covered over 16,800 kilometres. The trip to Argentina apart where there were, of course, special factors (cf. above, p. 108), this was one of the longest visits in kilometres traversed per day.[10]

There were, naturally, much shorter journeys too. On 3 November, for example, the Pope travelled to Northern Italy, spending three days celebrating the 400th anniversary of the death of St Charles Borromeo, the Cardinal Archbishop of Milan, and one of the Church's great reformers in the wake of the Council of Trent. The Pope described him as a symbol of the 'true reform', defined as one which 'loves and does not hate, succours and does not criticize, does not destroy but restores'. Was he contrasting, one cannot help wondering, sixteenth-century reform with that advocated by Liberation Theologians? If so, it was clearly to the disadvantage of the latter.

They were still on his mind when he came to write his response to the 1983 Synod on penance and reconciliation: the document was called *Reconciliatio et Paenitentia* and was dated 2 December, though it was published on the 11th. In describing the 'shattered world' John Paul highlighted violations of human rights, and especially of course the right to religious freedom, terrorism, the arms race and the unjust distribution of wealth. The root of all this was human sinfulness, sin both original and personal. A lengthy section of the apostolic exhortation was devoted to social sin, a concept much in use among Liberation Theologians, to describe the sinful, oppressive nature of the society in which people have to live and which adversely affects the way in which they can live. Although he acknowledges that there is a sense in which the term social sin can be used – indeed, he lists several different senses which are to his mind acceptable – he rejects the belief that 'practically every sin is a social sin in the sense that blame for it is to be placed not so much on the moral conscience of an individual but rather on some vague entity or anonymous collectivity, such as the situation, the system, society, structures, or institutions'. Such a notion, he says, 'can readily be seen to derive from non-Christian ideologies and systems – which have possibly been discarded today by the very people who formerly officially upheld them'. The legitimate senses of the term, however, are three (1) any sin is social because each such offence, no matter how private, adversely affects human solidarity; (2) a sin is social when it is directly an offence against another human being;[11] (3) social sin properly describes confrontation between groups (such as the class struggle) or blocs of nations.

There were other themes too. The Pope rigorously upheld the traditional distinction between mortal and venial sins. At the same time he rejected the notion of the 'fundamental option' which he interpreted as the belief that a person could not sin gravely unless he or she displayed 'explicit and formal contempt of God'. The rite of general absolution (cf. above, p. 126) was forbidden. The Church's penitential discipline (fasting and almsgiving) was reasserted and the practice of individual private confession, a sacrament much in decline in the Catholic Church, was insisted upon.

That was penance. As for reconciliation John Paul was clearly aware of divisions without the Catholic Church, and asked that we 'relinquish our subjective views and seek the truth where it is to be found, namely in the divine word itself and in the authentic interpretation of that word provided by the *magisterium* of the Church'. The Church would also work to overcome divisions within Christianity itself, but in relations with other Churches he warned against 'facile irenicism in doctrinal and especially dogmatic matters'.

Just at the time this apostolic exhortation was being released the Vatican announced the appointment of a new press officer. The person chosen was a layman, Dr Joaquín Navarro Vals, hitherto Rome correspondent of the conservative Madrid daily *ABC*. Dr Navarro Vals is a member of Opus Dei.

The year was not quite over. There was time for another onslaught on Liberation Theology. In his Christmas address to the papal Curia John Paul reflected, as he had done in *Reconciliatio et Paenitentia*, on divisions in the Church. There was room for pluralism, he emphasized, but healthy pluralism was that which contributed to the construction of unity rather than the opposite. Among the aspects of pluralism which he regarded as unhealthy was the calling into question of church doctrine, of tampering with the 'deposit of faith'. He was grateful, he said, for the help of the Congregation for the Doctrine of the Faith in its watchdog role. The Congregation, he said, was constantly inspired 'by rigorous criteria of respect for the persons with whom it enters into contact' – a view not necessarily shared by those who had been summoned before it. He defended the Congregation's instruction on Liberation Theology, and spoke particularly of the preferential option for the poor. He defended it, so long as poverty be extended beyond the materially poor.

He was soon to have an opportunity to renew his acquaintance with the continent that had given birth to the Theology of Liberation. On 26 January 1985 Pope John Paul embarked on an eleven-day tour of Venezuela, Peru, Ecuador and Trinidad and Tobago. The day before his departure, at a service in St Paul's Outside the Walls in Rome, the spot where John XXIII had called the Second Vatican Council, he summoned a special Synod to meet in November to 'draw up a balance sheet' of the Council, as Cardinal Casaroli put it to reporters on the papal flight to Venezuela.

The tour began on 27 January with an address in Caracas to the bishops of Venezuela in which the Pope made an outspoken attack on 'those who, abusing the mission to teach what they received from the Church, proclaim not the truth of Christ but their own theories, at times in open contrast to the *magisterium* of the Church'. There were, he said, priests who put the Gospel at the service of politics, seeking 'an illusory earthly liberation'. The following day in near-freezing temperature at Merida high in the Andes, he again warned against 'allowing oneself to be carried away by doctrines or ideologies contrary to Catholic dogma, as certain groups of materialistic inspiration or dubious religious content have desired'.

In Ciudad Guyana, a new industrial city, the topic switched to Catholic social teaching, and that was the main theme of his addresses in Ecuador. He arrived in the capital, Quito, on 29 January to be welcomed by a crowd of 60,000 in the city's football stadium before going on to celebrate mass for a further three-quarters of a million people in Carolina Park. In Ecuador's largest city, Guayaquil, he expressed sympathy for those who lived in the city's shanty town, and that evening (1 February) told priests, religious and lay leaders in Lima that the Church must work harder for the cause of justice and in defence of the poor, but urged them to adhere to the perennial teachings of the Church and not to ideologies which would pass. The following day, still in Lima, he told young Peruvians not to 'follow those who say that social injustice can disappear only through hatred between classes or the resort to violence and other anti-Christian methods'. A common theme in his addresses in Peru was the rejection of violence (though he made no direct reference to the government's own record of violence), clearly aimed at the Sendero Luminoso, the Maoist-inspired 'Shining Path' resistance movement. He stated it particularly strongly in Ayacucho, a town in the heart of the area dominated by these guerrillas. That was on Sunday 3 February: the following day the Sendero responded by plunging much of Lima, including the airport at which the Pope was due to arrive, into darkness.[12] From Peru John Paul flew on Tuesday 5 February to Port of Spain, the capital of Trinidad, and the following day continued his journey back to Rome.

On 19 February John Paul met the Prime Minister of Israel, Shimon Peres. They talked about the status of Jerusalem, upon which they could not agree, though the conversations were cordial enough and implied *de facto* recognition of the State of Israel.[13] Peres invited the Pope to visit Israel: he would not say what John Paul's reply had been. There was also once again talk of the establishment of diplomatic relations, apparently as a result of United States pressure. The Vatican, it seemed, had no objection in principle, it was simply there were a few problems in the way – like the status of the Palestinian Arabs.[14] Shortly afterwards John Paul interrupted his annual retreat to greet the Soviet Foreign Minister, Andrej Gromyko. On 23 February a meeting of the Association of Vatican Employees, a 1700-member trade union embracing all but a handful of the lay people who worked in the Vatican, called off a threatened strike over working conditions – they varied, along with pay-scales, from department to department – while on 5 March the commission of cardinals appointed to oversee the Vatican's finances met to discuss the latest deficit.

It was, therefore, business as usual in the Vatican, though outside Rome considerable anxiety was being expressed about the forthcoming extraordinary Synod which, it was felt by the progressives in the Church, had been called to turn back the clock on Vatican II. They were not mollified by the publication of a document proposed for discussion by the Church at large as a preparation for the 1986 Synod on the Laity. It was in three sections, each one ended in questions: 'Has the teaching of Vatican II concerning the place and task of the laity in the Church and the world been welcomed, understood and properly presented in the local churches?' was the first. Number four read: 'Has the conciliar interpretation of the figure of the lay-person been faithfully presented in your communities, or has it undergone substantial modification in the years succeeding the Council?' What was worrying was the import of words such as 'properly' and 'faithfully'. Who was to decide their content?

To anyone with experience of the Vatican, the answer was obvious. They had only to look at what was happening to the Discalced Carmelites. This group of religious, an Order effectively founded by St Teresa of Avila,[15] had a rule dating from 1581. This had been brought into line with Vatican II and the new version approved by Pope Paul VI. The revised rule had not been universally well received. There were some 800 convents of Carmelite nuns throughout the world and 20 per cent of them, mainly those in Spain, said they wanted to retain the original rule. An Order might have expected this problem to be resolved by the Order's own authorities, but the Pope had stepped in and instructed the Congregation of Religious and Secular Institutes to draw up a new constitution. The Vatican II Constitution had been in place for five years; the vast majority of the Carmelites accepted its provisions. Now the Pope was going to override it. He had, said the head of the Carmelites in a letter to the members of the Order, listened to a small group rather than to the overwhelming majority who understood their new Constitution not only to have already received papal approval from Paul VI but to be a faithful application of Vatican II to the ancient spirit of the Order. The Carmelite Superior General expressed his 'disgust' at the 'very hard tone and polemical content' of the letter of the Secretary of State, Cardinal Casaroli, informing him of the mandate given by the Pope to the Congregation of Religious. The Congregation in turn protested that it, too, would draw up a new Constitution in line with Vatican II. Once again, who was to be the interpreter of what was faithful compliance to the teaching of the Council? The Carmelites had thought they were being faithful: the Vatican apparently thought otherwise.

There was a similar problem with Holland, whither the Pope went on 11 May. A book published earlier in the year and consisting of fifty-six 'open letters' to John Paul made clear the authors' unhappiness with the way the Church was moving. The Church in Holland, they argued, had taken Vatican II seriously, with widespread consultation on ecclesiastical issues and a sharing of responsibility with the laity. The Vatican, on the other hand, was increasingly autocratic, centralized and determined to impose uniformity on the Church, especially where the liturgy was concerned, throughout the world.[16] On 12 May a trade union leader told the Pope that there was an increasing refusal on the part of the Church to engage in dialogue, while on the following day the Prime Minister himself complained that the 'word Rome makes some people uneasy if not downright suspicious' when the Pope called upon him at his residence in The Hague. The crowds were small to non-existent. Those who turned up at all were quiet, there were even some who booed the Pope though they were hurried away by the police. The final day of the visit to Holland was rather more upbeat, with a mass for 40,000 at Maastricht airport, and a smaller, but still sizeable, gathering of young people at Amersfoort.

That was 15 May. The following day, Ascension Thursday, John Paul went on to Luxembourg. He was there but briefly, visiting the offices of the European Community and praising Luxembourg for always being in the forefront of a united Europe. There was a meeting with steel workers, many of them immigrants. The following day there was an open-air mass for 50,000 and a warning against being dazzled by worldly wealth.

He flew to Brussels that evening, 16 May, and diplomatically avoided taking sides in the country's language dispute by waiting until he was in the (supposedly linguistically neutral) centre of Brussels before kissing Belgian soil. When he addressed the welcoming crowd he did so in French, Dutch (Flemish) and German. At the Menin gate the next day he defended the right to defend oneself against an unjust aggressor, and in Antwerp defended the Church's attitude to women: 'How could the coming of God's kingdom ever have started without Mary, the Mother of Jesus?' he asked. On his sixty-fifth birthday he was presented with a cake which had upon it models both of St Peter's and of the tower of Malines cathedral, while a choir of bishops sang 'Happy birthday'. The event took place in Beauraing, Belgium's major Marian shrine. The Pope venerated a statue of the Virgin of Beauraing, and met two of the seers of fifty years before. There was a mass at Malines cathedral where the Pope spoke about ecumenism. On 19 May he told trade unionists that 'a noble war should be waged for social justice', a war which required international solidarity. The word 'solidarity' he picked up when speaking to a Polish group. The following day, Monday, he met leaders of the European Council of Ministers, the European Commission and the European Parliament and made a plea for a unity within the continent which crossed the political boundaries between East and West. The contribution of the countries of the Eastern bloc to the heritage of Europe cannot be ignored, he told his audience. His last day of the tour he spent in Banneux, yet another shrine, and at the French-speaking Catholic university of Louvain-la-Neuve.

Just before the Pope left for Holland, on 8 May, Fr Leonardo Boff issued a declaration as he began a period of 'silence' imposed by the Vatican. 'By order of Rome I find myself prevented, for an indeterminate period of time, from making public statements. Before embarking upon this period of penitential silence it seemed appropriate to me to clarify fully certain positions which are liable to misunderstanding: I declare that I am not a Marxist. As a Christian and a Franciscan I am in favour of civil liberties and of the noble struggle for justice in the building up of a new society …' The ban, which also applied to Leonardo's brother Clodovis, came as a surprise: it had seemed that the Vatican would have been content with Boff's promise made in March to abide by the ruling the Vatican had made against him on the basis of his book *Church, Charism and Power*. But it was not only an individual Franciscan that the Pope had in his sights, it was the whole Order.

A General Chapter of the Franciscans opened in Assisi on 13 May. Dated 8 May, but only published in the Vatican newspaper on 13 May, there was a letter from John Paul to members of the Order, couched in language which the Franciscan press officer described as 'strong'. 'Men ask from you a clear evangelical witness and wish you to show to all the nobility of your vocation', he wrote. 'I urge you therefore to proceed with a careful revision of your theories and practices which have shown themselves to be an obstacle to meeting these expectations.' He feared that the Order was suffering 'a ruinous crisis of authority'. The poverty preached by Francis, he said, 'does not exhaust itself in proclamations in defence of the poor', but it had to be truly lived out. To ensure that there was adequate response to these criticisms in the course of the General Chapter, he was, he announced, sending Archbishop Virgilio Fagiolo, Secretary of the Congregation for Religious, to preside over it. John Paul had tackled the Jesuits, instructed the Carmelites to revise their rule, and was now determined to ensure that his vision of the Franciscan vocation be imposed upon the Friars Minor. The Friars responded by re-electing, under the eye of Archbishop Fagiolo, their Minister General to a further term of office. It was a vote of confidence in the way the Order had been run, despite papal criticisms.

At a Vatican press conference on 2 July there was launched *Slavorum Apostoli* (The Apostles of the Slavs) an encyclical to commemorate the eleventh centenary of the missionary work of the brother Saints, Cyril and Methodius[17] whom in December 1980 John Paul II had proclaimed to be patrons of Europe alongside St Benedict (cf. above, p. 91). The encyclical praised them for translating the Bible and the liturgy into the language of the people they were evangelizing. Old Slavonic 'became for many hundreds of years not only the ecclesiastical but also the official and literary language, and even the common language of the more educated classes of the greater part of the Slav nations'. The Saints constituted, he said, a bridge between East and West because, though born and brought up in the Eastern tradition they sought the authority for their labours from the Bishop of Rome. For that reason, went on the Pope, they are examplars of ecumenism: that they wished 'to preserve unity of faith and love between the Churches of which they were members, namely between the Church of Constantinople and the Church of Rome on the one hand, and the Churches which arose in the lands of the Slavs on the other, was and will always remain their great merit'.

In addition to the example they gave of ecumenism, even though at the time the Church was not yet formally divided, and of enculturation, went on the Pope, 'Their work is an outstanding contribution to the formation of the common Christian roots of Europe ... This diversity (of traditions, the one arising from Constantinople the other from Rome), when its origin is properly understood and when its value and meaning are properly considered, can only enrich the culture of Europe and its religious tradition, and likewise become an adequate foundation for its hoped-for spiritual renewal'. He seems to presume that this renewal will come from the East (his social encyclicals make the point that the Eastern bloc is less materialistic than the West), and in this task he clearly sees himself having a prominent role. His own special vocation is to be 'the first son of a Slav race to be called, after nearly two millennia, to occupy the episcopal see that once belonged to Peter in this city of Rome'. And he ended with a prayer: 'Grant to the whole of Europe, O Most Holy Trinity, that through the intercession of the two holy brothers, it may feel ever more strongly the need for religious and Christian unity and for brotherly communion of all its peoples, so that when incomprehension and mutual distrust have been overcome and when ideological conflicts have been conquered in the common awareness of the truth, it may be for the whole world an example of just and peaceful coexistence in mutual respect and inviolate liberty'.

Though published after, the encyclical was undoubtedly written before, a speech by John Paul to cardinals and Vatican officials on 28 June, the eve of the Feast of Sts Peter and Paul. 'The Church must learn to breathe again with its two lungs – the Eastern one and the Western one', but it fell to the Bishop of Rome, he said, to lead the flock of the whole Church. The Church, he insisted, was fully committed to ecumenism. Much had been achieved in the last quarter of a century, but there were still issues dividing the Churches and it was no use agreeing to easy solutions of these problems if this would not lead to anything 'stable or solid'.

The celebrations for St Methodius were held in Velehrad in Czechoslovakia on 7 July. John Paul had received an invitation to attend from the Cardinal of Prague, Archbishop Tomasek. The regime had vetoed it. 'The Pope is present in spirit', said Cardinal Casaroli, one of the few Cardinals able to obtain a visa to visit the country and there as papal legate. 'We want the Pope', chanted some of the 150,000 crowd, and when the Czech minister of culture compared the evangelizing activity of Cyril and Methodius to the liberation of the country by Soviet troops he was, not surprisingly, roundly booed and had hurriedly to revise his text. When, after the celebrations, Casaroli embarked on what he believed to be a round of meetings with government officials to discuss the situation of the Church, the appointments were abruptly cancelled – though the Cardinal managed to meet the President, Gustav Husak. Casaroli cut short his visit.

The Pope spent July as usual at Castel Gandolfo, though slipping off, on one occasion, for a 65-mile flight to allow him to do three hours hill-walking in the Apennines, and then, at the beginning of August, he began his 27th foreign journey and his third visit to Africa. Togo was the first stop. He

The exterior of the house in Wadowice where Karol Wojtyla was born in 1920. It now belongs to a school teacher. (© The Hulton Deutsch Collection)

The interior. (© Topham)

Karol Wojtyla was baptised in this church in Wadowice.

The young Karol Wojtyla (top left).

| Jozef 2nd name | |
Karol Wojtyla	
born: 18th May 1920	in: Wadowice
District: Wadowice	religion: Roman Catholic
pupil class: 8	

Marks in	First 6 months
General Behaviour:	Very Good
Religion:	Very Good
Polish:	Very Good
Latin:	Very Good
Greek:	Very Good
Classics:	———
German:	Very Good
History:	Good
Geography:	———
Nature:	———
Physics & Chemistry:	Good
Mathematics:	Very Good
Elem. Philosophy:	Very Good
Hygiene:	———
Drawing:	———
Singing & Dancing:	———
Handicrafts:	———
Writing:	———
Physical Training:	Very Good

No. of absences: Total: 6   Unexcused: ----
No. of times late: Total: —   Unexcused: ----

Date of report: First 6 months: 23.12.1937
Full schoolyear: —

A 1920 report of the 'very good schoolboy'.
(© Topham)

Karol Wojtyla's school in Wadowice. (© Topham)

Florian Church in Krakow, where Karol Wojtyla was curate in 1947.

(© The Hulton Deutsch Collection)

The young priest in 1948.

(© The Hulton Deutsch Collection)

Lover of the outdoor life, Karol Wojtyla is here pictured during a bicycle trip in the mountains on the Polish-Czech border.

(© Topham)

Karol Wojtyla prays in the Wadowice church following his ordination as bishop.

(© Topham)

Cardinal Wojtyla, Archbishop of Krakow, is pictured with the then Primate of Poland, Cardinal Wyszynski. (© The Hulton Deutsch Collection)

The Pope greets the crowds following his inauguration as Pope. (© Alain Keler/Sygma)

The new Pope's first outdoor audience in St Peter's Square in April 1979. He exchanged the traditional throne for a specially built car. (© The Hulton Deutsch Collection)

The Pope prays at the Krakow tomb of his parents in June 1979. (© Associated Press/Topham)

Banker Roberto Calvi at the beginning of his trial in May 1981.

The Pope collapses in obvious agony moments after the assassination attempt in May 1981.

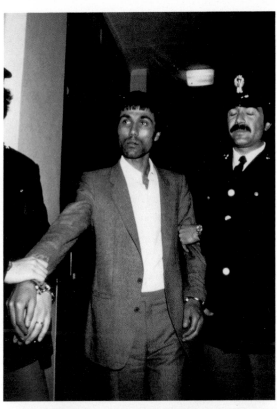

The arrest of the perpetrator, Mehmet Ali Agca.

(© Giansanti/Sygma)

The Pope visits his would-be assassin in prison.

(© Giansanti/Sygma)

John Paul II was the first Pope to attend a service in Canterbury Cathedral, in May 1982. He is pictured with Anglican Archbishop Robert Runcie.
(© The Hulton Deutsch Collection)

The Pope arrives at Westminster Cathedral, London, where he conducted Mass. He is accompanied by Archbishop Marcinckus. (© The Hulton Deutsch Collection)

A March 1983 meeting with Daniel Ortega, head of Nicaragua's ruling *junta*.

Dissident Archbishop Marcel Lefebvre. (© Associated Press/Topham)

The Pope had a brief meeting with President Reagan in Alaska on his way to South Korea, May 1984. (© Giansanti/Sygma)

John Paul II arrives in India in February 1986. He is flanked by President Zail Singh and Prime Minister Rajiv Ghandi. (© Associated Press/Topham)

The following day he met with Tibet's exiled God-King, the Dalai Lama, who presented him with the book he is reading. (© Associated Press/Topham)

John Paul II receives Yasser Arafat, then
leader of the PLO, at the Vatican in
December 1988.

(© Sygma)

The Pope gives the sacrament to Lech Walesa at Gdansk, June 1987. (© Giansanti/Sygma)

John Paul II kisses the ground on arriving in a new country – this time, Ireland – a gesture he would repeat all around the world.

(© Fabian/Sygma)

Mikhail Gorbachev's historic Vatican visit, December 1989. (© Sygma)

German Cardinal Joseph Ratzinger, Head of the Congregation for the Doctrine of the Faith, with the new Catholic Catechism in December 1992. (© Associated Press)

arrived there on 8 August, telling the crowds he had come to strengthen the links of the local community with the universal Church. He showed himself particularly sympathetic to indigenous customs, asking Christians to judge each one against their conscience and to hold on to whatever might be beneficial. The next day he got perhaps rather more than he had bargained for in the way of local customs, when seven masked priests of the traditional religion of Lake Togo escorted him from the lakeside.

The following day he spent five hours in the Ivory Coast, just long enough to consecrate the controversial cathedral in Abidjan, the foundation stone of which he had laid in 1980, then he was off to the Cameroon where, on 11 August, he met Muslim leaders and spoke on behalf of religious liberty as a fundamental human right. He met Muslims again the following day in Yaoundé and greeted Protestant leaders and the Polish community in the country. To the Muslims in Yaoundé he spoke of the elements of religious faith shared both by Islam and by Christianity:

One of the great challenges for mankind of today [is] to learn to live together in a peaceful and constructive manner. It must be acknowledged that we live in an era of 'polarization'. Certain racial and ethnic groups, certain religious communities, likewise certain economic and political ideologies across the world strive to make their points of view prevail, while excluding those which do not share them. They seek to defend their rights to the point of disregarding those of others, to reject proposals for cooperation and human fraternity. It is necessary for Muslims and Chrstians to resist those temptations for they do not lead mankind to those truly good acts, in conformity with the path which God has traced out for all from the beginning. For us, the true way remains that of dialogue. This presents numerous aspects. It means above all learning to respect each other's faith, to overcome prejudices and misunderstandings. It means being tolerant towards differences ...

The President, Paul Biya, and diplomatic corps he met the same day in the Presidential palace. In his address he called upon the international community to send aid to Africa, to take it seriously, to respect its cultural heritage – though he rather pointedly also attacked excessive bureaucracy, corruption, fraud and wastefulness.

The following day he travelled to Cameroon's largest city, Douala, accompanied by a bishop who had been exiled by Biya's predecessor on the charge of conspiring against the head of state. Biya had lifted the ban and the bishop and John Paul were given a rousing reception. He went back to

Yaoundé that afternoon to talk at the university about the need to assimilate the faith into the local culture, and that culture included the spiritual values of the African people. 'A rupture between the Gospel and culture would be a tragedy.' Admirable sentiments, no doubt, but the question remained how far he was prepared to adapt the Gospel, and its expression in the liturgy, into the indigenous culture.

There was another short stopover in the Central African Republic and then the Pope went on to Zaire – it was 15 August – for the beatification of a nun, Anuarite Nengapeta, who in 1964 had been murdered while resisting being raped. The Pope's journeys frequently bring him into contact with rather unsavoury regimes. Addressing President Mobutu of Zaire the Pope pointedly made an appeal for social justice and human rights. This trip to Africa had been timed to coincide with the close of the Eucharistic Congress being held in Kenya. On 18 August he presided at the closing mass of the Congress before going on to the headquarters in Nairobi of the United Nations Environment Programme, where once again, as he had done at the outset of the tour, he condemned South Africa's apartheid policy.[18]

The final stage of John Paul's journey was the most remarkable. He had been invited by King Hassan to visit Morocco. He touched down on Monday 19 August and was greeted by the King personally. It was the first time he had set foot in an Islamic state, apart from his visit to Turkey at the beginning of his pontificate (cf. above, pp. 70-1). King Hassan, who claims direct descent from the Prophet Muhammad, exchanged a kiss of peace with the Pope. He addressed 80,000 young Muslims in Casablanca's football stadium. 'We have understood each other badly and even exhausted each other in polemics and wars', the Pope told them. 'God invites us today to change our habits.' The Pope followed this with a call for mutual respect of religious differences. Later when the visit was over, a Vatican official described it as the most positive step ever taken in the long saga of Christian-Muslim relations. King and Pope met privately for far longer than expected, discussing the Middle East where Lebanon was still tearing itself apart, and the status of Jerusalem.

The position of Israel was obviously a matter which also deeply concerned the world's Jewish community. On 24 June, the Pontifical Commission for Religious Relations with the Jews published a set of 'notes' intended to guide Catholics in studying Judaism. They were entitled *The common bond: the right approach to Catholic-Jewish relations*. As the Chairman of the World Jewish Congress's Inter-religious Affairs Commission, Rabbi Pynches Brener, commented later, 'Some of us felt that some statements in the *Notes* meant we were going to go in a different direction, or were taking a step backward'.

Among the criticisms voiced, for example, by the Chief Rabbi of Great Britain, were a failure to condemn outright anti-Semitism, and in particular a reluctance to attribute any religious significance to the State of Israel. Others were dissatisfied with the 'vague' references to the Holocaust. When John Paul II addressed the liaison committee of the Catholic Church and the International Jewish Committee on Inter-Religious Consultation on 28 October as they celebrated together the 20th anniversary of *Nostra Aetate*, Vatican II's declaration on the Jews and other non-Christian religions, he showed himself conscious of these criticisms which had been made of the *Notes*. In his speech he commended the *Notes*, but he also called for a complete eradication of anti-Semitism, and for greater reflection by Roman Catholics on the Holocaust, and its significance for Jewish identity. The Catholic Church can change, he said. It 'is always prepared, with the help of God's grace, to revise and renew whatever in her attitudes and ways of expression happens to conform less with her own identity, founded upon the Word of God'. The Jews who heard him were encouraged – but were still disappointed at no mention of the State of Israel.

When John Paul returned to Rome from his African journey, however, it was relations with other Christian Churches rather than with other faiths that occupied his attention in the run-up to the Extraordinary Synod. The Secretary General of the Synod announced that ten Churches engaged in ecumenical discussions with Rome were to be invited to send observers to the gathering, though he did not disclose which ten these were. In a letter to an American Lutheran bishop, released on 27 September, the Pope had written 'Can we not aim at making the dawn of the third millennium the beginning of a special time for seeking full unity in Christ?' A few days later, during the meeting of the joint working party of the Catholic Church and the World Council of Churches held near Rome from 30 September to 5 October, the Pope addressed the members, saying that collaboration between the two bodies should be increased.

When the Synod eventually met, opening with a papal mass on 24 November, the ten non-Roman Catholic invitees were revealed. They were: the World Council of Churches and the World Reformed Alliance, the Disciples of Christ, the Lutheran, Anglican, Orthodox, Methodist, Baptist and Pentecostal Churches. That made nine: the Coptic Church had also been invited. Before the Synod began there had been a gathering of cardinals, which opened with a papal address on 21 November. Its agenda was to discuss a proposed reform of the Roman Curia. It also heard yet again about the parlous state of the Vatican's finances. As Pope John Paul pointed out, linking the meeting of the cardinals with the Synod, Vatican II had called for a reform of the Curia. This had been carried out by Paul VI in 1967, but, said the Pope, a further updating was now needed. One of the proposals would have implied a downgrading of the status of the Secretariat for Christian Unity. The status, and work, of the Secretariat was vigorously defended, and a counter-proposal made that it be raised to the rank of a Congregation. In the end the proposed reforms were postponed.

The Synod proper got under way on 25 November, with a lengthy report by Cardinal Godfried Danneels, the Archbishop of Malines-Brussels, based on the responses to the questionnaires filled in by Episcopal Conferences. It had not boded well for the Synod that, after a couple of these, including the response of the bishops of England and Wales, had been published, there was an instruction that responses were to be kept secret. Danneels summarized the positive and the negative responses to the questionnaire. For example, though the bishops in general had said there had been, as a result of Vatican II, greater participation in the liturgy by the laity, it was also the case that in the opinion of some, reported Danneels, the changes in the liturgy had been inadequately prepared. There was also, he said, a need to address the relationship of the local, or particular, Church to the universal Church, thus raising the issue of the theological status of Episcopal Conferences.

Pope John Paul did not speak throughout the Synod, though he attended it all and listened to the bishops' interventions, absenting himself only when voting took place. Danneels summarized the speeches, and proposed a number of points to be discussed by the nine language groups into which the members of the Synod were then divided. The responses of these groups differed markedly. The German-speaking group of which Cardinal Ratzinger was a member spoke of the decline of holiness in the Church, and of the powers of darkness ranged against it. There was too little reverence paid, too little talk of Christ and too much of the Church, they complained. One of the French language groups, that of which Cardinal Lustiger[19] of Paris was a member, also took a pessimistic view of the modern world, as did the report of the group which chose to hold its discussions in Latin. The English-language group of which Cardinal Hume was a member – the only European among them, most being from the Third World – was, on the other hand, far more upbeat in its assessment of the modern world. It called for the canonization of more laypeople, for greater stress on enculturation, and proposed raising the Secretariat of Christian Unity to the status of a Congregation.

The Synod revealed considerable differences of opinion between bishops from the same regions. There was, for example, both inside and outside the

Synod, a strong attack by some Latin American bishops on Liberation Theology, while others spoke equally vigorously in its support. The US bishops were likewise divided over the status of Episcopal Conferences, the president of the US conference arguing that they were an expression of collegiality, or co-responsibility for the Church, while the Archbishop of Philadelphia, Cardinal Krol, put forward the view that they were no more than a useful pastoral instrument.

There were a number of similar disagreements, but one common factor at least emerged: the feeling among the bishops that there was need for a new catechism for the Church. This was something to which John Paul drew attention when he spoke on 7 December at the closing of the formal business of the Synod. It should be, he said, 'a compendium of all Catholic doctrine, to which the catechisms or compendiums of all local Churches would need to refer'. He also highlighted the need for further study of the role of Episcopal Conferences, and commented on the publication of the Code of Canon Law for the Eastern Churches. The need for the catechism was referred to again in the Synod's Final Report. The Report itself took a somewhat gloomy view of the life of the Church twenty years after Vatican II, rather reflecting the perspective adopted by Cardinal Ratzinger and his German-speaking group. The 'Message to the People of God', on the other hand, a brief communiqué approved at the end of the Synod to represent the bishops' outlook as formed by the gathering, was a much more cheerful document, and sensibly urged laypeople to prepare themselves for the 1987 Synod on the Laity, which this Extraordinary Synod had replaced.

NOTES

1. A Vatican nuncio is *de jure* dean of the diplomatic corps in the country in which he is stationed. Where this position would be inappropriate, in non-Roman Catholic countries for example, his title used to be 'pro-nuncio' to avoid an automatic claim to the role of dean. This practice, however, has just been discontinued, unless the receiving government requests no change, and all Vatican ambassadors have the title of nuncio.
2. Three more were added in the course of the year.
3. Casimir (1460–83) was the son of King Casimir IV of Poland, and is also honoured as a patron of Poland itself.
4. For the intriguing story of the secret clergy of Czechoslovakia, see Felix Corley, 'The secret clergy in Communist Czechoslovakia' in *Religion, State and Society* 21, 2 (1993), pp. 171–206.

5. Which means 'the suffering which brings salvation'. The opening words of the English translation do not reflect its Latin title.

6. *The Tablet*, 17 November 1984, p. 1148.

7. Just over a month later Edward Schillebeeckx, the Dominican Professor of Theology at the University of Nijmegen, revealed that he, too, had been questioned by Cardinal Ratzinger, in his case about his book *Ministry: A Case for Change*. He had been accompanied to the interview by the Master General of his Order.

8. Ratzinger was clearly riled by this public display of support for Boff and Gutierrez. He criticized theologians who defended them but, more significantly, in an article in the November issue of the Italian magazine *Jesus* he criticized Episcopal Conferences, insisting, as he had done a year before to the US bishops, that such Conferences have no theological rationale, and that power should be restored to individual bishops in their dioceses.

9. The trip coincided with a letter sent by Mgr Mario Rizzi of the Congregation for Eastern-Rite Churches to Ukrainian-rite Bishop Isidore Borecky in Toronto asking for a list of priests who had been illicitly ordained because they were married. These priests, the Vatican said, were suspended from their functions. They were, went on Mgr Rizzi, provoking a scandal in the Church. The ordination of married men into the Ukrainian-rite priesthood had been banned in North America in 1929, though it was still permitted elsewhere. Some were being ordained in Yugoslavia and then transferred to North America. This, said Mgr Rizzi rather later, was something of a subterfuge.

10. The Jesuit General, Fr Peter Hans Kolvenbach, was also in Latin America in the month of October. In Rio de Janeiro and then in Caracas, he instructed Jesuits to back the preferential option for the poor, and told the *New York Times* that though there may have been mistakes in Liberation Theology, it must none the less be 'recognized as possible and necessary' (cf. *The Tablet*, 10 November 1984, p. 1126).

11. He includes in this 'sins of commission or omission on the part of political, economic, or trade union leaders, who though in a position to do so do not work diligently and wisely for the improvement and transformation of society according to the requirements and potential of the given historical moment; as also on the part of workers who through absenteeism or non-cooperation fail to ensure that their industries advance the well-being of the workers themselves, of their families, and of the whole of society'.

12. Archbishop Fernando Vargas Ruiz S.J., of Arequipa, called a conference on the 'Theology of Reconciliation' as a conscious rejection of the Theology of Liberation which Vargas had expressly forbidden his clergy to use in their pastoral work, following the example of the Archbishop of Cuzco, Alcides Mendoza.

13. Andrej Kreutz, *Vatican Policy on the Palestinian-Israeli Conflict* (New York, Greenwood Press, 1990), p. 161.

14. ibid.

15. 'Effectively' because the rule of the Discalced Carmelites was, at least in theory,

a return to the primitive observance of the Order.

16. Such was the hostility that a group was arrested for putting up posters advertising a reward for anyone killing the Pope: the price was roughly £3,500!

17. In fact it was the eleventh centenary of the death of Methodius. Cyril – after whom the 'Cyrillic' alphabet is named – had died in 869.

18. Rupert Murdoch, the newspaper magnate, claimed in July that the Pope might start writing a column for his chain of newspapers. The first of these appeared, with the by-line 'Pope John Paul II', in the conservative Madrid daily *ABC* on 7 September. It consisted of a selection of quotes from the Pope's addresses, in this instance on apartheid. The heading was later changed, at the Vatican's insistence, to 'Selected Observations of Pope John Paul II'.

19. On Lustiger's views, and their similarity to those of the Pope, see Paul Blanquart, 'Quand l'apologétique se fait au nom d'Auschwitz' in René Luneau (ed.), *Le rêve de Compostelle*, Paris, Centurion, 1989.

SEVEN

1986-7

THERE WAS the usual papal message for the 1 January World Day of Peace. It was entitled 'Peace is a value without frontiers. North-South, East-West: Only one peace'. Two weeks later in a letter dated 16 January 1986, John Paul instructed the Bishops' Conferences of Europe, headed by Westminster's Cardinal Basil Hume, to cooperate with each other so they might more effectively face 'the divisions from which Europe was suffering', divisions which included the religious East-West divide, and that between Catholicism and Protestantism. There should be a new evangelization of Europe, he said, and 'complete commitment to the cause of ecumenism'. On 25 January he announced that he would invite leaders of all major religions, Christian and non-Christian, to come to Assisi to pray with him for the peace of the world. On 1 February, he set off on a visit to India.

India's Catholic population is tiny in proportion to the total of 800 million citizens: but at 14,000,000[1] it was still a substantial body. Some early Jesuit missionaries had attempted, as they did in China, to adapt the faith to the essentially Hindu culture in which they found themselves. In so far as the Latin rite of the sixteenth- and seventeeth-century missionaries was concerned, such experiments came to an end in India, as had those in China, by decree from Rome. But there were – and still are – quasi-indigenous Churches in communion with Rome[2] that claim to trace their origins back to the Apostle Thomas. While Western scholars may be sceptical, there is no doubt that the Syro-Malabar and the Syro-Malankar Catholics have enjoyed a long and proud history. When bishops from the two Churches visited Rome shortly before John Paul set off for India, he described them as 'rooted in the Indian soil and adapted to the Indian way of life'. But they had their own problems to which the Vatican did not find an easy solution. They were concerned that when Catholics belonging to either of these two Churches moved from their Southern Indian heartland to other parts of the subcontinent or abroad, they were obliged to come under the jurisdiction of

Latin-rite bishops. In some of the larger cities of India Syrian-rite chaplains had been appointed, but there were demands for chaplains throughout the country and elsewhere, presenting Rome with a serious problem of double jurisdiction being exercised in that particular territory.

An even more tricky problem was that of relations with non-Christian religions. Militant Hindus – almost a contradiction in terms – had demanded that either the Pope was welcomed as a head of State, and therefore officially by the government, which was what the government intended, but then he must not be allowed to take part in religious ceremonies because that would amount to proselytizing; or he should be treated as a religious leader, and his presence therefore ignored by the state.

John Paul's first stop was New Delhi, to be welcomed by the Indian President, and to lay a wreath at the spot where Mahatma Gandhi had been cremated. Such a ceremony was required by protocol: to observers, however, it seemed that to John Paul this was much more than a necessary ritual. He knelt in prayer for nearly six minutes – he had to be roused from contemplation by the Papal pro-nuncio so that he would not fall behind his schedule – and made a speech in which he praised Gandhi and called for an end to terrorism. The following day at the Indira Gandhi Stadium he met Hindu, Sikh and Moslem leaders and called for collaboration in eliminating 'every enslavement of the human spirit'. He met – for the third time – the Dalai Lama. He met the 124 bishops of India and told them the Vatican would soon sort out the problems which had arisen over conflicts of jurisdiction among the rites. He also reminded them of the need for interreligious dialogue and respect for the other religions of India.

From Delhi he went to Bihar to speak to the tribes who, because they had found no place in the Hindu caste system, had turned to Christianity. Over 400,000 attended an open-air mass at which John Paul condemned discrimination based upon 'religion, caste, community or language'. From Ranchi[3] in Bihar he went on to Calcutta to a mass for a quarter of a million people. Next, he held his much-publicized meeting with Mother Teresa, spending an hour visiting her first hospice for the dying of the city, consoling and helping to feed those who lived there. What is the meaning of suffering? he asked the crowd who had gathered outside. He confessed he did not know, but through the ministrations of Mother Teresa and her Missionaries of Charity Christ had come to be loved by the people of Calcutta.

In Madras the Pope prayed at the spot where it was claimed the Apostle Thomas had been martyred, and in the cathedral believed to be built over his tomb. In Goa he venerated the body of St Francis Xavier, the sixteenth-century Jesuit missionary. In Kerala he beatified a Syro-Malabar priest, Fr Kuriakose Elias Chavare, and a nun, Sr Alphonsa, in a service conducted according to the local rite.

In Bombay he had a meeting with the Archbishop of Canterbury who was also visiting India at the time. Later, in the same teeming city, he spoke on the delicate topic of contraception. The government was actively promoting artificial birth control in an effort to limit population growth, and the campaign, at least in the decline in the number of births, was apparently particularly effective in some of the more Catholic regions of the country. The Pope was able to quote Mahatma Gandhi's endorsement of birth-control, but rejection of 'immoral and artificial means'. He left India on 9 February. Apart from a brief demonstration between the airport and the nation's capital as the Pope arrived, none of the threats which had been made before the visit materialized. It was on one level another triumph, but it left untouched problems between the Catholic rites, and problems between the Church and what was basically a Hindu society.

Which was not surprising. The Vatican was finding it difficult enough elsewhere to come to terms with traditionally Roman Catholic societies, for example in Latin America. The Brazilian Bishops' Conference, whose 289 members were divided for administrative purposes into fourteen separate regions, each region making a separate *ad limina* visit to Rome, decided that they ought to make representations as one single group. The president of the conference, Bishop Ivo Lorscheiter, went off to the Vatican to discuss the proposal, together with the presidents of each of the regions and the country's five cardinals. The three-day meeting began and ended with a papal address, though that at the close, on 15 March, was the more important. The avowed purpose was to assist the various offices of the Roman Curia ('the faithful associates of the pontifical ministry', according to John Paul) to understand better the problems of the country as a whole. The gathering met under the aegis of the Congregation for Bishops, but was attended every morning and afternoon by the Pope himself, and by ten cardinals representing their respective Congregations including Cardinal Ratzinger as head of the Congregation for the Doctrine of the Faith. It was of course this Congregation which had produced the much criticized Instruction on Liberation Theology. The Pope told the bishops that a more positive document was now being prepared by the same Congregation. The Theology of Liberation, said the Pope, was 'not only orthodox but necessary', and though he again warned the bishops against mistaking the Church's role as a political rather than a religious one, he urged the bishops to defend a

Liberation Theology cleansed of its distortions. This was all in his prepared text, but the Pope went on spontaneously for a full forty-five minutes, stressing the need for communion among the bishops, and for dialogue as a means to communion. It could have been interpreted as communion between Brazil and Rome but, given the tense relations with the Brazilian Bishops' Conference, it was to be taken both ways. Despite the tensions over Liberation Theology and the writings of Leonardo Boff, the Brazilian bishops generally regarded the March meeting as distinctly positive in tone: a year-long ban on new publications by Boff was lifted in the aftermath of the meeting, a month or so before the punishment imposed in 1985 would otherwise have run its full course.

And then, on 5 April, the Congregation of the Doctrine of the Faith published the much-heralded 'positive' Instruction on Liberation Theology. The warnings about the dangers of Liberation Theology contained in the first had not been superseded, it insisted, and in its first chapter pointed to 'serious ambiguities' in the meanings attached to the word 'freedom' in the modern world. It pointed out again the dangers of Marxism, and claimed that the poor understood 'instinctively' that the 'most radical liberation' is that from sin and death, achieved by Christ. The Church's essential mission, the document goes on, is to preach that message, but that preaching must also extend to justice, and the desire to assist people's temporal as well as spiritual needs:

Thus the Church is being faithful to her mission when she condemns the forms of deviation, slavery and oppression of which people are the victims. She is being faithful to her mission when she opposes attempts to set up a form of social life from which God is absent, whether by deliberate opposition or by culpable negligence. She is likewise being faithful to her mission when she exercises her judgement regarding political movements which seek to fight poverty and oppression according to theories or methods of action which are contrary to the Gospel and opposed to man himself.

The poor, claimed the Instruction, are the object of preferential love on the part of the Church which 'in spite of the failings of many of her members has not ceased to work for their relief, defence and liberation'. On the vexed question of 'social sin' the document insisted on the priority of conversion of heart for an individual, but acknowledged also that structures had to be changed in 'certain' countries because they could destroy 'all honest social life'. It was therefore essential to work both for conversion of heart and the improvement of structures. The Vatican also condemned violence, the class struggle, the 'myth of revolution' – because the last only too easily leads to the establishment of totalitarian regimes.

The document then shifts very largely to a typical example of the social teaching of John Paul II with its emphasis on work as the foundation of the social order: 'Just work relationships will be a necessary precondition for a system of political community capable of favouring the integral development of every individual'. Work must bring financial rewards sufficient to enable the worker and his family 'to have access to a truly human standard of living' materially, socially, culturally and spiritually – and the Instruction specifically applies this demand to agricultural workers in the Third World. The document ends on what is also a quintessentially papal note: an appeal to Mary and the Magnificat, a prayer much used by Liberation Theologians. It was dated 22 March, though it appeared a fortnight later.

When it was launched at a Vatican press conference Cardinal Ratzinger insisted that this later Instruction should be read in the light of the earlier one. The first, however, was basically a negative judgement from the perspective of a traditional theology. The new document was different in tone as well as perspective. It was well received. Gustavo Gutierrez, the founding father of Liberation Theology, welcomed it as putting an end to the 'painful debates'.[4] The Brazilian bishops, who had been expecting something of the sort, were equally positive. Moreover, a letter from the Pope to the Brazilian bishops as they met in conference, and dated 12 April, was hailed by one of the most progressive of the bishops (though himself a Spaniard), Pedro Casaldáliga of São Félix, as 'practically making [Liberation Theology] official within the Church'. The Instruction itself had been hopeful but the letter, with two explicit mentions of the value of Liberation Theology, had united the bishops, said Casaldáliga.

The Instruction was indeed remarkable. It had at least as much in common with a typical social encyclical of John Paul II as with a ukase from the Congregation for the Doctrine of the Faith. There was still evidence of an understandable papal fixation with Marxism, but if, as seems highly likely from the approach of the Instruction, the Pope had a hand in its drafting, then his travels, and his contacts with Peruvian and – especially – Brazilian bishops had undoubtedly taught him a great deal.

The document was also typical of the Pope's approach in the place it gave to the search for 'truth' through science, technology and so on, and that truth being the ultimate criterion against which all else must be judged: 'man becomes free to the extent that he comes to a knowledge of the truth, and to the extent that this truth – and not any other forces – guides his will'. As a philosophical statement it is something with which, no doubt, few would wish to disagree. Problems arise because of difficulties either in discovering 'truth', or in agreeing what, in any particular situation, the truth may be. These were, however, problems which the Pope, for all his philosophical training, does not appear to share.

Though in the immediate aftermath of its publication Leonardo Boff greeted the Instruction with enthusiasm, his second thoughts were more guarded, and arose specifically from the abstract, philosophical tone in which much of it was couched. In an open letter to Ratzinger published in a Brazilian newspaper and signed also by Leonardo's brother Clodovis, he wrote that while it was true that the essential Christian liberation was spiritual, it had to be linked to liberation from poverty: 'Without an insertion into concrete history, faith in God does not go beyond an "opium", and God himself is transformed into an "idol" '. Clearly the debate was not over.

At the beginning of April the John Paul II Institute for the Study of Marriage and the Family and the Academic Centre of the Holy Cross, a recently-opened study centre in Rome run by, and for members of, Opus Dei, joined forces in an international conference on moral theology. The Pope addressed the gathering on 10 April, using the occasion to attack 'moral relativism' which he described as 'distrust in the wisdom of God'. There were, he insisted, some moral norms which were always and in every case true: he instanced contraception or the direct killing of an innocent person. He went on to argue that philosophical ethics were by themselves inadequate, only in a theological form could they provide a complete answer to people's moral questions. This, he said, gave the Church an especial place in ethical debate because 'it enjoys the *charisma veritatis certum*, the sure charism of truth' (Dei Verbum 8). He had harsh words for those who appealed against the 'Church's moral *magisterium*' to the 'faith of the Church': 'One can also reach a point of violating the fundamental right of the faithful to receive from those teaching theology, with official approval, the doctrine of the Church rather than the opinion of theological schools'.

There was a particular context for the last remark. Charles Curran, a moral theologian and professor in the theology faculty of Washington's Catholic University of America, had been under investigation since 1979 for his views on sexual ethics. On 10 October 1985 he received a letter from Ratzinger as prefect of the Congregation for the Doctrine of the Faith requiring him to 'retract those positions which violate the conditions necessary for a professor to be called a Catholic theologian'. Curran had not lectured on sexual ethics at the Catholic University for fifteen years, and was prepared, if requested, never to do so again, a compromise approved by the chairman of the University's board of trustees, Cardinal Joseph Bernardin. The Archbishop of Chicago well understood the damaging debate that would arise about academic freedom in Catholic institutions of learning should Catholic University move to dismiss Fr Curran. To the Vatican, that solution was unacceptable: academic freedom was not something that mattered in the context. Curran denied that he had ever rejected any dogma or defined doctrine of the Catholic Church and insisted that if he ever came to deny the faith of the Church he would leave …[5] In his 10 April address the Pope was arguing that the duty of Catholic theologians to obey the *magisterium* (i.e., the teaching received from Rome) went beyond defined doctrine. But by implication he was also saying that if Catholic moral teaching depended upon the Church's theology, then the traditional position, traditional at least among Thomists, that ethics were founded on human nature and therefore in principle available to all, Christian and non-Christian alike, was inadequate. An ethical norm to be found in faith rather than in philosophy is not open to everyone to discover.

As has been recorded earlier (cf. above, pp. 111-13, 145-6), Pope John Paul had gradually begun to change his attitude to the State of Israel. On 13 April 1986 he gave the most dramatic evidence of a changing attitude to the Jewish people themselves when he visited the central synagogue of Rome, situated within the ancient Jewish ghetto of the city. In his address he made no mention of Israel but instead looked forward to better relations between Judaism and Catholicism as religious faiths. He cited Vatican II's declaration on non-Christian religions; he denied that the Jewish people could be blamed for the death of Christ or that there could be any theological justification for discrimination against them; he emphasized the close links, only then being rediscovered, between Judaism and the origins of Christianity. 'With Judaism', he said, 'we have a relationship which we do not have with any other religion. You are our dearly beloved brothers and, in a certain way, it could be said that you are our elder brothers.'

John Paul made no apology for the 'silences' of the wartime Pope Pius XII when confronted with evidence of the wholesale slaughter of Jews across Europe. Instead he expressed his horror at the genocide, and drew attention to the Catholic institutions, seminaries, convents, even the Vatican itself, which gave shelter to Jews during the Second World War. He did not mention – as the president of Rome's Jewish community did – that it was a Pope, Paul IV, who established the ghetto in the city in 1555, placing restrictions upon the Jewish community which were not entirely removed until the capture of Rome, and the final end of the papal states, in 1870. It was a delicate balancing act, especially for a Polish pontiff. John Paul was greeted with enthusiasm. He was the first pope to have entered a synagogue. It seemed as though a new era was dawning in Jewish-Christian dialogue. But, as events were later to show, the Vatican had not wholly grasped the reasonable sensitivities of the Jewish people. There was a Jewish-Christian conflict about to make headlines, and it arose within the jurisdiction of his old archiepiscopal see of Cracow.

The day after John Paul went to the Rome synagogue a delegation of French Jews met the Primate of Poland, Cardinal Glemp, then on a visit to France, to ask him to persuade a group of ten Carmelite nuns to move the convent they intended to build at Auschwitz to a site some miles away. A few days later the President of the World Jewish Congress declared that the idea for a convent 'offends us, saddens us, infuriates us'. The Superior General of the Sisters of Sion, a congregation of nuns whose purpose is to foster Jewish-Christian dialogue, commented that the proposal suggested 'a total lack of awareness of what Auschwitz is for the Jewish people'. Of the plan to erect a cross there she remarked that it showed 'ignorance of what the cross has meant in Jewish history and the bitter memories it still evokes'.

The project became almost as much an issue of Polish nationalism as a religious one, with the (male) Carmelite superior in Poland protesting about foreign interference in the affairs of his country. The proposal for the convent, he said, had the approval of the Polish government as well as Church authorities. The 'Church authorities' in this case was the Cardinal Franciszek Marcharski, the Archbishop of the Pope's former diocese, Cracow, within whose boundaries the concentration camp of Auschwitz lay. He was a vigorous defender of the convent, for which he had obtained permission in June 1984.[6] Pointing out that the Polish Franciscan Maximilian Kolbe, canonized by John Paul in 1982, had died there, as well as Edith Stein, a Carmelite herself but a convert from Judaism, he claimed in a sermon, later published in the Pope's semi-official newspaper *L'Osservatore Romano*, that Auschwitz 'belongs without distinction to all mankind and to every nation'.[7] Unhappily Edith Stein, to whom the Pope has a special devotion, saw the persecution of the Jews precisely as a curse which they had brought upon themselves through cooperating in the death of Christ.

For Pentecost Sunday, 18 May, Pope John Paul produced what he presented as the third part of his study of the Trinity, the encyclical *Dominum et Vivificantem. Redemptor Hominis* in 1979 had discussed the Second Person of the Trinity; the following year *Dives in Misericordia* had spoken of the Father; *Dominum et Vivificantem* dwelt on the Holy Spirit. 'The Conciliar texts', he wrote at the beginning of the new encyclical, 'thanks to their teaching on the Church in herself and the Church in the World, move us to penetrate ever more deeply into the Trinitarian mystery of God himself, through the Gospels, the Fathers and the liturgy: to the Father, through Christ, and in the Holy Spirit.' He does not here mention the Old Testament but it is, typically, much quoted, especially in the first part of the encyclical. He lays particular emphasis upon Isaiah, 'sometimes called "the fifth gospel" or "the gospel of the Old Testament" '. To read the Old Testament in the light of the New may be anathema to modern biblical scholars, but in doing so the Pope was in a long line of more traditional exegesis.

The era of the Church, went on the Pope, began with the coming of the Spirit at Pentecost. It is the Holy Spirit who provides continuity from the work of Christ in the redemption to the work of the Church in preaching Christ to the world. When Christ, in his last discourse in the upper room, promised to send the Spirit to 'convince the world concerning sin', this was part of the redemption. 'Convincing about sin and righteousness has as its purpose the salvation of the world.' This moves the Pope, by way of a discussion of the redemptive value of Christ's sacrifice, to consider conscience: 'In the depths of his conscience man detects a law which he does not impose upon himself, but which holds him to obedience'. This means that conscience is the voice of God, even if not recognized as such, and is not an independent means of deciding for oneself what is good or evil. It is possible to 'close oneself up in sin', says the Pope, and thus shut oneself off from redemption, but it is the action of the Spirit of truth to convince us of sin, and therefore to open us to the possibility of salvation.

In the final part of the encyclical John Paul returns to another common theme, the end of the second millennium and the celebration of the 2000th anniversary of the birth of Christ. This jubilee, he says, 'should be for everyone a special occasion for meditating on the Triune God', but unhappily there are obstacles in the way of coming closer to God through the Holy Spirit:

> The resistance to the Holy Spirit which Saint Paul emphasizes in the interior and subjective dimension as tension, struggle and rebellion taking place in the human heart, finds in every period of history and especially in the modern era its external dimension, which takes concrete form as the content of culture and civilization, as a philosophical system, an ideology, a programme for action and

for shaping human behaviour. It reaches its clearest expression in materialism ... The system which has developed most and carried to its extreme practical consequences this form of thought, ideology and praxis is dialectical and historical materialism, which is still recognized as the essential core of Marxism.

Materialism 'means the acceptance of death as the definitive end of human existence ... human life is nothing but an "existence in order to die" ', goes on the Pope, adding that 'the symptoms of death' have become increasingly part of our world – he mentions the nuclear arms race, poverty and famine, war and terrorism – 'of taking the lives of human beings even before they are born, or before they reach the natural point of death', practices, he says, which have become so widely established that in some places they are almost an institution. Against this culture of materialism are set Christians who,

> as witnesses to man's authentic dignity, by their obedience to the Holy Spirit contribute to the manifold 'renewal of the face of the earth', working together with their brothers and sisters in order to achieve and put to good use everything that is good, noble and beautiful in the modern progress of civilization ...

And then, after a reflection upon the Eucharist and a call to overcome the divisions which separate Christians at the Eucharistic table, Pope John Paul went on

> I trust that all will find in the teaching of this encyclical nourishment for their interior life, and that they will succeed in strengthening, under the action of the Spirit, their commitment to prayer in harmony with the Church and her *magisterium*.

And so, with a final call to obedience to the *magisterium*, the Pope ends. It was not a contentious document, indeed it has been widely praised by theologians for its teaching on the Holy Spirit. Otherwise it aroused little or no debate, though in Chile Señora Lucia Pinochet, wife of the dictator, quoted it at a press conference to claim that on Marxism the bishops of the country were out of step with the Pope, while the Patriarch of Moscow and All Russia complained that it pushed Catholics away from Marxism and in the direction of capitalism and consumerism.

The appeal for unity among Christians which was contained in the concluding part of *Dominum et Vivificantem* was no doubt heartfelt, but as the

Pope was only too well aware, there were new difficulties on the horizon which would make the search for unity, at least in the view of Rome, considerably more problematic. On 30 June, at a press conference at Lambeth Palace, the London home of the Archbishop of Canterbury, an exchange of letters between Rome and Canterbury was released on the subject of the ordination of women. The Church of England was moving, as other parts of the Anglican Communion had already done, to the elevation of women to the priesthood. The night before the press conference the Archbishop of Westminster, Cardinal Hume, said in a televised interview that the ordination of women would both make unity harder to achieve, and quite possibly lead to an unfortunate division within the Church of England itself. They were prophetic words.

The first of the four letters released on 30 June was from John Paul to Robert Runcie, the Archbishop of Canterbury, dated 20 December 1984. It was, as the Archbishop said in his reply, a 'frank' letter. The Pope insisted, citing Pope Paul VI, that the ordination of women within the Anglican Communion constituted 'an element of grave difficulty' to dialogue between the Churches – though he added, also quoting Pope Paul, that 'obstacles do not destroy mutual commitment to a search for reconciliation'. The Archbishop of Canterbury replied almost a year later, on 11 December 1985. The delay, he explained, was to allow time to consult the other primates of the Anglican communion. He admitted that the issue was 'a divisive matter not only between our Churches but within them', but he added that those parts of the Anglican Communion which had ordained women had done so for serious doctrinal reasons, and these he was outlining in a letter to Cardinal Jan Willebrands, as president of the Secretariat for Promoting Christian Unity.

In the letter to Willebrands, dated 18 December 1985, Archbishop Runcie honestly admitted his own hesitations about the appropriateness of the Church of England deciding for itself to ordain women, though he also cited the fact that where they had been ordained elsewhere in the Anglican Communion the experience was 'generally beneficial'. He isolated the central doctrinal argument as being about the priest representing Christ, and Christ having taken upon himself human nature. Though Christ was male, the presence of women in the ministerial priesthood would make the representative nature of the priesthood all the clearer, because it would then reflect the fullness of human nature as both male and female. Willebrands' reply, dated 17 June 1986, took up Runcie's observation on the propriety of one major part of the Christian Church deciding for itself that it would depart from the tradition and ordain women. The Roman Catholic Church had the same hesitation, he said, and so had the Orthodox. But to the substantive doctrinal argument which Runcie had used, he had little to say except to repeat that Christ's 'male identity is an inherent feature of the economy of salvation', and that the priest stands in *persona Christi* – 'in the person of Christ'. It was not an argument but an assertion. Ecumenists put the best face on it that they could, but movement towards reunion at least between the Roman Catholic and the Anglican Communions was effectively stalled.

From 1 to 7 July the Pope visited Colombia, his thirtieth trip overseas since his election, and his seventh to Latin America. As he flew from Rome he explained to journalists that he had refused to mediate with the M-19 guerrillas who the previous November had taken over the Palace of Justice in central Bogotá, a siege which ended in more than a hundred deaths, because such mediation was the responsibility of the government or the local hierarchy. The guerrillas, who had requested a meeting in a letter sent to John Paul in June, promised not to disrupt his tour. In this, perhaps the most violent of the countries the Pope had so far visited (some 300,000 people, it was estimated, had been killed in guerrilla activity over the previous 30 years), the chief message was an end to hatred and to violence. 'Put an end to the destruction and death of so many innocent people', appealed the Pope during an outdoor mass before a crowd of 800,000 on 2 July. The journey followed the established pattern. John Paul visited a slum on 3 July, and went on to the country's (and indeed one of Latin America's) best known Marian shrines at Chiquinquira. He spoke out on the rights of peasants. At Medellín, where in 1968 the Conference of Latin American Bishops (CELAM) had issued a lengthy document applying Vatican II to the situation in Latin America and thereby, at least indirectly, giving rise to the Theology of Liberation, he stressed that while the Church endorsed the preferential option for the poor it could not itself become political. He visited Armero where a volcanic eruption had caused the deaths, and buried the corpses, of some 23,000 people. The eruption had taken place only a few months previously and experts feared a repetition. The Pope's visit was limited to a ten-minute stay, followed by a trip to the nearby settlement of 3,000 survivors. On his last day he visited the shrine of the seventeeth-century Jesuit saint Peter Claver who had worked with the slaves imported from Africa into Cartagena. There the Pope condemned the trade in drugs, 'a new and more subtle form of slavery'. In a final speech he appeared to be claiming for the Church a major role in the abolition of the slave trade, then he was on his way back to Rome, via a brief stopover at St Lucia in the Windward Isles. It had been another success, judged by the size of the crowds and the enthusiasm with which John Paul was greeted. The violence, however, continued.

The Pope's determination that the Church should stay out of politics was demonstrated in July. The Archbishops of Chihuahua, Mexico, and of Mexico City had ordered all the churches in their dioceses to close on 20 July in protest against fraud in the recent elections. The Pope countermanded the decisions of the two archbishops. The mass should never be 'an instrument of politically-motivated pressure', said the apostolic delegate in Mexico, delivering the papal judgement.

But what did it mean for the Church to stay out of politics? Italian Catholic Action, well over half a million members strong, was criticized by the Pope at its annual general meeting for, in effect, being too discreet a presence in Italian politics. At one time Catholic Action had been a major force behind the Christian Democratic Party, and had produced some of that party's most distinguished leaders. It had supported the Church in campaigning vigorously against the divorce legislation (cf. above, p. 93-4), and had lost a battle which was seen by most Italians as an effort by the Church to prevent an advance in human rights. The option chosen by Catholic Action was to retreat as a body from the public arena, and to concentrate on the formation of its own members for service to the Church and world as individuals. The Pope's address seemed to be expressing a desire that Catholics should act together as a public force.

The implication could only be that John Paul was much more sympathetic to the activist role taken by Communione et Liberazione (CL), a movement originally founded for secondary schools in Milan by Fr (by this time Monsignor) Luigi Giussani but which spread to those in higher education after the student unrest of the late 1960s. CL's origins lay at least in part with Giussani's conviction that Catholic Action, which he had served as a chaplain, was ineffectual. By 1986 it not only had a political wing, Movimento Popolare, but a thousand or so town councillors, theoretically at least acting in support of the Christian Democratic Party. The Italian bishops were hesitant about support for CL: Pope John Paul was not. His criticisms of Catholic Action were couched in language that served as an endorsement for the activist role of CL; one of its members was the highest-placed layperson in the Roman Curia. John Paul stopped short of expressing support that there should be a Catholic political party. He was, however, sympathetic to CL's conviction that Catholic ideals and values should be given where necessary the force of law.[8]

On 4 October Pope John Paul few to Lyons: the President, François

Mitterand, was there to meet him. He had come, said the Pope, on a spiritual mission, to visit shrines and to pay homage to saints. It was therefore appropriate that the first event was an ecumenical service in honour of the martyrs of AD 177 in the Roman amphitheatre of the city. 'What have you done', he sternly asked the French, 'with the heritage of martyrs?' It was a good question. A poll on the eve of the Pope's visit revealed that while 81 per cent of the population would describe themselves as Catholics, over 60 per cent never practised, and 46 per cent of all Catholics did not agree with the Pope on sexual morality. There are laws, he said, styles of life, currents of thinking in France which undermine the Christian faith.

There was a risk that the Lyons gathering might not after all have been ecumenical. The non-Roman Catholic Church leaders invited to attend discovered their podium was not as high as that of the Pope: eventually he sat among them. Security was intense. There had been a terrorist campaign in Paris, and this, mixed with newspaper speculations about the Pope's safety based on the prophecies of Nostradamus, had the authorities on edge.

In the afternoon at Lyons there was a beatification of a French priest who had worked with the city's poor, and in his address the Pope emphasized the Church's commitment to the preferential option for the poor. The next day there was a trip to the ecumenical community at Taizé where priests form 57 different countries had been gathered to greet him. Taizé was followed by the shrine of the Sacred Heart of Jesus, at Paray-le-Monial, and yet another gathering at Lyons, this time of young people, animated by tableaux representing the Christian history of the city – and three long discourses by the Pope.

Monday 6 October the Pope spent mainly in Ars, the parish of the saintly curé who is patron of all diocesan clergy. It was the 200th anniversary of his birth, an anniversary that was the ostensible reason for this third visit to France. John Paul visited the house where John Vianney was born, and the church at Ars where his relics are now preserved. There was a retreat going on for 6,000 priests, student priests, and deacons. St John Vianney was a model for them all, said the Pope, in combating secularization. He consoled them with the thought – his conviction – that the identity crisis for priests which had arisen in the aftermath of Vatican II was now over. His final day, apart from a mass in Annecy, was spent in meetings in Lyons – with members of the Catholic University, with leaders of the Jewish and, separately, the Muslim communities, and with the French Prime Minister. He left for Rome at 8.00 pm.

It was a short flight. The brief visit may have cost the French Church a great deal in terms of effort as well as expense (the Archdiocese of Lyons having overestimated receipts and underestimated expenses had to appeal to the faithful for 3 million francs) but for the Vatican it was relatively cheap. Which was just as well. There was a meeting of the council for economic affairs of the Vatican – its fifteen members were all cardinals – on 20 and 21 October. The (limited)[9] figures it provided afterwards revealed that the Vatican estimated a budget deficit of $56.3 million against an income of only $51.9 million. It was, in other words, spending more than twice its income. Hitherto the loss had been made good, at least in part, by 'Peter's Pence', once a tax but now a free-will offering by the faithful to the Pope. But, quite apart from the propriety of using the money in this way, Peter's Pence itself had been falling in value, especially, it was said, since the Banco Ambrosiano affair: in 1985 $28.5 million had been donated and used to meet the Vatican's debt.

While Roman Catholic prelates are for the most part hesitant about criticizing Vatican theology, they are less inhibited about the Vatican's financial management. The Vatican's budget is smaller than some of the larger archdioceses, commented Cardinal Krol, Archbishop of Philadelphia and a member of the council for economic affairs. He clearly thought it about time a full and accurate statement was presented to the world at large. He noted one particular reason for the Vatican's predicament: there was no pension fund. Staff pensions had to be paid out of income. As it was, staff costs amounted to 55 per cent of the budget.

The Pope's next trip was also inexpensive: he went to Assisi for the meeting, on 27 October, of religious leaders of a wide range of faiths to pray for peace. It was an odd gathering. Pride of place – next to the Pope who was, after all, the host – was given to the Christian denominations, above all to Robert Runcie the Archbishop of Canterbury, but when they all came together they met in a circle. There were Buddhists and Moslems, Shintoists and Sikhs. There were African and Amerindian animists: the latter passed round a pipe of peace. There was a walk, supposedly a pilgrimage, around the streets of Assisi with John Paul at its head and Robert Runcie trying, not too successfully, to make conversation. There was also prayer, each in his or her own way, though the various strands of Christianity got together in the Our Father which the Pope led, a reading of the Beatitudes (by Runcie) and a prayer for peace from the Vice-President of the Lutheran World Federation who was, seemingly, the only woman entitled to call herself a religious leader in the sense of the meeting at Assisi. There was a waving of olive branches and a release of doves. Catholics, admitted the Pope with a sideways glance at the crusades which Francis of Assisi had tried, and failed, to halt, had not always been peacemakers. 'Either we learn to walk together in peace and harmony, or we drift apart and ruin ourselves and others', he said. 'We hope that this pilgrimage to Assisi has taught us anew to be aware of the common origin and the common destiny of humanity. Let us see in it an anticipation of what God would like the developing history of humanity to be: a fraternal journey in which we accompany one another toward the transcendent goal which he set for us.' It was, he told a gathering of Roman clergy in December, 'the religious event of the year'.

While Amerindian animists, whose belief in a transcendent God would be minimal, were invited on the 'fraternal journey', there was a group of Catholics who were being abandoned: the homosexual community. An (undated) letter was issued from the Congregation of the Doctrine of the Faith shortly after the Assisi gathering. Its first purpose was to tighten up on the 'Declaration on Certain Questions Concerning Sexual Ethics', issued by the same Congregation at the end of 1975 and given, in the view of Cardinal Ratzinger, an 'overly benign interpretation' as far as homosexuality was concerned: 'Although the particular inclination of the homosexual person is not a sin, it is a more or less strong tendency ordered towards an intrinsic moral evil; and thus the inclination itself must be seen as an objective disorder'.

The new document was uncompromising: the homosexual condition was condemned by Scripture and moral theology; those groups and pastors who worked on behalf of homosexuals were being misled; though violence against homosexuals was wholly wrong, it was not at all surprising; though there should be pastoral care programmes, no authentic one 'will include organizations in which homosexual persons associate with each other without clearly stating that homosexual activity is wrong'.

In the evening of Tuesday 18 November Pope John Paul set off on his 32nd, and longest, overseas tour. His first stop, the following morning, was Dhaka in Bangladesh. He said mass before 25,000 people and ordained 18 priests. He spoke of the spiritual resources Christians and Moslems had in common. He claimed that the day at Assisi demonstrated that the world's religions were evolving a 'harmony of mind' about justice and peace. In the evening he met the country's bishops in the papal nunciature.

On Thursday he flew to Singapore for a stay of only five hours, and so on to Fiji to be greeted by dead silence – though unnerving, it was a sign of deep respect – sat patiently throughout a two-hour ceremony of welcome from local chiefs, and was served at mass by men in grass skirts. He spent Friday in

Fiji, and arrived on Saturday in Auckland, New Zealand, to be welcomed by a Maori haka, a dance better known to the British by its regular performance before each match by the formidable New Zealand rugby team.

For New Zealanders the Pope's predominant theme was ecumenism, though an ecumenism which 'is not afraid to acknowledge the differences and divisions which still exist among Christians', speaking to the Catholic bishops, and one which 'makes new demands on the other Churches and ecclesiastical communities taking part in it', before an ecumenical gathering in Christchurch. He did not say that ecumenism made new demands upon the Catholic participants in dialogue. One aspect of the dialogue that the Pope chose to ignore was the prominent role played by non-Catholic women in the ecumenical service he attended. John Paul spent three days in New Zealand before flying on to Australia.

His first formal gathering was in Canberra, the country's capital, before going on to Sydney and to Hobart in Tasmania where he made a plea that women's work should be so structured that 'they do not have to bargain for advancement at the expense of their vital role in the family'. Nor should women who chose to stay at home to look after their children be financially penalized. It was a powerful plea for women's rights. The more militant advocates of sexual equality might have remarked that the same plea could have been made on behalf of men, but such radical sexual equality is not part of papal discourse. The land rights of the Aborigines was another matter. In a two-hour stopover at Alice Springs, beside the sacred Ayers Rock, he supported Aboriginal claims to their territories (a politically highly-charged claim as it was believed that considerable mineral resources lay in such areas), and in the right of their culture to survive, a culture which, he pointed out in a later address, predated Abraham: the Pope was promptly criticized in one newspaper for attempting to bring Liberation Theology to Australia.

The journey ended on 1 December, though there was a five-hour stopover in the Seychelles before the return home. It was the longest trip so far: over 40,000 air-miles and fourteen days away from Rome. In Fiji, in New Zealand and in Australia he had been given a taste of fast-disappearing indigenous cultures, which he had clearly relished, and which he had stoutly defended. But he did not announce, as the Maoris had hoped, the appointment of a Maori bishop. The degree of enculturation of Christianity that the Pope would support still remained an enigma. 'You do not have to be a people divided into two parts as though an Aboriginal had to borrow the faith and life of Christianity like a hat from someone else who owns them', he had said at Alice Springs, and he had told the Maoris much the same in Auckland.

What it meant in practice remained to be seen. In his message for 1 January, World Day of Peace 1987, entitled 'Development and solidarity: Two keys to peace', the Pope praised programmes which did not 'ignore the real linguistic, racial, religious, social or cultural differences among peoples'. It was not clear how far this referred to the Church. Meanwhile, in a homily in St Peter's that same day, he announced that the twelve months from Pentecost 1987 to the Feast of the Assumption 1988 would be kept as a Marian year, a time of special devotion to the Virgin Mary, in preparation for the third millennium of Christianity.[10]

The most important event on the calendar for 1987 as far as Pope John Paul was concerned, was his third visit to Poland, scheduled for June. On 13 January the Polish leader, General Wojciech Jaruzelski, called upon him at the Vatican. The last time they met had been in Poland in 1983. This time he was meeting the Pope on his own ground: Jaruzelski was at a disadvantage. The previous year had not been a good one for Church-state relations in his country, particularly in the aftermath of the murder in 1984 by the political police of the pro-Solidarity priest Fr Jerzy Popieluszko. Cardinal Glemp had held a number of meetings with Jaruzelski, but there was a widespread feeling that the hierarchy was simply seeking institutional privileges which touched the people little and left the Communist regime intact. Radical clergy such as Popieluszko were demanding much more, while state officials continued to remove crucifixes from classrooms and other public places and to censor the religious press. But before the papal visit the hierarchy was loath to go on the offensive lest the visit be cancelled. After the hour-long meeting Jaruzelski said it gave 'a strong impulse for the further improvement of Church-state relations'; the Pope called the meeting 'historic'. When Glemp called on the Pope in early March to fix final details he spoke kindly of Jaruzelski, describing him as 'an authentic Pole' and saying that his government was increasingly acceptable, at least as far as practicalities were concerned.

The Marian Year was celebrated in an encyclical, *Redemptoris Mater*, dated for the Feast of the Annunciation, 25 March. After an introduction explaining the origins of the encyclical with reference to the millennium and the desire, before the 2,000th anniversary of the birth of Christ, to devote a period to his mother, the Pope goes on to meditate on three New Testament texts concerning Mary – the annunciation, the birth of Christ, and Mary at the foot of the Cross. He went on to link devotion to Mary with pilgrimage – he made special mention of the great Polish Marian shrine of Jasna Góra – and with the search for Christian unity, though he acknowledged that there were 'discrepancies' among the Churches about the doctrine of Mary which had to be overcome if unity were to be achieved. 'Meanwhile', he went on, perhaps more hopefully than accurately, 'these Churches and ecclesial communities are finding agreement with the Catholic Church on fundamental points of Christian belief, including matters relating to the Virgin Mary.' He did, however, emphasize the similarity of doctrine between the Roman Catholic Church and Churches of the Orthodox tradition. The final section of the encyclical speaks of Mary's mediation – the Pope is careful to subordinate it to the mediation of Christ – of Mary as mother, and Mary as model for women in particular. Mary, he said:

> sheds light on womanhood as such by the very fact that God, in the sublime event of the Incarnation of his Son, entrusted himself to the ministry, the free and active ministry, of a woman.
>
> It can thus be said that women, by looking to Mary, find in her the secret of living their own femininity with dignity and of achieving their own true advancement. In the light of Mary, the Church sees in the face of women the reflection of a beauty which mirrors the loftiest sentiments of which the human heart is capable: the self-offering totality of love; the strength that is capable of bearing the greatest sorrows, limitless fidelity and tireless devotion to work; the ability to combine penetrating intuition with words of support and encouragement.

If women did not recognize themselves in that eulogy, the Pope promised further thoughts elsewhere on the 'unique relationship' between femininity and the Mother of the Redeemer.

On 30 March, in St Peter's basilica, the Pope beatified five Spaniards, two of them priests and three of them nuns. There was no question as to the admirable qualities of Cardinal Marcelo Spinola and Mgr Manuel Domingo y Sol who died in 1905 and 1909 respectively. The problem was about the Carmelite nuns who had been killed during the Spanish Civil War. A great many who had died in the course of that conflict had been proposed for eventual canonization as martyrs. Paul VI had put a stop to the process in 1975, believing the promotion of their cause to have been politically motivated and unacceptable to the government of Spain (cf. above, p. 127). John Paul had allowed the files to be reopened, despite protests from the left-wing government in Madrid, though only on an individual basis: the three Carmelites were the first whose process was complete.

Very shortly afterwards John Paul departed for his 34th overseas tour. He had promised the Argentineans during his brief visit during the Falklands War (cf. above, p. 108) that he would return; he made a similar promise to include Chile when the dispute over the Beagle Channel was settled. And now he fulfilled his commitments. The Beagle Channel accord was finally achieved in the Montevideo Act, and on 31 March the Pope arrived in Uruguay: the President, who was not a Catholic, declared the following day to be a national holiday. The Pope's stay in Montevideo was brief: he went on arrival to the cathedral to commemorate the Montevideo Act, and spoke in the evening with priests and religious. The following day he said an open-air mass, and departed for Chile.

Before the Pope's arrival in Santiago tension had been high between government and Church, and within the Church between the hierarchy and the more radical clergy working in the slum areas of Chile's capital city. The clergy felt their bishops were too sympathetic to the regime: the regime clearly felt the bishops were very far from being sympathetic enough. As soon as the Pope's plane touched down General Pinochet was in attendance, delivering an impassioned justification of the last thirteen years of military dictatorship. He no doubt chose his words thinking they would resonate with the Pope, speaking of 'aggression by international Communism' and 'the culture of death practised by atheist and materialist ideologies which threaten democracy'. John Paul remained unconvinced. After a triumphal journey into the city and a welcome in the cathedral, he blessed Santiago from a hill overlooking the city, making special mention of those driven into exile for political reasons.

The next morning there was a private meeting with Pinochet and his family followed by a visit to a slum. It was rumoured that the General had wanted John Paul to say a private mass for the dictator's family, and he had refused. He warned church workers against getting involved in politics, and said it again to senior churchmen whom he met over lunch. In the afternoon he travelled to Valparaiso; in the evening he told 100,000 young people not to fall into the trap of violence: it was a particularly emotive call, because the stadium where the gathering was held had been used after the fall of Allende to contain and torture political prisoners.

On 3 April a million people assembled in O'Higgins Park for the beatification of a nun, Sister Teresa of the Andes. The ceremony went on uninterrupted, but from the edges of the crowd stones were thrown and battles with the police developed which led to the firing of tear gas into the crowd from armoured vehicles. A cloud of gas hung in the air above the papal altar, but John Paul was physically unaffected, though clearly shaken, while well over 600 people were injured by the rioting.

There were three days filled with meetings with political leaders, diplomats, slum-dwellers and at least one hideously burnt victim of police brutality: she had set fire to herself, a government official explained. After the tension of Santiago, the papal trips to first the South and then the North of the country were relatively relaxed. From the far North, Antofagasta, John Paul left for Argentina: it was 6 April.

He arrived in Buenos Aires in the afternoon, joked with the crowd and told government leaders to protect human rights and reject violence – words taken to refer to the 'dirty war' waged by the military junta against its own people. One of the few liberal bishops in the country, Mgr Miguel Esteban Hesayne of Viedma, was rewarded the following day with a papal visit. He begged the Pope's forgiveness for the Argentinean Church which 'had not always identified itself with the poor and the persecuted'. The Pope restricted himself to calling for reconciliation, as later, on 8 April in Tucuman, he made a plea for national unity. On 10 April, Palm Sunday, the Pope celebrated an open-air mass in Buenos Aires, drawing a vast crowd for the first time on his Argentinean tour. He reminded them that Christ had been interrogated and tortured before the crucifixion. He said he had not forgotten the 'disappeared ones', and condemned explicitly the dirty war. Elsewhere, in Mendoza and in Cordoba, he spoke out in favour of the family and against divorce: the Argentinean Senate had undertaken not to consider a bill permitting divorce until after the Pope had left for Rome. He departed on 10 April, leaving behind a message for the bishops saying he understood the difficulties they had faced in dealing with the military junta, and commending them for their opposition. 'Opposition' was not what Bishop Hesayne would have called it.

The Pope was, as always, in Rome for Easter Sunday, but shortly afterwards, on 30 April, he set out on his second visit to Germany. The major event of the journey was to be the beatification in Cologne of Edith Stein, the Carmelite nun murdered in Auschwitz, and an author by whose writings the Pope had been much influenced.[11] But she was a Jew. The process designed to lead to her eventual canonization had been started in Rome in 1962: it had come to a halt because of the need for miracles directly attributable to her intercession. There was a way around this. Martyrs, those who have given their lives for the faith, do not need the support of the miraculous, and Pope John Paul was in a hurry. So Edith Stein, in religion Sister Teresa Benedicta of the Cross, was transferred to the ranks of the martyrs. But martyr of what cause? She had died because of her Jewish origins; she was being proclaimed a 'blessed' as a Christian witness. The ceremonies of beatification made a great effort to incorporate both the

Christian and the Jewish aspects of the life of Edith Stein. 'She never broke with her own people', said the Pope, and he met members of the Jewish community and of Edith Stein's family after the service.

In the afternoon Pope John Paul moved on to Munster where he prayed at the tomb of Cardinal Clemens August von Galen who, as Bishop of Munster, had been one of the very few among the German hierarchy to have openly opposed the Nazis. The Pope used von Galen's condemnation of Nazi extermination of the sick and incurable as the context for his own condemnation of euthanasia and abortion. The next day was spent in Kevelaer, a Marian shrine and Germany's most popular place of pilgrimage, and then in Essen. On 3 May there was the much less controversial beatification, in the Olympic stadium at Munich, of the Jesuit priest Rupert Mayer. Mayer died while saying mass on 1 November 1945, having been released from detention imposed for his constant opposition to the Nazis only five months previously. His anti-Nazi stand had been all the more impressive because no one could deny that he was a patriotic German, awarded the Iron Cross for bravery under fire during the First World War. But from as early as 1925 he had been a fearless opponent of Hitler. He was deeply disappointed with the German bishops' failure to condemn Nazism, but kept his disappointment largely to himself. Though he was remembered for his courage, he was beatified just as much for his dedicated service to the people of Munich.

The final day of the Pope's visit was spent in Augsburg and in Speyer – in which place he met the German Chancellor, Helmut Kohl – before leaving for Rome from Stuttgart airport. His final act, standing before the 900-year-old cathedral in Speyer, was to call for 'a new united Europe, from the Atlantic to the Urals'.

A month later the Pope was, for the third time in his pontificate, back in his home country. Poland's situation had greatly changed since his previous visit in 1983, a change brought about more by the arrival of Mikhail Gorbachev in the Soviet Union than anything that General Jaruzelski had done in Poland. Indeed, in some ways the omens in Poland were not good: the agricultural fund which the Church had striven for four years to establish had finally collapsed through government opposition; shortly before John Paul's arrival the minister with responsibility for religious affairs had been switched for a hardline atheist; there had been no major social or economic reforms to suggest that the Jaruzelski regime was itself sympathetic to the new Russian doctrine of *glasnost*. But at least there was no longer a threat of a Soviet invasion.

It was time, General Jaruzelski said to the Pope on his arrival in Warsaw on 8 June, for national reconciliation: he blamed 'foreign powers' for the 'turmoil' aroused by Solidarity. The turmoil, he said, had now subsided, and it was time for Church-state cooperation to solve Poland's problems. John Paul was not to be so easily won over. He reminded the General of the UN Charter of Human Rights: 'All violation and lack of respect for human rights constitutes a threat to peace'. Chief among those rights the Pope placed 'man's freedom to worship, associate and express his views'.

That was on Monday. On Tuesday the Pope went first to the extermination camp at Majdanek, and then on to his former university, the Catholic University of Lublin, an institution unique in the Eastern bloc. 'The nation still lives in its entire history', he told his audience, and that history as far as Poland was concerned included Lithuania to which, for 200 years after the 1569 Union of Lublin, Poland had been linked under a single parliament. On Wednesday John Paul was in Tarnow where he praised the Polish peasants and called upon the government to implement the agreements reached in 1981 with the agrarian equivalent of Solidarity. He beatified a girl, Karolina Kozka, killed while resisting rape by a Russian soldier in 1914. The same day he went on to Cracow where, during mass, he told the crowd to struggle patiently for freedom in Poland: 'keep us from hatred and prejudice when faced with those who hold different views'.

From Cracow the Pope's itinerary took him North to Szczecin where he encouraged the workers to continue the struggle for their rights, and to Gdynia where he spoke of 'Solidarity' as 'a word the world cannot forget'. From Gdynia he went on to Gdansk where, in the presence of Lech Walesa, he told the many thousands who came to greet him that workers had a right to trade unions, and that the Gdansk agreements still had to be fulfilled. He would, he said, support Solidarity's struggle: 'Every day, wherever I am, I pray for the great heritage of Polish solidarity'. Whether 'solidarity' was pronounced with a capital 'S' or a lower case letter, it was the same: he was greeted with cries of '*Solidarnosc*', and his controversial message was not one that Jaruzelski had expected to hear. Solidarity, as a trade union, was still banned.

There had been no official place on the itinerary for a meeting with Walesa, though one did take place. Nor had the Pope been permitted to visit the grave of Jerzy Popieluszko – whom he frequently mentioned in his homilies to great applause – but he went there all the same. That was on 8 June, the last day, when, before a congregation of a million, he presided at a mass to bring to a close the Eucharistic Congress he had inaugurated on his arrival. His final homily was an attack on 'programmed atheism'. Jaruzelski was at the airport to see him off; the papal tour had not gone the way he had hoped, following his visit to the Vatican in January. The visits to the Northern cities had been a concession by the regime: the Pope had made none. Now the General could scarcely control his anger or conceal his disappointment as he bade farewell, but in his departing address Pope John Paul held out the hope of the establishment of diplomatic relations between Warsaw and the Vatican, something which the Polish regime had long desired.

While in Cracow John Paul announced that he would not be attending celebrations in Lithuania, a largely Catholic country, to mark the 600th anniversary of the baptism of the Grand Duke Jagiello on his marriage to the Polish Princess Jadwiga. The clear implication was that the Soviet government, even in the era of *glasnost*, would not give permission. Instead he had to content himself with sending a letter to the President of the Lithuanian Bishops' Conference saying that through the Duke's baptism Lithuania had become part of the European family. He announced that, on 28 June, he would beatify the Lithuanian Archbishop Jurgis Matulaitis and, in the closing paragraphs, called for greater religious freedom for the country. This beatification was, by chance, the 200th performed by the Pope, and was consequently attended by a more than usual number of representatives of European Bishops' Conferences. The Pope took the opportunity to remind them that Lithuania was part of the family of European nations.

On 25 June Pope John Paul received the President of Austria, Dr Kurt Waldheim. It was not, on the face of it, anything more than the extension of the usual diplomatic courtesies, and that was how the Vatican tried to present it. Waldheim, Secretary-General of the United Nations when the Pope went there in 1979, had been elected Austrian President in 1986. Waldheim 'has repeatedly expressed the desire that his first official visit abroad should be to the Holy Father', said the Vatican's press officer. Undoubtedly protocol required that the audience, once requested, should take place – though there was no meeting between the President of Austria and the President of Italy as would normally have occurred with Waldheim present in Rome. Waldheim had been accused of being connected with the deportation of Jews from Greece to Nazi concentration camps when serving in the German army during the war. He had denied this charge, and the Austrian government had set up a commission of enquiry. But the papal audience deeply upset Jews both in Europe and the United States. Israel wondered publicly why the Vatican had allowed it to go ahead. Cardinal Decourtray of Lyons concurred. The Church's relations with the Jews, cemented, seemingly, by the Pope's visit to the Rome synagogue a year before, were again in jeopardy. *L'Osservatore Romano*, in a damage-limitation exercise the day before the audience, carried a long article on the Pope's solidarity with the Jewish people. The need was urgent. A meeting with Jewish leaders had been planned for 11 September in Miami, during the Pope's forthcoming tour of the United States. Now the Jewish delegation threatened to boycott the meeting. In a letter released towards the end of August to the President of the US Conference of Bishops, John Paul spoke of the Holocaust as 'a motive for sincere sorrow' for the Catholic Church. 'We seek to grasp its most authentic, specific and universal meaning', he wrote. He also agreed to see Jewish leaders just before setting out for the States.

After all the controversy John Paul might well have felt he needed a break. His residence for the summer of 1987 was, as always, Castel Gandolfo, but for six days in July he swopped his papal vestments for a pale-grey suit, a white cotton hat and walking boots and, discreetly protected by Italian security men, he went for a hike in the Dolomites. He climbed mountains, waved his stick companionably at astonished passers-by, lay down on the grass for an occasional nap, and ate the local food with gusto. In the village of Lorenzago di Cadore, where he lodged in a villa owned by the diocese of Treviso, he said Sunday mass and preached on the duty of Christians to protect the environment. It was refreshingly unpope-like.

That John Paul II did not live up to customary papal norms was also the view of Archbishop Lefebvre, still the only bishop in his Society of St Pius X. He had been formally suspended from performing priestly duties, but it was a suspension he ignored. He was by now 82 years old. To secure the succession of his self-styled Society he needed to consecrate another bishop who would in his turn be able to ordain new priests to the cause. He had met John Paul in 1978, shortly after his election: 'He didn't seem like a Pope to me. He had no character,' he reported to journalists. The following day, with the Pope safely elsewhere, Lefebvre went to Rome to call on Cardinal Ratzinger. They spent almost an hour and a half together, and the Archbishop left smiling. Both sides agreed there would be no communiqué.

The meeting between the Pope and Jewish leaders, arranged in an attempt to heal the wounds of the Waldheim affair, took place in Castel Gandolfo at noon on 1 September. The day before there had been a preparatory meeting in Rome of Cardinal Willebrands' Commission for Religious Relations with the Jews. The nine-member Jewish delegation to meet the Pope was led by the chairman of the international Jewish Committee for Inter-religious Consultation, Rabbi Mordecai Waxman. Cardinals Casaroli and Willebrands joined the Pope. The Jewish participants later described the meeting as 'historic': there had never before been a consultation at so high a level. The audience with Waldheim was not discussed; on the Holy See's recognition of the State of Israel they agreed to differ, but the Catholic representatives promised a document on the Holocaust, and on the roots of anti-Semitism. The way was clear for the Miami meeting to go ahead.

The Pope arrived in Miami on 11 September, just ahead of an electrical storm: his mass in front of a crowd of 200,000 had to be abandoned. In the afternoon he met representatives of the US clergy and listended silently to requests for an exploration both of celibacy and of the ministry of women in the Church. The following day the meeting with Jewish leaders took place. Not all of them had been mollified by the earlier diplomatic encounters in Rome and there were protests. Rabbi Waxman said the Catholic Church had not taken sufficient responsibility for European anti-Semitism, and urged diplomatic recognition of Israel. The Pope defended Pius XII's record, claiming that history would show how much he had tried to save them. He assured the Jews that they did indeed have a right to a homeland – but added that so did the Palestinians.

That was Friday. On Saturday he praised the example of Martin Luther King before a gathering of black Catholics in New Orleans. In New Orleans he also met presidents of US Catholic colleges. Many of them had expressed the fear that a document produced by the Vatican on the Catholic identity of such institutions would reduce them to the level of diocesan schools, and thereby run the risk of losing Federal aid. The Pope's address did not touch on the document directly, but his words seemed to bring a little comfort.

The following day John Paul was in San Antonio, Texas. Some 350,000 came to his mass, many of them 'Hispanics' but including Mexicans who had evaded border patrols to be present. He spoke in favour of the 'Sanctuary' movement, a Church-based organization giving refuge to political refugees from Central and South America: the US government regarded its activities as illegal. By Monday John Paul was in Arizona. In Phoenix he spoke to Indians gathered from 200 tribes and later met doctors, yet again attacking abortion, euthanasia and artificial insemination. Tuesday was for Hollywood, and an audience of film stars and movie executives. But on 16 September there was also a meeting with the Bishops' Conference, represented by four of its most distinguished members. The conference wanted to discuss with the Pope the relationship between the universal and the local Church; moral teaching, the role of the laity (the topic chosen for the autumn's Synod in Rome) and the 'crisis' in the life of American Catholicism – the Hunthausen affair had been settled just in time for the papal visit so that was one crisis out of the way, but other potential flashpoints remained. The four prelates read statements. The Pope had already seen them, and had been given ample time to produce his reply. It was predictably hardline, especially on moral issues.

The Pope went on to Monterey where he was welcomed by Clint Eastwood; he next visited the grave of Junipero Serra, the Spanish Franciscan who evangelized California. In San Francisco he spoke to religious and, the next morning, to representatives of the laity. Or rather that had been his plan: but Mrs Donna Hanson made it abundantly clear to him that in her view women resented the way they were treated by the Church: 'not to question, or to challenge, not to have the authorities involve me in the understanding is to deny my dignity as a person'. 'I do not feel I am being heard', she said. Yet among those who did not hear was the Pope himself. The US Bishops' Conference was preparing a pastoral letter on women (it was eventually abandoned), yet two other pastoral declarations of distinction had recently been produced, on war and peace (1983) and on economics (1986). Both were distinguished by the manner in which they had been produced, as much as by their content: drafts had been widely circulated, debated and amendments noted. The laity were involved, the results were impressive. To the great disappointment of American RCs the Pope made no mention of this achievement. His own discourse on economics, delivered in Detroit on 19 September, was heard by a far smaller crowd than had been expected. In Detroit he met the Polish community and, next day, five thousand Canadian Indians: a meeting with them planned for the Pope's earlier visit to Canada had been abandoned because of bad weather.

It had been an unusual visit. Television was present but – except when President Ronald Reagan greeted the Pope in Miami – the visit was only covered by local stations. Then people failed to turn out: only half the number that had been expected appeared on the appointed day, put off, it was said, by the security precautions, the weather, and the better view to be seen on television. Most notable was the semblance of dialogue. There were several set-piece occasions when the Pope listened and then replied. He certainly listened, but his replies seemed to have little to do with what he heard – except with the bishops in Los Angeles where he had been given plenty of time to prepare.

John Paul was back in Rome scarcely a fortnight before the Synod began. Its theme, the laity. Rarely had a gathering been more carefully prepared – it had been scheduled originally for 1986. There had been a Vatican questionnaire to which over 80 Bishops' Conferences had replied. Some few of these responses were published until the Vatican objected and secrecy once more descended. A working paper was drawn up said to be based on the replies, but given the secrecy, it was unclear how far it represented a balance of the bishops' comments. There had been a pre-Synod gathering at Rocca di Papa of more than 200 lay representatives of church organizations or 'movements' in May.

A novel element was the appointment of twenty 'assistants' and sixty 'auditors', of whom *in toto* fifty-five were laypeople. Five of the assistants were lay, and two of them were given the title of 'assistant special secretaries' to the Synod: one of these was M. Jean-Loup Dherse, until shortly before the synod chief executive of the consortium building the tunnel under the English Channel. Most of the auditors were lay and several represented individual movements of lay people within the Church. One should note that technically nuns are members of the laity. They had, of course, no voting rights, and were in any case outnumbered by the 231 official representatives, thirty of the most conservative directly appointed by John Paul II. They were allowed to address the gathering for twenty minutes each, though bishops were restricted to eight, and were permitted to take a full part in discussion groups which were, as usual, organized according to language.

The purpose of the Synod, which began work on 1 October with a mass presided over by Pope John Paul, was to 'revise' the teaching of Vatican II in the light of the working paper. That at least was the belief of Cardinal Thiandoum, Archbishop of Dakar, who presented the opening 'report'. He chose four topics as of special importance: the secular nature of the lay vocation, the relationship between lay movements and the bishops, the notion of lay 'ministries', and the role of women.

All of these themes were tackled in the course of the Synod, but the role of women and that of lay movements were particularly to the fore, with most of the speakers calling for a greater recognition of the part played by women in the life of the Church, and many of the bishops commenting upon the tension aroused within the parish by the rise of those lay associations which operated outside traditional Church structures.

The closing mass of the Synod was celebrated on 30 October. Cardinal Hume of Westminister described the gathering as 'an encouraging and positive experience'; a Canadian archbishop, in an angry interview given to the *Toronto Star*, said that nothing of significance had been achieved, and that participants in the Synod had been lectured to by Vatican bureaucrats. The list of propositions, prepared after group discussion, had been much pruned before presentation to the Synod fathers to be voted upon. Between the initial list and that presented for voting much had been changed. In particular, whole sections concerning the role of women in the Church recommending it be extended, had been cut out. In the end fifty-four 'propositions' were put to the Pope, the first of which asked 'humbly' that he might compose a final document on behalf of the Synod.

As ever the life of the Vatican went on. Tension was high between the Holy See and Czechoslovakia, but, oddly as things turned out, there were great hopes for a breakthrough with China. There were regular reports from Cardinal Ratzinger on the progress of the new catechism. Ecumenism, practically at a standstill as far as the Anglican Communion was concerned, seemed to flourish with the Orthodox – though it was made clear by the Patriarch of Moscow that John Paul would not be welcome in Russia for the celebration of the millennium of Christianity. The Pope had more luck with the Ecumenical Patriarch of Constantinople who was in Rome at the beginning of December. Nothing definite emerged, beyond a promise not to proselytize while working toward full union. When the Patriarch attended mass in St Peter's the *filioque* clause of the Creed, upon which East and West differ, was left out. In his homily, however, the Pope reaffirmed the primacy of the Roman See, 'a real responsibility to preside, guide in charity, and favour the maintenance of communion'.

NOTES

1. The total Christian population at the time was reckoned to be 20,000,000, or 3.5 per cent of the population.
2. Neither the Syro-Malabar nor the Syro-Malankar Churches has a continuous history of being in communion with Rome: the first went briefly into schism in 1653 in protest against the attempt to Latinize it; the second only returned to communion in 1930.
3. Critics pointed out that the visit to Ranchi, one of the poorest dioceses of India, lasted only two hours and cost four days' wages per head of Catholic population.
4. *The Tablet*, 19 April 1986, p. 414.
5. In the judgement against Curran, dated 25 July 1986, Ratzinger stated that the infallible *magisterium* was not restricted to matters of faith or solemn definitions. The faithful, he wrote, 'are to give religious submission of intellect and will to the teaching which the supreme pontiff or the college of bishops enunciate on faith or morals when they exercise the authentic *magisterium*, even if they do not intend to proclaim it with a definitive act'. Ratzinger concluded that 'in the light of your repeated refusal to accept what the Church teaches ... you

will no longer be considered suitable nor eligible to exercise the function of a professor of Catholic theology'. He added that this judgement 'might move you to reconsider your dissenting opinions'.

6. The nuns moved into Auschwitz the following autumn, taking up temporary accommodation in the building in which the Germans had stored the gas with which they massacred the Jews.

7. The sermon was preached on 14 January 1986 and published by *L'Osservatore* on 20 February. Of those who died in Auschwitz some 2.5 million were Jews, more than a third, in other words, of all Jews who died at the hands of the Nazis. Of the other 1.5 million people who died there, most were Polish.

8. cf. two articles by Desmond O'Grady, both in *The Tablet*, 'Born-again Catholics' and 'The Pope and the Laity', 26 April 1986, pp. 427f. and 2 August 1986, p. 800 respectively.

9. Some six months later Cardinal Giuseppe Caprio revealed that the Vatican's financial holdings amounted to some $570 million, a great deal of which was tied up in property that incurred costs (offices, schools and so on) rather than produced income.

10. There had been one other 'Marian Year', 1953–4, to mark the centenary of the declaration of the dogma of the Immaculate Conception of Mary.

11. cf. above, pp. 178-9. On the case of Edith Stein, see 'A question of martyrdom' by James Baaden, *The Tablet*, 31 January 1987, pp. 107–8. She was born in 1891, served as an assistant to the philosopher Edmund Husserl, and became a Catholic in 1930. She lost her teaching post at Cologne in 1933 because of her Jewish origins, and at that point decided to enter the Discalced Carmelites. She was sent to the Netherlands by her superiors for her own safety in 1938, but was deported to Auschwitz in 1942, where she was executed.

EIGHT

1988-9

IT WAS CLEAR, as 1988 began, that the failure of the Kremlin and the
Moscow Patriarchate to invite him to the millennial celebrations of the
Russian Orthodox Church still rankled in the Pope's mind. It was announced
that John Paul would be going to Austria in June, a 'prior engagement' which
would preclude such a trip, but it was hard to see why he was going to Austria
at all. He had been there in 1984; he would again compromise himself by
association with President Waldheim; and the occasion, the 50th anniversary
of the *Anschluss* when Austria was appropriated by Nazi Germany, scarcely
seemed an event that required the Pope's presence. But Waldheim had issued
an invitation, and somewhat precipitously the Vatican was taking it up.

John Paul was still hankering after a formal invitation from Gorbachev. He
said so quite openly on 17 January during a visit to the Foreign Press Club
in Rome. Catholics wanted to see their Pope, he insisted. The Catholics he
had in mind were those of Lithuania, Latvia, Byelorussia, the Ukraine and
Kazakhstan. There had, however, been no discussion of a papal visit to the
Soviet Union, said Gennadi Gerasimov, the spokesman for the Soviet Foreign
Ministry. Nor, he added, was there any likelihood of Gorbachev calling on
the Pope during a visit to Italy – but it happened in December 1989 and,
according to the Soviet leader himself, it was a significant meeting.[1]

That lay almost two years in the future. In the 1988 Week of Prayer for
Christian Unity John Paul's thoughts were particularly with the Orthodox.
He made an especial mention of his recent meeting with the Ecumenical
Patriarch of Constantinople (see above, p. 186), and as he brought the Week
to an end on 25 January with a homily in St Paul's Outside the Walls (the
Week ends on the Feast of the Conversion of St Paul), he offered the kiss of
peace to 'the sister Church of the patriarchate of Moscow which has assumed
a great share of the Christian inheritance of the land of Rus'. The words were
carefully chosen because he also spoke of the Ukrainians 'in full communion
with Rome while preserving their Eastern heritage'. And that, of course, was

the problem with a visit of John Paul or any Bishop of Rome to the territory of the Russian Orthodox Church. It was not that there was any personal antipathy to John Paul himself except that, being a Slav, this particular Bishop of Rome had an especial sensitivity to the issue. In 1946 the Ukrainian Catholic Church had been suppressed and, theoretically, incorporated into the Russian Orthodox Church though, as everyone knew, it still operated clandestinely, and vigorously, within the Ukraine and openly outside the Soviet bloc. The previous September John Paul had appealed for it to be allowed full liberty of worship. There had been no response from the Soviet leadership. Meanwhile, said the Pope, he was preparing two documents on the millennium of the conversion of Rus. He would give no details.

In February, however, a letter was released on the 1200th anniversary of the Second Council of Nicaea. Nicaea II had happened in 787, and *Duodecimum Saeculum* was dated 4 December 1987. The letter was addressed to the Bishops of the Catholic Church but at least in the Western half of that Church Nicaea II – as distinct from Nicaea I – was scarcely known about outside academic circles. The issue which it tackled was iconoclasm, the destruction of images, which had divided the Church in the eighth century. Iconoclasm had briefly affected the West, but was not a serious problem until the Protestant Reformation of the sixteenth century. The controversy in the East was finally won by the iconodules, those who approved of the veneration of images. Icons and their veneration have remained a much more central element in Eastern Christianity than they have in Western, despite the sacred statues and holy images that frequently adorned Catholic churches.

Nicaea II is the last general council of the Church to be recognized as such both by the Catholic and Orthodox branches of Christianity. The Pope's praise for the Council, therefore, was a reminder of what the two now divergent traditions had in common – not only the legitimacy of the veneration of images but also the efficacy of the intercession of saints, also insisted upon by Nicaea II. As the Pope pointed out, both were reaffirmed by the Council of Trent in the sixteenth century. He did not say so, though the implication was unmistakable, that such traditions shared by Catholics and Orthodox were not embraced by the Churches of the Protestant Reformation.

As has been noted above, on 25 January the Pope spoke of the Patriarchate of Moscow as a 'sister Church'. He repeated the phrase in a letter, *Euntes in Mundum*, (Going into the world) also dated 25 January but not released until the end of March. In it John Paul reflected upon the history of the Eastern Church, and particularly that which sprang from the baptism in 988 of Prince

Vladimir. He acknowledged that by the date of Vladimir's conversion the Church of the East and that of the West had diverged liturgically, but links between the two, he insisted, continued to be close. They are still close, he added, because the Orthodox Churches share with the Catholic Church the apostolic succession so that both have 'true sacraments' - he mentioned especially the Eucharist and the priesthood. This was yet another characteristic which marked off the Orthodox Churches from those of the Reformation.

John Paul had promised two documents to mark the millennium. The second, *Magnum Baptismi Donum* (The great gift of baptism), though not released until mid-April, was dated 14 February. It was addressed to Cardinal Lubachivsky, the exiled Major Archbishop of Lvov and primate of the Ukrainian Catholic Church who was living in Rome. Like *Euntes in Mundum* it traced the history of the relationship between the Churches of the East and that of the West, dwelling on the 1596 Union of Brest when some of the Kiev bishops re-established communion with Rome. The Pope spoke of the good relations now existing between Rome and the Orthodox Churches, and touched only in passing on the forcible absorption in 1946 of the Ukrainian Catholics into Russian Orthodoxy. 'No one ought to consider membership in the Catholic Church as incompatible with the good of the homeland', he said, and went on 'May your great numbers of faithful[2] enjoy true freedom of conscience and respect for their religious right to give public worship to God in their own rite and with their own pastors'.

The Pope has a penchant for anniversaries. 1988 was the twentieth anniversary of Paul VI's encyclical banning the use of artificial means of contraception, *Humanae Vitae*. John Paul praised it as 'part of the permanent inheritance of the Church's moral teaching' in an address to delegates attending the Fourth International Congress on the Family. Contraception, he said, arose out of an anti-life view of the world which led logically to the many thousands of legalized abortions being carried out around the world: wider use of contraceptives would, of course, have reduced the incidence of abortion, but upon that thought he did not dwell. Instead he had harsh words for those theologians who criticized Pope Paul's encyclical, thereby 'casting doubt upon the Church's certain teaching and clouding the perception of a truth which should be beyond discussion'. Truth, he added, was not decided by majority opinion. That is, no doubt, a good throwaway line, and one calculated to win assent. It is also true, however, that the Church in Council decides upon the truths of the Faith by the majority vote of the bishops, so the Pope's remark is not as self-evident as it might seem. Unfortunately it ranged very starkly the questionings of theologians against the seemingly impregnable truth emanating from the papacy.

The 20th anniversary of Pope Paul VI's encyclical *Populorum Progressio* (On the progress of peoples) had occurred in 1987.[3] John Paul's encyclical *Solicitudo Rei Socialis* (The social concern of the Church) was written to celebrate the event and dated 1987, but it did not become available until 1988: indeed, the Pope reflected in the course of the encyclical on the events which had been held the previous year to mark the anniversary. Twenty years ago, wrote John Paul, the outlook for development had been hopeful: now it was much less so. The gap between the countries of the North and those of the South had widened, and the responsibility for this deterioration fell squarely upon the richer nations and the means they use to increase their own wealth. A further problem, he went on, was the division of the world into two power blocs, the West with its liberal capitalism, the East embracing Marxist collectivism. The Church adopts a critical stance to both of them.

Development, he recognized, is not a simple forward process: it can be set back as it had been by two world wars. It can also be misled into seeing progress simply as a matter of 'having' more and more, rather than being directed to the totality of the human vocation. The Bible gives human beings dominion over all other created things and, in seeking true development, we are taking part in God's plan. Development can be hindered by 'structural sin', by an all-consuming desire for profit or a thirst for power. But there has been a growing recognition of humanity's interdependence, a growing sense of solidarity – solidarity with poor, alongside whom the Church is required to take its stand, and solidarity in international relations. Solidarity, said the Pope, is a Christian virtue, allied to charity and inspired by the Trinity. Through solidarity the structures of sin can be overcome.

The Pope acknowledged that it was not the Church's role to offer technical solutions. Its social teaching was an attempt to interpret reality in the light of the Gospel and in so doing to play a prophetic role in the condemnation of injustice. Opting for the poor is central to its message, which declares that the goods of this world are the property of all. Love for the poor has to be translated into deeds and, in Latin America, 'Liberation' has emerged as a fundamental category and principle of action. While no temporal achievement can be identified with the coming of the Kingdom of God, this fact itself cannot be used to justify a lack of concern for the integral development of people.

This was a remarkable document.[4] While many welcomed it, not least for its stirring endorsement of Liberation Theology, ecologists were unhappy at the unequivocal assertion of humankind's dominion over the rest of creation. That dominion, they felt, had led to the ecological mess in which the human race now found itself. There was much more controversy over the moral equivalence or parallelism the Pope appeared to find between the Eastern bloc and the West, between Marxist collectivism and liberal capitalism. He was obviously not going to give his blessing to the former, but nor would he endorse the latter. This aroused little comment in the United Kingdom, but it occasioned a good deal of upset in the United States.[5] On both sides of the Atlantic, however, journalists latched on to a throwaway passage about the Church divesting itself of its riches to help the poor – not a policy, it must be said, which has been much in evidence since the Pope enunciated it at the end of 1987.

On the theological spectrum from conservative to progressive, *Solicitudio Rei Socialis* ranked high up at the progressive end. But that is typical of John Paul II: conservative on doctrine while progressive on social issues, at the same time denying clergy the opportunity to involve themselves too closely in such matters except, apparently, in Poland. But like many, among the laity as much as in the hierarchy, the Pope considered himself to be holding the middle ground. In April he wrote to Cardinal Ratzinger about Archbishop Marcel Lefebvre and his 'Fraternity of Pius X' which, by now, existed in nearly thirty countries and had recruited some three hundred priests. The Pope rehearsed the efforts which the Vatican had made to reconcile Lefebvre, including the sending of Cardinal Gagnon as Apostolic Visitor to the Fraternity's seminary at Ecône in Switzerland. Lefebvre had difficulty in accepting the teaching of Vatican II: Pope John Paul set out to attempt to calm his fears. Though 'progressives' appealed to the Council, he said, it was a characteristic desire of such people that the changes they wanted were not in harmony with the teaching of the Council. 'Progress' that entailed a break with the past was unacceptable. 'Conservatism' or 'integrism' was the opposite tendency: holding on to the past without any attempt to develop the truths of the faith in the light of changing historical circumstances. The truth, said the Pope, 'is diligently safeguarded by the *magisterium*'. By which, of course, he meant himself.

On 7 May John Paul began his thirty-seventh foreign tour with a visit to Uruguay. He had been there a year before, but then only briefly (cf. above, p. 177) when he had promised to return. In the stadium at Montevideo a tenth of the capital's population turned up to greet him. Uruguay was not a country suffering from crushing foreign debt, internal terrorism, or harsh dictatorship. It had, however, almost zero population growth and the Pope urged the government not to penalize fecundity. He went down to Melo, a town on the Brazilian frontier, to tell workers they had both a right and a duty to work and to tell the wealthy that their riches were for the good of all, and that the welfare of the workers was more important than profits. He moved on to Florida, some fifty miles north of the capital, where he appealed for more vocations, and told Catholics to go to mass more often. Uruguay is a highly secularized country; or as the President put it to the Pope on his arrival: 'We are a humanist country, here you are at home'. Yet the papal party took heart from the fact that government ministers turned out for papal events. At Salto on Monday 9 May, John Paul called for an evangelization of Uruguay before he left for Bolivia that afternoon.

Bolivia is one of the poorest of Latin American countries. When the Pope said mass at Oruro, at the centre of the mining area where many had lost their jobs as the price of copper fell, he was presented with an empty saucepan and a miner's helmet. He met the young in the sports stadium at Cochabamba and the sick in the cathedral at Sucre. He met Jewish leaders in the nunciature at La Paz and called on the President. He spoke of the unemployment of the poor and the greed of the rich; he criticized the levels of infant mortality and the poor standards of nutrition. He also denounced divorce and concubinage. During his first mass he called upon young people not to seek refuge in drink or in the liberation of women 'which only brings woman to worse slavery'.

From Bolivia he flew to Peru on 14 May to close the 'Marian' Eucharistic Congress attended by many bishops from the neighbouring states. The Pope preached social justice, along the lines of *Solicitudo Rei Socialis*, and a gospel of non-violence. It was particularly apposite in Peru where the 'Shining Path' guerrillas, shortly before his arrival, had managed to cut off the power supply to much of the country, and, on the day before his plane touched down, had exploded bombs in the streets of Lima.

The Pope's stay in Peru was brief, just long enough to close the Congress and greet the President before going on to Paraguay to be received by possibly the most unpleasant of Latin American dictators, Alfredo Stroessner. He arrived in pouring rain on 16 May, and knelt on a plastic bag to kiss the ground at the airport. He drove through streets full of excited crowds and past posters which proclaimed 'Blessed are the Peacemakers - Pope John Paul II and President Alfredo Stroessner'. The President, however, was greeted with a handshake rather than with the customary embrace. Those in power had an obligation 'to respect the rights and legitimate freedom of individuals', he told Stroessner, quoting John XXIII. His first engagement was the canonization of a Spanish Jesuit missionary, martyred near Asunción in 1628.

On the second day of his stay the Pope met agricultural workers and Amerindians from the Chaco region. In Asunción he met opponents of the regime whom the government had tried to ban (one of their leaders was arrested). The Vatican had insisted that, if the visit was to go ahead at all, Stroessner's political opponents should be allowed to greet the Pope. Stroessner had been forced to relent. The country needed a moral clean-up, the Pope told the opposition, but they knew that already. Government control of the media prevented his message going further. Stroessner's attempt to exploit the papal visit for his own political purposes had been unsuccessful, however, and opponents of the regime - which included the Church - were able to take heart. On 19 May Pope John Paul flew back to Rome.

He arrived back in the Eternal City to the usual problems. There were protests over the appointment of a conservative bishop - this time in Chur, Switzerland, where the controversy was to become peculiarly nasty. The Vatican was still expecting a reconciliation with Archbishop Lefebvre - before the summer, Cardinal Gagnon promised confidently. There were cardinals to be created - twenty-five of them, of whom only ten hailed from Western Europe and two came from behind the Iron Curtain. On 22 May, there was a letter to all members of religious communities and secular institutes, in which the Pope meditated on the Marian Year which, he thought, 'may mark a reawakening of vocations through a more trusting recourse to Mary . . .' There was a speech to the United Nations' special session on disarmament - delivered for John Paul by Cardinal Casaroli - and, more remarkably, a letter from the Pope to Mikhail Gorbachev written by hand.

This was to be delivered at the millennial celebrations of the Russian Church. The Pope had not been invited, but he sent ten cardinals and sundry other bishops, the most imposing Vatican delegation ever. Events began on Sunday 5 June with an elaborate liturgy in Moscow's Cathedral of the Epiphany, presided over by Patriarch Pimen of Moscow and All the Russias. Cardinal Casaroli was there, along with representatives from many other Churches including the Archbishop of Canterbury - though not the Ecumenical Patriarch Dimitrios I of Constantinople who felt that the Moscow Patriarchate was attempting to undermine the primacy of honour which the Patriarch of Constantinople traditionally enjoyed.

Also present in Moscow, and distinctly not welcome to the Russian Orthodox, was a delegation of two bishops, three priests and three laymen of the Ukrainian Catholic Church. They were also something of an embarrassment to the delegation from Rome whose primary business was improving Vatican relations with Moscow, but they could scarcely be ignored. Despite

Soviet attempts to prevent it, the Ukrainians were received by Cardinal Willebrands and the American Jesuit John Long at their hotel - Casaroli joined them towards the end of the ninety-minute meeting. The Ukrainians wanted Casaroli to put their situation on the agenda when they met Gorbachev.[6] But it was still uncertain whether he would receive them. There was some good news for the Vatican's delegation when Metropolitan Filaret of Kiev announced that the Russian Orthodox Church would discuss the future of the three million Ukrainian Catholics. But it was clearly not something which the Metropolitan relished, and he warned that in any case the legalization of the Ukrainian Catholic Church would be a matter for the Soviet State rather than the Russian Orthodox Church. A government official said at a press conference that the question could no longer be ignored, and proposed a joint Orthodox-Catholic commission.

Matters were moving less smoothly with the delivery of John Paul's letter to Mikhail Gorbachev. A meeting with the Soviet President, Andrei Gromyko, was scheduled, but not one with the General Secretary of the Communist Party. When it took place, in the Kremlin on 13 June, it was attended also by the Soviet Foreign Minister Edward Shevardnadze who had just returned from New York: it was quite possibly Shevardnadze's influence that persuaded Gorbachev to receive the delegation from the Vatican.[7] The ninety-minute meeting went well. Casaroli handed over the papal letter, which Gorbachev read on the spot, together with a rather longer memorandum, which he did not. The letter spoke of the need for formal contacts between the Vatican and the Soviet Union, an idea which the Communist leader did not reject out of hand, though he added later that much would have to happen before John Paul came to visit Russia. The memorandum listed specific difficulties of Catholics, the first time, said Casaroli, that the Soviet leadership had accepted representations from outsiders about the wellbeing of their own people.

Gorbachev had encouraged the millennial celebrations as an example of his policy of *perestroika*. Two days before the meeting with Gorbachev, at a gathering held in the Bolshoi Theatre, Casaroli had praised the new recognition being given to the role of the Church in Russian society. At the meeting with the Soviet President he was told that the Soviet government would put no barriers to the work of the Roman Catholic Church in its territories. It was all very hopeful although when a delegation from the Eastern Catholic Churches met with representatives from the Soviet Council for Religious Affairs to ask for the recognition of 15 'religious associations', they were urged to be patient. 'Our sole concern is to avoid conflicts between different social groups', said a spokesman for the Council, and added that they would have to take into account the views of the Russian Orthodox Church.

Back in Rome the Pope held his own celebrations of the millennium. On 10 July he concelebrated mass in St Peter's with the leader of the Ukrainian Catholics, Cardinal Lubachivsky, Archbishop of Lvov, together with seventeen other bishops gathered from exiled Ukrainian communities. He told the Ukrainians that he would insist upon their Church's right to exist, but reminded them also that his aim was unity with the Orthodox Church. The Pope took part in various celebrations four times in the second week of July which were broadcast by Vatican Radio to the Ukraine. It was critical to furthering the cause of the Ukrainian Catholics that Vatican-Soviet relations be improved. On the last day of the events to mark the millennium John Paul received the Soviet ambassador to Italy in private audience.

In between the Moscow and the Rome festivities, however, much else had been going on. The Pope had undertaken his controversial second visit to Austria, and, on 30 June, Archbishop Lefebvre had made his final break with the Holy See.[8] This in spite of Cardinal Gagnon's prophecy that all would be well (cf. above, p. 194). A dramatic last-minute offer from Cardinal Ratzinger to lay on an immediate meeting with the Pope had also failed. Shortly afterwards the Vatican announced reconciliatory terms for those who left Lefebvre's Fraternity to return to the obedience of Rome.

The Austrian tour took place from Thursday 23 June to Monday 27 June. The excuse had been to return President Waldheim's visit to the Vatican, but meetings with Waldheim were kept to the bare minimum – on arriving, on leaving, and a courtesy call at the presidential palace – and the Pope was distinctly cool.[9] At the presidential palace he spoke of bringing before God in prayer the heavy heritage of the past, and working for reconciliation. John Paul also spoke of reconciliation when he met leaders of the now tiny Austrian Jewish community for a kosher breakfast on 12 June, and in the afternoon he visited the Mauthausen concentration camp where he made an emotional speech, addressed in part to the 120,000 who had died there. 'Tell us, were we too quick to forget your hell?', he asked rhetorically. 'Do we not delete from our memories and consciousness the traces of past misdeeds? What direction should Europe and mankind take after Auschwitz, after Mauthausen?' But as the Chief Rabbi of Austria remarked, he never once named the Jews but spoke of only one: Jesus Christ. The Jewish community was disappointed that he had yet again failed to respond to an appeal for diplomatic recognition of the state of Israel and had not openly condemned Austrian anti-Semitism.

The major event of the Austrian visit was an open-air mass at Trausdorf airport attended by an estimated 100,000 people. The airport was close to the border with Hungary, and half the crowd were Hungarians, who were joined by their new Cardinal and nine bishops.[10] There was also a scattering of Czechs and Slovaks, Poles, Croats and Slovenes. The Pope, clearly at ease in this company, called for a Europe united in faith across the boundaries which divided West from East. It was something of a public relations triumph for John Paul. Czech television even broadcast the mass.

But during his visit the Pope did not address the question which Austrian Catholics were asking with some asperity: why had Hans Gröer been appointed to succeed the immensely popular Cardinal König as Archbishop of Vienna, and why had Kurt Kremm been appointed to assist him? If Gröer was unknown, Kremm was renowned for his conservatism. Under König the Church had pursued an independent policy on contraception and the remarriage of divorced Catholics, now Austria was being brought into line.

After Austria there was a break at Castel Gandolfo to recoup, and then it was back on the road again, to Africa for the fourth time. John Paul arrived in Harare, the capital of Zimbabwe, on 10 September to be greeted by its Prime Minister, Robert Mugabe. Mugabe had been one of the leaders of the armed struggle against white rule in what was once Southern Rhodesia. The campaign to end minority rule had received considerable support from Catholic sources, not least Rhodesia's own Justice and Peace Commission, and Mugabe was himself of a Catholic background. As he welcomed the Pope he defended the armed struggle as an example of the just war theory. They had resorted to war, he said, 'because we felt we could not achieve justice through a peaceful solution'. The Pope responded by congratulating Mugabe on the efforts his government had made to achieve national reconciliation – not only with the white population, it must be said, but with political opponents within the black community. But the Pope, with the proximity of South Africa in mind, explicitly rejected armed struggle as a means of overcoming apartheid. He condemned apartheid, but he also called upon all who were struggling against it to renounce the use of violence to achieve its overthrow. He returned to the theme that evening, when he addressed the bishops of Southern Africa, gathered for an inter-regional conference. It was a message which all but a few leading churchmen of any denomination would have endorsed, and something which they had long been repeating – despite the fact that it seemed an increasingly unrealistic option. In Matabeleland some years previously troops loyal to Mugabe had been accused of carrying out massacres of Mugabe's (black) political opponents. The Pope went there, and sympathized with the victims of violence, but once again went out of his way to support the Prime Minister's efforts at reconciliation.

The entire three-day tour of the country took place in a particularly festive atmosphere. The Pope spent 13 September in Botswana, and his plans were to spend the next two days in Lesotho. Here he was to beatify a nineteenth-century missionary who helped make it very largely a Catholic country. But then it all began to go wrong. En route to Lesotho his plane was forced to make an unscheduled stop at Pretoria's Jan Smuts airport. The Vatican had been busily trying to avoid South Africa: when the Pope landed he was greeted by a delighted Foreign Minister, Pik Botha, who had arranged for him to be escorted into Lesotho by a squad of South African security men. It was a propaganda triumph for South Africa: for the Holy See it was a disaster. The South African Government could also take heart from the Pope's fervent appeal to reject violence. 'To choose non-violence', the Pope told a youth gathering in Lesotho on 15 September, 'means to take a courageous choice in love, a choice which includes the active defence of human rights and a firm commitment to justice and ordered development.' How, he did not say, and the South African press made the most of the complete rejection of violence even against a violent oppressor. As leading South African churchman, Alan Boesak, said later, it was not enough simply to tell people not to use violence. One had to offer practical strategies for combating violence by non-violent means, and that the Pope had failed to do.

Lesotho was followed by a five-hour stopover in Swaziland before John Paul travelled on to Mozambique, and possibly the most controversial part of any of his African tours hitherto. In the capitol, Maputo, the Frelimo party held sway; in much of the countryside Renamo guerrillas, backed by the South African government, were fighting Frelimo forces in one of the bitterest civil wars in Africa. Under the previous Portuguese administration the Church had enjoyed a highly privileged position, but Frelimo had deprived it of that status. The Church had been urging the government to open talks with Renamo in the belief that they might be more sympathetic.

Yet the Mozambican authorities had shown considerable enthusiasm for the papal visit. Possibly it provided a welcome distraction both from the war and from the wretched economic conditions resulting from it. The local hierarchy was pleased at this sign by Frelimo of a retreat from its anti-Catholic stance. Accordingly, the Pope's message must be framed with care. He gave only a passing mention of the need for dialogue to end the war, adding that the conditions for evangelization were 'difficult'. He chose Mozambique to insist that the Gospel must be rooted in local culture, but he added the immediate rider that the liturgy must 'respect, with loving and total fidelity, [to] the texts and rites which the legitimate authority has decided to exclude from the creativity of individuals and groups'. It was not the Gospel which must change, he said as he departed Maputo for Rome on 19 September, but local cultures must make an effort to assimilate the Gospel. It was a distinctly conservative message, both politically and theologically. That, at least, was how it seemed to a delegation from the South African Council of Churches which met the Pope briefly on his last day in Mozambique, after attending the final rally. Before he started on this journey representatives of the SACC had been to Rome to brief the Pope about the situation particularly in South Africa. They were disappointed at the outcome, and Alan Boesak made no attempt to hide it.

The clash was not helped by remarks the Pope made to journalists during one of his flights in the course of this tour, in which he appeared both to reject the policy of economic sanctions against South Africa, and to deny the value of boycotting elections. These were tactics actively supported by South African opponents of apartheid. It was little wonder that people asked whether he had really understood the situation, despite his verbal condemnations of apartheid. Though still opposed to the use of force, John Paul took the opportunity of his first public audience after his return to condemn once again and unequivocally the apartheid system. 'Getting rid of discrimination', he said, 'is an integral part of liberation and the self-determination of the African people.'

By this time, however, another sort of liberation was on the papal mind. The previous year's Synod had given considerable attention to the role of women in the Church, and the Pope had recently praised the attempts of the US Bishops' Conference to produce a pastoral letter on the subject which in the end came to nothing. As September came to a close, John Paul published *Mulieris Dignitatem* (On the dignity of woman) as a response to this as well as to the Marian year which had given the topic a 'special thrust'. The Pope described the apostolic letter as more a meditation on certain passages of Scripture than a doctrinal or practical discussion of the role of women in the Church. In this sense he takes up the two quite separate accounts of the creation of Adam and Eve that occur in Genesis. The 'unity of two', he says, 'are called to live in a communion of love, and in this way to mirror in the world the communion of love that is in God'.

But this 'communion of two' for John Paul implies a 'specific diversity' between men and women. While that diversity does not entail male domination, the struggle of women to free themselves from that domination must not involve their appropriating 'to themselves male characteristics contrary to their own feminine originality'. Male domination, he argues, arises not from the natural state of the relationship between women and men, but from original sin. John Paul emphasizes Christ's own attitude to women – he 'became a promoter of women's true dignity and of the vocation corresponding to this dignity'.

The Pope reflects next on motherhood and on a virginity that has been chosen freely, which he describes as a spiritual motherhood. And, in a section on the Eucharist, he comments on St Paul's analogy of the Church as the bride of Christ, where he considers why women cannot be ordained to the priesthood. Arguing against those who say that Christ only chose men to be his apostles because, in the society of the time, it would have been impossible to have done otherwise, John Paul insists that He chose twelve men acting in a 'completely free and sovereign manner'. Using Paul's analogy he declares the Eucharist 'expresses the redemptive act of Christ the Bridegroom towards the Church the Bride'. The priest at the Eucharist, acting *in persona Christi*, therefore has to be male to give expression to that relationship between bridegroom and bride. Having reached this point, the Pope then goes on to comment on the role that women can play in modern times. The sensitivity of women, he argues, can humanize the technological world in which we find ourselves.

It was an spiritually inspiring document, no doubt, but as a blueprint for the future role of women in Church and society it failed to provide any positive guidance. The delicate issue of the ordination of women was a matter of great ecumenical concern. Had the Pope argued that a male priesthood was only a question of discipline, there would have been no new obstacle to unity with the Anglican Communion. He insisted, however, that it was a doctrinal matter, and it was embarrassing that a supposedly doctrinal argument was built upon a biblical metaphor, without even recourse to modern exegesis – though that, it has to be said, is typical of the Pope's style.[11]

It was also very much the papal style to call Europe back to its Christian roots, and to argue that the Eastern bloc countries had every reason to be regarded as part of a common European culture. On 8 October John Paul began his fourth tour of France. This journey took him, not only on a pastoral visit to Alsace-Lorraine, but to agencies of the European Community based in Strasbourg: on 8 October to the Council of Europe and the European Court and on the 11th, the final day of his stay, to the European

Parliament - where the Reverend Ian Paisley, Democratic Unionist member for Northern Ireland, was removed from the chamber for abusing the Pope as Antichrist.

Before the Council of Europe John Paul spoke of a common European identity, and of the present threats to that identity. He mentioned in particular economic and social developments which, in his view, put at risk the stability of family life. Before the judges of the European Court he argued that respect for human rights was one of Christian Europe's chief legacies to the rest of the human race. Traditionally, he said, there had been two types of rights, political ones and social ones. But now there had to be a third kind, those to do with the quality of the environment, with health and security.[12]

John Paul spoke in praise of the Single European Act, insisting that, far from submerging member states into one super-state, the Act would provide a guarantee of the cultural identity of each member. If Europe's Christian roots were ignored, he said, it would be a denial of the continent's heritage and would put at risk a future worthy of the people of Europe. He also warned the member states not to have too narrow a notion of what constituted Europe. 'Other nations could certainly join those which are represented here today', he said. 'My wish as supreme pastor of the universal Church, someone who has come from Eastern Europe and who knows the aspirations of the Slav peoples, that other "lung" of our common European motherland, my wish is that Europe . . . might one day extend to the dimensions it has been given by geography and still more by history.'

The Pope had reason to be hopeful for the signs were encouraging. As Mikhail Gorbachev's policy of *perestroika* began to take hold, the new Prime Minister in Poland, Mieczyslav Rajowski, told Parliament that his government intended to press ahead with the establishment of diplomatic relations with the Vatican, and to regularize the position of the Catholic Church within the country. Meanwhile in Vilnius, capital of Lithuania, the cathedral was handed back to the Church, and mass was said there for the first time since 1950.

In Rome itself, however, neither *perestroika* nor *glasnost* were much in evidence. In a religiously pluralistic Europe, marriages across denominational and faith boundaries are common. Yet by contrast in Poland, an almost wholly Roman Catholic country, such marriages are inevitably rare. Addressing an ecumenical group from Switzerland the Pope commented unfavourably on the effects on the religious lives of families by permitting 'mixed' marriages. Meanwhile the Pontifical Council for the Family called a conference to celebrate the twentieth anniversary of Paul VI's encyclical condemning artificial means of contraception, *Humanae Vitae*. There was a gathering of sixty bishops from round the world to whom John Paul spoke of 'unjustified criticisms and unacceptable silences' about the encyclical, whereas it had, over the years, demonstrated its 'prophetic meaning and living relevance'. The John Paul II Institute for Studies on Marriage and the Family, together with Opus Dei, sponsored a similar gathering for moral theologians, paid for by the American Knights of Columbus. There should be no exceptions to the teaching on contraception for any reason, the Pope told them: that is what Pope Paul intended when he described contraception as 'intrinsically evil'.[13] Because this teaching was 'written by the creative hand of God in the nature of the human person', it was not possible to disagree with it except by 'refusing to God himself the obedience of our intelligence'. It seemed as if he were saying that to reject the teachings of the disputed encyclical was to reject the entire teaching of the Church, for such teachings he insisted, ignoring Vatican II's assertion of the 'hierarchy of truths', form a 'unitary whole'. It was the role of theologians and teachers simply 'to defend and deepen' what had been taught in *Humanae Vitae*.

What was at issue, apart from the validity of the encyclical's arguments in themselves, was the role of theologians and how that is viewed by the Pope and his Curia. In mid-November the US bishops met to discuss a draft document sent by the Vatican on the status of Episcopal Conferences. It had been circulated earlier in the year by Cardinal Gantin of the Congregation of Bishops as a response to the request of the 1985 Synod for a better appreciation of the theological underpinning of Episcopal Conferences. The document played down their role, drawing attention to three dangers inherent in appearing to grant them more authority than they, in reality, possess; restrictions on the freedom of individual bishops in their dioceses; making bishops into simple executives of conference decisions; and thirdly appearing to give such conferences autonomy from the Holy See on disciplinary or even doctrinal matters. On this last point the document drew a distinction between the merely collective nature of decision-making within a conference, and the collegial nature of the decision-making when bishops are gathered around the person of the Pope.

Such, briefly, was the gist of the Congregations's arguments against the authority of Episcopal Conferences. The US bishops found the document so deficient that it was not even suitable as a basis for discussion, and they asked that it be withdrawn and rewritten. The voting was 205 against the draft, and 59 in its favour.[14] In addition, the bishops had before them a statement drawn up for them on the relationship between bishops and theologians. It had been carefully prepared over a long period of time, and had been sent to the Vatican more than a year before the conference was scheduled to meet to discuss it. Just before the meeting took place the Vatican sent a five-page fax of criticisms (the document, it said, seemed to place bishops and theologians on the same level). The late arrival of the Vatican's observations made it impossible for them to be taken into consideration. If the American bishops were not to appear as if on a collision course with the Vatican, debate about the role of theologians had to be postponed, and it was.

The role of theologians was also addressed in the revised draft of a document issued by the Congregation for Catholic Education. The earlier version had been much criticized by heads of Catholic universities. The concern of the Congregation had been to preserve the Catholic identity of the Church-related institutions of higher education: the worry of the university authorities had been that the way the document was phrased might put such institutions outside the sphere of national education systems, particularly by appearing to restrict academic freedom. The new version gave theologians more independence, though it insisted that theologians 'recognize and accept the right of bishops as the authentic interpreters of Catholic doctrine to judge whether their theological research and teaching conform with authentic Catholic doctrine and divine revelation'. The document acknowledged the juridical independence from the bishops of institutions of higher education, and equally acknowledged the right to theological research, provided 'theories and hypotheses' were not allowed to disturb the faith of the ordinary Catholic in the pew.

On 8 December the Vatican issued the Pope's message for the World Day of Peace, 1 January 1989. It dealt movingly with the rights of ethnic minorities. Meanwhile, in Berlin, a new and conservative Archbishop was being imposed upon the diocese of Cologne, contrary to the rights of the cathedral chapter, contrary to the terms of the Vatican's concordat with North Rhine Westphalia and, to judge by the protests, contrary to the wishes of the people of the diocese. In the Heenan Lecture, delivered at Heythrop College, University of London, Paul Sieghart, a distinguished law reformer and international jurist, described John Paul II as the 'best known, and most powerful, consistent and persistent protagonist' of human rights in the world. Why was it, he wondered, that 'my own Church – that is, the Church of Rome – has not yet even begun to practise what it has so forcefully preached for twenty-five years and more in the matter of human rights?'[15]

That was not, of course, how the Pope saw it. As he looked back over 1989 in his customary address to the Roman Curia, he took delight in the Marian

Year, in the millennium celebrations in Russia, in his social encyclical *Solicitudo Rei Socialis*, and in the apostolic constitution *Pastor Bonus*, due to come into force the following March, which revised the structures of the Curia. He had a special word for the 'courageous' *Humanae Vitae*. Of course there were black spots: the schism of Lefebvre, naturally, and the decision by the Anglicans to ordain women to the priesthood. It was a setback to ecumenism, but, he added, he hoped that painful consequences might be avoided, both in ecumenical relations and within the Anglican Communion.

On the Feast of the Epiphany, in the course of the ordination of thirteen new African bishops, John Paul announced that a Synod of the African Church would take place. It was an idea which had long been mooted in Africa itself,[16] and there were very different points of view about the proposal, given the wide variety of problems facing the continent, its poverty, and its political fragmentation. The theme announced by the Pope was 'The Church in Africa on the threshold of the third millennium', which meant, presumably, that it would have to meet before the end of the century, but no date was mentioned and, perhaps more importantly, no place.

The threshold of the third millennium was also part of the theme of *Christi Fideles Laici*, published at the end of January. It was the papal response to the Synod on the Laity which had taken place over a year earlier. Everyone, said the Pope in this apostolic exhortation, is called to be a labourer in the vineyard of the Lord. But Christians are not simply labourers, he insisted, they are themselves branches of the vine, a symbol not only of the people of God but of Christ himself. The ministries which lay people undertake, much more various than they used to be, are 'in communion and on behalf of the communion' – though he makes a point of asserting that the ordained ministry has a primary position in the Church and is a participation in the ministry of Jesus which is different in kind, and not simply in degree, from the participation of the laity. Certain pastoral roles can be performed by the laity 'when the necessity of the Church warrants it and when [ordained] ministers are lacking', but the danger of clericalizing the laity by too indiscriminate use of the word 'minister' ought to be avoided. The Pope goes on to talk about forms of participation which the laity may share, such as parish and diocesan pastoral councils, and he included participation in 'lay movements', stressing as one of the five basic criteria which such movements must fulfil, total adherence to the proposition that the Pope is 'the perpetual and visible centre of the unity of the universal Church'. The laity had a right to form such groups, as affirmed in the Code of Canon Law, but the Pontifical Council for the Laity was drawing up a list of those with official approval.

Having established the nature of lay participation in the life of the Church, John Paul focuses on the task it has to perform, that of re-evangelization of those countries where secularism and atheism now hold sway in place of Christianity. He is thinking, he says, of the First World, with its economic wellbeing and consumerism, but the same holds true to some degree for other regions affected by the same spread of secularism and, says the Pope, 'the spread of sects'.

The task to be rendered to humanity by the Church is 'to rediscover and make others rediscover, the inviolable dignity of every human person'. The Pope lists the rights inherent in this dignity – the right to life, to religious freedom. There must be support for the family, and Christians have a duty to play an active part in political life, the fruit of which is peace. He next describes the specific role to be played by different groups in society, the young, the elderly, the sick, women and men. The Pope demanded in particular, and in line with the Synod's deliberations, that ways might be found to foster a greater role for women in the life of the Church – though that, he added again, does not include the role of priest. He ended the exhortation with a prose poem to Mary.

The issue of rights within the Church was addressed in a document which appeared at the same time as *Christi Fideles Laici*, though from a very different source. The 'Cologne Declaration' as it came to be called was published on 27 January, signed by 163, mainly German-speaking, theologians, though later endorsed by distinguished scholars from around the world. There were three main criticisms of the Church developed in the Declaration, and clearly stated in its opening paragraphs:

(1) The Roman Curia is energetically filling episcopal sees throughout the world without respecting the suggestions of local churches and neglecting their established rights.

(2) Throughout the world qualified theologians are being refused official Church permission to teach. This is a significant and dangerous intrusion into the freedom of research and teaching and into the dialogue-like structure of theological thinking which the Second Vatican Council emphasized in many passages. The granting of official permission to teach is being abused by being made a means of discipline.

(3) We observe an attempt, theologically highly questionable, to enforce and overstep in an inadmissible ways the Pope's competence in the field of doctrinal teaching alongside that of jurisdiction.

Some bishops - most notably perhaps the Episcopal Conference of Latin America (CELAM) - rallied to the side of the Pope and his Curia. The Vatican tried to brush off the theologians' complaints as a little local difficulty, but as support for the declaration increased - fifty-two members of the Catholic University of Louvain, a hundred and thirty French theologians - the Vatican's response grew equivalently sharper.

Rome had in any case a new weapon to hand, the oath of fidelity to be taken by all in positions of authority in the Church, even including deacons about to be ordained and those with a teaching office, especially a post where faith or morals had to be taught. In addition to the oath, the profession of faith taken by the same group of people was revised to include the sentence 'I adhere by religious assent of the will and intellect to the teachings which either the Roman pontiff or the college of bishops declare when they exercise the authentic *magisterium*, even if they do not intend to proclaim them by definitive act'. The instructions of the '*magisterium*', in other words, did not have to be infallible for theologians to be required to give 'religious assent of the will and intellect'. The oath and revised profession of faith came into force on 1 March.

Shortly afterwards, from 8 to 11 March, there was a meeting of the American bishops in Rome, presided over by the Pope, ostensibly to discuss evangelization but in practice to hear criticism from the Curia of the way in which things were being done in the American Church. Theologians were replacing bishops as teachers of doctrine, warned Ratzinger, and that must stop. His views received short shrift from the President of the US Conference of Bishops, Archbishop John May of St Louis, who told Ratzinger that, in the USA, the divine right of bishops was regarded as being as outmoded as the doctrine of the divine right of kings.

Too many nullities of marriage were being given by the American marriage tribunals, complained the Curia. It is because nuns are qualifying as canon lawyers and are too soft-hearted, surmised Cardinal Gagnon of the Pontifical Council for the Family, whereas men are more objective, a remark which the US bishops regarded as sexist and gratuitously insulting. Women came in for a hard time from the Curia, and were stoutly defended by the US bishops. The bishops, it must be said, were on a spectrum from the conservative to the liberal; yet the Vatican's criticisms of the US Church managed to unite them as rarely before.

As the US bishops met in Rome to listen to criticisms of the state of the American Church, it was announced that Archbishop Marcinckus was to leave the 'Institute for the Works of Religion', better known as the Vatican

Bank, where he had been president for eighteen years. Ultimate control of the IOR was to be put in the hands of a commission of five cardinals who would hold office for five years. They in turn would give oversight of the IOR to five bankers or economic experts who in turn would delegate day-to-day control to a director and deputy director, together with three auditors.

All this was happening seven years after Roberto Calvi had been found hanging under Blackfriars Bridge following the crash of the Banco Ambrosiano (cf. above, p. 109). Meanwhile the Vatican's finances were getting ever deeper into the red: a loss of $68 million in 1988 was announced, and one of $78 million was predicted for the current year, 1989. It was always hoped by the Vatican that the faithful would stump up the money through Peter's Pence. This they had constantly failed to do, at least in sufficient quantity to wipe out the deficit. The Vatican had to take steps to cut back its expenditure, said Cardinal Krol, turning a critical eye upon the Vatican's publishing activities in general and L'Osservatore Romano in particular. It was revealed that a fund set up to finance the Holy See's diplomatic activity had been exhausted: there were now 118 nunciatures around the world.

The Pope's forty-first visit outside Italy began in the evening of 28 April in Madagascar. A week earlier there had been deaths in the capital city, Tannanarive, as opposition parties went on to the streets to protest against the government of the socialist President Didier Ratsirak. The Churches had called for an end to the conflict at least for the duration of the papal visit, and the truce was observed. The opposition groups wanted their own audience with the Pope as had happened in Paraguay (cf. above, p. 194), but unlike Paraguay this was refused by the Vatican. Instead they met Cardinal Casaroli. The Pope spent two full days in Madagascar, and on Monday 1 May flew on to Réunion, where the French Prime Minister turned up to congratulate John Paul on his second visit to French territory in a year.

The following day the Pope arrived in Lusaka by Concorde, sent especially by Air France, the 2,000 mile flight from Réunion taking just two-and-a-half hours. In the Zambian capital he was welcomed by Kenneth Kaunda as a champion of 'the hungry, the poor, the sick and the homeless', before the President went on to condemn apartheid in South Africa as 'a sin against the whole of humanity'. With that description the Pope concurred, but insisted then, as he did the following day in his customary address to the diplomatic corps, that any change in the system would have to be brought about peacefully. He was more eloquent on the topic of international debt: 'Is it merely a rhetorical question', he asked, 'how many infants and children die every day in Africa because resources are being swallowed up by debt repayments?' He went on to congratulate both Zambia and Malawi, to which country he was going next, on their care for refugees from the civil wars in Angola and Mozambique.

In Zambia the Pope visited the Copper Belt town of Kitwe and blessed the cornerstones of six new churches; he held a rally with the country's youth, and attended an ecumenical service in Lusaka's Anglican cathedral where he called on the Churches to 'avoid all forms of competition and rivalry' in Africa. The President of the African National Congress, Oliver Tambo, attended this service, but did not meet the Pope.

Religious rivalry, the Pope found, was much in evidence in parts of Malawi, where the competitor was not another Christian body but Islam. He held a prayer service which was attended by representatives of fifteen different faiths including Islam. The Catholic Church wanted dialogue, he told them, and to work with others to build Malawi. This building up, he said in his final mass before leaving for Rome on 6 May, must not be at the expense of the African traditional way of life: 'I put before you a challenge', he told his congregation at mass in Lilongwe, 'to reject a way of living which does not correspond with the best of your local traditions and your Christian faith.' What did not correspond, it was clear, was the Western version of progress.

On his arrival in Malawi on 4 May the Pope had the unusual experience of being upstaged by his host, President-For-Life Hastings Banda who, in a distinctly extempore speech praising the contribution of Catholics to the life of his country, managed to claim that Malawi was the best governed country in Africa. Banda stayed behind to dance with the crowds as the Pope drove off. The following day the Pope's first outdoor mass in the country was delayed for fifteen minutes until Banda turned up, complete with a troupe of dancing women. The Pope appeared to take it all in good part, and opened the service with a blessing for Banda and his party.

On the flight out to Africa a journalist, formerly of *L'Osservatore Romano*, had asked John Paul what he thought had been the effect of his many travels. It was, said the Pope, a deep question[17], but he had thought about it and, on the way back to Rome, supplied an answer. First of all, there was the question of conflict in the Church between conservatives and progressives – he believed it to be particularly true of Europe. By ignoring that conflict, he said, and going directly to the People of God, he was pushing the two extremes to the margins. Again his travels demonstrated the Church's universality, preparations for them benefited local churches and improved religious practice. It was also more effective when speaking of peace to do so in Hiroshima. He acknowledged some of the problems, including that of meeting dubious political leaders, but he dismissed the charge of triumphalism and claimed to dialogue every day with those he met on his journeyings. Overall, however, he felt he could not give a general assessment. His journeys were still developing. The assassination attempt had convinced him that he should make as many of them as he could while he still had the strength, so much did he believe in their usefulness.

Back in Italy there was trouble among the country's theologians. Inspired by the Cologne Declaration (cf. above, p. 205), sixty-three of them had produced their own version, published in the Catholic monthly *Il Regno*. Some of their themes were the same though their tone was more conciliatory than that of the German-speaking theologians: indeed, they urged that the debate be less polemical. On the other hand, they made some sharp observations on the tendency to describe Vatican II simply as a 'pastoral' Council, thereby playing down its doctrinal implications. They also spoke of the 'readjustment' in the notion of *magisterium* which had happened since Vatican II, and called for respect for the 'hierarchy of truths' which the Council had insisted upon. Conciliatory or not, the document was swiftly rebutted by Cardinal Ugo Poletti as chairman of the Italian Episcopal Conference. The Church, he said, was not underestimating the importance of Vatican II. It was simply a question of how to interpret the Council.

The theme was taken up in an apostolic letter from the Pope, published on 14 May to mark, belatedly, the twenty-fifth anniversary of the Council's Constitution on the Liturgy. The Pope recognized the difficulties that had occurred as a result of the introduction of the revised forms of the liturgy – active participation had been found by some, he said, to be too demanding. He criticized those who had simply gone back to traditional forms of worship, but he was more critical of 'deviations' such as omissions from, or additions to, liturgical texts, such as general absolution, a confusion between ministerial priesthood and the priesthood of the laity. Such deviations, he insisted, had to be rooted out by the bishops.

Since Vatican II, however, a generation had grown up with little or no memory of what went before. There was an urgent task of liturgical and biblical formation, above all of the clergy but also of the laity. A more difficult question was that of liturgical adaptation in different cultures. There were parts of the liturgy not open to change, but other parts might be adapted. Such adaptations might be a source of enrichment, but must not be allowed to harm unity. Yet it was not only the liturgy which might be adapted: cultures themselves had to change. 'Cultural adaptation also requires con-version of heart and even, where necessary, a breaking with ancestral customs incompatible with the Catholic faith'.

It was an age-old problem. The Jesuits had fallen foul of it when, in the late seventeenth and early eighteenth centuries, they had tried to adapt Christian liturgy to the ancestral customs of the Chinese. Their efforts had been reported to Rome by more orthodox Franciscan missionaries. However much the Pope praised the possibility of adaptation, he was much more concerned that deviation from the Roman norm would be inconsiderable. And however much he exhorted the people of Africa, say, not to get carried away by Western consumerism and retain their own culture, that culture had to shift significantly if there was evidence of a conflict with Christian norms of faith and morals as they had developed in Europe.

Not that, as he made clear yet again, this time to George Bush, the Pope had any high opinion of Western culture as a whole. The American President was in Europe at the end of May for a meeting of NATO, and he took the opportunity of calling on the Pope. John Paul spoke highly of the United States, but dwelt more upon the President's efforts to eradicate the evils from which the country was suffering, especially drug abuse and poverty. These, however, 'are only symptoms of a deeper moral crisis eating away at the texture of society in almost every part of the world', he said. In return, President Bush congratulated the Pope on the recent legalization of the Church in Poland. It was, he insisted, 'a tribute to your enduring commitment to freedom'.

Shortly after the meeting with Bush, John Paul set off from Rome on his forty-second foreign tour to a Christian region where the faith and morals of his own Roman Catholicism was little represented. Because the Catholic population of Scandinavia is less than two per cent in any of the countries he was to visit, he described the trip as ecumenical, rather than the more usual pastoral.

The first country to receive him was Norway, where the Pope arrived on Thursday 1 June. It was not an easy visit. No crowds on the street to greet him, awkward questions from the country's prime minister about the Church's attitude to contraception and to the prevention of AIDS, a boycott by seven of the eleven Lutheran bishops at an ecumenical meeting in the royal palace. While the Pope talked about the Catholic Church's irrevocable commitment to ecumenism, about the dangers of secularization, and the need for the Churches to make common cause in the fight against religious indifference, the Lutheran bishops raised practical matters such as intercommunion, mixed marriages, and the failure of Rome unequivocally to recognize in the Lutheran Churches true ecclesial communities.

The bishops who had failed to turn up in Oslo still remained absent when the following day John Paul went to an ecumenical service in Trondheim. One of them explained that, in their view, the ecumenical process had stopped with the accession of Wojtyla, and that his view of reunion was getting the other Churches to acknowledge his own spiritual leadership.

Next he went to Iceland for a day. A day was enough. There are only eighteen hundred Catholics on the island, and two churches, one of them a cathedral, served by seven priests. He said mass in the cathedral, and presided at an open-air ecumenical service. And then on to Finland where he was more at ease. Helsinki had given its name to an agreement on civil rights in Europe. The Pope made a point of criticizing Russia for the denial of the right of freedom of worship to the Catholics of the Ukraine.

The next stop was Denmark for two days where the Archbishop of Copenhagen called upon him to cancel the excommunication of Martin Luther. John Paul who must have been warned replied directly. The excommunication had caused deep wounds, but simply cancelling the excommunication, he said reasonably, will not cure them. There had to be a rethink of Luther's legacy to the wider Church. In Roskilde the Bishop would only let him into his cathedral for vespers provided he did not speak. John Paul accepted the discourtesy humbly, and won much sympathy from the local press.

In Sweden, where John Paul spent two and a half days, the atmosphere was warmer. The Church, though still very small in numbers, had undergone a rapid growth in the country largely through immigration and the arrival of refugees. It was also well respected and, as the Pope told the widow of the assassinated socialist prime minister, Olaf Palme, it had been Palme who had first invited him. The invitation from the bishops had come later and, it seemed, only after they had been prodded by the prime minister. Swedish interest in the Church had been confirmed by the recent decision to establish a resident ambassador at the Vatican.[18] When an ecumenical service was held in Uppsala cathedral, attended by the King and Queen, the archbishop pleaded for intercommunion. The Pope was uncomfortable at this suggestion, but was firm in rejecting it. He had, it transpired, his own proposals for speeding ecumenical advance. In Norway and Sweden the respective monarchs are titular heads of their Lutheran Churches. The kings and the Pope should go skiing together, suggested John Paul to journalists on 10 June, during the flight back to Rome.

In July the Pope took a walking holiday in Piedmont. It was while he was away that the restoration of full diplomatic relations between the Holy See and Poland was announced, on 17 July. The Pope, who had in April, even before the 'normalization' of Church-state relations there, written to Warsaw's Archbishop, Cardinal Glemp, saying the time had come for just such a step, made no comment.

There were other signs of a changing relationship between the Vatican and what was still the Soviet bloc. The Czechoslovak government had in the past insisted that any new bishops in that country would have to be chosen from priests in the pro-government *Pacem in terris* group. They now waived that requirement though they still accused the Vatican of contravening the Helsinki Accord on Human Rights by discriminating against the *Pacem in terris* clergy in making the appointments when new bishops were created to fill some of the vacant sees. At the end of July a priest was appointed, with the rank of bishop, as apostolic administrator of Minsk, his responsibility included the whole of the Soviet Republic of Byelorussia. It was a difficult choice. Most Catholic priests in Byelorussia are of Polish origin, and proud of it: the number of Byelorussian clergy is small, so the Vatican's room for manoeuvre was limited. After consulting Moscow and Minsk, the Pope opted for Tadeusz Kondrusiewicz, ethnically a Pole. The 'Byelorussian National Front for Perestroika', which had been campaigning for religious liberty, was also pressing for a restoration of national language and identity through, among other means, the translation into Byelorussian of religious texts. The National Front had links with the more developed national movement in Lithuania: the appointment of a Polish, rather than a Lithuanian priest to the post of apostolic administrator was calculated more to please the Soviet authorities than Byelorussian Catholics.

Among the Pope's other problems in the summer of 1989 was the continued existence of the Carmelite convent at Auschwitz (cf. above, p. 165). An agreement had been reached according to which the nuns should have moved out by the end of February, but when Jewish leaders went to the Vatican in May to discuss the Vatican document on racism, and what was to be said about the Jews in the Catechism then in preparation, the move had still not taken place. Another date had been fixed – 22 July 1989 – but the Jewish representatives were far from hopeful. They were also clearly disturbed by the failure of the Pope to intervene personally. John Paul's insistence that it was purely a local matter for the Polish episcopate was not taken kindly. The new date came and went, with the nuns still in place – planning permission for their new centre outside the former concentration camp was given only in June. Jewish militants invaded the site in protest at their continued presence, and Pope John Paul's successor as Archbishop of Cracow, Cardinal

Macharski, made things worse by blaming the 'Jewish media in the West', and talking of 'unrealistic deadlines'. 'I know the Pope has made some very positive statements', said the Vice-President of the European Jewish Conference, Théo Klein, 'but I think he should make them more strongly – and in Polish.' When Macharski's August statement that his Archdiocese was to suspend work on the new centre because of the Jewish groups' 'violent campaign of accusation and slander' was broadcast on Vatican Radio it was seen as a sign that his stance had papal support. It did not help relations with the Jews when, on 2 August, during one of his regular Wednesday audiences, the Pope insisted that God's covenant with the Jews had been superseded by the Christian covenant, signed in Jesus' blood. Nor did it help when Cardinal Glemp, speaking at the Marian shrine of Jasna Góra, talked of a Jewish invasion of Polish sovereignty. He wanted the whole matter to be renegotiated by 'competent people'. But the 'competent people' who had negotiated the original agreement upon which Cardinal Macharski had reneged had been four cardinals: Macharski himself, and the Archbishops of Brussels, Lyons and Paris, the last, Cardinal Lustiger, himself Jewish by birth. They were, not surprisingly, incensed by the attitude of the Polish Cardinals. John Paul still said nothing. On 19 September, however, the Vatican Commission for Religious Relations with the Jews issued a statement in support of the 1987 agreement about the removal of the Auschwitz convent to a site outside the camp, and promised to contribute funds. The following day Cardinal Glemp fell into line.

If the Pope's morale needed a boost as the summer of 1989 drew to a close he received it in Santiago de Compostela, the shrine on Spain's northwest coast to the Apostle St James, and for centuries one of Europe's most popular destinations for pilgrims. A 'World Youth Forum' had been summoned there, to be addressed by John Paul. They arrived in their tens of thousands – over half a million young people finally gathered to greet the Pope when he arrived on 19 August – and cheered him to the echo. His first visit was to a church in the city to meet handicapped pilgrims, and in the evening he went to meet the vast crowds camped out on a mountainside. They stayed there all night – it turned bitterly cold – and the Pope came back the following morning to say their Sunday mass. 'Do not be afraid to be saints', he told them. That was Sunday. On Monday he went to the shrine of the Virgin at Covadonga, which commemorated the decisive battle when Islamic forces began, slowly, to be driven back out of Spain – and therefore out of Western Europe. 'With confidence I lay before the feet of the Saint of Covadonga the project of a Europe without frontiers that does not renounce its Christian roots', he said.

As he came to reflect at the end of August in an apostolic letter written on the fiftieth anniversary of the outbreak of World War II, John Paul recalled events which he had himself witnessed 'at the side of the Archbishop of Cracow, Adam Stefan Sapieha'. He mentioned the fate of Poland, and of Polish Jews in particular. But, he added, 'The new paganism and the systems related to it were certainly directed against the Jews, but they were likewise aimed at Christianity, whose teaching had shaped the soul of Europe'. He attacked the two ideologies of Nazi paganism and Marxist dogma, called for respect for people's rights and for disarmament and, in a letter addressed to 'all people of good will', spoke directly to Catholics. They should, he said, 'make an examination of conscience about the quality of Europe's evangelization. The collapse of Christian values that led to yesterday's moral failures must make us vigilant as to the way the Gospel is proclaimed and lived out today.'

Shortly afterwards there was another apostolic letter to all bishops in which the Pope appealed for freedom and independence for Lebanon. Peace in the civil war there had been a constant theme both of Paul VI and himself, he said. It was incumbent upon the Church to make known that collaboration between Christians and Muslims which had been a feature of Lebanese political life, and an example to all. The letter was dated 7 September: bearing the same date was an unprecedented message 'to all followers of Islam', calling both for prayer and for action to bring the war to an end, and promising Christian cooperation for that purpose.

From 29 September to 2 October the Archbishop of Canterbury, Dr Robert Runcie, was in Rome for a series of meetings with the Pope. On the first day there was a private encounter between Pope and Archbishop, followed by a reception given by the Council for Christian Unity. The following day there was a more formal meeting between John Paul and Dr Runcie and an ecumenical service at vespers in the monastery from which St Augustine set out to convert the English. On Sunday Dr Runcie first celebrated the Eucharist in the church of All Saints with Cardinal Willebrands of the Unity Council in attendance, and then he went to the Vatican for mass in St Peter's, during which the Pope and he exchanged the kiss of peace. The final meeting occurred on Monday 2 October, with the reading out of a joint declaration.

If the intention was to forward ecumenical relations, then the visit of the Archbishop was only a modest success. Indeed, it was almost only the participants, apparently surprised by the warmth with which they were received, who seem to have thought it to have been any sort of success at all.

At vespers in San Gregorio the Pope dwelt upon the authority of his own office, encouraged perhaps by a remark of the Archbishop's, published in *Il Regno*, that 'Anglicans are beginning to recognize and welcome a petrine universal primacy in the office of the Bishop of Rome'. Though the final declaration committed the two Churches 'to the restoration of visible unity and full ecclesial communion', it could not disguise the problems in the way of that unity, most particularly the ordination of women to the priesthood.

Meanwhile there was a Eucharistic Congress taking place in Seoul, South Korea. John Paul went there for the closing ceremonies. He arrived in the capital on 6 October, to find an atmosphere a great deal less tense than at the time of his previous visit in 1984. Nevertheless, when he said a mass for young people on 7 October, he was presented with a (miniaturized) tear gas canister and a Molotov cocktail. The closing celebration of the Congress took place the following day. In his homily John Paul expressed the desire, for the first time aired in public, to visit the People's Republic of China. In speaking of the Church there he recognized the difficulties of healing the breach between Catholics who had suffered for their loyalty to Rome and the Patriotic Association, the breakaway National Catholic Church set up by the government. A delicate task remained, he said, of fostering reconciliation within the ecclesial community.

While in Korea the Pope spoke publicly as well as privately to the President of the need for greater democracy and greater respect for human rights, themes to which he returned in Indonesia. He flew there on 9 October and warned the President and his ministers (several Catholics being among their number although the proportion of Catholics in the population was only 3 per cent) that they should not 'disregard human rights in a misguided search for political unity'. The most difficult part of his journey was to East Timor, a former Portuguese colony which Indonesia had annexed in 1975 a mere week after it had been granted independence. Attempts to regain its sovereignty had been brutally crushed, and the site chosen for the papal mass in Dili, the capital, had been one of the killing fields.

John Paul needed to tread with the utmost caution. The Vatican, in line with the world community, had not recognized the annexation, and the Bishop of Dili was not a member of the Indonesian Bishops' Conference. The population was largely Catholic, and had become more so because of Indonesian oppression and efforts to convert them to Islam. The Pope, however, had to think of the position of the Church in Indonesia as a whole. When he arrived on 12 October he did not kiss the ground nor, much to the disappointment of his hearers, mention the question of sovereignty. Perhaps the Pope had delivered only what the people had expected: it was thought that 200,000 would come to the open-air mass, but only some 80,000 turned up. Banners of the independence movement were unfurled during the service: the congregation was ill at ease. From East Timor the Pope went on to Mauritius, and then back to Rome.

If by this time John Paul was in need of another fillip to his morale – though it did not appear unduly low – it came with the long-awaited visit to the Vatican by Mikhail Gorbachev on 1 December. It was described as an 'official but non-state' occasion, but the Swiss Guard and monsignori were out in force. Mr Gorbachev's wife wore red, instead of the customary black for a papal visit, but that raised not an eyebrow. Some significance was made of the Pope walking out of his library and through other reception rooms to meet the President; and when he saw him off, he walked a good way with him rather than exchange formal goodbyes at the library door. The meeting was distinctly cordial, and lasted half an hour longer than scheduled. It took place in Russian and Polish, languages which naturally both understood, but most of the time views were exchanged through the medium of interpreters.

The main thrust of the papal message to the Soviet President – and, it would seem from Gorbachev's own memoirs, equally true of their private conversation – was that of religious freedom. The Pope sought this not only for Catholics, but for Baptists whom he mentioned particularly, other Protestant groups, for Jews, and there was an especial word for Muslims. Gorbachev promised that a new law on religious freedom was being promulgated in the Soviet Union, and he hoped the Pope would pay a visit to Moscow. The invitation was made publicly, but in an unscripted remark. Any such visit would require the collaboration of the Orthodox, and that, as the Pope knew, could not be guaranteed. Indeed a meeting between the two Churches had just been postponed.

The context of this warm encounter between Pope John Paul and President Gorbachev was against a background of increasing tension in the Ukraine between the Orthodox and the Catholics, where the latter had been accused of illegally seizing an Orthodox church. The Ukrainian Catholic account was that the congregation had gone over to Rome *en masse*. Immediately following the conversations in Rome, Moscow radio reported that Eastern-rite Catholic congregations, a category which included Ukrainians – would be allowed to register as legally constituted entities. But, the report continued, if congregations decide to change their allegiance, it did not follow they could take their churches with them: ownership of such buildings lay within the State's competence rather than that of the Church.

In his customary pre-Christmas message to Vatican officials the Pope spoke of his hopes for the restoration of the Ukrainian Catholic Church, and for religious freedom in the Soviet bloc which was, as 1989 drew to a close, rapidly collapsing. In his Christmas Day message he made particular mention of Rumania where the Communist dictatorship had just been overthrown. As he prayed 'for this old Europe of ours', he reminded his hearers yet again of Europe's Christian roots, so well evidenced, he declared, in its art, its culture, and in its belief in human rights. The message was broadcast to fifty countries and the Pope used fifty-three different languages.

These had been the constant concerns of his pontificate. As John Paul prepared for his Christmas midnight mass he was presented with something totally new. On 20 December American troops invaded Panama to overthrow its ruler, General Manuel Noriega. Though they undoubtedly wanted rid of Noriega, the Catholic bishops of Panama were not particularly sympathetic to the American action which they regarded as a contravention of their national sovereignty. The US government, however, was after Noriega personally, to put him on trial for drug trafficking: on Christmas Eve the former dictator asked for asylum in the papal nunciature in Panama City. He was admitted, though only provisionally. The Panamanian bishops demanded he be handed over for trial for his human rights record without specifying to whom he should be surrendered. The Americans played loud rock music outside the nunciature. The nuncio complained, and so did the Vatican, describing US troops as an occupying force.

Pope John Paul might have had a satisfactory meeting with the President of the fast disintegrating Soviet Union at the beginning of December. Yet as the year came to a close his problems were, unexpectedly, with the government of the United States.

NOTES

1. Mikhail Gorbachev, 'La perestroijka e Papa Wojtyla', *La Stampa* 3 March 1992. Cf. also *La Stampa* of 15 February 1993. I am grateful to Desmond O'Grady for supplying these references.
2. The Ukrainian Catholic rite is the largest of the 'Uniate' Churches.
3. *Populorum Progressio* was dated 26 March 1967.
4. The text, with brief commentary, of *Solicitudo Rei Socialis* and of all other encyclicals on the social teaching of the Church, can be found in *Proclaiming Justice and Peace: Papal Documents from 'Rerum Novarum' through 'Centesimus Annus'*, edited by Michael Walsh and Brian Davies, Mystic, Connecticut,

Twenty-Third Publications, 1991.

5. When the encyclical was criticized by the *New York Times* for the 'moral equivalence', the Pope was vigorously defended by the Moscow weekly *Literaturnaya Gazeta*.

6. cf. Desmond O'Grady, *The Turned Card,* to be published by the Ave Maria Press.

7. Ibid.

8. This he did by consecrating four bishops in order to secure the succession – an act that put him formally into schism with the Holy See. This was confirmed formally by a *motu proprio* on 2 July.

9. None the less, President Kurt Waldheim was created by Pope John Paul a Knight of the Order of Pius in a ceremony in Vienna on 6 July 1994. The title, which is awarded for 'outstanding services to the Church or society', was conferred by the Apostolic Nuncio.

10. It was afterwards claimed the Hungarian authorities had allowed some 100,000 Hungarians to cross the border during the Pope's visit.

11. On the Pope as an exegete, cf. Terrence Prendergast's article, 'A vision of wholeness', in John M. McDermott (ed.), *The Thought of Pope John Paul II* (Rome, Gregorian University Press, 1993) and the 'Response' by James Swetnam, pp. 69-97.

12. To claim the concept of human rights as part of the Christian inheritance of Europe is somewhat to overstate the case. They are much more part of the inheritance of the French Revolution and, as such, had been regarded by the Church with hostility. For the Church's attitude on human rights, see, for example, Paul-Émile Bolté's introduction to his collection of documents, *Les droits de l'homme et la papauté contemporaine* (Montreal, Fides, 1975).

13. The term is *intrinsice inhonestum*.

14. They were of course not the only Episcopal Conference which was of that opinion: the Brazilian bishops were of like mind. Others, such as the Mexican Episcopal Conference, were more sympathetic.

15. The lecture was given on 6 December: Mr Sieghart died of lung cancer on 12 December.

16. The idea went back to a 1972 meeting of the Permanent Committee of the Symposium of Episcopal Conferences of Africa and Madagascar (SECAM), when the proposed topic was 'Black civilization and the Catholic Church'. The proposal had been urged on John Paul II by the bishops of Zaire in their 1980 *ad limina* visit. When in 1987 SECAM carried out a survey of African Episcopal Conferences they discovered that half of those who answered at all – and approximately a third declined – wanted no such gathering. The decision to go ahead none the less was taken in December 1988 when the Pope met the heads of SECAM Episcopal Conferences. See Joseph G. Donders, 'Ambiguity about Africa: from council to synod' in *America*, 15 January 1994, pp. 10-12.

17. His actual words were it was a 'sea question'.

18. The Holy See, which had by this time diplomatic relations with 117 states, did not intend immediately to open a nunciature in Stockholm. Of the 117 states, thirty had established diplomatic relations during the pontificate of John Paul II.

NINE

1990–1

T HE NEW YEAR began on a high note. The Pope's New Year message, 'Peace with God the Creator: Peace with All of Creation', with its ecological theme, was well received. Unlike far too many papal documents this one was readable. As one commentator in *The Tablet* remarked, it 'is written in a lively style; its coverage of ecological problems is comprehensive; the analysis is incisive and the text reverberates with a note of urgency'.[1] There was, he noted, only one obvious, though crucial, omission: no mention at all of the population problem.

With its emphasis on the moral issues arising from ecological problems, above all that of an uneven distribution of the world's resources, the 1990 New Year message deserves to be counted among the best of papal social teaching. But there was an added element, no doubt reflecting John Paul's own passion for the countryside: 'The aesthetic value of creation cannot be overlooked', he wrote. 'Our very contact with nature has a deep restorative power; contemplation of its magnificence imparts peace and serenity.' It was more difficult, he admitted, to find the same aesthetic satisfaction in the 'works of human ingenuity' but, he went on, 'even cities can have a beauty of their own'. Against the background of this document it was particularly disappointing to Catholic ecologists that the Church was sending only twenty non-voting observers to the World Council of Churches' conference in Seoul on 'Justice, Peace and the Integrity of Creation'.[2]

The Panamanian dictator, General Noriega, who had done little to advance either Justice or Peace or the integrity of creation, was finally winkled out of the papal nunciature in Panama City on 3 January, leaving behind him a personal letter for the Pope. He had been given refuge by the nuncio (not asylum it was stressed) on condition that he put an end to any resistance to the Americans by forces loyal to him. The nuncio, Archbishop José Laboa, who before his posting to Panama had spent all his working life either in the Congregation for Divine Worship or that for the Evangelization of Peoples, escorted the General to the place where he was handed over to the US commander. Vatican diplomacy had scored a minor coup.

The changing pattern of world politics was curiously reflected as Pope John Paul set off yet again for Africa: among the fifty journalists travelling with him was one from a Russian newspaper. It is the Pope's practice on overseas tours to talk to journalists in the course of the flight out, and again on the return flight. This time his topic was the need for the West to support development in Africa. The emergence of the new democracies in Eastern Europe from the ruins of the Soviet bloc, he said, should not be allowed to divert aid from the Third World, and specifically from Africa. He and the Vatican could be called Africa's allies, he claimed, because it fell to them to represent to the wealthier nations the needs of the poor on the continent of Africa.

At Praia airport in the Cape Verde Islands, where he arrived on 25 January, the Pope took up the theme with the country's civil and religious leaders who had gathered to greet him. The goods of the world, he said echoing one of the topics he had addressed in his New Year message, are meant for all. He called for solidarity among peoples to redistribute wealth to meet the needs of the poor. In São Vicente he called upon those who had emigrated from the Cape Verde Islands – emigration being one of the country's major problems – to be faithful 'to their culture, to their faith and to their healthy traditions and customs'. The question was, which customs. President Aristide had married only a fortnight before the Pope arrived, even though he and his wife had three grown-up children. Back in Praia, John Paul attempted to reinforce the Church's teaching on marriage and the family. But even in this predominantly Catholic enclave in Africa, many husbands and wives had not been wed in church.

The problem of a clash of cultures between Roman Catholicism and local mores was yet more evident in Guinea-Bissau where the Pope arrived on 27 January. Even among the small Catholic population the custom of polygamous marriage was common. The Pope denounced it. He visited a leper colony run by Franciscans, and told sufferers that their fate was a 'scandal' brought about by poverty and neglect. Later the same day he declared that while freedom in Eastern Europe had been threatened by the Marxist ideology – Guinea-Bissau was still technically Marxist – in Africa it was undermined by poverty and ignorance.

John Paul spent the next two days in Mali, a predominantly Islamic country, thus half his audience were Muslims. Catholics, he told them, would contribute as best they could to solving their national problems. He praised the good relations which existed between members of the two faiths which, he declared, shared the same basic beliefs.

Ten years previously the Pope had visited Upper Volta. The country was by now renamed Burkina Faso. It remains one of Africa's poorest, bordering the Sahara. John Paul chose Burkina Faso to make the major speech of this tour. When he addressed economists in Ouagadougou, the capital city, he pleaded for help for Africa from the world's richer economies. What would be the judgement of history, he asked, if countries which were able to relieve the famine in Africa left their brothers and sisters to starve? This was for international ears. His burden to the local people was as before, in an address at the Marian shrine of Yagma: the restoration of family values; the rejection of artificial contraception.

The final stop on this tour was Chad, where a civil war had recently ended and a peace agreement had just been struck with neighbouring Libya. Hence the Pope's topic as he arrived in N'Djamena on 30 January was one of reconciliation: reconciliation within the country, and reconciliation between Muslims and Christians. Again he expressed his concern that preoccupation with Eastern Europe might distract attention from the needs of Africa. He also spoke, as he had in each of the countries visited, about family values and on the problem of contraception. On this occasion at least, however, he recognized that many of those who heard him were practising polygamy or had not otherwise contracted marriages valid in the eyes of Western canon lawyers. On 1 February he flew from Chad back to Rome.

On 23 January, shortly before John Paul had left on his sixth African tour, the Hungarian National Assembly had voted to allow freedom of religious practice, and to forbid state interference.[3] This action was swiftly followed on 9 February by the establishment of diplomatic relations between Hungary and the Holy See. Hungary was only the second country after Poland of the former Soviet bloc to have gone this far. There could hardly have been a clearer symbol of the changing character of Eastern European political alignments. In 1949 Hungary had been the focus of one of the most dramatic 'show trials' of the Communist bloc, when Cardinal Mindszenty was condemned. On the eve of the agreement establishing diplomatic links a requiem mass was celebrated for Mindszenty in Esztergom, the official residence of the Hungarian primate, and the town's main square in front of the primate's palace was renamed, by the acting President of Hungary, Mindszenty Square.

In Czechoslovakia too, the Pope had at long last been able to appoint bishops to all vacant Sees. The situation in the newly-freed Rumania, by contrast, was unclear. The law of 1948 which outlawed the Uniate Church in the country was repealed, but no positive steps could be taken to reinstate the Uniates largely for reasons – similar to those in the Ukraine – of the ownership of church buildings.

While the Church might play politics as the socialist regimes collapsed in Eastern Europe, the Vatican maintained its pressure on South America to ensure that any left-wing tendencies were kept well under control. The – admittedly enormous – diocese of São Paulo was in 1989 divided up, effectively restricting the influence of the diocese's charismatic Archbishop, Cardinal Evaristo Arns. One of his closest collaborators, who had been expected to take over as bishop of one of the new dioceses, was moved away. In Recife, the highly successful Theological Institute started by Dom Helder Camara was shut down by Dom Helder's successor as bishop. At the beginning of 1990, Brazil's bishops started their *ad limina* visits to Rome. Pope John Paul, though praising their pastoral programme and emphasizing the need for Catholics to be instructed in social ethics, again warned the bishops to stay out of politics. The clear distinction must be made, 'between the action of the faithful, individually or in groups, guided by their Christian conscience, and the action they undertake in communion with their pastors in the name of the Church'. A bishop's ministry, he told another group from Brazil, must not be based on choices 'made to the measure of man'. People had the right to hear from bishops the authentic word of God.

In Rumania Catholics of both Eastern and Western rites were once more able to hear the word of God from their bishops, of whom only one, the 81-year-old Bishop of Alba Julia, had survived through the Communist repression. On 14 March Pope John Paul named bishops for the seven Latin-rite dioceses (the Bishop of Alba Julia retired) and for five of the Eastern-rite dioceses. As soon as the Eastern-rite Church was formally legalized, it claimed back the churches belonging to it before the merger. Not surprisingly the Rumanian Orthodox Church was incensed. Nor was the Ministry of Religious Affairs too pleased with the speed with which the Vatican had acted over its appointment of bishops.

At the same time, it was formally announced that diplomatic relations between the Holy See and Russia, agreed upon in principle when Gorbachev met the Pope the previous December, were to be established with Archbishop Francesco Coasuonno as nuncio. It was he who had helped to negotiate the abrogation of the decree which in 1948 had forcibly merged Rumanian Eastern-rite Catholics with the Orthodox Church. He also had wide experience of the Eastern bloc in general. Which was a help, because he immediately encountered similar problems in the Ukraine (at this time still part of the Soviet Union) as those experienced in Rumania. On 13 March the Eastern-rite Catholic bishops had walked out of talks between the Vatican and the Russian Orthodox Church complaining, in the words of a leading Ukrainian politician, that the Vatican was using the Uniate Church in his country as a bargaining tool with the Moscow patriarchate. The Vatican, the Uniate delegates said, was concentrating too much on the minor issue of the ownership of churches and not tackling the central one of the right of the Uniates to exist as a fully legal Church. They wanted the Russian Orthodox to accept that the Synod of 1946, which merged the two Churches, had been invalid. Not surprisingly, this the Moscow patriarchate was steadfastly refusing to do. But after more than forty years of suppression, the Uniate Church came out fighting.[4]

The steadfastness of Catholics under Communist regimes was a major theme of Pope John Paul when, on 21 and 22 April, he paid a brief visit to Czechoslovakia. He spoke frequently and bitterly of the attempt by Communism to suppress religion, but warned the newly-freed nations of Eastern Europe not to be contaminated by the culture of secularism and materialism that had overtaken the West. He was greeted in Prague by President Vaclav Havel as 'the apostle of spirituality'. The Pope presented his visit as a sign of triumph for spiritual values over 'one of the most serious attempts to deprive man of the freedom to which he is destined'. In Bratislava he spoke in Slovak, praising the people for the tenacious way in which they had clung to their national identity. He did not, however, give support to Slovak separatists and argued – in vain as it was to turn out – for the unity of the Czechoslovak republic. Between Prague and Bratislava the Pope visited Velehrad and the shrine of Saint Methodius who, with his brother Cyril, John Paul had proclaimed co-patrons of Europe at the start of his pontificate (cf. above p. 91). The visit to the tomb was the Pope's excuse for coming to Czechoslovakia first among the post-Communist countries: he had wanted to come in 1985 for the 1100th anniversary of Methodius, but had been refused. He had promised to make the journey as soon as he possibly could. At Velehrad he announced a special Synod for representatives of the twenty-five Episcopal Conferences of both parts of Europe to discuss the role of the Church in the aftermath of the collapse of Marxist ideology and the emergence of the new democracies.

But was Marxism alive and well elsewhere in the world? The Mexican Bishops' Conference thought so, as it dismissed a letter signed by more than four hundred priests and religious in Mexico because they judged it to be influenced by the Marxist notion of class conflict. The Pope began a visit to Mexico – his forty-seventh foreign tour – on 6 May. The letter was sent to him before he set off. It expressed a worry that those in charge of the papal visit would not expose the Pope to the true situation in the country – to the crippling effect of foreign debt on the spending power of the poorer sections of society, and to the situation of the native Indians to whom, they said, should be returned all that the Church had taken from them after the conquest. They wanted, they said, a Church more clearly committed to the service of the poor.

The Pope had an opportunity to see a slum, that of Chalco on the outskirts of Mexico City, when he celebrated mass there on the second day of his visit. The Mexican hierarchy had described it as home to the poorest of the poor, but a government programme to improve services just happened to coincide with John Paul's arrival. 'The option for the poor continues to be in the heart of the Church', he told his hearers. He also attacked fundamentalist sects, a theme that would surface again. The day before, as the Pope stepped from his aircraft, he was greeted by the President himself, in place of the Minister for Foreign Affairs as had been foreseen by the programme. It was taken as a sign of the country's desire, despite the latent anti-clerical articles of its Constitution, to establish better relations with the Holy See. The Pope allowed himself to be moderately critical both of the Constitution for some of its anti-Catholic legislation (on church schools for example) and of the ruling party for its corruption. Despite this, the President turned up again to see him off.

The Holy See was also doing its best by the people of Mexico themselves who, whether practising their faith or not, have a deep devotion to the national shrine of Our Lady of Guadalupe. On the first day of his visit John Paul beatified five Mexicans, one of them being the Mexican Indian Juan Diego, the visionary who had seen the Virgin and who had insisted to the bishop that a shrine be built in her honour. But the abiding theme of papal homilies seemed addressed to the Third World in general and not to Mexico in particular. It was that countries of the Third World should take note, when developing their own social structures, of the failure of the Communist model in Eastern Europe. At the same time they should not think that the only viable alternative was the system of liberal capitalism prevalent in the West.

The theme of solidarity with the poor the Pope raised again during a seven-hour stopover in Curaçao on 13 May on his way back to Rome. The Church should help the poor, he said, by selling off superfluous goods – though, he added, these did not include art treasures in its keeping.

The Pope was scarcely back in Rome than he was off again, though this time only as far as Malta. He arrived for a visit on 25 May and began with a call for the Church's freedom to be respected – during the administration of the Maltese Labour Party under Dom Mintoff prior to 1987 the government had forbidden Catholic schools to accept fees, and had attempted to confiscate Church property. Despite this earlier antagonism, both opposition and government parties were represented as the Pope arrived, and at every stage of the three-day tour of the islands (he also visited Gozo). The Pope's chief concern was indeed to improve relations between Church and state, but he also issued a renewed warning to the newly-independent democracies of the East not to be seduced by the Western way of life. Alone of the Western democracies apart from Ireland, Malta banned both divorce and abortion. In that regard, therefore, it was an example in the West of at least some of the spiritual values which the Pope wished to urge upon the post-Communist governments of the East.

On 26 June (though dated 24 May) 'An Instruction on the Ecclesial Vocation of the Theologian' was released in Rome. It was signed by Cardinal Ratzinger, head of the Congregation for the Doctrine of the Faith, the Vatican department responsible for its publication, but it represented the attitude of John Paul II, as expressed constantly in his writings and homilies, on the status of the *magisterium*.[5] The document has much that is excellent to say about the task of a theologian in the Church: the need to marry prayer and scholarship, the tools he or she has to acquire in order to undertake this study, the problems of the culture against which theological study is carried out. It has a valuable comment on academic freedom: 'Freedom of research, which the academic community rightly holds most precious, means an openness to accepting the truth that emerges at the end of an investigation in which no element has intruded that is foreign to the methodology corresponding to the object under study'.

Further reading, however, makes it clear that, so far as theological research is concerned, the freedom of inquiry is limited. The task of the theologian, says the Instruction, is to present the doctrine of the faith 'in its integrity and its full accuracy'. And how does one know in what its 'integrity and full accuracy' consists? The *magisterium* ('an institution positively willed by Christ as a constitutive element of his Church') tells the theologians so.

When the *magisterium,* not intending to act 'definitively', teaches a doctrine to aid a better understanding of Revelation and make explicit its contents, or to recall how some teaching is in conformity with the truths of faith, or finally to guard against ideas that are incompatible with these truths, the response called for [from the theologian] is that of the religious submission of will and intellect.

225

This kind of response cannot be simply exterior or disciplinary but must be understood within the logic of faith and under the impulse of obedience to the faith.

In other words, even when the *magisterium* (i.e., the teaching of the Pope or his Curia) is not acting 'definitively' (i.e., might be wrong), theologians have still got to accept that teaching with the 'submission of will and intellect'. The Instruction acknowledges that in some instances theologians may not be able readily to give that submission, but urges them to try patiently to do so, to take to prayer, and to remember that conscience is not the final arbiter. The final arbiter is truth but truth, it would seem, is what the *magisterium* declares to be such, not what the theologian discovers at the end of the research to which the document urges him.

Dissent from the views of the *magisterium*, the Instruction continues, does harm to the community of the Church. Dissenting theologians cannot argue, for instance, that the views of the Vatican are simply other theological opinions because, even though it may reflect a particular theological perspective, it 'has a validity beyond its argumentation'. The Vatican, in other words, may not win the theological argument, but one has got to believe its teaching none the less because otherwise 'there arises a kind of "parallel *magisterium*" of the theologians'. Nor may theologians point to the *sensus fidei*, the faith of the people, because 'not all the ideas which circulate among the People of God are compatible with the faith. This is all the more so, given that people can be swayed by a public opinion influenced by modern communications media.'

Rather curiously, in the light of the general tenor of the document, theologians are told that tensions between their views and those of the teaching authority of the Church, can become a 'dynamic factor', a 'stimulus' both to the *magisterium* and the work of the theologians. In practice that 'tension' is ruled inadmissible. What is required of theologians is submission of will and intellect, even to the 'non-irreformable' teaching of the Vatican.

The definition of 'freedom of research' quoted above from the document, would be acceptable in any context. But academic research is carried on in open dialogue, through the 'media' of academic journals. Truth, or the nearest approximation to it, is finally decided by its acceptance by the community within which the research is carried out, whether of historians or physicists or any other similar group. These are principles which the Western culture has embraced, or attempted to embrace, since the Enlightenment. They are part of modern culture. Yet the Instruction rejects them. The Pope, whose views the document undoubtedly reflects, makes use with great skill of the technical achievements of the modern world, of the communications media, of means of transport, even, in his summoning of Synods for this and that, of the modern propensity for conferences.[6] But in this document he appears thoroughly anti-modern.

This rebuke to theologians was followed by a pastoral letter to the religious Orders of Latin America dated 29 June, though released only at the end of July. He praised the efforts that the religious were making to evangelize the people of their continent, but warned them, as the Instruction had warned theologians, not to set up a parallel *magisterium* to that of their bishops. There had, he said, been misunderstandings between bishops and religious. The independence of the local hierarchy traditionally enjoyed by the Orders must not be 'a pretext for apostolic activity with only a marginal connection' to the bishops. They had become politicized, he complained, and were being manipulated for purposes foreign to the mission of the Church. Some of the theologies of liberation were not approved by the Church because they were still too Marxist-oriented, and this had led to a misunderstanding of the Church's option for the poor.

The ostensible purpose of the letter was to guide religious in their preparations for the 500th anniversary celebrations of the arrival of Catholicism in the Americas, about which many of them had considerable doubts as they considered the devastating effect of the *conquistadores* on the indigenous peoples. The Pope had no such hesitations. The evangelization of the continent, he said, had 'more light than shadows', and one must not judge the work of the first missionaries by standards more appropriate to the present day. Those early missionaries, for the most part members of religious Orders, had brought to Latin America its 'profound sense of community, its desire for social justice, its fidelity to the faith of the Church, its deep Marian piety and its love of the successor of Peter'.

This particular successor of Peter set off on his 49th foreign tour with his seventh visit to Africa and his second of the year, on 1 September. The ten-day journey began in Dar-es-Salaam where he was met on landing by the President of Tanzania. In response to the President's words of greeting John Paul expressed the hope that the easing of tensions between East and West would free resources to be spent on the world's poor. From the diplomats he spoke to a few hours later he called for help to fight the battle against AIDS in Africa. The Church would help, he said, but only in the context of a return to traditional morality: condoms were out as a means of preventing the disease. Indeed, he said, their use simply encouraged the kind of sexual behaviour which led to the disease spreading.

Four days were spent in Tanzania, during which time the Pope criss-crossed the country, met Julius Nyerere, the country's retired president and a devout Catholic, ordained forty-three priests, blessed a pastoral centre and celebrated the centenary of the arrival of Catholic missionaries on Mount Kilimanjaro.

AIDS was again the topic during the Pope's next stop, Burundi, though he also talked of national reconciliation – the country's two main tribes had gone to war with the loss of 150,000 dead and vast numbers of refugees fleeing to neighbouring states. In Gitega John Paul urged couples to limit the number of their children, though by natural means rather than by artificial ones. Natural forms of contraception was also a theme in Rwanda which, even more than Burundi, had a severe problem with overpopulation. The bishops had established centres for natural family planning, largely in response to an increased campaign for birth control on the part of the government. But, warned the Pope, donor nations should not put pressure on Rwanda to adopt contraception in return for the grant of aid.

The final stop on the tour was a return visit to the Ivory Coast, in Yamoussoukra. Here he was to dedicate the massive basilica of Our Lady of Peace built at President Felix Houphouet-Boigny's home town, built with his own money (or so he claimed). The Vatican had insisted on a proper endowment to pay for its running costs plus a number of ongoing social services run from the cathedral. Here the President was eventually buried in February 1994. The papal blessing, *L'Osservatore Romano* later claimed, was an 'historic gesture' on behalf of the poor of the African continent. They would, the paper's anonymous contributor went on, be 'privileged guests' in the £50m basilica. After the service on 10 September John Paul attended a meeting to plan for the forthcoming African Synod, and then he returned to Rome.

In Rome the Jesuits were quietly celebrating the 450th anniversary of the papal bull which formally established their Society. Pope John Paul sent them a letter. Given that in 1981 the Pope had removed the official vicar-general of the Jesuits and installed his own delegate, Fr Paolo Dezza (cf. above p. 97), it was a remarkably friendly letter. The Pope recalled the history of the Society – he described it as 'glorious' – praised its current work, especially that for refugees, and urged them to strengthen their commitment, stemming from the time of Pope Paul VI, to combat atheism, a task, said the Pope, all the more important after the collapse of Communism in Eastern Europe. There was not a sour note in the letter, though the papal emphasis on the

Jesuits' traditional loyalty to the Pope went somewhat beyond what most Jesuits would think of as being implied by their Constitution.

The Pope also had a letter, or more properly an apostolic constitution, for Catholic universities. It had been a long time in the making (the first draft had been issued four years earlier), and in its various versions had been subject to much criticism. But this was an instance when the Vatican had listened. The document was published on 25 September and was on the whole well received. The Pope's words in the first part of the constitution are reformulated as norms or rules in the second part. The norms recognize the 'autonomy' of the institutions, and its freedom in teaching and research 'so long as the rights of the individual and of the community are preserved within the confines of the truth and the common good'. There was, inevitably, an insistence that theologians should be 'faithful to the *magisterium* of the Church as the authentic interpreter of sacred Scripture and sacred tradition', but that *magisterium* was not identified with the teaching of the Vatican.

On the last day of September Pope John Paul presided and preached at the opening mass of the 1990 Synod of Bishops. Two hundred and thirty-eight participants had gathered in Rome to discuss 'the formation of priests in the circumstances of today'. When, two days later, Cardinal Lucas Moreira Neves, the Archbishop of São Salvador da Bahia in Brazil, presented his position paper at the opening of the Synod proper he announced that some of the most significant themes – celibacy, the ordination of married men, the role of priests who had been freed of their vows, the ordination of women – had already been definitively dealt with elsewhere, and need no longer be debated. Yet this did not prevent bishops saying what they thought. Another Brazilian bishop, for example, asked that very same day why it was that older men, married or celibate,[7] could not be ordained when there were vast parishes without clergy doomed to celebrate only the Word and not the Sacrament: Just like the sects, he added, touching a favourite subject of the moment of the Pope's, which were gaining ground because there were no priests. He had said more or less the same thing at the Synod of 1971, and still there had been no change.

Many members of the Synod were concerned that the number of vocations was declining. Not so, said bishops from the former Eastern bloc, and from parts of the Third World. There would soon come a time, said a bishop from Chad, when Europe would be re-evangelized by priests from Africa and Asia. But there was a problem. The priests of Africa and Asia had first to adapt the Gospel to their own culture. Just what this 'enculturation', as the process of local adaptation has come to be called, might require was spelled out in various ways. One bishop, for instance, pointed out that in the culture in which he worked, celibacy, optional or not, was so unusual that it was likely to be misinterpreted by those among whom the priests were required to work. Another bishop said that the notion of seminary education was quite alien to the Indian population of Ecuador, and other styles of formation had to be sanctioned were priests to be drawn from this group. There were mixed feelings about the value of seminaries as a whole. As another Brazilian bishop pointed out, a large proportion of recent popes, including John Paul II, had not been put through the seminary system and were, he suggested, none the worse for that. As a bishop from Indonesia was to put it, 'Imposing a foreign system or method in priestly formation which is bound to a certain culture means putting Christ into the prison of that culture, and that is indeed a crime'.

And so the debate continued for two weeks, with the Pope silently present except when on a few occasions he was summoned away by the requirements of his diary. At the end of the two weeks Cardinal Moreira Neves summed up the discussion in a thirty-five-page Latin document. It had fifteen questions in four sections, two of which focused on training for the priesthood. The document was debated again and then the bishops broke up as usual into language groups: this time there was one for the Slavs. The secretaries of the groups presented their reports on 17 and 18 October and a composite list of propositions was drawn up for the consideration of the synodal fathers. There were debates about the propositions, amendments proposed, and a final list of forty-one propositions published internally for their vote.

Despite the secrecy, the general drift of what was being put forward was widely known: a focus on the spiritual life of the clergy in a manner which assimilated diocesan priests to those belonging to religious Orders with a form of noviceship, a commitment to the evangelical counsels of poverty, chastity and obedience, a rejection, stated explicitly by the Pope in his final address on 3 November, of the ordination of married men: 'The possibility of calling upon *viri probati*' said John Paul, 'is often evoked within the framework of a systematic propaganda hostile to priestly celibacy', which seemed a little hard on those bishops who had supported the idea simply because there were not enough priests to go round.

Papal endorsement of priestly celibacy was echoed in the statement of the synodal fathers, read out at mass in St Peter's the following day. It had 'shone out for us in a new light and with a new clarity ... Observing the evangelical counsels remains a sure way of acquiring virtue and attaining a true and complete freedom of spirit'. And with that the fathers went home. Almost the last thing they heard was an announcement that the Vatican had completed, and had promulgated, a code of canon law for Eastern-rite Catholics. As far as these were concerned, it was not good news.

On Sunday 25 November President Mikhail Gorbachev paid a return visit to the Vatican. Gorbachev had come to Rome to collect a peace prize, while *en route* to Paris for the conference on Security and Cooperation in Europe, the conference which was hailed as putting an end to the Cold War. That the Cold War was indeed over was agreed by Pope and President in the course of their forty-minute meeting, and a visit to Russia was no longer out of the question though the date still had to be fixed. They talked about the crisis in the Gulf, and the Pope linked settlement of that with the wider problems of the Middle East: peace in the Lebanon, peace between Israelis and Palestinians.

At the Paris conference Cardinal Agostino Casaroli made his last formal appearance as Secretary of State. He retired on 8 December and Archbishop Angelo Sodano took over, a papal diplomat who had served almost entirely in South America. Casaroli's chief successes by contrast had been in Eastern Europe, and his ability there had won the Pope's confidence and dispelled any initial doubts. Indeed it was Wyszynski, the Polish cardinal, who had advised the newly-elected Wojtyla to retain the services of Casaroli. A Polish pope needed an Italian second-in-command if only to keep the loyalty of the Curia. It had proved a wise decision, as the praises John Paul heaped upon him on his retirement amply illustrated. The high point of Casaroli's long years of service came at the end when he went to Moscow (cf. above, pp. 194-5), and when Gorbachev came to visit the Pope. His patient diplomacy in Eastern Europe had indeed paid dividends.

On 14 December Pope John Paul issued an Apostolic Letter (in Spanish) entitled 'Master in the Faith' on St John of the Cross, the subject of the Pope's first doctorate long years before. With St Teresa of Avila, he had been the founder of the Discalced Carmelites in the sixteenth century and the letter began a year of celebrations to mark the 400th centenary of the Saint's death. But the Carmelites of John and Teresa's reform had little to celebrate. Nearly three-quarters of the Carmelites who had voted on a new Constitution drawn up by the Vatican's Congregation for Religious had turned it down. A new Constitution, prepared by a commission set up by the Order's Superior General, had been submitted to the Vatican for approval in June 1990. Now, however, almost simultaneously with the Apostolic Letter of John of the

Cross, the Pope approved a further version of new Constitutions drawn by the Congregation for Religious, which reflected in detail the original version of 1581. It was accepted by less than a hundred Carmelite houses: another seven hundred rejected it. The Vatican had engineered a split in the ranks of the Order, making those who accepted the Vatican's version responsible to the Holy See, with the local bishop having more direct oversight, while the majority of houses remained under the control of the Superior General.

In contrast, as conflict in the Gulf between Iraq and the Western alliance because of the occupation of Kuwait seemed increasingly likely, the Pope was trying to bring reconciliation to the opposing forces. He spoke of it in his Christmas message to the crowd gathered in St Peter's Square. There was even an official hint that the Holy See might be prepared to act as mediator in order to prevent war breaking out. Meanwhile the Holy See had announced that it was establishing diplomatic relations with Bulgaria – the fifth country of the former Soviet bloc with which diplomatic links were forged in 1990. The allegations that Bulgarians had been involved in the plot to kill Pope John Paul in May 1981 had clearly been forgotten, or forgiven.

Giving his customary address on 12 January to all diplomats accredited to the Holy See, John Paul spoke of his belief that a peaceful solution in the Gulf was still possible. He warned that an outbreak of hostilities would be an ecological, political and economic disaster for all concerned. He also spoke of the Middle East more generally, regretting that Christians in too many countries there were barely tolerated. He added a word, too, about the Palestinians. He condemned some of the means they had used in the past to make their voice heard – a delicate reference to terrorism – but he insisted that for the state of Israel to rest secure, the Palestinians must be granted their rights. The overall message was clear: the Middle East had been badly treated by the Western nations. And the response to the invasion of Kuwait by the Iraqis was yet another example of it.

The Gulf War broke out on 16 January, when by chance Iraqi Christian leaders were in Rome to present the Pope with an appeal for peace. He called for all foreign armies to be withdrawn from the Gulf, and described the United Nations' trade embargo against Iraq as a 'ghastly crime against humanity'. John Paul had already made numerous appeals for peace[8] before the fighting broke out. He had called upon Iraq to withdraw its troops from Kuwait, had written to both Presidents Saddam Hussein and George Bush, and had offered to mediate if asked. There was little more that he could do beyond exhorting the combatants to limit the horrors of modern warfare. But even that had its dangers. When the Pope condemned the bombings, the

Chief Rabbi of Rome complained that John Paul should have made special mention of Israel which had been attacked by Iraqi rockets, and the fact that he did not do so, thought the Rabbi, implied that the Holy See was still not prepared to recognize the state of Israel. There were diplomatic difficulties in the way of explicit recognition of Israel, said a Vatican spokesman, such as the status of the occupied territories and the Palestinians, the position of Jerusalem, and the status of the Church, but recognition of Israel had long been implicit.

Shortly after the Gulf War broke out Pope John Paul issued his eighth encyclical, *Redemptoris Missio* – 'The mission of Christ the redeemer' – which was a powerful call to Catholics to engage in the evangelizing mission of the Church, twenty-five years after the decree of Vatican II on the same topic entitled *Ad Gentes*, 'To the nations'. In a context where Iraqi Muslims were bombarding Israeli Jews, the Pope asked whether missionary work among non-Christians had not been replaced by inter-faith dialogue. His answer was negative. Jesus was the self-revelation of God and 'This definitive self-revelation is the fundamental reason why the Church is missionary by her very nature'. There were three quite distinct areas for missionary activity, he went on. There were those regions which had not yet known Christ; there were those areas where the Christian community was conscious of its mission to spread the Gospel and were doing so; and there were those parts of the world where the faith was long established, and had grown cold. But missionary activity proper was directed to the first group, to the non-Christians, and he mentioned in particular Asia as a field for missionary endeavour.

On the charge of 'proselytizing', John Paul would not compromise: 'Everyone has the right to hear the "Good News" of the God who reveals and gives himself in Christ, so that each one can live out in its fullness his or her proper calling', he insisted. Missionary activity which simply tried to help people be faithful to their own religion, and built communities which worked for justice, was not good enough. What he was talking about was conversion, and a conversion which was completed in baptism. Division among Christians makes this activity more problematic, he admitted, and especially the existence of Christian sects. On the other hand he had kind words to say of 'basic Christian communities', a structure of the Church fostered in Latin America by Liberation Theology, which he now recognized as an excellent base for evangelizing the underprivileged. It is the Church's task to offer people the opportunity not so much to have more as to be more 'by awakening their consciences through the Gospel'. The third millennium draws near, said the Pope, and 'God is preparing a great springtime for Christianity', of which he claimed to be able to see the first signs. These 'first signs' were an acceptance of what he took to be Christian values: 'the rejection of violence and war; respect for the human person and for human rights; the desire for justice and brotherhood; the surmounting of different forms of racism and nationalism; the affirmation of the dignity and role of women'.

The encyclical insisted strongly that the work of a Christian preaching the Gospel of Christ should be in deeds – in liberation – as much as in words. Yet Christians also need to understand the faith and the practice of other religions. On the other hand the figure of Christ presented in the document seems not to have moved on from the sixteenth century. John Paul does not address the conviction of those belonging to other faiths that theirs is also a sure road to salvation. In that context, which is one in which missionaries have to work, it is not enough to say that Jesus is the 'definitive self-revelation of God', without asking how that definitive revelation can be found in other faiths, as so many adherents of such faiths firmly believe. The encyclical likewise fails to ask what the Gospel would be like were it to be fully 'inculturated' in the different regions of the world. On the contrary, when it presents the Gospel as a 'liberating' force it implies that the local culture is an oppressive one, and it explicitly warns against the danger of overestimating the value of a particular culture. Cultures are always human creations, and therefore of necessity marked by sin. The Gospel is seen as 'purifying' such cultures, but those preaching the Gospel must come from a particular context (mainly Europe and North America), and understand the Gospel in accordance with their own culture. In other words, the Pope is implicitly giving an especial place to Western culture in a manner which appears imperialistic. From the text of *Redemptoris Missio*, it seems he does not really mean what he constantly preaches to the peoples of the Third World, the need to foster their own culture.

Meanwhile the war in the Gulf went on. On 19 February John Paul decided to summon together representatives of all the Episcopal Conferences whose countries were involved. The meeting was called for 4 and 5 March and he intended to preside. Those invited included the seven patriarchs of the Churches in the Middle East, at least one of whom, Patriarch Raphael I Bidawid of Baghdad,[9] was an enthusiastic supporter of the campaign launched by Saddam Hussein. The Pope was not: he had called repeatedly for the restitution of Kuwait's sovereignty, and although he wanted peace, he did not mean, as he explained to some school children in a Rome parish he was visiting, peace at any price. He was not, he insisted, a pacifist even though he appealed every Sunday for the warring parties to come to the conference table to discuss peace.

In the end the war was over before the Patriarchs and the heads of seven Western-rite Episcopal Conferences turned up in Rome. The purpose of their meeting remained the same: to promote peace, and to encourage inter-religious dialogue in the Middle East, a region where there were some ten million Christian Arabs. There was considerable concern expressed that the war would have irreparably damaged Christian-Muslim relations. To put the participants' minds at rest, at the start of the conference there was a letter from the Secretary General of the Pan-Islamic Organization of Islamic Conferences, based in Saudi Arabia, promising to do everything possible to promote Christian-Muslim dialogue. But then Saudi Arabia had been on the side of the Western allies against Saddam Hussein, and was not inclined to see the attack on Iraq as a Christian crusade against Islam.

That the Gulf War had not been a crusade was the theme of Pope John Paul's opening address. But he also appealed powerfully on behalf of the Palestinians and for the territorial integrity of Lebanon. Patriarch Bidawid none the less voiced his fear that Arab Christians might from now on be unwelcome citizens of their homelands, and be driven out – a worry which the Latin Patriarch of Jerusalem, Michael Sabbah, himself a Palestinian, had already frequently expressed. A couple of weeks later, during a general audience, the Pope told his hearers that he hoped one day to visit Jerusalem and from there, with Christian, Jewish and Muslim leaders, to appeal for peace throughout the world. He had made $80,000 available for emergency aid, by far the larger part of it going to Iraq and to Kuwait.

When talking of the Gulf War the Pope spoke of the need for dialogue and mutual trust. Unhappily, it was in short measure within his own Church, and the blame for this must fall squarely upon his shoulders. At almost the same time as the Synod met to discuss the Gulf War, the bishops of Switzerland were meeting for a three-day conference to discuss the case of Mgr Wolfgang Haas, Bishop of Chur. Haas had been appointed an assistant bishop with right of succession two years earlier despite an outcry from the priests and people of the diocese. A year later his Bishop unexpectedly resigned, and Haas therefore succeeded to the diocese. Complaints increased. He sacked popular clergy from their posts, including the director of the diocesan seminary. He blocked the appointment to the theological college of a rector who had opposed his nomination to the bishopric; yet the man had been unanimously elected by professors and student representatives alike. Many priests had asked to be transferred out of the diocese of Chur and there had been public demonstrations against the bishop. The canton of Zürich within Chur diocese voted to cut off all payments to the diocese.

Haas, a canon lawyer by profession with little experience of pastoral work, seemed impervious. He refused all dialogue and avoided all meetings. The president of the Episcopal Conference had taken up the matter with the head of the Congregation for Bishops, but had been referred to the Pope. The Pope had said the case would be looked into immediately and still nothing had happened. Haas said he would retire only if asked to do so by the Pope. But then, it was widely believed, he had been appointed by Rome precisely to implement a conservative programme in sympathy with the Pope's own spiritual vision. Now, at the end of their conference, the Swiss announced that they wanted to meet the Pope in person to discuss the case of Bishop Haas. The bishop was unrepentant, claiming that he had already discussed his position with John Paul. 'If one accepts fully the *magisterium* of the Church, an essential condition for Catholics, then one comes under fire', he declared.

When the Swiss bishops went to Rome for their meeting with the Pope, on 29 and 30 April, John Paul began by recalling the significance of his 'petrine ministry': 'a local Church that does not nourish a deep and sincere communion with the see of Peter cannot exist'. The published agenda of the meetings made no mention of Haas, but his case was none the less discussed – and forcefully – by the Swiss bishops. 'We set out for Rome in a thick fog', said the secretary to the Episcopal Conference on his return to Switzerland. 'We are still in a fog, but the visibility has increased.' In November, at the winter meeting of the Episcopal Conference, a letter was received from Rome, signed by the Secretary of State Angelo Sodano, and by the Prefect of the Congregation of Bishops, Bernardin Gantin, insisting that Bishop Haas would stay in charge of the diocese of Chur. There was no question of his resigning his see, said Cardinal Gantin in a telephone call, but the Pope wanted it to be known that he was always ready to meet the bishops of Switzerland.

In April, however, John Paul had other things on his mind. The suggestion he threw out that he might visit Jerusalem (cf. above, p. 235) was not well received either by Archbishop Jean-Louis Tauran, who was the nearest thing the Vatican had to a foreign minister, or by Archbishop Michael Sabbah, Latin Patriarch of Jerusalem. The Israelis would not welcome such a visit unless the Vatican established diplomatic relations. The Vatican would not agree to diplomatic representation until Israel had sorted out its problems with the Palestinians. The Pope wrote about it all to the Secretary General of the

United Nations, Xavier Pérez de Cuellar. He hoped that the peace negotiations in the Gulf would not lead to the humiliation of any of those involved, and added that true peace could not come until the situation in the Lebanon and with the Palestinians had been resolved, and the status of Jerusalem settled. Jerusalem should not be forgotten, he insisted, in the midst of all the other problems of the region.

The Vatican was doing its bit. The Congregation for the Causes of Saints, which prepared candidates for beatification and eventual canonization, and had been working overtime during John Paul's pontificate, announced that it was not proceeding, at least for the time being, with the case of Queen Isabella of Spain. The fact that during her reign Granada, the last Muslim stronghold in Spain, had been conquered, and Jews in Spain had been given the alternative of conversion to Catholicism or expulsion from the country, weighed heavily against her. There had been protests, especially from Jewish groups but also from Muslim ones, and the Holy See had deemed it politic to bow to such pressures in the name of good interfaith relations. Isabella's supporters were outraged. They had wanted her beatified for the 500th anniversary of Columbus's discovery of the Americas – she had sent him on his way and thereby, argued her protagonists, had brought the faith to the New World. 'In my opinion', said the promoter of the cause, Fr Anastasio Gutierrez, 'all Jews are against her because they are anti-Catholic'.[10]

The papal appeal to Muslims was more direct. Each year the Pontifical Council for Inter-religious Dialogue send a message to Muslims to mark the end of Ramadam – the Islamic equivalent of Lent. This year it came as a personal message from the Pope. He recalled the sufferings of the Gulf War and went on to say that among those things which led people away from God are unwillingness to enter into dialogue and to negotiate.

John Paul's ninth encyclical, and his third expressly on social issues, was released on 2 May. It had been expected. The year 1991 marked the hundredth anniversary of the publication of what has been widely hailed, though perhaps inaccurately, as the first encyclical on social problems, Leo XIII's *Rerum Novarum*. It had become the custom to mark each decade, and the Pope's contribution this time[11] was entitled *Centesimus Annus*, 'A hundred years ...'. It is presented as a 'rereading' of Leo's encyclical and certainly begins that way, but the document quickly develops into a treatise about what had happened to Europe (it is distinctly Eurocentric) since the Second World War. One half of Europe has been under Communist domination, while the other half armed itself in defence against Communism. It was a period of 'non-war' rather than one of peace. He analyses three ways in which the threat came to be met: the development of democracy, the establishment of national security states, and the promotion of a consumer society. Only the first way is valid, he says, the other two share in some of the worst features of the Communist regimes. He devotes chapter three of his letter to the collapse of Communism in Eastern and Central Europe, identifying the forces which brought it down. Pride of place goes to Solidarity, as a workers' movement overthrowing a system which claimed to represent the dictatorship of the working class.

He was also practical: the second factor was the simple inefficiency of the Marxist economic system. But the true cause of Communism's downfall, he insists, is the spiritual void which atheism brings in its wake. His earlier encyclicals had been criticized for what was called the 'moral equivalence' he seemed to find between capitalism and Communism. There is little of that in *Centesimus Annus*. John Paul upholds the free market 'as the most efficient instrument for utilizing resources and effectively responding to needs', and recognizes 'the legitimate role of profit'. Yet he is critical of some aspects of advanced capitalist societies – drug abuse, pornography and environmental problems. The latter he divides in two – the natural environment and the human one, including in the second category threats he perceives to the family. He says expressly that the Church 'values the democratic system' (paragraph 46), but he is distinctly unhappy with democracy when states make decisions of which he does not approve, such as the legalization of abortion.

John Paul shows himself in this encyclical to be very well aware of the possible flash points in the former Communist bloc, and is eager that the Western powers assist in putting structures in place which will contain such disturbances. His warnings came too late, but they put this document into a somewhat different category from those which had gone before. He pays lip service, as popes have always done, to the insights of his 'venerable predecessors', but he parts company with them in *Centesimus Annus* in both content and style. He is far less insistent on the right to private property, for example, and although he does not approve of 'the class struggle' as such, he clearly understands that something like a class struggle was taking place in the overthrow of Communism. It reads rather like the manifesto of somebody who was determined to play a leadership role within Europe.

The encyclical marked the triumph of democratic capitalism over Communism. The Pope gave more practical evidence of this triumph by establishing five new bishoprics throughout the territories of the former Soviet Union, including one in Moscow itself. The Russian government was irritated. Its objection was not against the papal action as such, but it felt it had a right to be consulted. That was the local tradition: clearly they had yet to come to terms with Rome's way of doing things. The Pope then went off to Portugal to visit for a second time the Marian shrine at Fátima; it was the fiftieth foreign journey of his pontificate. He went, he said, to thank Mary for delivering Eastern Europe from Communism, for protecting the Church from repression, and for saving him, ten years before to the day (13 May), from the assassin's bullet.

John Paul made his way to Fátima via Madeira and the Azores. Both on these islands and in Lisbon he talked about the role of Portugal in spreading the Gospel through the missionary activity which went hand-in-hand with the country's colonial expansion. He chose not to dwell upon the contemporary problems which this colonial empire had left behind it in Angola, Mozambique, Indonesia and elsewhere. In Fátima he met the bishops of Angola celebrating five hundred years of Christianity in their country, at the same time, the Mozambican government was conducting talks with the UNITA rebels in nearby Estoril. After his mass in Benfica's stadium on 10 May East Timorese lifted placards accusing him of forgetting their plight. He prayed for them every day, he told journalists on his flight to the Azores.

Scarcely a fortnight after returning from Portugal John Paul began his fourth visit to his homeland. He went first to Koszalin on the Baltic coast. He arrived there on Saturday 1 June to be greeted by President Lech Walesa. Without Walesa, the Pope declared, Solidarity would not have existed, and without Solidarity the Communist regime would never have fallen. It was a changed country – though economically poorer – to which the Pope came, a change symbolized above all by his meeting with the army on the second day of his tour. Then he flew south west to Rzeszow, where he beatified Jozef Sebastian Pelczar, bishop of the Latin-rite diocese of Przemsyl, who died in 1925. Inter-rite feuding preoccupied the Pope in this corner of Poland. The church of St Teresa in Przemsyl had belonged to the Ukrainian Catholics until they were suppressed in 1946, at which point it was handed over to the Latine-rite Carmelites. In January 1991 it had been handed back to the Ukrainians for five years, until, that is, a group of Latin-rite protestors forced a change of plan. John Paul told the Ukrainians they could have a totally different Latin-rite church as their cathedral, thus neatly side-stepping controversy. And there he said mass. It would be 'a glaring anachronism', he told his congregation, to try to revive nationalism, or to divide the Church: it was a lesson he had to repeat elsewhere. The Cardinal Archbishop of Lvov, Myroslav Lubachivsky, crossed the border to visit him with an estimated

9,000 other Ukrainians. He would like to visit the Ukraine, said John Paul hopefully, but he did not know when it would be possible. His new Secretary of State, Angelo Sodano, one of the twenty-two new cardinals named by the Pope shortly before leaving for Poland, had told journalists on the flight from Portugal to Rome that a visit to the Soviet Union was under active consideration, and it might take place as early as 1992. Clearly the Pope himself was being more realistic.

The papal itinerary through Poland by way of a dozen cities to Warsaw should have been something of a triumphal progress. It was, however, marked by controversy. He upset the remaining Jewish population of the country by comparing abortion – on which the Polish parliament was scheduled to make a decision in the Autumn – to the mass killings in the Nazi concentration camps. He was evidently profoundly disturbed by what he saw as an aping of Western European standards in his newly-liberated homeland. Western freedom meant, apparently, licence to commit abortions. It had nothing to do with democracy, the political system much lauded in *Centesimus Annus* and never mentioned by him in Poland. Nor, for that matter, was his latest social encyclical. He was, he admitted in Warsaw at the end of his stay, still a Polish patriot at heart. He could not bear to see his countrymen and women departing from the high moral standards the Church had been able to impose on them during the long years of Communist domination. And he was particularly distressed by the apparent condescension of the Western European nations. 'We do not have to become a part of Europe', he said at Wroclawek on the morning of 7 June, 'we created it. We created it, incurring greater hardships than those who are credited with, or who credit themselves with, being the keepers of the European spirit'. The Pope shouted, the crowd roared its approval. This was political demagogy rather than spiritual guidance, even if he went on to complain about abortion. He was scathing of Western European standards with which the Poles were – he believed – being taken in. 'Is it a civilization or an anti-civilization, a culture or an anti-culture?' he asked his hearers. Poland, it seemed, was not only to be part of Europe, but Europe's moral paradigm. It was an unlikely vision.

The tensions to which John Paul was referring between Latin and Eastern-rite Catholics in Poland and the Ukraine were repeated in Rumania, where the Orthodox Patriarch called on the Orthodox Churches throughout the world to boycott ecumenical contact between Roman Catholicism and Orthodoxy as long as John Paul remained Pope. He accused Rome, and the Pope in particular, of pursuing a policy of expansionism in Eastern Europe at the expense of Orthodoxy. Patriarch Teoktist had been angered by the

Catholic takeover of an Orthodox church. He did not mention that Catholic Christians had been forcibly incorporated into Orthodoxy during the Communist regime, that their property had been seized, or that talks between Catholic and Orthodox leaders in Rumania about restoring churches to Catholics had broken up without agreement. Romanian Orthodoxy had hardly covered itself with glory during the years of Communist domination. It was not surprising that here, as elsewhere in the former Eastern bloc, the Catholic Church was making gains at the expense of the Orthodox. No other Patriarch, however, had made so personal an attack on the Pope's ecumenical credentials, at least not in public. John Paul's response was a letter to bishops preparing for the Synod on Europe he had announced at Velehrad. All religious believers had suffered under Communism, he said, but the Catholic Churches of the Byzantine tradition in the Ukraine, Rumania and Czechoslovakia had suffered most of all. It had been a great grace for him to be able to appoint bishops to those Churches, but he regretted it had led to disputes over buildings. The aim, he insisted, was full ecclesial communion between the Catholic and Orthodox communities, but in the meantime he hoped a solution might be found to local difficulties, one 'that is fair and worthy of the Christian calling'.

Nowhere, perhaps, had the 'glaring anachronism' of ancient nationalisms about which the Pope had spoken in Poland reached so dangerous a point as in Yugoslavia. In his general audience on 3 July the Pope called for an end to the cycle of violence in the country. The Orthodox Patriarch of Serbia wrote to the Catholic Archbishop of Ljubljana, Alojzij Sustar, proposing a joint appeal with the Archbishop to 'our brothers, Slovenes and Serbs, Orthodox and Catholics, and especially those who have the power, and all men of good will to do everything to have peace'. There was no response from Archbishop Sustar. The Vatican, however, sent an emissary. The Holy See's foreign minister, Archbishop Jean-Louis Tauran, travelled to Yugoslavia on 5 August 'to express the Holy Father's solidarity', to let the bishops know what the Vatican had been doing about the crisis in their country, and to listen. Talks were held in Zagreb with the Catholic bishops on 6 August, and with the Orthodox Patriarch in Belgrade the following day. The Pope continued publicly to deplore the violence, and asked Catholic bishops the world over to set aside Sunday 8 September as a day of prayer for Yugoslavia. Serbs, however, chose that day to parade up and down outside the papal nunciature in Belgrade waving placards proclaiming 'Vatican Satanic State'. The Catholics had already decided to support the independence of Croatia and Slovenia from Yugoslavia, an independence – so Serbs believed – which had been bolstered by Vatican funds.

What funds, Vatican officials might well have asked. In 1990 the Vatican incurred a deficit of $78m, and despite an increase in 'Peter's Pence' and an anonymous donation of $12.5m, the Holy See had to dig into its reserves for the first time in half a dozen years. There were more obvious cost centres than Croatian and Slovenian independence. Papal journeys ranked high. In mid-August John Paul went back to Poland for the fifth time. He prayed at the grave of his parents, he visited Wadowice and chatted to old friends, he even attended a meeting of theologians from Central and Eastern Europe, but the purpose of the journey was to pray at Czestochowa on 14 and 15 August with over a million young people gathered from every corner of Europe and beyond – including, it was estimated, some 70,000 from the Soviet Union – and four hundred bishops. Many in the East, said John Paul during his homily at the Assumption Day mass, had been left bereft by the collapse of the Communist ideology. He upbraided the youth of the West for losing their purpose in life, and for a lack of interest in public affairs. It was their job, he told them, to ensure the future liberty of religion, respect for the personal dimension, respect for the right to life, the defence of the family and of diversity of cultures, and the maintenance of the ecological balance.

It was a spectacular, if chaotic, gathering. On 16 August the Pope left it all behind him and flew off to Hungary. His first stop was another Marian shrine, at Mariapocs in the north east of the country where the papal mass, said in the Greek rite, brought pilgrims from a number of Eastern bloc countries some of whom afterwards, like a number of those in Czestochowa, refused to return home because of the attempted coup in Russia against Mikhail Gorbachev. When the Pope proclaimed at Mariapocs that the 'dark period is over' the coup had not yet taken place, and his chief concern in his homily was for minority rights, respect for diverse cultures, and reconciliation between the Orthodox and Roman Catholic Churches.

In Pecs, near to the border with the – by now former – Yugoslavia, the Cardinal of Zagreb came with four Croatian bishops as well as a large number of Croatian laity. 'I am close to your legitimate aspirations', he told them, 'and I renew my appeal to the international community to help you in this difficult hour in your history'. He also said, to everyone's surprise, that he hoped soon to visit Croatia: the Serbian fears of a Catholic conspiracy against them were clearly not diminished by the Pope's words. In Debrecen, which is Calvinist, he came close to apologizing for past Catholic persecution of Protestants and called for unity as a prerequisite for evangelization. He went on to Budapest – which is where he learnt of the attempt to unseat Gorbachev – and met

Hungarian Jews who criticized the Church for failing to defend the Jewish community during the Second World War. The bishops had done what they could in the circumstances, he told them.

The four-day visit ended in Esztergom, the country's former capital and still the primatial see. He prayed at the tomb of Cardinal Mindszenty, whose body had been brought back to Hungary only a couple of months earlier, and pleaded for an effort by Catholics to overcome tensions and suspicions left over from the past: the Church, more perhaps in Hungary than elsewhere in the former Eastern bloc, was divided between those who had confronted the regime and refused to compromise and those, including the former Cardinal of Hungary, Laszlo Lekai, who had believed in a step-by-step approach in dealing with the regime.

Some of those from the Soviet Union who had attended the youth rally in Czestochowa had returned to take part in the defence of the Moscow White House under Boris Yeltsin, which led to the collapse of the coup attempt. The Vatican was relieved at the return of Gorbachev, and made no bones about saying so. The Pope sent a telegram of support to the Russian President, saying that he hoped he would continue his work for the economic and spiritual renewal of the peoples of the Soviet Union. But 'peoples' was already becoming outdated. The USSR fell apart and Rome no longer had to refer matters to Moscow that, it believed, could be dealt with at the level of the individual Republics. Patriarch Aleksei could be bypassed.

The Patriarch, however, had emerged from the coup attempt with increased authority, partly because some of his younger clergy had taken an active part in the defence of the regime against the coup, and partly because his own support for Gorbachev never wavered. Whatever the Latin-rite Archbishop of Moscow might have thought remained unknown. He made no comment whatsoever, though he conducted a requiem for those killed in the defence of the White House before leaving for Italy to take part in a conference of Communione e Liberazione. In Moscow itself Archbishop Tadeusz Kondrusiewicz was keeping a low profile. The mayor of Moscow was not too pleased with Kondrusiewicz's appointment. Nobody had bothered to tell him, he complained, that there was to be such a person as a Catholic Archbishop of his city. Meanwhile a spokesman for the Orthodox Church, Metropolitan Kirill of Smolensk, had also criticized the Archbishop for opening parishes for ethnic Russians. Such parishes should, he said, serve foreigners, the diplomatic community, and those of ethnic minorities who were traditionally Catholic. Russians were to be left to the Orthodox.

That was, indeed, how L'Osservatore Romano presented the Catholic position when, on 14 October, it responded to criticisms of the Church's policy in Russia contained in a message from Patriarch Aleksei rejecting the invitation to send observers to the Synod of European Bishops, due to open in November. There were, the message said, serious differences between the Orthodox and Catholic Churches, especially in relation to the Uniate Church in the Ukraine – though whether Moscow had any longer any say in such matters Rome may well have doubted. The Moscow Patriarch accused the Catholic Church of setting up 'parallel missionary structures'. Not so, said *L'Osservatore*. The parishes serve established Catholic communities which owe their existence to the wholesale deportation of peoples under Stalin. And as for the Ukraine, efforts had been made to reconcile differences between the two Churches and the problems which had arisen sprang from the suppression of the Uniate Church under Stalin, and the confiscation of its property.

By the time this article appeared Pope John Paul was in Brazil. His fifty-third foreign journey, and his second to Brazil, ran from 12 to 21 October, and took in ten cities. On the flight he talked to journalists about his disappointment at the Moscow Patriarch's rejection of the invitation to attend the European Synod, and of difficulties over the establishment of diplomatic relations with Israel. But naturally he was chiefly concerned about the situation in the country he was about to visit. His anxiety concentrated on the expansion of fundamentalist sects and the ability of the Catholic Church to meet the challenge these presented. He was clearly not hopeful, and he let his worries be known as soon as he arrived at his first venue, the city of Natal in the north east of Brazil. To make use of married priests, he said, was no way to solve the shortage of clergy in Brazil; priests should preach the faith, not turn it into false prophecy; there should be a preferential, but not exclusive, option for the poor; priests should stay out of politics leaving that to the laity. A local newspaper had carried out a survey before John Paul arrived, and one of its conclusions was that more than half the population thought the clergy spent more time on politics than on religion.[12] (Rather fewer, but still a good forty per cent it turned out, did not know who the Pope was.)

The warning to churchmen to stay out of politics was a recurring theme of the visit. He denounced social injustice of all kinds, including the unfair distribution of land, though he insisted it was not the Church's task to try to rectify this inequality. The Archbishop of Rio de Janeiro, Cardinal Eugenio Sales, one of the most conservative of an increasingly conservative Episcopal Conference, claimed after the Pope left that his message had been to condemn the occupation of over-large estates by landless peasants, and to condemn Liberation Theology. In fact neither was true, and the Pope's words though generally conservative in tone on religious issues, were as usual more liberal on social ones. To seminarians in the country's capital, Brasilia, he insisted on the value of the traditional structures of priestly formation – the Vatican a couple of years before had closed Dom Helder Camara's theological institute and seminary in Recife (cf. above, p. 222) – and he endorsed the value of priestly celibacy. He warned the bishops about the dangers inherent in adapting the liturgy to local cultures.

At Cuiba he met some of the indigenous people of the Amazon. They complained about the way the 500th anniversary of the coming of Columbus was to be celebrated: for them it had led to five hundred years of suffering, they explained. John Paul was not of the same mind. The missionaries had given their all, he said, they deserved respect, even if they were not perfect. He also chose this visit to Cuiba to plead for the protection of the environment.

There were to be no politics on the agenda when the Pope opened the special Synod of European Bishops on 28 November. The forty-four page summary of replies by bishops and others to a Vatican questionnaire on the situation in Europe suggested that the central problem was one of freedom: freedom to love God, or freedom to love oneself. To a certain extent freedom had returned through the fall of Communism. The Church had built up in Eastern Europe a considerable standing because of its opposition to Communism, but now lacked resources to fill the gap left by the disappearance of that particular ideology. In Western Europe, on the other hand, the real problem was not lack of resources but indifference and materialism – some bishops, apparently, had also added theological dissent as one of the difficulties that stood in the way of the Church being recognized as the way to salvation.

As the representatives of the Episcopal Conferences, and a few lay people, had their say in a series of eight-minute speeches, the main theme of the Synod, at least as far as its participants saw it, became clear: the integration of the former Eastern bloc, and particularly, perhaps, the integration of Russia, into a new Europe, and the 'exchange of gifts' between Eastern and Western Europe, meaning the ability of each to learn from the experience of the other. When the final statement was approved on 13 December the Church's role in the unification of Europe was given pride of place. Evangelization had to uncover the Christian foundations of Europe, and to build upon them a new Christian, and therefore humane, civilization. It would not be easy, for although ideological atheism had disappeared with the collapse of Communism there remained a practical atheism – people think and act as if there were no God. The Church, the Synod insisted, is tied to no one political system, but it favoured a 'correctly understood democracy', the free movement of goods and the market economy – though it accepted that such concepts, especially the economic ones, had to be introduced with discretion into the former Eastern bloc.

On the 'exchange of gifts', the Synod appreciated the witness of the Churches of the East under their persecution, and the abundance of vocations to the priesthood and the religious life which had sprung from their living faith. The Western Churches, living in a greater freedom, had developed pastoral structures which they could now share with their fellow Churches of the East. All of this, it was stressed – and the Pope made special mention of it in his closing address – was to be done under the close control of the Pope himself.

The Synod had talked about ecumenical relations, and expressed regret in particular that only one Orthodox Church had felt able to send a 'fraternal delegate'. That delegate was Metropolitan Spyridion Papagheorghiou of Venice, representing the recently-elected Patriarch Bartolomeos II of Constantinople. He had explained to the Synod why the other Churches had stayed away – because the revival of the Uniate Churches had been accompanied by violence, especially in the occupation of churches in the Ukraine and Rumania, and because of the creation by the Roman Catholic Church of 'parallel missionary structures' in Russia. In sharp contrast, he said, to the bad relations between Orthodoxy and Rome, relations between Orthodoxy and the Protestant Churches were excellent.

The omission of any reference to Protestant-Orthodox relations was commented upon by delegates from the non-Roman Churches at the end of the Synod. They also regretted that the Synod had failed to mention that non-Roman Churches had also suffered under Communism; or that such Churches talked to each other, said the Anglican Bishop Mark Santer of Birmingham, without any reference to Rome. It was a pity, said Bishop Santer, that some of the propositions put forward by the non-Roman Catholic delegates had not made it to the final list; on the other hand one had to be grateful for small mercies: the proposition attributing the fall of Communism to the intervention of Our Lady of Fátima had been omitted.

It was not a good month for ecumenism. Soon after the Synod got under way the Congregation for the Doctrine of the Faith issued its response to the *Final Report* of the first Anglican-Roman Catholic International Commission (ARCIC I) which had been published in 1981. The reply, for which the

Church had waited a decade, was distinctly unhelpful. It was 'a significant milestone' said the CDF, but the Catholic Church judges 'that it is not yet possible to state that substantial agreement has been reached ... There still remain between Anglicans and Catholics important differences regarding essential matters of Catholic doctrine'. While the Anglican Communion had accepted that ARCIC I was 'consonant' with its doctrine, remarked the Archbishop of Canterbury, George Carey, somewhat tartly, Rome wanted to know whether it was identical with Roman doctrine – and had judged that it was not. As Canon Christopher Hill, Anglican co-secretary to both ARCIC I and ARCIC II, commented in *The Tablet*,[13] 'what seems to have happened is that the Council for Unity has persuaded the CDF to accept a genuinely positive and ecumenical tone, while failing to persuade it to modify its substantive judgements.' Those judgements were generally negative. The tone of the document was warm, and in desperation the English Catholic bishops seized upon that; reception by the Anglican communion was decidedly cool.

Roman Catholic relations with other Christian Churches had also reached a low ebb. They were destined to sink even lower particularly with the Orthodox Churches. Relations were good, however, with Russia itself as distinct from its Church. President Boris Yeltsin had decided not to be outdone by his former rival, Mikhail Gorbachev. On 20 December he had a sixty-five minute audience with the Pope. He had prepared himself for the occasion by consulting the Patriarch of Moscow, Aleksei II. Aleksei was far from happy with the Church of Rome for establishing five new bishoprics in the former Soviet territories and for appointing Archbishop Tadeusz Kondrusiewicz as Apostolic Administrator of the new diocese of Moscow. Ecumenical cooperation, which was what Yeltsin wanted, was not high on Aleksei's list of priorities and Yeltsin found it impossible to repeat Gorbachev's invitation to the Pope to visit Russia – though, it was intimated, the original invitation still stood. Yeltsin undertook to carry out the promises made to the Catholic bishops which, it was believed, included the return to the Catholics of two churches in Moscow itself. There was only one available, and there, on Christmas Day, Archbishop Kondrusiewicz presided at a mass televised by the Italians. The promises made by Mary at Fátima were coming true, he told his congregation. Since those promises were commonly interpreted as including the conversion of Russia, this was not a particularly diplomatic thing to say in the circumstances, nor to dwell as he did on the crisis of Moscow's shops empty of goods. The Catholic Church would help out, he told his congregation.

NOTES

1. Sean McDonagh, 'The greening of the Church', in *The Tablet*, 13 January 1990, pp. 40-42.
2. The Vatican's explanation for turning down the invitation to co-convene the Seoul conference was that it was being asked as a Church to put itself on a par with the World Council of Churches, a wholly different entity, and that co-sponsorship would therefore be on an unequal footing. The Catholic Church had taken part in the earlier, preparatory, gathering in Basle in May 1989 because delegates were then invited from individual Churches. The Vatican's rejection of the invitation to co-sponsor the Seoul conference came so late that it caused a delay in planning the conference. In the event, quite a number of Catholics turned up at Seoul, sent by religious orders or other Catholic organizations.
3. The law laid down that a Church might gain legal recognition so long as it had 100+ members. While this seemed reasonable enough to the mainline Churches, in effect it discriminated against 'sects' or New Religious Movements.
4. There was a remarkable lack of diplomacy about the whole affair, with mistakes made by all sides and a good deal of gerrymandering by the Orthodox. See Michael Bordeaux, 'Ukrainian imbroglio' in *The Tablet*, 12 May 1990, p. 579.
5. The term '*magisterium*' has a complex history, but has come to mean the teaching, to be regarded by the faithful as authoritative, of the Bishop of Rome and, by extension, of the Vatican departments or Congregations which serve him. Much has been written on the meaning of '*magisterium*', but for a brief summary, cf. Robert Murray, 'Further reflections on magisterium and "Magisterium" ' in *Commentary on the Catechism of the Catholic Church*, edited by Michael Walsh (London, Geoffrey Chapman, 1994), pp. 34-5.
6. Not to mention the telephone. It was announced in 1990 that you could dial (010 39) 7779 3020 and get the Pope – a recorded message in English (there were different numbers for other languages). You heard the bells of St Peter's, a Vatican Radio announcer saying that you were about to hear the voice of the Pope, *Christus vincit* played on the glockenspiel (it was Vatican Radio's signature tune) and then a few chosen words from the Pope. Profits – and the calls were reported to be expensive – went to defray the costs of papal travels.
7. It was confirmed in Rome during the Synod that two married men had been ordained, both of them in Brazil. John Paul had given his approval on condition that the husband did not live in the same house as his wife; that celibacy was accepted with full awareness of what it entailed; and that wife and children gave their consent. The Pope, explained Archbishop John Foley of the Pontifical Council for Social Communications, had not annulled the marriages but had given those involved 'permission to suspend their marital rights'.
8. For papal interventions in the Gulf conflict, see Jean Toulat, *Le Pape contre la guerre du Golfe*, (Paris, O.E.I.L., 1991).
9. Bidawid had not been in Baghdad during the war – he had been absent when

fighting broke out and claimed he could not get back. The papal nuncio, on the other hand, had stayed at his post throughout.

10. Gutierrez circulated a letter to drum up support, listing Isabella's virtues and explaining away her apparent failings: cf. *The Tablet*, 1 June 1991, pp. 675-6.
11. *Laborem Exercens* had marked the ninetieth anniversary.
12. They also thought that the clergy lived in luxury and had sexual relations.
13. 7 December 1991, pp. 1525-6.

TEN

1992-3

WHILE THE Apostolic Administrator of the (Latin-rite) diocese of Moscow may not have been the most diplomatic of individuals, he observed the courtesies. Representatives of the Church attended the Orthodox Christmas liturgy, presided over by Patriarch Aleksei, on 7 January. The Holy See, meanwhile, granted formal recognition to the Russian Federation. On 13 January the Holy See also recognized the independence of Croatia and Slovenia from the Yugoslav federation – much to the annoyance of the rump of the Yugoslav government. The Croatians announced their intention of quashing the conviction for treason and for collaboration with the Nazis of Archbishop Stepinac, the former Primate of Yugoslavia, who, under the Tito regime, had been sentenced to sixteen years imprisonment. The Catholic Church had been pressing for his rehabilitation. The Orthodox were unhappy about it, and argued that the Archbishop's[1] role in the genocide of Serbs should be investigated before the verdict against him was overturned. Relations with the Orthodox, whether in Russia or beyond, were delicate in the extreme, and the Pontifical Council for the Promotion of Christian Unity was making every effort to build bridges.

They were not particularly successful. On 4 February the Holy Synod of the Greek Orthodox Church denounced 'the dishonest tactics of Rome' in Eastern Europe, tactics which were designed, in the view of the Synod, to further the Pope's ambitions as a player in world affairs. 'He is sly and personally interested', insisted the Synod, and called upon the Greek government to break off diplomatic links with the Holy See. The Greek Orthodox Patriarch, Archbishop Seraphim, described the Vatican's activities as deceitful and perfidious. 'The Orthodox will never tolerate the conspiracy of the Pope and the Trojan horse which is the Uniate Church.' The particular occasion of this Greek irritation seems to have been the Pope's Christmas greeting in the language of Macedonia, which was interpreted as an attempt to take over the Macedonian autocephalous (or independent) Church, a body not recognized by the rest of the Orthodox world.

The Greek government reacted with irritation to the Holy Synod's call for the cessation of diplomatic relations with the Vatican. The new Greek ambassador hurried to present his credentials, and to assure the Pope that it was his government's hope that ecumenical dialogue would continue 'in a spirit of due respect'.

The Pope's 54th foreign journey began on 19 February with his arrival at Dakar in Senegal. His message to Catholics was to be true to their land and their culture. He went on to encourage members of the archdiocesan synod of Dakar, and others gathered in the cathedral to greet him, in the adaptation of the liturgy to 'expressions that are natural to Africans' – though he warned them at the same time not to go too far, and to keep in mind the requirements of the Church. Inculturation was a prominent theme of this visit. Islam was steadily spreading among the peoples of Africa, and presented itself as the religion most consonant with the spirit of the region. 'The Catholic faith does not make its followers any less African than their neighbours', insisted the Pope in Dakar, but he also went out of his way to cultivate good relations with Muslim leaders in all three countries he visited on this tour, countries where Catholicism represented only a tiny proportion of the population.

From Senegal the Pope made an excursion to the Gambia on 23 February, and on the 24th, back in Senegal, he travelled to the island of Goree whence very many thousands of Africans had departed for the Americas, and a life of slavery.

The final stage of this eight-day tour was in Guinea where, until his death in 1984, President Sekou Touré had persecuted the Church in the name of Marxism, imprisoning Conakry's archbishop, expelling missionaries and sequestrating ecclesiastical property. That the Church had managed to survive, said the Pope, was due under God to the work of the lay catechists.

The Pope had left for his latest excursion to Africa reassured by the words of the Greek ambassador to the Holy See. Shortly after he came back yet another attack was launched upon him by the Orthodox, this time from a meeting in Istanbul from 12 to 15 March of the leaders of all the Churches. Among the forces which threatened the Orthodox Church, they declared in their final communiqué, were schismatics, Protestant fundamentalists, and the Catholic Church. They had expected fraternal support after all the sufferings they had gone through during Communist rule, instead of which Rome was sending missionaries into Eastern Europe, and – what was apparently worse – was aiding and abetting the Uniate Churches. The 'violent actions' of the

Uniates could not have taken place without the support of Rome, insisted Metropolitan Spyridion Papagheorghiou. There were those in the Roman Catholic Church who understood the exigencies of ecumenical dialogue, he said, instancing the Jesuit Cardinal Archbishop of Milan, Carlo Martini, but not those in the upper reaches of the Vatican.

John Paul's concerns at that particular moment, however, were elsewhere. He was putting the final touches, so that it would be out in time for Easter, to *Pastores Dabo Vobis* ('I will give you shepherds', a citation of Jeremiah 3:15), a two hundred and twenty-four page apostolic exhortation summing up the October 1990 Synod of Bishops on priestly formation (cf. above, pp.229-31).

The Pope begins his exhortation with a chapter on the cultural context in which vocations arise. While he recognizes the pressures of a consumer society he also sees opportunities in 'the recent collapse of ideologies': 'For many young people the question of religion and the need for spirituality are becoming more explicit.' Priests, he accepts, do not necessarily exhibit a greater degree of holiness than the laity, their role is to serve the laity, to proclaim the Gospel and to build up the Church. Priests are expected to demonstrate in their lives some of the 'radicalism of the Gospel', which he finds encapsulated in the evangelical counsels, particularly the counsel of celibacy. Celibacy, he insists, is not just a legal requirement for ordination but is theologically motivated – the priest gives himself to the Church totally just as Christ gave himself totally to the Church, and the priest is thereby made like Christ.

The Pope appears by implication to recognize that celibacy can have deleterious effects on priests' emotional lives. They must be able to relate well to others, he insists, and for that they need 'an affective maturity which is prudent, able to renounce anything which is a threat to it, vigilant over both body and spirit and capable of esteem and respect in interpersonal relationships between men and women'. For this to be achieved a priest needs education and spiritual formation. This spiritual formation, he adds, should include especially training in the preferential option for the poor.

Education, naturally enough, has above all to be in theology. John Paul comments on the problems which had arisen with theologians. The framework should be one of co-operation, but it had to be remembered that there was only one *magisterium*, 'that of Peter and the Apostles, the Pope and the bishops' – the theologians themselves, who in practice do most of the teaching, are not included. It was important to distinguish, he said, 'the common teaching of the Church from the opinions of theologians and from tendencies which quickly pass'. There was a particular problem where priestly studies were conducted in academic institutions. He was clearly happier, as the Synod had been, with the traditional seminary, 'a continuation in the Church of the apostolic community gathered around Jesus'. The formation received in a seminary is not simply theological but spiritual as well, and that intellectual and spiritual formation should continue throughout the life of the priest – though the Pope recognizes such continuing education is difficult to arrange in the busy life of a modern clergyman. That, he says, makes it all the more imperative that it be taken seriously, both by priests and by bishops. Nothing in *Pastores Dabo Vobis* suggested that the pattern of priesthood – or of priestly formation – in the future would differ markedly from that of the past.

On 17 May Pope John Paul beatified in St Peter's Square, before a crowd estimated at 20,000, 'an exemplary priest who succeeded in opening up new apostolic horizons and of missionary and evangelizing activity', Mgr Josemaría Escrivá de Balaguer, the founder of Opus Dei. Never had there been so contentious a beatification. Opposition was aroused as much by the nature of Opus Dei itself, a distinctly conservative organization of, it is frequently alleged, considerable political as well as ecclesiastical, clout,[2] as by the life of Escrivá himself which to many critics seemed anything but exemplary.

Arguments about the appropriateness of the beatification – there were none about the suitability of the one-time African slave, Giuseppina Bakhita, who was beatified on the same occasion – focused attention on the changing character of saint-making in the Church during the pontificate of John Paul II.[3] There had been other controversial beatifications and canonizations, those of Maximilian Kolbe and Edith Stein, for example. Commentators had observed a rapid increase in the number of Poles elevated to saintly status. The Pope had also changed the pattern of the ceremonies. They were no longer conducted exclusively in Rome but frequently took place in the course of the Pope's foreign journeys. It was remarked that John Paul II had canonized more saints than all his predecessors put together, at least since the process had been put firmly under the control of the Congregation of Rites at the end of the sixteenth century.

In some ways the statistics were misleading. It was true that the Pope had canonized more people than his predecessors, but his average, year by year, was not significantly greater than that of Pope Paul VI. If he had made more people into saints it was at least in part because he had canonized large groups of martyrs. The Congregation for the Causes of Saints, the successor to the Congregation of Rites in the business of making saints, had streamlined its procedures. Escrivá had gone through the process remarkably quickly, which was not surprising given the money and effort Opus had put into it, but every cause had speeded up, particularly those in which the Pope had a personal interest. That interest was not without its problems as far as the Congregation was concerned. It had not been happy to transfer Edith Stein from the ranks of the confessors to that of martyrs, but the Pope had wanted to conduct the beatification while in Germany, and the matter was pressing. The Congregation itself, or at least some of its officials, were quite aware of the problems that would ensue (cf. above, pp. 178-9), but the Pope was insistent. He has an unshakeable conviction in the 'exemplary' value of the lives of holy men and women, and is eager that the Congregation promote more lay people, and especially more women, to the ranks of the officially holy to serve as models for the lives of modern Catholics. Whether Mgr Escrivá was an appropriate model many people doubted; others – including Cardinal Oddi, one of the most conservative of ecclesiastical figures – wondered whether the beatification was opportune; there were also questions about whether the Congregation had been manipulated in the interests of Opus. But the Pope decided to proceed. His doing so despite all the controversy was generally interpreted as a sign of the favour which Opus Dei enjoyed in the highest echelons of the Vatican.

On 24 May Pope John Paul was visited by Dr George Carey, the new Archbishop of Canterbury. Dr Carey's evangelical churchmanship did not make him particularly sympathetic to the claims of the Roman Church. In an interview he gave to the London *Daily Telegraph* a week or so before leaving for Rome he had taken issue with Catholic teaching on contraception as expounded by Paul VI's encyclical *Humanae Vitae*, and vigorously upheld by John Paul. The context of his remarks was the forthcoming 'Earth summit' in Rio de Janeiro, to be held under the auspices of the United Nations' Conference on Environment and Development. Dr Carey told the *Telegraph*, he had talked to the UN Secretary General and other officials about the Summit – at which the Vatican was to be represented – and had asked why the question of population control was not on the agenda. He had been answered, he said, by 'an uncomfortable silence'. It had been left off the agenda, he concluded, because of the opposition of Catholic 'dogma' about birth control, a dogma which, he confessed, he did not understand. The Archbishop's views were, said the Catholic Archbishop of Liverpool 'for the most part unhelpful', while the papal pro-nuncio' described them as 'untimely – that is putting it mildly'. Other British Catholic leaders hastened to be more diplomatic than the Vatican's own diplomat.

In the event the Archbishop's views on population control did not figure in his hour-long conversation with the Pope – though for a time they were alone and without interpreters and the Archbishop remarked afterwards that he disagreed with the Pope on a number of important matters. It was not birth control but the ordination of women to the priesthood, which Dr Carey supported, that he named as the most problematic. 'We're at a stage in the friendship', he claimed about relations between the Anglican and Roman Churches, 'where it is possible to say tough things about one another without entering into polemics.' The toughest thing for the British Catholic hierarchy may well have been the revelation that the Archbishop had invited the Pope to make a second visit to England. There was talk in the official communiqué issued afterwards by the Vatican Press Office of the Christian responsibility for 'stewardship of God's creation', and of the need for collaboration on issues of justice and peace, but for the most part it concentrated on ecumenism, and the response to ARCIC I. Although the Vatican had not been able to endorse ARCIC's claim to have achieved 'substantial agreement', this was not intended as putting a brake on the dialogue. Clearly the issue of women priests was a problem, said the statement, and a 'grave obstacle' to reconciliation, but talks should go on.

After a decent interval the Vatican's official spokesman denied that there had been an attempt to prevent discussion at Rio of the problem of population. Quite the contrary. He insisted that the Vatican wanted the topic on the agenda because of its opposition to enforced birth control. A note sent to all governments taking part in the Earth Summit asserted that population growth in itself was rarely the cause of environmental problems, though richer nations often seized upon it as an easy alternative to a fairer distribution of the earth's resources. Development aid, the note went on, 'should not be made conditional on acceptance of programmes of contraception, sterilization or abortion'.

Rejection of the 'sly propaganda' for abortion was one of the themes of the Pope's 55th foreign tour, which took him, between 4 and 10 June, to Angola and to the islands of São Tomé and Principe, all former Portuguese colonies. He arrived in Luanda to be photographed between the president Eduardo dos Santos and his rival Jonas Savimbi. The former represented the (originally Marxist) MPLA, the latter the South Africa-backed UNITA, opposing parties in the fifteen-year-long civil war which had cost thousands of lives, including those of priests, nuns and catechists, and had reduced the country to starvation. A treaty of peace had been signed a year before, and elections were planned for the coming September. The primary message of the Pope was, therefore, one of peace and reconciliation, but there were other topics. In the course of the war the MPLA had been supported by Cuba. Foreign intervention, said the Pope in Lubango, had caused enormous damage to the family, to respect for life and motherhood. He told young people gathered in a stadium in Luanda not to be deterred from marriage by the cost of church weddings. He attacked cohabitation and polygamy, and warned his hearers not to be attracted by Protestant sects but to 'follow in the one Church founded and desired by Christ'. This remark had not been meant as a criticism of mainline Protestant Churches, a Vatican official hurriedly denied afterwards.

He came back to Rome to yet another ecumenical problem, once again with the Orthodox over the problem of Uniates. In a letter of 23 June the Ecumenical patriarch of Constantinople, Bartholomew I, complained about clashes between the Uniates ('the so-called Greek-rite Churches' as he called them) and the 'traditional ancient Orthodox Churches'. The letter criticized the Vatican for its support of the Uniates, and made it clear that dialogue with the Orthodox could not continue unless the support were withdrawn – which, clearly, the Pope was not prepared to do. Instead he replied diplomatically to Metropolitan Ivakovos, who had come to Rome as a representative of the Patriarch, that Rome was fully prepared to continue dialogue, and that the 'practical difficulties' to which the Patriarch referred had arisen out of the 'sad legacy of the long and tragic persecution that Christian communities in various countries have experienced in this century'.

The Pope, it transpired, had other things on his mind. Towards the end of June he began to experience some pain in his abdomen which gradually got worse. His personal physician, Professor Renato Buzzonetti, was called in. Buzzonetti in turn sought the assistance of Professor Francesco Crucitti, who carried out tests at the Vatican and decided there was sufficient cause for concern for more tests to be made, and that they should take place in hospital. During the Angelus address on 12 July John Paul announced he was going into Rome's Gemelli hospital that evening. Three days later, at 6.25 am on 15 July, he was operated on for the removal of a tumour of the lower intestine. The operation lasted four hours; the tumour that was removed from his colon was seven centimetres long, two centimetres high, and was non-malignant – though had it been left much longer, the doctors declared, it would have developed into a malignant growth. At the same time a number of stones were removed from the gall bladder. The operation was a complete success and the Pope recovered at least as well as any one of his age (he was now seventy-two) could have been expected to do. Less than twenty-four hours after the operation he was allowed out of bed to sit in an armchair. On 19 July he spoke on Vatican Radio in a pre-recorded, seven-minute broadcast of the Angelus to thank those who had sent him 'messages of solidarity'. In the evening of 28 July he was discharged from hospital and went directly to Castel Gandolfo for a month's convalescence. On 17 August he left for a small house in the woods at Lorenzago di Cadore in the Dolomites, where he had spent his holidays in 1987 and 1988. He returned to Castel Gandolfo on 2 September.

The Vatican machine continued without him. The day after John Paul departed for the papal Summer residence it was announced that a 'permanent bilateral working commission' had been established between the Holy See and the state of Israel to discuss Church issues in Israel and in the occupied territories. The establishment of the commission – which had not one Palestinian representative – was described by Archbishop Jean-Louis Tauran, the Holy See's equivalent of a foreign minister, as a 'qualitative leap' forward. The Palestinian Latin-rite Patriarch of Jerusalem, Michael Sabbah, at first welcomed the commission while noting that the Vatican was concerned about the status of Jerusalem and the rights of Palestinians, both of which topics had been left out of the terms of reference for the commission. Shortly afterwards, however, he signed a letter published in an Arabic newspaper in Jerusalem, alongside the Anglican Bishop of Jerusalem, the imam of the Al-Aqsa mosque, and the mufti of Jerusalem, warning the Vatican to be cautious in its dealings with the State of Israel. An Islamic-Christian committee had been set up, said the letter, to monitor the workings of the Vatican-Israel commission.

The Pope's state of health continued to improve. He began to receive official visitors; he resumed his Wednesday public audiences earlier than expected; his journey to Santo Domingo from 9 to 14 October for the Conference of Latin American Bishops (CELAM), it was decided, would go ahead, though visits to Mexico, Nicaragua and Jamaica planned as part of the same trip were cancelled.

The Santo Domingo meeting had been arranged to coincide, in time and place, with the 500th anniversary of the arrival in the New World of Christopher Columbus. Whether Columbus's coming was a matter of celebration was itself debatable: many of the indigenous peoples of the continent clearly did not think so (cf. above, p. 245). But the Pope, it was made clear, was not visiting Santo Domingo to mark the arrival of the Europeans but to celebrate the 500th anniversary of the evangelization of the continent. And as he remarked in his speech at the opening of the CELAM gathering, they were not really celebrating the beginning of evangelization either, because missionaries did not travel with Columbus until his second voyage.

The Santo Domingo meeting itself was highly contentious. The Latin American bishops had managed to force upon the Vatican, and upon the CELAM executive, a working document in the tradition of the earlier conferences at Medellín and Puebla. They were disappointed, however, that references to the martyrs of El Salvador, Archbishop Oscar Romero and the Jesuits, had been removed. They were further irritated by the appointment as co-secretary to the conference (a hitherto unheard of post) of a friend of the Chilean dictator General Pinochet, and equally by the appointment as an expert to the conference of only one – and he the most conservative – of the eight theologians who had drawn up the working document. They were also upset by the banning – on the specious grounds that he had retired as a diocesan bishop – of Mgr Cándido Padin, O.S.B., who was renowned for having protested, over a decade earlier, at the Vatican's unilateral alteration of the agreed text of the Puebla conference.

The Pope did not kiss the ground as he arrived in Santo Domingo, an omission which was generally attributed to his delicate state of health. On 11 October he said mass in front of the vast lighthouse, shaped like a cross, which had just been built to serve as a monument to the five hundred years, and as a mausoleum for the bones of Columbus – which had been moved there on 6 October. The following day John Paul opened the fourth CELAM conference[5] with an hour-long speech which he clearly struggled to finish. It was an inspiring address, insisting on the need to see the Church's social teaching as an integral part of the Church mission of evangelization. It contained a proposal that the more radical bishops looked at askance: the notion of a Synod of all the bishops of the Americas, both North and South.

Whether their suspicions were groundless has yet to be shown, for at the time of writing no firm plans have been made for such a gathering. It seemed, however, to place CELAM into a context where its own concerns might be subsumed under the concerns of the richer Churches to the north. It would, moreover, as a Synod be organized from Rome, giving the local hierarchies much less of an opportunity to control the agenda and determine the outcome – though there has hardly been a meeting of bishops which the Vatican had made a greater effort to control than that of Santo Domingo. Whether the control was exercised at the behest of the Pope or by Vatican officialdom acting independently was one of the topics much debated by those who attended, bishops and journalists alike. The Pope himself, however, had returned to Rome by midnight on 14 October and the following day was back in harness, his busy life giving the lie to suggestions that his health had been irreparably harmed by the illness of July.

On 23 October he received the Israeli Foreign Minister, Shimon Peres. In the course of the forty-five minute conversation, described by the Vatican rather oddly as 'cordial and serene', Peres invited John Paul to visit the Holy Land, an invitation, he added, which the Pope had 'accepted with great emotion'. The Vatican itself was cooler. The Pope had frequently made it clear he wanted to go to the Holy Land, said a statement. He had long wanted to go to Jerusalem, 'the holy city for Jews, Christians and Muslims, and the crossroads of peace for all the peoples of the Middle East', which was not quite how Mr Peres saw it. For him the rapprochement between the Catholic Church and Israel was of 'historical, political and psychological' importance, because it was another step in the reduction of the 'anti-Israeli camp'. Peres was upbeat on the possibility of a visit by the Pope in the near future. The Vatican itself was more circumspect. There was talk of 1994 as a possible date, because that would be the 30th anniversary of Paul VI's historic journey. In the meantime much had changed. Paul VI had studiously avoided anything which might have seemed like recognition of the state of Israel. After his meeting with John Paul, Shimon Peres claimed that diplomatic relations were in the offing, and that as a first step there would be an exchange of less formal representation. On this, the Vatican forbore to comment.

That was on Friday. On Sunday 25 October the Pope presided at the lengthy ceremonies of beatification of a further 122 martyrs of the Spanish Civil War – forty had already been elevated to the status of blessed by John Paul (cf. above, p. 176), even though Paul VI had halted the process 'for fear of opening old wounds'. The event attracted only seven thousand pilgrims from Spain, which rather suggested that devotion to the martyrs, technically a prerequisite for beatification, was not great. The causes of some 6,500 others were being considered.

Six days later came a formal retraction from the Vatican of the 1633 condemnation of Galileo. 'We cannot deny that Galileo suffered greatly at the hands of churchmen', John Paul had said in 1979, on the occasion of the centenary of Albert Einstein's birth. Two years afterwards he established a commission to look into the affair. On 31 October, at a meeting of the Pontifical Academy of Sciences, it was declared that Galileo's judges made a 'subjective error of judgement'. We cannot be certain, commented the Pope, that the same thing would not happen again. To prevent it happening 'will require both sides to have an informed awareness of the limits of their own competencies'. It was therefore incumbent on theologians, went on the Pope, to be aware of scientific advance, in case their teaching might have to be altered in the light of it – which, of course, was what many had been saying about the doctrine of birth control.

That Catholic teaching on sexual morality had not changed, and was not about to change, was part of the message of the much-heralded *Catechism of the Catholic Church*, which eventually saw the light of day on 15 November when it was published in its French edition. The original intention had been to publish simultaneously in French, English, German and Spanish, but the French had been allowed to appear early, explained the Vatican spokesman, to prevent unnecessary speculation about the *Catechism's* content. French had been the language in which it had been composed, and therefore was the first version available. It proved to be a curiously mixed compilation.[6] Though the strictures on sexual morality were as harsh as ever, there were welcome sections on social morality – on careless driving, for example, or on business ethics – of a kind not hitherto found in official catechisms. Jewish-Christian relations were excellently treated, otherwise there was little or nothing on world religions, or even on ecumenism. The section on the liturgy was widely praised; that on creation and original sin roundly criticized. Scattered throughout were a profusion of texts from the Scriptures, from the fathers of the Church, from saints, and from Church Councils, all treated as if of equal value – which they are not – and, especially in the case of Scripture, with little or no reference to the context in which they were composed.

The Pope, who had given his formal approval to *The Catechism of the Catholic Church* on 25 June saying that he had read ten drafts and that the suggestions he had made for the *Catechism's* improvement had been 'accepted with great openness and carried out with careful fidelity', contributed a short apostolic constitution, *Fidei Depositum* (The deposit of faith). This served as an introduction, explaining the genesis of the project, and its purpose. It was, he said, linked closely to Vatican II – a remark with which some commentators quite reasonably took issue – and was intended as a general guide: there would be need for local conferences of bishops to adapt it to local needs. When the British and American hierarchies commissioned a translation into inclusive language, however, Rome took fright, produced a new translation in which 'man' replaced 'people' or 'human beings', and held up publication for well over a year. Rather oddly Cardinal Ratzinger managed to hand the Pope a translation of the *Catechism* in English – as well as in Italian and Spanish – during the solemn promulgation of the text in the Vatican palace's Sala Regia on 7 December. The Pope shortly afterwards told the bishops of the Netherlands the *Catechism* would help to settle the minds of Dutch Catholics, confused by much of the recent theological debate in their country.

On 1 December Pope John Paul called a meeting of the twenty-four presidents of the Episcopal Conferences of Europe. In the course of the one-day meeting the Pope announced that the Council of European Episcopal Conferences would be restructured with all the presidents of such conferences as full members, to make it a more effective coordinating body for the Church's work throughout the continent. The meeting also called on European Catholic Churches to declare 1 January 1993 a special day of prayer for peace, and particularly for peace in the Balkans. In addition an invitation was issued to representatives of all Christian Churches in Europe – and the invitation was explicitly extended to Jews and Muslims – to meet in Assisi on 9-10 January 1993 for a vigil of prayer and fasting for peace. Speaking shortly afterwards to health and agriculture ministers of more than 160 countries meeting in Rome, John Paul appeared to give his approval, though without explicitly saying so, to the use of military force, presumably under the aegis of the United Nations, to bring humanitarian aid to those civilian populations where the distribution of such aid was being impeded by war. The immediate situation to which the Pope's words applied was Somalia, to which the US President George Bush was proposing to send troops, but it was clear he was also thinking of Bosnia.

Bosnia was certainly on his mind as he composed his message for the 1 January 1993 World Day of Peace. 'Nothing', he said, 'seems able to halt the senseless violence of arms' there. 'The aberrant logic of war is prevailing over the repeated and authoritative calls for peace.' But the situation in Bosnia seems to have been added as an afterthought. The central argument of his message was that poverty itself was a grave threat to peace: 'To allow situations of extreme poverty to persist is to create social conditions ever more exposed to the threat of violence and conflict.'

Among the causes of poverty he listed, in the first place, the burden of foreign debt on Third-World countries. He pointed out that drug-dealing arises out of situations of poverty, and argued that the best way to deal with the cultivation of drugs by the poor was to find alternative sources of income for them. Migration, too, was a consequence of poverty, but migration gave rise to social tensions in the receiving countries. It was of 'fundamental importance', wrote the Pope, to recognize that war had never solved anything, but simply caused new forms of poverty. If poverty were to be alleviated, he went on, this could be done only by a reduction in the consumption of the world's resources by the industrialized nations. In place of consumption he recommended 'evangelical poverty', freely chosen. It is, he said, 'the source of peace, since through it the individual can establish a proper relationship with God, with others and with creation'.

Bosnia was again the focus of concern as the Pope, representatives of European and North American Episcopal Conferences, delegations from other Christian communities and leaders of Jewish and Muslim communities again gathered at the Pope's invitation in Assisi – he had, it was known, wanted to hold the meeting in Sarajevo, but was firmly advised against doing so. Much to the Pope's disappointment there were only two representatives of the Orthodox Churches present, both of them from Skopje in Macedonia. However, both the Ecumenical Patriarch Bartholomew I and the Serbian Patriarch – who against his wishes had been prevented by his Synod from attending – sent letters, the Serbian Patriarch saying that he would send a delegation to the Vatican in the near future.

At the opening ceremony on 9 January the Pope said that the purpose of the occasion was to pray according to each group's tradition to the 'Lord of history', since prayer was the proper response of the believer, whether Christian, Jew or Muslim. He asked five people, including a teenage girl and a Muslim leader from Sarajevo, to give testimony to what they had observed. As he spoke in the course of the vigil service, presided over by Cardinal Martini of Milan in the church of St Clare, he described the war in the Balkans as a 'special accumulation of sins', and attributed it to 'a society based on selfishness and greed against the civilization of love'.

On Sunday morning, 10 January, John Paul met the Muslim leaders, promising that the Catholic Church would cooperate to 'promote social justice, moral values, peace and freedom'. To use religion as an excuse for violence, he said, must be condemned 'by all true believers in God'. Shortly afterwards the Archbishop of Sarajevo, in Rome for his *ad limina* visit, invited the Pope to travel to Bosnia. The Pope accepted. The Vatican is 'studying concrete possibilities' for a trip in the near future, said the Archbishop hopefully.

Bosnia was again on John Paul's mind when, on 16 January, he gave the annual papal address to diplomats accredited to the Holy See. (There were by the beginning of 1993 145 governments with full diplomatic relations, plus the Russian Federation, which had a 'special mission'.) What he had meant by 'humanitarian intervention' (cf. above, p. 261) now became clear. 'States no longer have "a right to indifference"', he insisted. 'It seems clear that their duty is to disarm the aggressor if all other means have proved ineffective.' He had, he said, received appeals from Catholic, Orthodox and Muslim leaders in the former Yugoslavia. A 'practical indifference' in the face of such appeals was a 'culpable omission'.

The Balkans even made a brief appearance in the papal homily on 25 January during the closing mass for the Week of Prayer for Christian Unity. He recalled the letter addressed to him from their Patriarch Bartholomew on the occasion of the Assisi gathering, and thanked the Orthodox for their support through prayer for peace in Europe and in the Balkans, even though few of them had been able to be present in person. In an attempt to defuse misunderstandings between Rome and the Orthodox he referred to the Pontifical Commission for Russia's directive, issued on 1 June the previous year, that 'the way to realize the unity of Christians is not by proselytism but by fraternal dialogue'. The Vatican would soon, he announced, be producing an 'ecumenical directory'[7] as a guide to dialogue with Christian Churches. In the course of his homily the Pope sent special greetings to Patriarch Aleksei of Moscow who had been particularly vociferous in condemning 'proselytism' on his 'canonical territory'.

At least at this point in his pontificate, John Paul appeared to be winning greater favour with the Muslim community, who had less to fear from his high view of the papal office, than with his fellow Christians. The Secretary General of the World Islamic League led a delegation to see the Pope on 28 January, and afterwards praised him for his efforts for peace in the Middle East. The Pope's forthcoming visit to the Sudan would, he hoped, bring better relations between Christians and Muslims in that country.

The journey to the Sudan – specifically a nine-hour stopover in Khartoum, belatedly tacked on to an eight-day tour of Benin and Uganda, was scheduled for 10 February. The Pope's tenth visit to Africa began in Cotonou, the capital of Benin, on 3 February. One of John Paul's themes was an insistence that, because the Catholic Church recognized what was good and true in other religions, people could become Christians without denying their cultural heritage. Only a small percentage of the population of Benin had converted to Catholicism, though a slightly higher percentage than had converted to Islam. At Parakou in central Benin a Muslim leader thanked the Pope for his work for peace, and asked Catholics to recommit themselves to dialogue and cooperation with Muslims. The Pope in his turn stressed the similarities between the two faiths. Both, he said, were based on prayer, the need for an upright life, and respect for human dignity.

Respect for human dignity was a regular theme both in Benin, where he linked it to the earlier trade in slaves, and in Uganda, where he recalled the

abuses of human rights under the former regime of Idi Amin. He visited
AIDS patients in a hospital in Kampala – Uganda being the African country
worst afflicted by the disease. He also attended a meeting of the secretariat
working on preparations for the African Synod which, it was announced,
would be held in Rome the following April. This proved a great
disappointment to the African bishops who very much wanted an African
location. There was also a visit to the site of the martyrdom in 1886 of
thirteen Catholics and nine Anglicans. Their deaths side by side was a sign of
the faith they shared, said the Pope, 'by our divisions the credibility of the
Gospel is weakened'.

His theme in Khartoum had long been signalled. Speaking to the
diplomatic corps in Kampala he had said 'I wish to raise my voice in support
of peace and justice for all the Sudanese people, and to comfort my brothers
and sisters in the faith, so many of whom are affected by the conflict going
on in the South'. On 6 February, while in Northern Uganda, he had met a
bishop, Paride Taban, from the South of the Sudan, who brought a letter
from the new Sudanese Council of Churches which operated in the area
under the control of the Sudanese People's Liberation Army. In the letter the
Council of Churches invited the Pope to be their 'voice', to make their views
heard to the fundamentalist Islamic government in control of the Northern
part of the country. The government would try to blindfold the Pope with
the red carpet, said Bishop Taban. He would be greeting a leader 'whose
hands are full of the blood of innocent people'.

The Sudanese government had made promises about the extent of
toleration during the papal visit which, for the most part, were kept, though
printing of the Mass booklet for the public celebration of the life of Blessed
Giuseppina Bakhita was held up by censorship – it was forbidden to say in the
Sudan that this nun, beatified by the Pope on the same day as head of Opus
Dei, Escrivá de Balaguer (cf. above, p. 253), had been kidnapped and sold
into slavery. There were other problems, but at least the Islamic law was
suspended to allow a parade of Christian banners, and for the mass itself, for
which the government made available their principal gathering place of
Green Square. Anti-Christian demonstrators were held back by the police.
The security forces were out in force, and machine guns were pointed at the
vast crowds – which included Muslims – who turned up to hear the Pope.
Travel restrictions were lifted for the occasion.

'When people are weak and poor and defenceless', said the Pope after he
had kissed the ground at Khartoum airport, 'I must raise my voice on their
behalf.' In response to the banners which called for justice and peace, the

Pope during his homily in Green Square said: 'Today the successor of Peter and the whole Church renew their support for the pressing plea of your bishops for respect of your rights as citizens and believers'. For the oppressed Christians of the Sudan, and for moderate Muslims opposed to the fundamentalist government, the papal visit was an enormous morale boost and, for a brief period, focused world attention upon the persecution from which they had long been suffering.

For the Pope it had been a particularly strenuous eight days. John Paul was clearly deeply moved by his encounter with AIDS sufferers in Uganda; he had taken a courageous stand in Khartoum during his first visit ever to a fundamentalist Islamic state; he had delivered over two dozen major addresses. It was no wonder that, at the end of this first full-scale journey abroad since his operation, he should be tired. But his energy in pursuit of his mission was unabated. It gave the lie to rumours circulating in the press that he had been receiving chemotherapy for cancer, and had been told that he had, at most, four years left to live.

The Pope had a number of surprises in store for his return. The case of Bishop Haas of Chur, appointed, it was believed, because of his sympathy with papal perspectives on the Church (cf. above, pp. 194, 235), had dragged on. In 1991 a special envoy, Archbishop Karl-Joseph Rauber, had been sent to bring peace to the Swiss hierarchy. His mediation while it had been welcomed had failed. At the beginning of March, as much to the astonishment of the Bishop of Chur as of everyone else, the Pope announced that he was appointing two auxiliary bishops to assist Haas, help which he had not requested. Both were Swiss priests who had been working in education, both were members of religious Orders, neither had been involved hitherto in the controversy, and neither could be accused of being notably conservative. One of them achieved certain notoriety by letting slip that John Paul had told him he had come to realize that the nomination of Haas to the bishopric had been a mistake. The new appointments were greeted with huge approval in Switzerland – as was the replacement, announced shortly afterwards, of the serving papal nuncio with Archbishop Rauber.

The Pope had, he said, learned a great deal from his meetings with the Swiss bishops. He had also, it seemed, learned much from the Dutch, for immediately after their *ad limina* visit to Rome in mid-January the retirement was announced 'on health grounds' at the age of sixty of Johannes Baptist Mathijs Gijsen, the arch-conservative Bishop (since 1972) of Roermond.

On 25 April John Paul flew for the day to Albania to consecrate four new bishops for that country, the last in Europe to throw off Communism, and the one where persecution, not just of Catholicism but of all religions in the name of atheism, had been the most severe. Five bishops, one hundred and sixty priests, one hundred and thirty nuns, and many lay people had died for their faith during what the Pope called, in the course of the ceremony in the cathedral of the Sacred Heart at Shkodèr, the 'painful and prolonged winter of solitude and persecution'.

Albania has a large majority of Muslims (some seventy per cent of the population), and more Orthodox than Catholics. On his arrival in Tirana, the Pope was greeted by the Muslim President, as well as by the Grand Mufti and the Archbishop of the Orthodox Church. His welcome was particularly warm and enthusiastic. And the Pope was clearly moved, both now and later, by the ceremonies in the cathedral establishing a Catholic hierarchy in the country.

From one nation where there was little religion to another where, said the Church's critics, there was a danger of there being too much. Spain had been through a general election just before the Pope arrived on Saturday 12 June. Felipe González's Socialist Party had won, against all European trends, by playing upon fears that the centre-right Popular Party would be dominated by Catholic dogmatism – or so González's adversaries alleged. The Pope's arrival was timed to coincide with the close of the Seville Eucharistic Congress; before a crowd of 700,000, the Pope celebrated the closing mass on Sunday morning. When the mass ended, it was announced that the next eucharistic congress would take place at Wroclaw, in Poland. On the Sunday evening, he opened a home for the elderly a few miles from Seville. He called upon those in public office to 'make a renewed effort in favour of justice, freedom and progress; giving the very best of themselves to strengthen the basic values of society – solidarity, defence of the truth, honesty, dialogue and the responsible participation of citizens at every level'. There was nothing in these sentiments to which either Sr González or his erstwhile opponent Sr José María Aznar could take exception. On the following day, however, when John Paul travelled to Huelva, he delivered a homily asserting that ignorance of God, leading to a loss of moral values, gave rise to economic structures aimed at making money to the destruction of human dignity. As unemployment was affecting the lives of millions of Spaniards, and Felipe González was a self-proclaimed agnostic (while Aznar was a devout Catholic), these papal sentiments had a much more direct political import.

That afternoon the Pope visited a shrine to the Virgin at El Rocío, one of the most popular in Southern Spain, and then on to the Franciscan monastery of La Rábida, where Columbus had prayed before setting out on the journey which took him to America. As the King of Spain remarked when he greeted the Pope at the airport in Seville, it was the five hundredth anniversary of the beginning of evangelization of the New World that had brought John Paul back to Spain.

The following day, Tuesday, the Pope moved on to Madrid for the consecration of the city's cathedral of Our Lady of La Almudena now at last completed, on which work had first begun in 1879. On the final day of his visit the Pope received Felipe González at the nunciature, followed by José María Aznar. Since there is in Spain no such thing as a 'shadow cabinet' and Sr Aznar had no formal status beyond that of a member of Parliament, his reception raised eyebrows.

The final event of the visit was the canonization of Enrique de Ossó. The lengthy service in the Plaza Colón,[8] another reminder of the 500th anniversary of the discovery of America, took place in temperatures of around one hundred degrees or more. Posters around the city had urged the people of Madrid to attend: 'The Pope is coming to see you', they proclaimed. Thousands turned up for the event, but having seen the Pope, went away again without staying for the lengthy ceremonial of the canonization.

John Paul himself had, of course, to stay until the end. Commentators reported he looked tired, which was hardly surprising. On 7 July he went back to the presbytery in Lorenzago di Cadore in the Dolomites for ten days holiday. It rained most of the time, which gave him opportunity to read the twenty or so books he took with him – mostly books on spirituality, but also on marriage and the family. He needed the break because he had ahead of him a particularly busy summer. Though how much of a break one may doubt, since he is said to have received fifty calls a day on a specially installed telephone line.

On Monday 9 August he was in Jamaica, a visit which he had intended to make in 1992 but which had been omitted from the itinerary as a consequence of his operation for the removal of the intestinal tumour. The dropping of Jamaica may have been inevitable, but it was also regrettable. One of the complaints about the celebration of the 500th anniversary of the arrival of Columbus had been that the indigenous peoples had little to celebrate and much to regret. In Jamaica the indigenous population had been entirely wiped out. This was a theme which he took up immediately on his arrival, accepting that, alongside the efforts to evangelize the peoples of the region, there had been 'sins and errors'. He also acknowledged that the population of Jamaica was now largely the descendants of slaves, and he recalled his visit to Goree in Senegal eighteen months before (cf. above, p. 251).

On Wednesday he flew on to Mérida on the Yucatán in Mexico. In May Cardinal Juan Jesús Posadas had been shot at Guadalajara airport – by accident said the Mexican government, he was caught in the crossfire between rival drug gangs. The Mexican bishops were not so sure. Some thought the Cardinal's assassination had been intended as a warning to the Pope from drug barons not to travel to Yucatán; others believed it to have been a protest at improving relations between Church and state in the aftermath of John Paul's earlier visit; the most sceptical saw it as a warning to the Church not to be so critical of the Mexican government's economic policy, or of its record on human rights. Whatever the reason for the Cardinal's death, the apostolic nuncio, who had announced that 'God has returned to Mexico' when agreement between Mexico and the Holy See on diplomatic links was reached in 1992, assured the Vatican that the Pope would be in no danger.

So, indeed, it proved. The theme addressed in Jamaica, that there had been 'sins and errors' in the treatment of indigenous peoples in the aftermath of the conquest, returned in the Yucatán: the Pope visited a shrine to the Virgin which had been built by the Franciscans amid the ruins of a Mayan temple. The Mayas had a duty to defend their culture, the Pope told them, and governments throughout the Americas had a duty to respect the rights and cultures of the survivors of those who had been there before the *conquistadores* arrived.

The purpose of the Pope's latest transatlantic voyage was to visit Denver, Colorado, for the celebration of World Youth Day. He arrived on 12 August to be greeted by a youthful President of the United States, Bill Clinton, with a speech in which he claimed all Americans were grateful to the Pope for his moral leadership. The Pope's response contained a vigorous attack on abortion, a right which the US President publicly upholds. Pope and President met afterwards in private for thirty-five minutes, and with their advisors for a further three-quarters of an hour at the Jesuit Regis College to survey the world scene from Bosnia to Haiti. Abortion was not touched upon.

Nor was it, except in passing, when the Pope addressed the vast crowds of young people from around the world who had gathered in Denver to greet him. Estimates put the number of 'pilgrims' at around 186,000 and some 375,000 people came together for a vigil and closing mass. There were moral strictures in plenty, but generally contained within more positive exhortation. 'The Pope has not spoken against American civilization, American society, American television', he said in the course of a dialogue with the crowd during the final vigil. 'He has spoken for the authentic promotion of what is civilization, what is culture, for human dignity.' He was, though, being a little too generous to himself. When he met members of the Denver diocese he inveighed against the violence of US society, blame for which he placed in part on the media. He was roundly applauded.

The World Youth Day was an enormous success. The Pope responded willingly to the enthusiasm of the crowd. There were protestors about the Church's stand on abortion or on homosexuality, for example, but the occasion was, for a gathering of such numbers of young people, remarkably peaceful. It was, said one commentator, like a spiritual Woodstock, with all the virtues and none of the vices of that 'sixties celebration of popular music.

The Pope left for Rome, and thence to Castel Gandolfo, on 15 August; on 4 September he was in Lithuania, for his first visit to any part of the territory which had once formed the Soviet Union. The clergy of Lithuania gathered in Vilnius cathedral to hear him praise their Church for its courageous defiance of Communist rule, but also hear him warn them not to get too deeply involved in politics. The Church had, not unnaturally, been closely associated with the resurgence of Lithuanian nationalism, and its clergy had been openly supportive of the nationalist leader Vytautas Landsbergis, recently defeated in a general election by a party dominated by former Communists. John Paul also urged the Lithuanian clergy to be more active in social work, and to deepen their knowledge of Catholic social teaching – a theme he repeated the following day during a meeting with Lithuanian intellectuals.

The major event of the day was Sunday mass in the pouring rain at Vignis Park, attended by 100,000 people. He used the homily, given in Russian, to call for better relations with the Russian Orthodox Church, praising the 'historic importance and glorious tradition' of Orthodoxy. On the same day he also visited the cemetery where those who had died resisting the Soviet army had been interred in January 1991. He praised their courage, but also noted that nearby were the graves of Polish and Lithuanian soldiers who in 1921 had died fighting each other for control of Lithuania: one of the themes of his visit was reconciliation between Lithuanians and the Polish minority population which had existed there ever since the two nations had been part of one kingdom. When he visited the Polish community at their church of the Holy Spirit he was greeted ecstatically. His message, however, was less welcome: he urged them to identify with the future of Lithuania rather than dwell upon their Polish past.

On 8 September he moved on to Latvia, where only a quarter of the population, as against three quarters in Lithuania, identified themselves as

Catholics. Again the message was one of reconciliation, this time with the remaining Russian minority. You are called upon, he told his congregation at an open-air mass in Riga, 'to confirm your faith through your generous total offering of fraternal forgiveness'. Forgiveness of the Russians was also a theme during the brief visit to Estonia (where only a tiny proportion of the population are Catholics) on 10 September. It was a policy in all three Baltic states to ban the use of Russian in public life. The Pope, who had learned Lithuanian for the visit to add to his numerous other languages, said language should be a bridge rather than a barrier between nations.

In the Baltic states the Church, especially the Church in Lithuania, had emerged heroically from the years of Communist oppression. But it had also emerged largely untouched by the renewal of Vatican II, or by the current emphasis upon Catholic social teaching. Despite his frequent and much applauded condemnations while in these states of Western consumerism and materialism, he had also a great deal to say about updating the Church to handle modern problems.

Whether or not the Catholic Church as a whole needed updating to deal with modern problems was, of course, a question in itself, and one which the publication on 5 October of the Pope's encyclical, *Veritatis Splendor*, 'The splendour of truth', gave added point. An encyclical on the moral issues facing Christians had long been signalled, and the text had been six years in preparation.[9] A draft, leaked to the German press in 1989, laid claim to infallibility for its teaching and had caused alarm. All references to infallibility had been removed in the text the Pope signed on 6 August, the Feast of the Transfiguration, though the claim to infallibility in moral, as well as in dogmatic, pronouncements by the Pope had been present in the decree on infallibility at Vatican I.

In his introduction to the document, John Paul insists that 'No one can escape from the fundamental questions: What must I do? How do I distinguish good from evil? The answer is only possible thanks to the splendour of truth . . .' But, he goes on, many objections have been urged against the traditional moral teaching of the Church. 'It is no longer a matter of limited and occasional dissent, but of an overall and systematic calling into question' of that teaching. There is, he says, a genuine crisis.

The encyclical proper begins with a typical papal meditation on a Scripture text, that of the rich young man of St Matthew's gospel (19:16). He went away sorrowing, the Pope concludes, because he could not live up to the moral demands which Jesus set before him if he were to seek perfection. He goes on to pay tribute to those theologians who have tried to communicate the Church's moral teaching in a manner more appropriate to the needs of the day, as Vatican II requested. 'The Church's *magisterium*', he goes on, 'does not intend to impose upon the faithful any particular theological system, still less a philosophical one', but, he points out, there are some such systems which are incompatible with the revealed truth.

One of the major problems, he continues, is a misunderstanding of the notion of conscience: 'Conscience is no longer considered in its primordial reality as an act of a person's intelligence, the function of which is to apply the universal knowledge of the good in a specific situation ... Instead there is a tendency to grant to the individual conscience the prerogative of independently determining the criteria of good and evil and then acting accordingly'. Reason has a role in discovering the moral (natural) law, but that does not mean that reason creates moral values and norms. The natural law extends to every individual; its negative precepts are universally valid, there are some actions which are always wrong – the Pope lists some of them (abortion, genocide, torture, prostitution, degrading conditions of work to name but a few), but makes special reference to birth control, and to Pope Paul VI's encyclical *Humanae Vitae*. 'Circumstances or intentions can never transform an act which is intrinsically evil by virtue of its object into an act "subjectively good" or defensible as a choice', he concludes.

In the last chapter of the encyclical the Pope sums up what has gone before in a quotation from an address to the International Congress of Moral Theologians in 1986, 'Only the freedom which submits to the Truth leads the human person to his true good. The good of the person is to be in the Truth and to *do* the Truth', though he recognizes that 'faced with the many difficulties which fidelity to the moral order can demand, even in the most ordinary circumstances, the Christian is called, with the grace of God invoked in prayer, to a sometimes heroic commitment', which John Paul compares to martyrdom. But such morality is essential, for without it society, as well as individuals, is in danger whether in the political or in the economic sphere. There is a 'risk of an alliance between democracy and ethical relativism', says the Pope in words that suggested that, in his mind, the risk has already been realized.

Much of the commentary in the secular press likened the publication of *Veritatis Splendor* to Paul VI's *Humanae Vitae*, but that was to give too much emphasis to the condemnation of birth control which John Paul's encyclical contained, but which was cited simply as an instance of something 'intrinsically evil'. John Paul was laying out moral norms, and not, except in passing, discussing individual moral precepts. In that sense, a closer comparison would be Pius XII's 1950 encyclical *Humani Generis* which condemned a whole school of dogmatic theologians, and sent many of them into (usually) temporary exile from their teaching posts. From this exile they returned in the late 1950s to prepare the way for Vatican II, which triumphantly rehabilitated them. Various schools of moral theologians were explicitly criticized in *Veritatis Splendor*, in accounts of their views which, their defenders claimed, were travesties of what they actually taught. The danger that some of these moralists might be 'exiled' as a result of the encyclical was a real fear. So far this does not seem to have happened.

Rarely, however, can an encyclical have aroused such interest both inside and outside the Catholic community. Leader writers in the daily press clearly liked the smack of firm government, so long, presumably, as they did not have to submit to it themselves. One of the most interesting comments appeared, rather oddly, in the 'World View' column of *The Times Higher Education Supplement* penned by a German academic, Wolfgang Lepenies, who confessed himself to be 'not a religious person' but from a Protestant background. He had read the encyclical – his first – in preparation for a discussion with the chairman of the German Episcopal Conference. Despite himself, he had been impressed: the encyclical 'shows that, in post-modern times, you have only to remain old-fashioned long enough in order to become up-to-date in the end'. 'If you feel that somehow you have lost your orientation in the modern world, you should read *Veritatis Splendor* to learn that a case for faith can still be made', he went on, 'there are not many documents around in which bold statements occur so often – and some of them are even testable.' He faulted it, however, for despising culture, regarding it as a 'prison' above which human beings must arise; for being 'Eurocentric'; and for demonstrating 'a curious spirit of anti-democratic sentiment'.[10]

Though the encyclical was formally addressed to the bishops of the Catholic Church, there is a sense in which the Professor Lepenies of this world are the real audience the Pope would like to reach. His fundamental argument, in which he differs not at all from his predecessors, is that in matters of morality what the Church teaches applies to all, and not simply to those who share the Catholic faith. That is why the basis of the encyclical had to be the natural law for that – at least in so far as natural law philosophers are concerned – applies to the whole of humanity. The Pope said in the course of the document that he did not want to impose any particular theological, or still less philosophical, system upon the Church, recognizing that he would have no authority to do so. But in practice he attempted to do exactly that. It was no wonder that Cardinal Ratzinger spent so much time, at the packed press conference which launched the encyclical, expounding the concept and history of the natural law, or that the encyclical itself defended the natural law against the charge it had been reduced in papal teaching to biological determinism.

This last issue about biological determinism is an important one in understanding John Paul. The argument, put simply, is as follows. There are two quite different understandings of the natural law. According to both of them, human beings must act in such a way as to fulfil their nature. The difference between the two concepts arises when one asks what the nature is: is it to be defined in terms of biological necessities, or is it to be defined in terms of biological necessities as mediated through a human being's rational understanding of what is best for him or herself? It had been argued by some moral theologians that whereas the second form of the natural law operated in the field of social ethics as found in papal writings, the former was used when talking of sexual ethics. The Pope was having none of that, or of the theologians who put such views forward: 'doctrine which dissociates the moral act from the bodily dimensions of its exercise', he wrote, turning the tables on his critics, 'is contrary to the teaching of Scripture and tradition'.

Dissident views received short shrift. The question of dissent arose at the press conference, to be answered by the Polish theologian Andrej Szostek, professor of ethics at the University of Lublin and thought to be close to the Pope: his presence at the press conference suggested that he had taken a hand in writing the encyclical.[11] The text, he said, did not close the dialogue between *magisterium* and moral theologian: the latter was invited to reflect upon it, pray about it, and review his work in the light of it. *Veritatis Splendor*, one cannot help thinking, insists upon the freedom of conscience to follow the truth, and then declares that what the truth is, is determined by the Pope and his Curia, defined in the document as the *magisterium*. That there was no longer room for dissent was asserted in the pages of *The Tablet* by Germain Grisez, Professor of Christian Ethics at Mount St Mary's College, Maryland, and a stalwart defender of the *magisterium*. 'Theologians who have been dissenting from the doctrine reaffirmed in this encyclical', he wrote, 'now have only three choices: to admit that they have been mistaken, to admit they do not believe God's word, or to claim that the Pope is grossly misinterpreting the Bible.'[12]

The Pope has been saying these things for fifteen years without persuading people, commented Hans Küng, so now he has resorted to an encyclical so that instead he can impose his views. It was a timely reminder that, on 16 October, John Paul II celebrated the fifteenth anniversary of his election to the papacy. To mark the event he gave an interview to his old friend Jas Gawronski, a Polish emigré and journalist on *La Stampa*. He commented on the charge that the Polish media were turning against him. True to some extent, he said, but it in no way reflects the 'heartfelt feelings' of the population as a whole. He was still very much a Pole. His country's culture and language were still with him. When he had to write something he drafted it in Polish. He did not deny it when Gawronski remarked that he sometimes appeared more opposed to capitalism than he was to Communism in which, he admitted, there was a 'kernel of truth'. At the root of many of the social problems of the world, he said, are the 'distorted manifestations' of capitalism. Not, he added, that any third way could be found between Communism and capitalism: 'It is the abusive practices of capitalism which are to be condemned'. From the interview there was little of a personal nature to be learnt, beyond the fact that he had no time to keep a diary, and that he was not lonely. He had friends, he said, and did not make decisions on his own but collegially, with the episcopates – something they may have been surprised to discover – and with the Curia.[13]

As his schedule for 1994 clearly indicated, the Pope might have been fifteen years and more in office, but there was to be no diminution of his activities. Was his age beginning none the less to take its toll? On 11 November, as he walked down the steps of the podium in the Hall of Benedictions, to greet delegates attending a UN Food and Agriculture Organization conference, he slipped on the newly-laid red nylon carpet, dislocating and partially breaking his right shoulder. He was taken to the Gemelli clinic where the shoulder was reset. Though the operation, under a general anaesthetic, lasted less than a quarter of an hour, he was detained in hospital overnight, and his right arm was to remain in plaster for a month. He was told to take things easily for a week.

Addressing the Roman curia just before Christmas the Pope sketched out some of his plans for 1994. In late May he intended to travel to Lebanon, he said, and he hoped for a second visit to the Middle East, 'to all the principal sites linked with the Christian faith'. Both the Chief Rabbi of Israel and the Latin Patriarch of Jerusalem had recently added their voices to Shimon Peres' invitation to the Holy Land (cf. above, p. 259). As he said this he knew that the hope of returning – he had visited there as a bishop – he had entertained ever since he was elected (cf. above, p. 28) was now more realistic. On 30 December 1993 a 'Fundamental Agreement' was signed between the Holy See and the State of Israel.

The signing in Jerusalem was a low-key affair, though the Israeli negotiators had wished to have a much more public ceremony, because the Vatican did not want to alienate Christian groups in the Middle East who would be unlikely to view the accord with sympathy. Nor did it want to annoy other Christian groups in the Holy Land itself: a note issued just before the signing insisted that the Vatican had negotiated on behalf of nobody but itself, and that the status of the Holy Places, together with the rights therein of the different Churches, would remain as they were. In the Agreement both sides undertook 'to uphold and observe the human right to freedom of religion and conscience'. That was fundamental. In addition, the State of Israel recognized the right of the Church to carry out its mission, and assured it of the freedom to employ the usual means of doing so, guaranteeing freedom of expression, as well as the right to own property, run schools and so on. In turn the Church solemnly reaffirmed its opposition to anti-Semitism, and both sides committed themselves to combating it. But the joint campaign against anti-Semitism was linked to a wider commitment to oppose all kinds of racism and religious intolerance.

This was not yet the establishment of diplomatic relations between Israel and the Holy See, but it was a necessary prelude. The Israeli Prime Minister, Yitzhak Rabin, was given a full ceremonial reception when he visited the Pope on 17 March. And he repeated the invitation to visit Israel. The Pope, said the statement afterwards, sincerely hoped that circumstances would permit it. Meanwhile Yasser Arafat and the PLO also sought formal recognition from the Vatican. Archbishop Jean-Louis Tauran went to talk to Arafat in Tripoli as Rabin was being greeted by Swiss Guards in the Vatican.

'Ethnic cleansing' was just another form of that racism the Holy See had agreed with Israel to combat wherever it might be found. In 1993 and into 1994 it was being found in some at least of the republics which had once formed Yugoslavia. At the beginning of January John Paul called a meeting of twenty-four experts, including the nuncios from Croatia, Slovenia, Bosnia and what remained of Yugoslavia, to discuss the situation in the Balkans. People have 'the right to live where they were born and where they have their roots', said the statement at the end of the meeting. 'Peace founded on the accentuation or manipulation of nationalisms would be a false peace', it insisted. There were, of course, those who believed that the Vatican's readiness to recognize the independence of Croatia and Slovenia in particular had not helped the peace process in Yugoslavia.

The Pope's constant concern with the 'Christian roots' of European civilization, and the need to preserve a people's cultural identity might likewise have been used to defend ethnic cleansing, should any side in the conflict felt a need to justify itself by appeal to the teaching of the Church. In his annual address to the diplomatic corps (of whom there were by this time 150[14] accredited to the Holy See) on 15 January John Paul pre-empted such criticisms. The deification of the nation, he said, was a new form of paganism. It was but a short step from nationalism to totalitarianism. 'Every time Christianity – whether according to its Western or Eastern tradition – becomes the instrument of a form of nationalism, it is as it were wounded in its very heart and made sterile', he went on.

Meanwhile the Pope had problems nearer home. The Italian government had collapsed in a welter of accusations about corruption which had touched some senior figures in the Christian Democrat Party, as well as, tangentially, the Vatican Bank for laundering money given in bribes and Cardinal Fiorenzo Angelini for accepting for his Vatican office large sums of money illegally obtained by the donors. (The Vatican denied the Cardinal's involvement in financial scandals, but promised otherwise to cooperate.[15]) There was still need, even after the disappearance of Communism, for Christian-inspired politics in Europe, said the Pope in a letter to the Italian hierarchy that was seen as an effort to re-establish the Christian Democrats. It must never be forgotten, he added, that in Italy the Christian Democrats had kept the Communist Party out of power. And, with an eye to the electoral success of the Northern League which wanted a separation of the economically successful North from the South of Italy, he warned against separatist tendencies.

The Pope's exhortation, the most explicit papal support for the erstwhile Christian Democrats since 1948, was in vain. Elections took place towards the end of March. The rump of the Christian Democrats (though now known as the Popular Party) was crushed between a left-wing alliance and a triumphant right-wing grouping, which included the Northern League.

The express papal policy seemed to be facing defeat also at the UN conference on population and development scheduled to be held (at the time of writing) in Cairo in September 1994. There was too much in the draft document about the promotion of unacceptable methods of birth control, and the right to abortion on demand, and too little about integral development, said the Pope. On 25 March the Pope met the secretary general of the Cairo conference, and handed her a letter explaining how the draft document contradicted basic ethics. The right to abortion, the Pope said, went beyond what was agreed at the 1984 conference on population in Mexico, where it was agreed that abortion should not be promoted as a method of family planning. In another facet of the Vatican's offensive the

Cardinal Secretary of State took the unusual step of calling together ambassadors accredited to the Holy See, and explaining the Church's position.

After all his fifteen years in what he had made for the world's most public office, John Paul II had lost none of his combativeness over issues that were close to his heart.

NOTES

1. He was made a Cardinal in 1952.
2. On Opus Dei and its founder see my *The Secret World of Opus Dei* (London, Grafton, 1989) – in the U.S. edition, *Opus Dei* (San Francisco, HarperCollins, 1991).
3. It has been studied by Kenneth Woodward in his *Making Saints* (London, Chatto & Windus, 1991). Woodward, the religion editor for *Newsweek*, was one of the most active campaigners against Escrivá's beatification.
4. A country with full diplomatic links with the Vatican has a 'pro-nuncio' rather than a nuncio where it would be impolitic to have the Vatican's representative as the doyen of the diplomatic corps. Such is generally the case in countries where the Catholic Church is a minority religion. That, at least, was the case until November 1993 when the decision was made to call them all nuncios no matter what the precedence, providing the receiving country agreed.
5. It ended on 28 October.
6. For a survey of its contents, see Michael Walsh (ed.), *A Commentary on the Catechism of the Catholic Church* (London, Geoffrey Chapman, 1994).
7. It was published the following June.
8. Columbus is known in Spanish as 'Cristobal Colon'.
9. The Pope explained that the long delay in producing the encyclical had been to allow for the prior publication of the *Catechism of the Catholic Church* which, in its English-language edition, still had not appeared. Publication for that was eventually scheduled for 31 May 1994.
10. 18 February 1994, p. 14.
11. For the record, the other members of the panel at the press conference were: Cardinal Ratzinger, Bishop Dionigi Tettamanzi, secretary of the Italian episcopal conference, Mgr James Stafford, Archbishop of Denver, and a member of the Congregation for the Doctrine of the Faith, Albert Chapelle, S.J., professor of dogmatic and moral theology at the Brussels Institute for Theological Studies, and Fr Szostek.
12. 'Revelation versus dissent' in *The Tablet*, 16 October 1993, pp. 1329–31. This was the first in a series of articles, most of which were unsympathetic to Grisez, and to the encyclical. A revised version of them has been published in John Wilkins (ed.), *Understanding 'Veritatis Splendor'* (London, SPCK, 1994).

13. 'States of savagery, seeds of good', *The Guardian*, 2 November 1993.
14. Diplomatic relations were established with Jordan on 3 March, taking the number of different countries to 151.
15. Cf. Giancarlo Zizola, 'De l'argent sale lavé à l'eau bénite?' in *Actualité religieuse*, 15 November 1993, p. 13.

ELEVEN

1994

Nो ONE is likely to describe that doyen of dissident theologians, Hans Küng, as a disinterested observer of the present pontificate. Nevertheless, in the remark cited towards the end of the previous chapter (cf. above, p. 273) he has a point. There is no doubt that Pope John Paul II came to the papacy saying the sort of things he said in his encyclical *Veritatis Splendor*, that he has reiterated them frequently, and that they have made little impact upon the Church at large.

This has been especially true of contraception. The use of artificial means of birth control was condemned by *Humanae Vitae*. Pope Paul VI put his authority on the line in publishing this encyclical and then, when what he had insisted upon in the document was very largely ignored, never wrote another, though he had plenty of opportunity. In the process, however, a great number of devout Catholics were caused considerable distress as they tried to reconcile their consciences with what they understood to be the teaching of the Church as contained in *Humanae Vitae* with the practice of contraception that they believed to be, for them, the most appropriate way of living out their marriages. John Paul has constantly restated the prohibitions of Pope Paul's encyclical. He has had just as little success in making them stick as had his predecessor. When *Veritatis Splendor* says there is a crisis in the Church, that is exactly what the crisis is: a large proportion of Catholics are simply not obeying what the papal *magisterium* has laid down. The way to make them obey, it was seemingly thought at one point in that encyclical's preparation, was to endow this bit of papal teaching with the charism of infallibility. Even the Vatican, despite its inflated notion of what constitutes the *magisterium*[1] drew back from such a step.

It is an interesting situation. At a reception to mark the one hundred and fortieth anniversary in 1990 of the founding of the Jesuit magazine *Civilità Cattolica*, a journal whose pages are censored by the Secretariat of State, John Paul informed the staff of writers that they ought to support Vatican policies and opinions even when they were personally not in sympathy with them. There has of course been a great deal of talk during this pontificate about 'dissent' and, as has been seen in the case, for example, of the Cologne declaration (cf. above. p. 205), there has been a good deal of open opposition.[2] But in terms of numbers, the great mass of dissent lies not with the intellectuals, those who were called to heel in general terms in the Instruction on the role of theologians (cf. above, pp. 225-7) or in the moral theologians whose thought was censored in *Veritatis Splendor*. The intellectuals may have received the column inches, but the great mass of dissent is among the faithful at large. They have chosen their own inter-pretation of Catholicism, and yet choose to remain more or less happily within the family of the Church.

'Family of the Church' is a phrase that the Pope would use to describe the almost one billion Catholics over whom he rules. When Archbishop of Cracow, comments Blazynski,[3] 'he did not wish to "rule" in any author-itarian, autocratic manner. He sought to lead – that is to say, to create the opportunity for people with initiative, people of independent mind, and possessed of a creative and healthy imagination, to work together. One has to bear in mind that Wojtyla's spell as Archbishop of Cracow marked the start of a brave new style of government in that archdiocese . . .' And given his intervention in the conciliar debate on the text of *Lumen Gentium* (cf. above, p. 47), one would have expected no less. But that is not how he thinks he can run his Church as Supreme Pontiff. Nothing is more striking in the present pontificate than the use of episcopal appointments to impose his own rigid views of authority upon the faithful. The example of Chur in Switzerland has been dwelt upon, but there have been many other instances in Austria, in Brazil and elsewhere.

These impositions upon the local churches are bad enough, but one can understand that a pope who believes deeply in the righteousness of his cause would wish to have like-minded men in positions of authority. What is less excusable is the use of episcopal appointments to reward Vatican civil servants for years of faithful dedication to the interests of the papacy. There was the case of Mgr John Magee, former missionary, chosen by Archbishop Bennelli in 1976 to be English-language secretary to Paul VI, then, briefly of John Paul I, and for a good deal longer of John Paul II. He was rewarded in 1987 with the bishopric of Cloyne in County Cork, a diocese with which he had hitherto no connection. Or more recently there was the case of Archbishop Justin Rigali, secretary of the College of Cardinals and of the Congregation of Bishops, appointed by the Pope in January 1994 to be new Archbishop of

St Louis, after the see had been vacant over a year. The Congregation of Bishops had sent the Pope a list of three names: Rigali's was not on it. This was a personal appointment by the Pope of someone close to him, a trusted advisor who accompanied John Paul on his travels. It was a reward for services rendered entirely in Rome, except for three years in the nunciature in Madagascar in the 1960s. Against such 'provision' of benefices the English parliament in the fourteenth century had passed the four Statutes of Provisors. The Pope seems to be treating the Church as one enormous medieval fief, behaving in exactly that 'monarchical' way against which he had spoken out during the debate on *Lumen Gentium*.

Whether the Pope himself is aware of the paradoxes in his behaviour may be doubtful, but others certainly are. The apparent contradiction between his open support for clearly political objectives, and his constant reiteration of the ban on priests and religious playing an active part in the political life of their country, is often commented upon. The Pope's exhortations are based upon his philosophical convictions about the nature of the human person, who both needs society and transcends it. The action required to achieve the ideal he puts before his audience he thinks it best to leave to the laity, for political life, he argues, is their proper sphere. He clearly has little sympathy with the contrary argument frequently invoked by politically committed churchmen and women that there does not exist in their particular context sufficient, or sufficiently educated, laity to undertake all the political tasks necessary to make the papal vision into a reality. He may be right about leaving it to the laity. His own two major interventions in Italian political life, the referendum over abortion, and his letter to the country's hierarchy about the 1994 elections (cf. above, pp. 93-4), have both proved disastrous for the Christian Democratic Party he was intending to support.

It is the same high ideal of the human person which led him to lambast both liberal capitalism and Communism in his encyclical *Solicitudo Rei Socialis*, and, oddly enough, it is the same ideal which makes him suspicious of democracy. The individual's greatest dignity is achieved in pursuit of the truth, he believes, and truth is not determined by democratic vote. That at least is a view commonly expressed, and one to which the Pope firmly adheres, as he made clear in *Veritatis Splendor*. But it is not as self-evident as it seems (Church dogma, after all, is determined in Councils by majority verdicts), and it is a view which does not sit comfortably with the Pope's basic phenomenology. According to that, each question has to be examined from as many different aspects as possible for the truth to emerge. It has to be probed by all appropriate techniques of investigation – among which the study of culture ranks high, hence its importance in papal exhortations – so that a full understanding may emerge. It is this exhaustive examination which the Pope, from his philosophical background, thinks essential, that accounts for the considerable length of his encyclicals and other writings.[4]

Yet even here there is a contradiction for John Paul frequently speaks of 'truth' as somehow given, out there to be seen by those who have eyes to see it, rather than to be arrived at by close inquiry, employing all the means at one's disposal. There is, in other words, an unresolved tension between the Pope's phenomenology and his Thomism – though the inability to produce a synthesis, or reconciliation, of such views, may reflect a failing in the reader rather than in the proponent.[5] As one commentator put it, while wading about in the phenomenological fog, one occasionally bumps into bits of Thomistic steel.

It is undoubtedly one of the Pope's achievements that he has put his own particular form of philosophy on to the Church's agenda. No longer do encyclicals read as if they were scholastic manuals. There is a new perspective on issues, and the nature of the human person (or of man, as the Pope prefers to say) has been put at the centre of ecclesiastical reflection. He may not be a brilliant philosopher – his best known work, *The Acting Person*, is a very difficult book to read and interpret – but he is certainly one to be reckoned with. As the citation said for his honorary degree at the Johannes Gutenberg University, conferred upon Cardinal Wojtyla on 23 June 1977, he has 'demonstrated new methodological paths for the Christian ethic through a phenomenological foundation and continuation of Christian personalism ... he has convincingly portrayed the inviolable dignity of Man in an original demonstration of philosophical-theological anthropology.'[6]

John Paul's intellectual itinerary formally began with Polish literature and moved on, during his seminary days, first to philosophy, then to theology and finally back to philosophy. But as he reminded Andre Fossard,[7] he had been attracted to the spiritual theology of St John of the Cross long before he entered Cardinal Sapieha's secret seminary. It had been nurtured under the supervision of Carmelite friars, and then by studying the Spanish mystic under the guidance of Jan Tyranowski (cf. above pp. 10-11). More time has been spent by commentators on his philosophical (and of course literary) work, but his theological output as Pope has been extraordinary both in its approach, in its scope and in its quantity: his encyclical on the Holy Spirit, *Dominum et Vivificantem,* in particular has been highly praised. The content of his writings on Christian morality has been unashamedly conservative in tone, but his theology, informed as it is by his personalist phenomenology, is fresh and inspiring – and even if still fundamentally conservative, it is clearly based on the Pope's understanding of the teaching of Vatican II.[8]

Much more problematic is his use of Scripture.[9] No student of the papal theological output can fail to notice the way in which the Pope uses biblical texts, laying quotation upon quotation, rarely with reference to the historical context in which they were written.[10] He appears to take the infancy narratives as if they are accurate accounts of the events of Christ's birth, and the frequently-cited first chapters of Genesis, particularly the story of the Fall are treated as if they really happened. 'There is not a great deal', remarks Terence Prendergast, 'that formally links John Paul and modern biblical scholarship'.[11] Fr Prendergast, however, loyally goes on to provide an apologia for the Pope's approach. His Jesuit colleague, James Swetnam, is rather less sympathetic: 'Not only does John Paul seem to be unconvinced about the commonly agreed-on results of source criticism as helpful for illumining the meaning of the biblical text, he also seems to think that the results are not as assured as they should be to warrant drawing inferences from them'.[12]

It is not simply that John Paul, more often than not, ignores the results of the historico-critical method when handling biblical texts, but he has no compunction about drawing from the texts theological or spiritual conclusions which the texts themselves will not sustain. It is not that he is not appreciative of biblical scholarship: he regularly praises exegetes and when, in 1993, the Vatican's Biblical Commission came out with a splendid document encouraging biblical research in all its forms the Pope contributed an introduction. Yet he makes little or no use of such research himself. It is as if the theological opinions come first, and then scriptural texts garnered to support those opinions with little or no attention to whether, in the eyes of the scholars, they effectively do so. The undiscriminating use of 'proof texts' is a long tradition in the Church. The Pope's citing the Bible in this way is yet another example of his innate conservatism.

Among the books of the Bible, John Paul has his clear favourites. From the Old Testament it is the book of Genesis – especially the first chapters – and in the New Testament John is the gospel which he most frequently quotes. This is readily understandable. At the heart of the Pope's thinking and, presumably, his personal reflection, which might be called his spirituality, lies the notion of the human person. This, too, can easily be understood. His philosophical outlook, quite apart from the specifically philosophical mentors he had, was forged in a Poland dominated by Marxism, and he came from a region of Poland in which lay Auschwitz. It is hardly surprising that he has been concerned above all with the basis of human dignity, a dignity rooted in the individual's relationship with God in Christ. In the opening of Genesis he found, and finds, the basis of human dignity in the creation of the person in the image of God, a dignity reinforced by the Incarnation when the Son of God became man. The exposition of the doctrine of the Incarnation he finds most conveniently to hand in the fourth gospel.

The individual's self-realization is to be found through relationship with others ('solidarity' is a spiritual requirement as well as a political expedient). But the primary focus for that relationship is union with Christ, to be found most satisfactorily within the family of the Church. Hence the Pope's concern for the Church to be allowed to be Church, and not to be distracted into other paths such as that of politics where – he believes – that union with Christ, and therefore the self-realization of the individual, is not to be found. 'The state has the practical, and thus subordinate, function of serving the common good. The Church, however, is concerned with the meaning of human existence in all its profundity, not in a theoretical mode but in the lived expression of the sacramental encounter with Christ and its extension precisely through the Church to the whole human community.'[13]

The author from whom the last quotation has been taken describes the fundamental attitude of the Pope's spirituality as 'an optimism rooted in the cross of Christ'. 'Optimism', however, does not seem to be the prevailing trait. Although John Paul writes movingly about the redemptive work of Christ, more commonly to be found in his encyclicals is a harping on the failures of human beings to live up to the high moral standards which their nature demands of them. There is no escaping original sin, 'the hereditary sinfulness of human nature', as he calls it in his encyclical on the Holy Spirit, *Dominum et Vivificantem*.[14] The Pope's encyclicals constantly catalogue the moral failings of individuals, and of societies. The Fall and its consequences are central to the papal view of the world. From these failings people can be rescued only by obedience to their consciences, informed by the Church's *magisterium*.

There are, of course, saints – and John Paul is eager to put before the Church more and more exemplars of sanctity – who achieve holiness by following their own consciences, but the Pope has little confidence in the constructs of human society. He praises culture, but clearly distrusts it. He has praised democracy, but distrusts that likewise. He damns Communism because it suppresses human dignity, and damns capitalism because it leads inexorably to materialism. He talks of 'a third way', but does not know what it is.

The tensions mentioned earlier are many and varied. He is the most modern of the Popes in his use of the media, yet his message is sternly traditional. He talks of collegiality, power sharing among the bishops of the world, yet under his pontificate the Church has become constantly more centralized. He speaks of ecumenism, yet the ecumenical movement is in the doldrums, ARCIC put on hold (even before the issue of women priests in the Anglican Communion became a live one) and relations with the Orthodox could scarcely be worse. He is the first Slav pope, and self-conscious about it. He believed that he could draw closer to the Eastern-rite Churches, but he has totally failed to do so. In part, as has been seen, it is the problem of the Uniates whom he could hardly repudiate. But in part also it is the exalted view of the papal office and the role of the *magisterium* which the present Pope professes.

The problem has been exacerbated by the collapse of the Soviet empire. As the republics of the former USSR recovered their independence, the Orthodox churches have squabbled among themselves. But is is not surprising if the years of apparent compromise between the national churches and the Communist regimes should have turned people away from Orthodoxy to seek some other way to express their faith, whether in the Catholic or in the other mainline Churches, or in new religious movements.

The Pope's own attitude to this development is complex. Clearly he has supported in the Russian Federation and in other territories of the former Soviet Union the emergence of a Latin-rite Church alongside the Orthodox Churches, much to the obvious irritation of the latter. But he has not been as sensitive as he could have been to the problems which would be posed by the re-emergence of the Uniate Churches in the Ukraine in particular but also elsewhere. Then there is the problem of culture. He has spoken frequently of the religious foundations of culture, especially of the culture of Europe. He has encouraged his hearers to rediscover their culture and to embrace it wholeheartedly. But he seems ill at ease when that culture is not allied to that of Western Europe in which the Latin rite of the Roman Church has developed, no matter how much he criticizes it for its materialism. He speaks of himself often as a Slav, and therefore a bridge between Eastern and Western Europe, but his own culture is very much more Western than he seems ready to acknowledge.

The fact that he was a Slav, a citizen of one of the countries then within the Soviet bloc, caused consternation in the Kremlin when he was elected in 1978. A fortnight after the conclave there was a report ready, produced by the director, Professor Oleg Bogomolev, of the Institute for the Economy of the World Socialist System, part of the USSR Academy of Sciences. In order to forestall papal statements hostile to the USSR, suggested Bogomolev, relations with the Catholic clergy of Lithuania, the Ukraine and Byelorussia should be improved, and means sought to prevent the adherence of the Uniate Churches to the Catholic Church. Another report, produced by the KGB, expressed the belief that the election of Wojtyla had been partly the result of pressure by cardinals from the USA acting in concert with President Carter's security advisor Zbigniew Brzeinski.[15]

The USSR's Council for Religious Affairs, aided by similar bodies in the satellite countries, closely monitored the Pope's doings. His visit to Mexico for the Puebla meeting, for instance, was described as 'antidemocratic and antisocialist' because of the way the Pope had condemned 'progressive Catholics'. When the Pope eventually went to Poland in 1979 the Kremlin was sent hourly reports. It was decided, in the aftermath of the visit, to provide notes to explain why the visit had been allowed to go ahead and to counter what was thought to be a new level of activity by the Catholic Church in countries of the Soviet bloc. Communist parties in Europe and Latin America were ordered to discredit the Pope whenever they could. The Russian Orthodox Church was instructed to strengthen links with Catholics in Western Europe who were critical of John Paul.

There was, of course, the particular problem of Solidarity. When Ronald Reagan visited the Pope on 7 June 1982, support for Solidarity was high on the agenda, and the Vatican and the USA agreed to cooperate. When the Pope was asked about this, after Carl Bernstein's article appeared in *Time* magazine in February 1992, he chose his words carefully. He did not deny that there was a degree of agreement with Reagan over support for Solidarity, but balked at the suggestion that this amounted to political action on the Vatican's part. In fact the KGB judged that 'destabilization' in Poland was chiefly the consequence of American action rather than Vatican support. None the less the Kremlin actively gathered intelligence about the Vatican's doings, and went on doing so until tensions eased sometime after the election of Mikhail Gorbachev as General Secretary of the Communist Party in Russia.

It is difficult to judge just how far the Pope has influenced the collapse of Communism in Eastern Europe. Certainly, his visits to Poland inspired hope that there might be a change, and his support for Solidarity undoubtedly encouraged that hope. It is possible to argue that if Solidarity had not received so much support from outside Poland, support which in part at least the movement owed to the patronage of John Paul, it would not have survived. But as one of its leaders, Jacek Kuron, observed (cf. above, p. 91), the Soviet

Union was facing so many internal problems that it was in no position to put down Solidarity in Poland even had it wanted to do so – which, at least after the arrival of Gorbachev with his policies of *glasnost* and *perestroika*, it did not.

It is easy to overestimate the influence of Pope John Paul in world affairs. It has been remarked that some unsavoury leaders – Pinochet or Stroessner for example – disappeared from the scene soon after a papal visit, the suggestion being that the Pope's presence, and message, encouraged the opposition. But other, equally unsavoury, leaders with whom he shook hands are still in place. The Vatican mediated in the case of the Beagle Channel, but other attempts at mediation, in the Middle East for example, have been rebuffed. The Pope is apparently a major figure on the world stage, and governments have hurried to establish diplomatic representation with the Holy See, but it is difficult to know what they gain from doing so – except that, as everyone admits, Rome is a particularly good listening post.

The more diplomats there are accredited to the Vatican, the more time the Pope has to spend in seeing them, in his daily round of 'private audiences' which begin at 11.30 each morning that the Pope is in Rome, and go on until lunch at 1.30. They may indeed go on during lunch, for the Pope does not eat alone as his predecessors have generally done, apart from their private staff. John Paul starts his day with an hour's prayer before mass at seven, which will usually be attended by visitors to Rome as well as by his personal entourage, and this is followed immediately by a working breakfast of coffee, bread and fruit with his secretaries and guests. The guests at lunch, the main meal of the day, may very well be visiting bishops, journalists, old friends with whom he is good at keeping in touch. The third meal is at eight, again usual with guests. The food is cooked by nuns who came from Cracow. It is described as 'plain'. As a concession to the Rome location, the first course at lunch is commonly pasta, and white wine – the Pope prefers white. There is also usually a dessert – perhaps of fruit, but the Pope is also fond of puddings.

It is another of the paradoxes of John Paul that although he is very conscious of the high calling of the petrine office, and is clearly determined to hand it on with its authority increased, he wears the office lightly. Unlike his predecessor Paul VI he is naturally outgoing. Pope John XXIII might have wished to reach out to others as the present Pope has been able to do, but he felt constrained by the formalities of his office. John Paul feels much less constraint, which may be the advantage of his comparative youth on his election, or the influence of his formative years in Nazi-occupied Cracow.

Whether his attempt to assert his own understanding of the authority of the papal office will survive him will depend very much on the theological stance of his successor. But it is difficult to believe that whoever is elected at the next conclave will be able to return to the almost sacral image of the Pope which has been cultivated during this century, and which John Paul has discarded. There is a revealing portrait of him from Bishop Magee, Magee's impression of him the first time they met. The Pope was sitting at what had been, in the previous pontificate, Magee's own desk in the papal apartments on the fourth floor of the Vatican Palace.

His *zucchetto* [skull cap] was just thrown to one side, his cassock was all unbuttoned down his chest, no collar, and he was sitting sideways on to the desk, writing, not as Pope Paul VI did, upright and elegant, but slouched, his hand on his head, like a man more used to physical action than to scholarship. I knocked, and, as he turned it was the physical posture of a man of the world – it was un-Popish. This was a very human, down-to-earth man. He jumped up and came over. He wouldn't let me kiss his ring. He caught hold of me, put his arms around me. 'Welcome home,' he said. 'Now you stay with me.' He didn't ask me whether I wanted to or not. He just said, 'Now you stay with me!'

That night at supper he explained to me that he wanted me to help them to get started and to train his Polish secretary Father Stanislav [Dziwisz]. He said, 'I won't keep you always here. Eventually I'll put you out.'[16]

He has remained throughout his pontificate just as 'un-Popish', and just as authoritarian.

At about 11 o'clock, the time at which he normally retires for the night, on the evening of 28 April, Pope John Paul II slipped as he was getting out of the shower in his apartment and fractured the top of his right thigh bone. He called Mgr Dziwisz who in turn called in the Pope's doctor, Renato Buzzonetti, and John Paul, for the sixth time in his pontificate, was taken off to the Gemelli hospital. The fracture was a bad one, and needed pinning. He would no longer be able to ski, said Buzzonetti (the Pope being by this time almost 74 years old that was hardly a surprise), but he could continue swimming[17] and otherwise lead a normal life.

Naturally, there had to be changes made to the papal diary. A trip to Sicily was put off, as was a visit to Belgium for a beatification. An extraordinary consistory of Cardinals, originally scheduled for 9-10 May, was postponed until 13-14 June, by which time the Pope should be able to attend. Consistories occur from a variety of reasons, particularly for the creation of new cardinals, but John Paul has made them into something more practical and rather less formal. Would one of the topics on the agenda be his possible resignation?

A Pope has resigned before. It may have been back in the thirteenth century, but if it has happened once it can happen again. There are rumours that the Pope is not in the best of health, that he suffers from temporary blackouts (which could explain his two falls), that there is evidence of the onset of Parkinson's disease. John Paul would not resign his office simply because of age, but he might very well do so if he felt himself physically incapable of carrying it out in the manner which he has made his own. He sets great store by, and clearly relishes, his pastoral visits. Should they be significantly curtailed he might consider giving up his office. When in 1982 he was asked by a journalist whether he would ever retire he brushed it aside with a joke; when the same question was put in 1987 he said: 'Let us leave it to Providence'. His retirement would almost certainly be back to Poland, and very probably to spend his last years in prayer in a Carmelite monastery, once again studying the works of St John of the Cross.

One question over which he certainly will pray – though will not agonize, for that is not his style – in the course of any future retirement is the success or failure of his tenure of the papacy, measured against the ends which he set himself.

He came to the papacy with more than his fair share of talents. Bishop Magee said he did not look like a scholar (cf. above, p. 288), yet he certainly has been one, with major academic studies to his credit, as well as books of poetry, theatre criticism and plays. He was more of a scholar in the formal sense of the word than any of his predecessors this century. But he had also been well schooled in the pastoral responsibilities of the Church, from curate to Archbishop. He came to the Vatican with an extraordinary linguistic ability which someone, sometime, may well describe as the gift of tongues, and the distinct advantage of being the first non-Italian in four and a half centuries. As a consequence he succeeded to the pontificate with the immense good will of the Catholic faithful, and an enormous sense of excitement about what was to happen.

That excitement, and much of that good will, was soon dissipated. The many foreign tours were remarkably successful in drawing crowds, but their long-term impact is much harder to gauge. It was certainly part of the Pope's purpose to bring the Catholic faithful more into contact with the person of the Pope. The journeys have done that. But his intention also was to unite the Church around the figure of the pontiff, and in that sense he has failed. In his early years as Pope a great effort was undertaken to win back the (eventually) schismatic Archbishop Lefebvre who was, as it were, leaving the Church on the right. Far less effort has ever been put into reconciling those who are leaving the Church on the left perhaps because, in a sense, they do not leave: their understanding of the unity of the Roman Catholic Church allows them to remain within it while being out of sympathy with the direction taken by Vatican theology. If what the Pope set out to do was to unite the Church, then that is to be chalked up as a failure. He has polarized it.

He has also polarized relationships between the Churches. It may be that he cannot be blamed for the breakdown of ecumenical relations with the Anglican Communion over the issue of women priests. It is hard to imagine any pope in this century being ready to accept the ordination of women, when the Church has not come to terms with the ordination of married men. But the failure with Anglicanism goes back further than that, to the unsympathetic treatment of the Final Report of the ARCIC by the Congregation for the Doctrine of the Faith. Relations with the Orthodox, on which John Paul set even greater store, have simply gone from bad to worse. It was always going to be difficult to deal with the problem of the Uniates, but it is hard to escape the conclusion that the situation in Russia, in the Ukraine particularly, in Rumania, has been badly handled, and that responsibility for this lies perhaps even more directly at the door of the papal private office than does the question of the Anglican Communion. One cannot help contrasting the skilful way political relations with these states has been handled by Casaroli, Poggi and others, with the manner in which religious links have been dealt with – to the considerable disadvantage of the latter.

John Paul came to the papacy with a clear vision of what he wished to achieve. He came well-versed in the documents of Vatican II as his book *Sources of Renewal* abundantly demonstrates, but his interpretation was that formed in a Polish Church under siege. In North America or Western Europe, or, for that matter, in South America and in Africa, clergy and faithful alike had read those documents as providing for a dispersion of authority from the administrative centre of the Church to the periphery. The Pope has attempted to reverse that trend, whilst paying lip-service to the concept of collegiality. The trend has indeed been reversed, which the Pope would presumably consider a success. Many in the Church judge it otherwise.

The Pope has written some outstanding encyclicals, apostolic exhortations and the like. Not all have commanded the same admiration, but that is only to be expected. It is not surprising, given his background, that he should not be as sensitive on the problems facing missionaries for example, as he was competent to account for the fall of Marxism as an ideology in *Centesimus annus* (cf. above, p. 238). On the other hand, his moral outlook, also forged in a rigidly disciplined Polish Church (a discipline which is itself rapidly disappearing to John Paul's obvious dismay), has failed to win acceptance – even among the bishops, as the African Synod, still meeting as this is being written, gives evidence.

The African Synod will draw up its propositions and, as is now customary, hand them over to the Pope for a final document to be produced. To judge by the debates at the Synod, high on the list of topics John Paul will have to discuss will be that of *enculturation*. Culture is an issue to which he has returned time and again. He has urged nations, particularly those of Africa but others as well, not to let their indigenous culture be swamped. He has stressed how close to the centre of culture religion finds itself – no doubt true, but a dangerous doctrine, as conflict in Northern Ireland, in the former Yugoslavia and in several other areas of the world bears witness. Even within Europe it is problematic now to insist upon the Christian elements of its culture, when the people who make up the continent's population clearly no longer share a common faith. The states of Europe, East or West, are not about to return to the old principle of *cuius regio, eius religio*. Despite the frequency with which Pope John Paul returns to the theme of culture, he appears ambivalent towards it. As Dr Lepenies remarked in the article quoted in the previous chapter (cf. above, p. 272), '*Veritatis Splendor* is almost an anti-ethnological tract, despising culture as nothing but a prison for man and his true nature'.

No one can accuse the Pope of not understanding culture. There has rarely, if ever, been anyone on the papal throne who displayed the same linguistic and literary gifts, as well as the more clerical learning of philosophy and theology. He is moreover unashamedly a Polish nationalist, and there is much of value that his own background in Poland brought to the papacy. Perhaps there has never been a time in the Church when it was more important to have a Pope who understood from first-hand experience the particular problems of Central and Eastern Europe. But he has failed to rise above his own culture when addressing the rest of the world. He is aware that his Polish, or even his European, paradigm for the expression of the faith of the Roman Catholic Church fits uncomfortably on the peoples of Africa, of Asia, even of Latin America. But he seems afraid to follow the implications of this through to its conclusion.

Possibly without even realizing that he has done so, Pope John Paul has made one enormous change in the culture of the Roman Catholic Church. He has recast, into the personalist and phenomenological language he finds most congenial, much of the religious discourse of the official documents of the Church. Since such language comes most naturally to him as he writes, he may not appreciate how different his writings seem to those who read them from the writings of his predecessors. His successors may not share the same philosophical preferences, but it is unlikely that the Church will return permanently to the Thomistic style which has dominated for the last century or so. That is a relief. It is itself a broadening, albeit a modest one, of the culture in which the faith may be expressed.

But the question of culture – of *enculturation* – is the greatest challenge which faces the Church today. The Pope has constantly demonstrated that he realizes this, but he has failed to face up to it. In the English translation of the *Catechism of the Catholic Church* destined for the Anglo-Saxon world of the British Isles and North America where it is increasingly common to express the faith as far as possible without using gender-specific terms, the Vatican has objected to the use of inclusive language. If even so minor a matter of diversity of culture is deemed unacceptable, however is Rome going to deal with the vastly more complex issues presented to it by the Church outside the confines of Western Europe and North America? The omens are not good.

Enculturation is closely allied to evangelization, another issue which Pope John Paul has regularly addressed – though never as well, it should be said, or at such length, as did Paul VI in his apostolic exhortation of 1975, *Evangelii Nuntiandi*. The last ten years of the present century, and of this millennium, were declared by John Paul to be the 'decade of evangelism', and he was followed by leaders of other Christian denominations. It was a phrase which sounded alarm bells among those of other faiths. They need not have worried. The impact of the decade of evangelism has been so slight for it to have reached the halfway stage without anyone noticing. The new millennium is almost upon us, and the Church has still made little impact upon the growing number of unbelievers.

Liberation Theology was one movement within the Church in the last quarter of a century which seemed likely to have a mass appeal. As has been seen (cf. above, pp. 50-1) it was received with little sympathy at Rome, especially in the first part of the pontificate. It is commonly suggested that the reason for Vatican hostility was the use of Marxism as a tool of social analysis. Obviously that is true: the Pope has frequently warned against the insidiousness of Communism. But Liberation Theology poses a much more fundamental challenge, for it reminds the Church that all of its doctrine – just like all of the Scriptures upon which that doctrine is based – is historically conditioned. They need to be rethought in the light of tradition, but in the context of a particular place and a particular time. Liberation Theology, in other words, is an attempt to enculturate the Gospel in diverse cultures. There are some who have not yet given up the struggle to do this but as the Vatican's manipulation of the Santo Domingo meeting of CELAM demonstrated (cf. above, pp. 257-8), a struggle it is forced to remain.

When the Roman Catholic faithful are faced with a decision from Rome to which they object, they commonly turn their ire, not upon the pope of the day, but upon the Roman Curia just as, in medieval times, unjust laws were blamed on 'evil counsellors', never upon the king. However true in the past such an understanding of authority in the Catholic Church may have been, it is not an accurate assessment of Rome's authority today. There has rarely in modern times been a pontiff who has so quickly and decisively stamped his own character upon the Church – or attempted to do so. He has chosen to have about him like-minded men whom he can trust, otherwise he could not so often spend time away from the Vatican. The line from Rome, whether it be in an encyclical or some other papal document, in a decision of a Vatican tribunal or in an instruction which emanates from one of the Congregations or Secretariats which make up the Vatican bureaucracy, reflects the outlook of Pope John Paul II. And, as it has been remarked earlier, on some crucial issues that outlook is steadfastly anti-modern.

Who is to say that Pope John Paul is wrong to adopt such a stance? There are many who sympathize. Yet, under God, the Church has survived for two millennia because of its ability to adapt to the world about it at different stages of its existence.[18] No matter how immoral, how violent, how unbelieving the society in which the Church has found itself, it has remained a part of that society, evangelizing from within. It is precisely because the Church has been world-affirming rather than world-denying that it has remained a Church and not degenerated into a sect. If the Church is to remain true to itself and true to its history the urgent need to enculturate the faith in the modern world will not go away.

John Paul has had much to say that is inspiring, especially about the dignity of the human person and the demands of solidarity among people and between nations. But there is another side to his teaching which displays a deep pessimism about the human condition, and demonstrates a refusal to come to terms with some aspects of the modern world which no amount of preaching will ever reverse. He has changed the Church's notion of what it is to be Pope, while asserting an authority for the papal *magisterium* which goes well beyond the ability of theologians to demonstrate or historians to justify. He has been the most politically active of modern pontiffs, while constantly exhorting bishops and priests to stay out of the political arena. He has been the first Pope since the Middle Ages who could have understood the Churches of the Orthodox tradition, yet relationships between Orthodoxy and Roman Catholicism have rarely been so poor. He is the most travelled of pontiffs, yet remains suspicious of cultures other than that in which he grew up. He has been a vigorous critic of Communism yet, as Communism has disappeared, he has come to regret the changes which have taken place consequently even within his own beloved country.

The approach of the millennium has been a constant theme of papal catechesis. John Paul looks upon anniversaries as occasions to remind people of their roots, and opportunities for reflection and conversion. What more obvious an occasion for such renewal than the two thousandth anniversary of the birth of Christ?[19] He wants to send a renewed Church into the third millennium, and he has his vision of what the Church might become. Unhappily for Pope John Paul, that vision has divided the Roman Church rather than united it.

NOTES

1. On the notion of *magisterium* cf. the articles by John P. Boyle, 'The "ordinary *magisterium*": towards a history of the concept' in *The Heythrop Journal*, vol. xix, 1979, and vol. xx, 1980, pp. 14-29, and the excursus on *magisterium* by Robert Murray in Michael Walsh (ed.), *A commentary on the Catechism of the Catholic Church* (London, Geoffrey Chapman, 1994).
2. cf, for example, Leonardo Boff's statement dated 27 June 1992 on his leaving his Order and the priesthood: 'I am leaving the priestly ministry and the Franciscan Order not to be free from the Church, which I love and shall never abandon, but to be free to work without impediment ... Since 1971 I have suffered continuous tribulations, restrictions and punishments from the doctrinal authorities of the Church and from the Franciscan Order ... Let us never forget: Christ called us to freedom, not to slavery' (quoted from *The Tablet* 4 July 1992, p. 850).
3. *John Paul II* (London, Weidenfeld & Nicolson, 1979), p. 84.
4. cf. John J. Conley, 'The philosophical foundations of John Paul II' in *The Thought of Pope John Paul II*, edited by John M. McDermott (Rome, Gregorian University Press, 1993), p. 25.
5. cf. John M. McDermott in his Introduction to *The Thought of Pope John Paul II*, p. xxiii.
6. Quoted by Blazynski, p. 151.

7. *Be Not Afraid* (New York, Doubleday, 1985), pp. 16-18.

8. See a number of the contributions to *The Thought of Pope John Paul II*, edited by John M McDermott (Rome, Gregorian University Press, 1993), especially those by John McDermott himself, Gerald A. McCool, Joseph Murphy and Avery Dulles.

9. Also studied in the book edited by McDermott: cf. Terence Prendergast's 'A vision of wholeness', and the response to this article by James Swetnam, pp. 69-98.

10. The same curious tendency can be found throughout the *Catechism of the Catholic Church*.

11. art. cit., p. 83.

12. art. cit., pp. 94-5.

13. Gary Gurtler, 'The spirituality of Pope John Paul II: a Response', in John M. McDermott (ed.), *The Thought of John Paul II*, p. 119.

14. Section 44.

15. See Felix Corley, 'Soviet reaction to the election of Pope John Paul II' in *Religion, State and Society* 22 (1994). This section had been based on Mr Corley's fascinating article, which he kindly let me see in advance of publication.

16. Quoted from John Cornwell, *A thief in the night* (London, Viking, 1989), p. 200.

17. He had built a swimming pool at Castel Gandolfo early in his pontificate. When one of his secretaries wondered aloud whether spending that much money would not give rise to criticism, John Paul responded that a swimming pool was cheaper than a conclave.

18. This was a central theme of my book *The roots of Christianity* (London, Collins, 1986).

19. He must of course be aware that the most likely date for the birth of Christ is 6 BCE.

AFTERWORD

O N 4 APRIL, 1994, the day after Easter, a preparatory meeting for the September population conference was held at the UN in New York. The offensive which John Paul had begun with a meeting with the Secretary General of the Conference, Nafis Sadiq, and with a meeting on 25 March of the 151 ambassadors accredited to the Holy See (cf. above, p. 276) continued unabated. He had little success. The USA had backed papal opposition to abortion at the 1984 population conference (cf. above, p. 268), but President Clinton was not going to emulate President Reagan. Though the head of the US delegation insisted that abortion should be 'safe, legal, and rare', Clinton refused to condemn it and the Holy See found itself in an opposition group of less than a dozen states – including Turkey, Iran, and a small number of Latin American countries.

1994 had been declared the International Year of the Family: the Pope proposed to write to all heads of state about the threats he saw to family life in the modern world, and he opened his campaign with a letter to Clinton. The draft document for the Cairo meeting, he wrote, focused so strongly on population that it practically ignored development issues. He foresaw a general moral decline were the draft to be adopted at Cairo, 'a serious setback for humanity'. At the beginning of June the Pope again had an opportunity to put his point of view to the American President when Clinton called on him at the Vatican. The Cairo conference was chief among the topics they discussed. There are, said Clinton afterwards, 'some genuine differences between us on the role of contraception and population policy'.

On 10 April the African Synod began with the throbbing of drums and dancing in St Peter's: piety, said the Pope, was expressed somewhat differently in Poland. There were over 300 representatives – though none from Rwanda, whose bishops preferred to stay (and three of them to die) with their people. The civil war in that country was a sobering event for the Church, a sign that the blood of the tribe was proving stronger than the water of baptism, as

Bishop Albert Obiefuna of Nigeria put it in the course of the Synod, though not speaking specifically about Rwanda. Cardinal Hyacinthe Thiandoum from Senegal, highlighted five key issues: proclaiming the gospel, enculturation, dialogue, justice and peace and the means of social communication. The topic which quickly put itself at the heart of the agenda was enculturation. This was a constant theme of the bishops' interventions: even Cardinal Ratzinger had something rather theoretical to say on the matter. The most obvious question was that of the liturgy. Somewhat less obvious, though very much to the forefront of the African bishops' concerns, was enculturation and justice, the notion that 'culture' is not simply the artistic representation of a people. The West seems to regard, as Cardinal Ratzinger has argued that indeed it is − Western culture as the norm for the Christian faith.

Even democracy is often seen by Africans as simply another Western importation. Dialogue could mean ecumenical relations with other Christian Churches, but that with Islam was at least as pressing. A statistic on everyone's mind at the Synod was that, by the year 2000, it was likely the population of the African continent would be 48 per cent Christian and 42 per cent Muslims. Dialogue with Islam was not simple, one delegate pointed out fiercely, when Muslims are slaughtering your fellow Catholics.

The Synod ended on 8 May as it had begun, with drums and dancing in St Peter's, this time in the absence of the Pope, still confined to his hospital bed after his fall (cf. above, p. 288). Propositions − secret, as the Vatican requires − were laid before the Pope for his consideration and a committee formed to help prepare the papal response, and to implement the Synod's conclusions. Whether the Synod had been a success there were mixed feelings, depending upon how much hope had been placed in it. No similar gathering had been so long in preparation, and from that perspective the achievements were perhaps somewhat limited. But the synodal fathers had not shied away from issues of priestly celibacy, polygamous marriages and other similar problems on which they displayed a sympathetic attitude not to be found in the upper echelons of the Vatican. While it was clear that enculturation had a long way to go, it seemed as if the African Church might be about to take a firmer hand in its own liturgical and theological development. Above all, the representatives of the different countries had come to realize their common problems, and to grow in a spirit of continental solidarity, that in itself may prove a formidable challenge to the Vatican.

The Pope had been expected to leave hospital in time for Pentecost. In the event he returned home a week later, on 27 May, looking frail but cheerful.

Two days afterwards he spoke at the Sunday Angelus. In the Catholic Church the month of May is linked to devotion to Mary: John Paul thanked Mary for 'this gift of suffering' in the Marian month. He remembered the attempt on his life. Cardinal Wyszinski had told him, he said, that he had been called by God to lead the Church into the year 2000. 'I have understood that I have to lead the Church of Christ into this third millennium with prayer, with various initiatives. But I saw (in his hospital bed) that this was not enough: I must lead her with suffering, with the attempt on my life of 13 years ago, and now this suffering . . . Precisely because the family is threatened, the family is attacked, the Pope must be attacked, the Pope must suffer, so that every family and the world should see that there is, I would say, a higher Gospel: the Gospel of suffering, with which one must prepare the future, the third millennium'. Theologians (and psychologists) may reflect upon John Paul's mystical vision of himself as suffering for the good of humankind.

Theologians, at least, had little time to do so before the bombshell of an apostolic letter 'On reserving priestly ordination to men alone', addressed to the bishops of the world, and issued to them on 13 May but publicly released on 30 May. It concluded 'In order that all doubt may be removed . . . in virtue of my ministry of confirming the brethren (cf. Luke 22:32) I declare that the Church has no authority whatsoever to confer priestly ordination on women and that this judgement is to be definitively held by all the Church's faithful'.

As the Archbishop of Canterbury commented, the arguments advanced in the letter were perfectly well known, had been fully considered, and had not been found convincing. Even the Pontifical Biblical Commission had responded in 1976 that it could find no argument in Scripture against the ordination of women. It was another example of the Pope, having failed to persuade by exhortation, attempting to impose his views by an act of authority. Anyone who did not accept the teaching, said Cardinal Ratzinger, 'obviously is separated from the faith of the Church'. It sounded more than ever like a return to the Modernist crisis at the beginning of the century. On 18 November 1907 Pope Pius X – now a canonized saint – declared that everyone was obliged in conscience to accept the definitive decisions of the Biblical Commission, those already issued and those still to be published, on matters of scriptural interpretation. Those decisions have since been disavowed. When risking 'definitive' judgements the Vatican has a short memory.

Cardinal Martini, the Jesuit Archbishop of Milan and a distinguished Scripture scholar, remarked that the letter did not close discussion, but the ordination of women was not a question for this millennium. This millennium, it was promptly remarked, had only half a dozen years to run.

Martini, the Italian press's most favoured candidate for succession to the papacy, also pointed out that the third millennium of Christianity begins in 1994, the most likely date of Christ's birth being 6 BCE. This cautionary comment did not deflect John Paul from calling a conclave of cardinals to discuss his plans for celebrating the year 2000.

There were 114, of the 139 living, cardinals present when the Pope walked, with difficulty but without the aid of the stick he had been using since his release from hospital, into the consistory on 13 June. His lengthy speech touched a variety of topics. He looked for ecumenical progress, something not evident thus far in his pontificate. He wanted to improve relations with China and Vietnam; the Church needed a conversion, to acknowledge its past failings and do penance for them; the vision of Vatican II had yet to be realized. It was left to the Cardinal Secretary of State, Angelo Sodano, to put before the consistory the Pope's more visionary ideas for celebrating the millennium: a gathering of Christian leaders in Jerusalem, a meeting with Jews and Muslims (for whom, one would have thought, the millennium of Christ's birth was scarcely a matter of enormous significance) on Mount Sinai. There was considerable support, said Sodano, for declaring 1999 a year of special devotion to Mary. Where this support was coming from was unclear, but once the idea was mooted the Cardinals fell into line. They also spoke of the possibility of another Council of the Church

It would all, of course, cost money, but for once Cardinal Edmund Szoka, the Vatican's equivalent of a minister of finance, had good news for their eminences. The Vatican was out of the red. The surplus was small, $1.5m, but it was a considerable turnaround. The extra to balance the books, it was said, had come from the local Churches. Was this the profits from the *Catechism of the Catholic Church* which, wherever it had been published (and the English language edition had finally appeared in a pedestrian translation with gender-specific language) had been a best-seller? The Vatican had prudently reserved copyright to the Administration of the Patrimony of the Holy See (APSA): APSA was collecting the royalties.

As June ended it was announced that the Pope had just completed another book. *Crossing the Threshold of Hope* was to be published in Italy by Mondadori, a firm in which the Italian Prime Minister, Silvio Bertusconi, had a 47 per cent stake. It was rumoured that Random House of New York had bought English-language rights for an astonishingly large sum which, if the rumour were true, would keep the Vatican out of debt for the foreseeable future. Increasing frailty might curtail papal travels, but new apostolates were opening for the ever-resourceful Pope John Paul II.

BIBLIOGRAPHY

The list which follows contains only the main books and articles which I have consulted in the course of writing this book. References to shorter articles, frequently from *The Tablet*, are given in full in the footnotes. Encyclicals have also been omitted: I have usually consulted the version published by the Catholic Truth Society, though for some papal documents I have turned to that estimable US publication, *Origins*.

Acta Synodalia Sacrosancti Concilii Oecumenici Vaticani Secundi, Rome, Vatican Press, 1970-9.

Blazynski, George, *John Paul II: A man from Krakow*, London, Weidenfeld & Nicolson, 1979.

Burns, Gene, *The Frontiers of Catholicism*, Berkeley, University of California Press, 1992.

Burns, Tom, *The Use of Memory*, London, Sheed & Ward, 1993.

Carroll, Michael P., *The Cult of the Virgin Mary*, Princeton University Press, 1986.

Cornwell, John, *A thief in the night: The death of Pope John Paul I*, London, Viking, 1989.

Cornwell, Rupert, *God's Banker: The life and death of Roberto Calvi*, London, Victor Gollancz, 1983.

Craig, Mary, *The Crystal Spirit*, London, Hodder & Stoughton, 1986.

d'Onorio, J.-B. (ed.), *Le Saint-Siège dans les relations internationales*, Paris, Cerf, 1989.

Greeley, Andrew M., *The Making of the Popes*, London, Futura, 1979.

Grootaers, Jan and Selling, Joseph A., *The 1980 Synod of Bishops 'On the Role of the Family'*, Louvain, Leuven University Press, 1983.

Hebblethwaite, Peter, *Paul VI*, London, HarperCollins, 1993.

Hebblethwaite, Peter, *The Papal Year*, London, Geoffrey Chapman, 1981.

Hebblethwaite, Peter, 'Pope John Paul II as philosopher and poet' in *The Heythrop Journal XXI* (1980), pp. 123-36.

Hebblethwaite, Peter, *Synod Extraordinary*, London, Darton, Longman & Todd, 1985.

Hebblethwaite, Peter, *The Year of Three Popes*, London, Collins, 1978.

Hellman, John, 'John Paul II and the personalist movement' in *Cross Currents* XXX, 4 (198-81), pp. 409-19.

Herman, Edward S. and Brodhead, Frank, *The rise and fall of the Bulgarian connection*, New York, Sheridan Square Publications, 1986.

Johnson, Paul, *Pope John Paul II and the Catholic restoration*, London, Weidenfeld & Nicolson, 1982.

Kalser, Robert, *The Encyclical that never was*, London, Sheed & Ward, 1989.

Kreutz, Andrej, *Vatican Policy on the Palestinian-Israeli conflict*, New York, Greenwood Press, 1990.

Lake, Frank, *With respect: A doctor's response to a healing Pope*, London, Darton, Longman and Todd, 1982.

Luneau, René, *Le rêve de Compostelle*, Paris, Centurion, 1989.

McDermott, John M. (ed.), *The thought of Pope John Paul II*, Rome, Gregorian University, 1993.

Michel, Patrick, *Politics and Religion in Eastern Europe*, Oxford, Polity Press, 1991.

Montclos, Christine de, *Les voyages de Jean-Paul II*, Paris, Centurion, 1990.

Penanster, Alain de, *Un papiste contre les papes,* Paris, La Table Ronde, 1988.

Raw, Charles, *The Money Changers*, London, Harvill, 1992.

Schmitz, Kenneth L., *At the Center of the Human Drama: The philosophical anthropology of Karol Wojtyla/Pope John Paul II*, Washington DC, Catholic University of America Press, 1993.

Toulat, Jean, *Le Pape contre le guerre du Golfe*, Paris, Oeil, 1991.

Walsh, Michael and Davies, Brian (eds.), *Proclaiming Justice and Peace*, Mystic CT, Twenty-Third Publications, 1991.

Weigel, George, *The Final Revolution*, New York, Oxford University Press, 1992.

Whale, John (ed.), *The Pope from Poland*, London, Collins, 1980.

Willey, David, *God's Politician*, London, Faber, 1992.

Williams, George H., *The Mind of John Paul II,* New York, Seabury, 1981.

Wojtyla, Karol, *The Acting Person*, Dordrecht, D. Reidel, 1979.

Wojtyla, Karol, *The Collected Plays and Writings on Theater*, Berkeley, University California Press, 1987.

Wojtyla, Karol, *Easter Vigil and other poems,* London, Hutchinson, 1979.

Wojtyla, Karol, *Sign of Contradiction*, London, Hodder & Stoughton, 1979.

Wojtyla, Karol, *Sources of Renewal*, London, Collins, 1980.

INDEX

Prefatory note: This index is arranged alphabetically, letter by letter, except for the section headed '*Life*' under the main subject, **John Paul II.** This is the only section arranged chronologically. The abbreviation 'JP' = 'John Paul II'. His encyclicals, other papal writings and books by him mentioned by the author are in a section under the main subject, **John Paul II.** Encyclicals and writings by other popes appear in the main index. Papal themes have their headwords in bold. Saints: the convention has been followed whereby saints are indexed under their Christian names unless they are known by both Christian name and surname (e.g. St Charles Borromeo), in which cases they appear under their surnames. Places commencing with the prefix St appear under the letter 'S'. Names commencing with 'de' or 'von' appear under the letters 'D' or 'V' accordingly.

Aborigines 174
abortion JP speaks on 66, 190, in Arizona 183, in Canada 142, in Germany 179, in Italy 93–4, in Japan 93, in Poland 240, in Spain 113; protest in USA 269; UN conference 276, 296
absolution *see* penance
Adalbert, St 59
Administration of Patrimony of the Holy See (APSA) 70
Africa *see under individual countries*
Agca, Mehmet Ali 71, 94, 95–6
AIDS (auto-immune deficiency syndrome) 210, 227, 228, 264, 265
Alaska: papal visit 93, 135
Albania: papal visit 265–6
Albert the Great, St 89
Albertine Order 19
Aleksi II, Patriarch of Moscow 244, 247, 250, 263
Altotting (Bavaria) 89
American Church, criticism of 206
Analecta Cracoviensia 31, 46
Analecta Husserliana 33
Angelicum college, Rome 13
Angelicum (journal) 14
Anglican–Roman Catholic International Commission (ARCIC) 104–5, 255
antisemitism 35, 36, 153, 183, 196
apartheid: condemned by JP 152, 197, 199; by Kenneth Kaunda 207
apostolate of the laity 28–9 *see also* laity
Arafat, Yasser 111, 112
Argentina 106, 108–9, 178; Beagle Channel 48, 132, 176–7
Ariccia 29, 30
Aristotle 32
Arns, Archbishop Evaristo (São Paulo) 83, 85, 127, 141, 222
Angola 255–6
Aquinas, St Thomas 13–14, 32, 97 *see also* Thomism

Arrupe SJ, Pedro 62–3, 85, 97–8, 101n41, 104
Assisi 172
Association of Vatican Employees 115, 146
atheism 30, 246, 266
Auschwitz concentration camp 5, 37, 60–1, 165, 187n6–7, 212
Australia 37, 174
Austria 125, 188, 196–7
authority, papal 47, 84–5, 91, 287–8 *see also* magisterium
Azores 239

Backis, Mgr Audryss 56
Baggio, Cardinal Sebastiano 74, 135
Banco Ambrosiano 109, 172 *see also* Vatican Bank
Bsnda, Hastings (President of Malawi) 208
Bangladesh 173
Barcelona 114
Bartholomew, Patriarch 246, 263
Bäumer, Professor Remigius 88
Baziak, Archbishop Eugeniusz 20, 24, 27
Beagle Channel dispute 48, 132, 287
beatifications: Alphonsa, Sister 160; Bakhita, Giuseppina 253, 264; Chavare, Kuriakose Elias 160; Chmielowski, Adam 122; complaints about 253; Escriva de Balaguer, Josemaria 253; 40 killed in Spanish Civil War 127; French priest in Lyons 171; Kalinowski, Rafael 122; Kolbe, Maximilian 37; Kozka, Karolina 180; Ledochowska, Ursula 122; Lesotho missionaries 198; martyrs of Angers, France 130n34; 122 martyrs Spanish Civil War 259; Matulaitis, Archbishop Jurgis 181; Mexicans (5) 224; Nengapeta, Anvarite 152; Pelczar, Jozef Sebastian 239; Ruiz, Lorenzo 92; Spaniards (5) 176; Teresa of the Andes 177
Belgium 14, 147–8
Belo Horizonte 83
Benedict, St 91
Benelli, Cardinal Giovanni 44

JOHN PAUL II (Karol Wojtyla)
Attributes/characteristics: appearance 4; altar-server 4; acting 4, 5, 9–10, 17; cinema 4, 18; conservative 52–5, 68, 74, 192; devout 3; diplomat 67, 88; theatre director 4; energetic 45; extrovert 287; faith, deep 43; girl friends 5, 11; health 6, 94, 256–7, 274, 288, 289, 297, 299; humility 43; informality 287–8; intelligence 43; linguistic gifts 4, 13, 125, 148, 223, 270, 291; literature 4; mortification 18; music 5; nationalism, Polish 9–10; piety 10; poverty 4; prayer 10–11, 12; progressive 192; pragmatic 122; scholarly 4, 289; spirituality 284; sportsman 4, 18; translator 7, 20, 31; traveller 289; writer 290
Family: aunts, maternal 5, 17; Kaczoronowska, Emilia (mother) 3, 6; Wojtyla, Edmund (elder brother) 4; Wojtyla, Karol (father) 2, 6, 17–18; Wojtyla, Maciej (paternal grandfather) 3
Early life: (chronological) birth 1; High School 3; bereavement 4; moves to Cracow 5; enrolled at Jagellonian University 5; road-building work 5; military training 5; philology student 6; labouring jobs 6, 12; founded Rhapsodic Theatre 7; playwright 4, 7–8, 9–10; theology student 10, 13; decides to study for priesthood 10; joins theology discussion group; aids Jews in Cracow during Second World War 12; enters seminary 12; ordination 13; doctoral studies in Rome 13; investigates worker-priest movement 14–15; returns to Poland 17; curate at Niegowic 17; holidays 17–18, 24; second doctorate 20; university teaching 23–4; becomes professor 23; pastoral work in Cracow 24; student chaplain 24; becomes youngest Polish bishop 24; writes new play 'The Jeweller's Shop' 25; becomes administrator of diocese 27; attends Second Vatican Council 27; appointed Archbishop of Cracow 28, 280; named Cardinal 30; vice-president Polish episcopal conference 31; publishes handbook on Vatican II 31–2; attends synod of bishops in Rome 35, 37; travels to Australia and New Zealand; intervenes in Gdansk riots 38–9; elected Pope 43–4; installed as Pope 46
Themes of papacy: in alphabetical order, in bold throughout main index
Travels: countries in alphabetical order throughout main index
Writings: Encyclicals: *Centesimus Annus* 237; *Dives in Misericordia* 90, 166; *Dominum et Vivificantem* 165–6, 282; *Laborem Exercens* 96–7; *Redemptoris Missio* 233; *Redemptoris Mater* 175–6; *Slavorum Apostoli* 149; *Solicitudio Rei Socialis* 191, 193, 204, 281; *Veritatis Splendor* 170–3, 279, 281, 291
Other writings: *Christi Fideles Laici* (apostolic exhortation) 204; *Duodecimum Saeculum* (letter) 189; *Euntes in Mundum* (letter) 189; *Familiaris Consortio* (apostolic exhortation) 87–8; *Fidei Depositum* (apostolic exhortation) 260; *Magnum Baptismi Donum* (letter) 190; *Master in the Faith* (apostolic letter) 231; *Mulieris Dignitatem* (apostolic letter) 199–200; 'On reserving priestly ordination to men alone' (apostolic letter) 298; *Pastor Bonus* (apostolic constitution) 204; *Pastores Dabo Vobis* (apostolic exhortation) 252–3;

Reconciliatio et Paenitentia (response to synod) 143–4; *Redemptoris Donum* (apostolic exhortation) 134; *Redemptor homines* (written as Karol Wojtyla) 52–4, 165–6; *Salvifici Dolores* (apostolic letter) 134
Books and plays: *Acting Person, The* 32, 282; *An Assessment of the Possibility of Building a Christian Ethic on the Principles of the System of Max Scheler* (doctoral thesis) 20; *Crossing the Threshold of Hope* 299; *David* (first play) 8; *Jeremiah* (play) 8, 9; *Jeweller's Shop, The* (play) 25, 106; *Job* (play) 8–9; *Love and Responsibility* 25–7; *Our God's Brother* (play) 18, 19; *Sign of Contradiction, A* 38; *Song of the Hidden God* (poems) 13; *Sources of Renewal* 31
Justice and Peace Commission 30, 79, 135, 197
justice *see* social justice

Kalinowski, Rafael 122
Kalwaria Zebrzydowska 60
Kane, Sister Theresa 66, 73n26
Katholikentag (Congress of German Catholics) 82
Kaunda, Kenneth (President of Zambia) 207
Kenya 79–80, 152
Khaddoumi, Frank (PLO) 112
Kim, Cardinal Stephen (Seoul) 135
King, Martin Luther 183
Kissinger, Henry 95
Klein, Théo 213
Kluger, Jerzy 12
Knock, Eire 64, 65
Köhl, Helmut (German Chancellor) 179
Kolbe, St Maximilian 10, 37, 40, 60–1, 113, 122, 129n17, 165
Kolvenbach SJ, Pieter-Hans 125, 156n10
Kondrusiewicz, Archbishop Tadeusz (Moscow) 247
König, Cardinal (Vienna) 43, 55, 133, 141, 197
Korea, South 135, 215
Korec, Bishop Jan (Czechoslovakia) 133
Kotlarcyzk, Dr M 4, 6, 9, 10
Kremm, Kurt 197
Krohn, Juan Fernandez 128n4
Krol, Cardinal (Philadelphia) 155, 172, 207
KUL *see* Lublin, Catholic University of
Küng, Hans 27, 55, 74–5, 82, 88–9, 138–9, 273, 279
Kurón, Jacek 39, 286
Kydrynski, Juliusz 5, 6

Laboa, Archbishop Jose (Panama) 219–20
Labour Organization, International (ILO) 109
Lagos 103
laity 28–9, 30, 76–7, 142, 146, 154–5, 184–6, 204
Latin America 38, 49–51, 63 *see also under names of countries*
Latin America, Conference of Bishops of (CELAM) 49, 50, 116, 117, 119, 142, 169, 257–8, 293
Latvia 269–70
Leadership Conference of American Religious 66
Lebanon 112, 214, 235
Ledochowska, Ursula 122
Lefebvre, Archbishop (France) 81, 182, 192, 194, 196, 204
Leo XIII, pope 94, 237

Kane, Sister Theresa 66; in Latin America 227; in Lyons (France) 171; implied at Medellin conference 49, 51; in Mexico 224; in *Solicitudo Rei Socialis* 191–2
Opus Dei 111, 144, 163, 253–4
Oraison, Marc 139
ordination of women *see* women, ordination of
Ortega, Daniel 118
Orthodox Churches *see* dialogue with Orthodox Church
Osoba I Czyn (The Acting Person) see under John Paul II
Osservatore Romano, L' 46, 95, 110, 123, 165, 182, 228
Ostaszeewski, Tadeusz 7

Pacem in Terris (encyclical of Paul VI) 67, 212
Padín, Mgr Cándido 258
Paisley, Rev Ian 63, 200–1
Palazzini, Cardinal Pietro 83
Palestine Liberation Organization (PLO) 111
Palestinians, rights of 257
Palme, Olaf 211
Panama 118, 217, 219–20
Papagheorghiou, Spyridion (Metropolitan of Venice) 246, 252
Papua New Guinea 135
Paraguay 193–4, 207
participation in natural community 34
Patriotic Catholic Association in China 92, 93
Paul VI, pope (Giovanni Battista Montini) 28, 30, 32, 34, 37, 38, 39, 52, 67, 76, 77, 111–12, 176
Pax Christi 117
peace, JP on: Falklands dispute 107; Gulf crisis 232, 235; Lebanon 214; New Year messages 48, 67, 158, 175, 203, 219, 261; to United Nations 108–9
penance 54, 121, 126, 143–4
Peres, Shimon (Prime Minister of Israel) 145–6, 259
Perez de Cuellar, Xavier 237
personalism 20–1
Peru 144, 145, 193
Peter's Pence 115, 172, 207
phenomenology, JP's 282
Philippines 91–3
Pignedoli, Cardinal Sergio 82
pilgrimage of Polish priests to Rome 37
Pilsudski, Marshal 11–12
Pinochet, General 177, 258, 287
Pinochet, Lucia 167
Pires, Archbishop José (Brazil) 83
Pironio, Cardinal Eduardo 135
Pittau SJ, Giuseppe 97–8
Pius X, St, pope 11, 298
Pius XI, pope 11
Pius XII 26, 164, 183
Poggi, Archbishop Luigi 49, 108, 133
Poland: explosive situation 38; Gdansk arrests 39; government reaction to JP election 44–5; historical background to JP life 1–3; inter-rite disputes 237–8; Jaruzelski crushes uprising 96; martial law suspended 115; political changes 179, 239; politically disturbed 35, 91; situation worsens 137; papal visits 17, 57–61, 121–3, 175, 179–81, 239–40, 242; Soviet troops enter 13

Poletti, Cardinal Ugo 68, 209
Polish Theologians, Congress of 37, 39
politics, JP on Church and: 50–1, 62, 83–4, 102, 119, 170, 177, 222, 244, 269
Pontifical Council for the Family 121, 201–2
Pontifical University of St Thomas Aquinas *see* Angelicum
Popieluszko, Fr Jerzy 175, 180
population *see* birth control, contraception
Population Conference, International 139
Populorum Progressio (encyclical Paul VI) 67, 191
Portugal 106, 239
Posadas, Cardinal Juan Jesús (Yucatan) 268
Potocki, Andrzej 32
Potter, Dr Philip 138
Poupard, Bishop Paul 83
poverty 67, 83, 88, 135, 161, 163, 221, 161–2
see also option for the poor
Pozniak, Jan 5
Prefecture for Economic Affairs of Holy See 69–70
priesthood: conference of US bishops 47; Dutch Church 75, 76; laicization 47, 83; letter from JP to all priests 54–5; ministerial 28, 32; synod 1990 229–31; universal 28, 32
priests, married: Africa 78; Brazil 244, 248n7; Dutch Church 75, 76; laicization 47; Switzerland 138; Ukrainian Rite 156n9 *see also* celibacy
Puerto Rico 143

Rabin, Yitzhak (Prime Minister of Israel) 275
racism 66, 275
Radom riots 38
Rahner SJ, Karl 14, 73n29
Rajowski, Mieczyslav (Prime Minister of Poland) 201
Ratsirak, Didier (President of Madagascar) 207
Ratzinger, Cardinal Joseph (Munich): African synod 1994 297; Brazilian Bishops' conference 160, 162; catechism, new 261; Curran, Charles 163; damns general absolution 126; guidance at 1980 synod 87; on homosexuality 173; on liberation theology 140, 141, 156n8; on *magisterium* 225–6; 'Message to the People of God' 155; on ordination of women 298; at papal visit to Germany 90; Prefect of Cong. for Doctrine 99; president of ARCIC 105; and Schillebeeckx, E 156n7; on *Veritatis Splendor* 272–3; vetoes appt. Johannes Metz 73n29, 75; warns US theologians 206
Rauber, Archbishop Karl-Joseph (Switzerland) 265
Raw, Charles 110
Reagan, Ronald (US President) 102, 135, 184, 286
Recife 83
reconciliation, papal messages of 143, 144, 156n12, 196, 197–8, 228, 242, 256, 269
redemption, JP on: 52–3, 134, 284
religious orders 70, 105, 134, 146–7, 227 *see also under names of orders*
Religious and Secular Institutes 146–7, 149
Rerum Novarum (encyclical Leo XIII) 237
Rhapsodic Theatre, Cracow 7–10, 17, 18
Rigali, Archbishop Justin (USA) 280–1
rights *see* human rights

280; Jesuits 63; Latin American 38, 49; letter
from German-speaking 88–9; liberation
theologians 140; moral 30; papal praise of
270–1; rebuked by JP 225–7; Schillebeeckx, E
256n7; woman unnamed 89
theology; JP studies 10, 13, 282–3; hard line on
184, 202: homosexuality 173; international
conference 163–4; international congress 271
see also liberation theology, theologians
Theology of Liberation (Gutierrez) 49
Thérèse of Lisieux, St 11, 81
Thiandoum, Cardinal Hyacinth (Senegal) 297
Thomism 14, 21–2, 33, 116, 282
Togo 150–1
Tomasek, Cardinal (Prague) 133–4, 150
Tomko, Joseph 74
Toronto Star 185
Toure, President Sekou 251
tradition as a source of teaching 22, 26
travels of Pope John Paul II *see under names of
countries*
Trinidad and Tobago 144, 145
Trinity, JP study of 165–6
Trujillo, Cardinal Lopez (Medellin) 50, 56,
116–17, 127
truth, search for 162–3, 282
Tucci SJ, Roberto 52
Tudlinski, Tadeusz 7
Turkey 70–1
Turowicz, Jerzy 20, 36–7
Tutu, Archbishop Desmond 137
Tygodnik Powszechny 7, 19–20, 36
Tymienecka, Dr Anna-Teresa 32–3
Tyranowski, Jan 10–11, 13, 14, 15, 282

Uganda 263–4
Ukrainian Church 77–8, 189, 194–5, 196,
216–17, 239, 240–1
Uniate Church 221, 244, 246, 256
United Nations 53, 65, 66–8, 112, 139, 276, 194
United Nations Environment Programme 152
UNESCO, papal address to 81–2
United Nations University, Japan 93
United States of America 31, 34, 65–6, 131,
183–4, 268–9
unity among bishops, JP insistence on 35, 52
unity of Church 118, 168, 294
Uruguay 177, 192–3

Vagnozzi, Cardinal Egidio 69, 70
Vaivods, Cardinal (Riga) 116

Vatican II *see* Second Vatican Council
Vatican Bank 70, 115, 206–7, 276
Vatican Employees Association 115, 146
Vatican Radio 28, 52, 196, 213, 257
Venezuela 144, 145
Vianney, St John 171
Vietnam 136, 299
Villot, Cardinal Jean 56
violence, JP condemnation of 64–5, 84, 93, 119,
120, 142, 145, 162, 170, 177, 193, 197, 198,
241–2, 269
vocations, religious 229, 246, 252
Volk, Cardinal 39
von Galen, Cardinal Clemens August (Munster)
179

Waldheim, Kurt 66, 181–2, 188, 196
Wadowice 1, 2–3
Walesa, Lech 36, 90, 123, 180, 239
Warsaw uprising 12–13, 38
Wawel 13
Waxman, Rabbi Mordecai 182–3
Weigl, Gustave 95
Wicher, Wladyslaw 22
Willebrands, Cardinal 74, 76, 124, 168–9, 182–3
Willey, David 66, 78, 95, 118, 119
Williams, G H 32, 33
Wojtyla, Karol Josef (nickname Lolek) *see* John
Paul II
women, JP attitude towards: 26–7, 148, 174, 176;
ordination of 88, 128, 200, 298; and CofE
168–9, 204, 215, 255; status in the Church 66,
89–90, 128, 138, 184–6, 206, 199–200
Woodrow, Alain 43
worker-priest movement 15
workers' defence committee (KOR) 39, 81
World Council of Churches 138, 153, 219
World Jewish Congress 152, 165
World Youth Day 1992 268–9
Worlock, Archbishop Derek (Liverpool) 126
Wright, Cardinal John 47
Wyszynski, Bishop Stefan (later Cardinal) 23, 30,
36–8, 44, 49, 57, 58, 59, 96, 122

Yeltsin, Boris 243, 247
Young Christian Workers 15, 111
Yugoslavia (former) 133, 250, 263, 275

Zaire 78–9, 152
Zambia 207–8
Zimbabwe 197–8